TEXT AND LOGOS

Scholars Press
Homage Series

Israelite Wisdom: Theological and Literary Essays in Honor of Samuel Terrien
    John G. Gammie, editor

Selected Papers of Lionel Pearson
    Donald Lateiner and Susan A. Stephens, editors

Mnemai: Classical Studies in Memory of Karl K. Hulley
    Harold D. Evjen, editor

Classical Texts and Their Traditions: Studies in Honor of C. R. Trahman
    David F. Bright and Edwin S. Ramage, editors

Hearing and Speaking the Word: Selections from the Works of James Muilenburg
    Thomas F. Best, editor

Greek Poetry and Philosophy: Studies in Honour of Leonard Woodbury
    Douglas E. Gerber, editor

Nourished with Peace: Studies in Hellenistic Judaism in Memory of Samuel Sandmel
    Frederick E. Greenspahn, Earle Hilgert, and Burton L. Mack, editors

Early Jewish and Christian Exegesis: Studies in Memory of William Hugh Brownlee
    Craig A. Evans and William F. Stinespring, editors

Language and the Tragic Hero: Essays on Greek Tragedy in Honor of Gordon M. Kirkwood
    Pietro Pucci, editor

Justice and the Holy: Essays in Honor of Walter Harrelson
    Douglas A. Knight and Peter J. Paris, editors

Faith and History: Essays in Honor of Paul W. Meyer
    John T. Carroll, Charles H. Cosgrove, and E. Elizabeth Johnson, editors

Collected Works of Leonard Woodbury
    Leonard Woodbury

Cabinet of the Muses: Essays on Classical and Comparative Literature in Honor of Thomas G. Rosenmeyer
    Mark Griffith and Donald J. Mastronarde, editors

Text and Logos: The Humanistic Interpretation of the New Testament Essays in Honor of Hendrikus W. Boers
    Theodore W. Jennings, Jr., editor

TEXT AND LOGOS
THE HUMANISTIC INTERPRETATION
OF THE NEW TESTAMENT

edited by
Theodore W. Jennings, Jr.

Scholars Press
Atlanta, Georgia

TEXT AND LOGOS
The Humanistic Interpretation of the New Testament

edited by
Theodore W. Jennings, Jr.

©1990
Scholars Press

Library of Congress Cataloging in Publication Data

Text and logos : the humanistic interpretation of the New Testament /
    edited by Theodore W. Jennings.
    p. cm. -- (Scholars Press homage series)
    Festschrift for Hendrikus Boers.
    Includes bibliographical references.
    ISBN 1-55540-508-8
    1. Bible. N.T.--Criticism, interpretation, etc. 2. Christianity-
-History of doctrines--Early church, ca. 30-600. 3. Bible as
literature. I. Jennings, Theodore W. II. Boers, Hendrikus.
III. Title: Humanistic interpretation of the New Testament.
IV. Series: Homage series.
BS2361.2.145   1990
225,.6--dc20   90-41203
                                                CIP

Printed in the United States of America
on acid-free paper

CONTENTS

Introduction

Jennings ix
What is Humanistic Interpretation?

Part One: Theoretical Issues

Lührmann 3
Rudolf Bultmann and the History of Religion School

Beardslee 15
Ethics and Hermeneutics

Vorster 33
The Function of Metaphoric and Apocalyptic Language
about the Unobservable in the Teaching of Jesus

Part Two: Rhetoric and Structure

Kraftchick 55
Why do the Rhetoricians Rage?

Patte 81
"Love your Enemies—Woe to you Scribes and Pharisees":
The Need for a Semiotic Approach in New Testament Studies

Merritt 97
The Angel's Announcement: A Structuralist Study

Hellholm
The Visions He Saw or: To Encode the Future in Writing 109
An Analysis of the Prologue of John's Apocalyptic Letter

Part Three: Theological Themes

Lategan 149
Some Implications of Hebrews 2:5-15 for a Contextual Theology

Schottroff 165
The Seduction of Eve and Adam's Sin:Social Historical Feminist Interpretation of Paul's Understanding of Sin and Freedom

Hartman 175
Is the Crucified Christ the Center of a New Testament Theology?

Part Four: Critique of Christology

Betz 191
The Problem of Christology in the Sermon on the Mount

Weder 211
"But I say to you... "Concerning the Foundations of Jesus' Interpretation of the Law in the Sermon on the Mount"

Jennings 229
The Martyrdom of the Son of Man

Part Five: Translation and Transformation

Tannehill 247
Paul Outside the Christian Ghetto: Stories of Intercultural Conflict and Cooperation in Acts

Beker 265
The Pastoral Epistles: Paul and We

Delorme 273
Text and Context: "The Gospel" according to Mark 1:14-15

Sölle 289
Loving Bach in a World of Torture

Annotated Bibliography of Boers' Published Works 295

CONTRIBUTORS

WILLIAM A. BEARDSLEE, Director: Center for Process and Faith, Claremont; Emeritus Professor of New Testament, Emory University

J. CHRISTIAAN BEKER, Professor of New Testament, Princeton Theological Seminary

HANS DIETER BETZ, Professor of New Testament, The Divinity School and Chair, Department of New Testament and Early Christian Literature, The Division of the Humanities, The University of Chicago

JEAN DELORME, Professor of New Testament, Institut Catholique de Lyon; Director of the Centre pour L'Analyse du Discours Religieux; Director of *Semiotique et Bible*, Lyon, France

LARS HARTMAN, Professor of New Testament Exegesis at the University of Uppsala, Sweden

DAVID HELLHOLM, Professor of New Testament, University of Bergen, Norway

THEODORE W. JENNINGS, JR., Independent Scholar, Bakersfield, California

STEVEN J. KRAFTCHICK, Assistant Professor of New Testament, Princeton Theological Seminary

BERNARD LATEGAN, Professor of Biblical Studies, The University of Stellenbosch, Republic of South Africa

DIETER LÜHRMANN, Professor of New Testament, University of Marburg, Federal Republic of Germany

WAYNE MERRITT, Assistant Professor of New Testament, Interdenominational Theological Center, Atlanta

DANIEL PATTE, Professor of New Testament and Chair, Department of Religious Studies, Vanderbilt University

LUISE SCHOTTROFF, Professor of New Testament, Gesamthochschule, University of Kassel, Federal Republic of Germany

DOROTHEE SÖLLE, Professor of Theology, Union Theological Seminary, New York; and University of Kassel, Federal Republic of Germany

ROBERT C. TANNEHILL, Harold B. Williams Professor of Biblical Studies, Methodist Theological School in Ohio

WILLEM VORSTER, Head of the Institute for Theological Research, University of South Africa, Pretoria, Republic of South Africa

HANS WEDER, Professor of New Testament, University of Zurich, Switzerland

WHAT IS HUMANISTIC INTERPRETATION?

The occasion for the writing and collecting of these essays was the sixtieth birthday of Hendrikus W. Boers who is professor of New Testament at Emory University. The essays do not however seek to honor one who has brought his career to a conclusion but to honor a set of questions which have been and continue to be persistently and provocatively raised by his teaching and writing. These questions have essentially to do with what we have called a humanistic interpretation of the NT. Briefly, the issue is whether the study of the NT is something which concerns only confessing Christians on the one hand or historians of antiquity on the other. If it is only the former who are involved then the NT seems not to have a place in academic inquiry. But if, in order to secure a place within academe, we think only of documents of antiquity then it is difficult to justify the place given to their study, the restriction of study to just these documents, and so on.

The work of Hendrikus Boers has been concerned with raising the possibility of a non-confessional, an extra-ecclesiastical, interpretation of the meaning and assessment of the truth or validity of that meaning. That is, he has been concerned with the meaning of these texts not for confessing Christians alone but for human beings who seek to understand their existence simply as human beings. Is the NT simply the book of the church, or is it a book for human beings irrespective of their relation to a particular religious institution or creedal confession?

It is out of the issues raised by this sort of question that a humanistic interpretation of the NT arises. In this introductory essay I want to indicate something of the character of such a form of interpretation, the relationship between such a project and some of the work of Boers, and indicate how the essays collected in this volume are related to one another and to this issue generally.

A humanistic interpretation of the NT is situated between an historical-critical inquiry into the texts in terms of their production and cultural environment on the one hand, and the dogmatic or confessional appropriation of these texts for contemporary Christian teaching on the other. It precludes neither of these enterprises; but it has a different aim and function.

An historical-critical inquiry is typically motivated in one of two ways: either as an attempt to free the texts from ecclesial tradition so that the text may serve to criticize and reform that tradition (the aim of the reformation) or, to associate the study of the NT with accepted canons of academic-historical inquiry so that it may have a place within the context of the university. In the first case such an inquiry has theological motivation. In the second case it has a non-theological motivation. Both however require the pursuit of rigorously historical aims and methods.

But in either case the text is more and more treated as a datum for historical investigation, and is fixed more and more firmly in the receding past. When attention is turned to the question of the present meaning and truth of these texts this inquiry is generally made in terms of the meaning of the text for that group who ascribe to these texts a certain a priori authority. As such a reflection on the contemporary meaning of foundational texts for the religious community this inquiry is theological in the general sense of a clarification of the authoritative teachings of a religious community.

A humanistic inquiry however supposes that it is possible to inquire into the contemporary meaning and truth of these documents without presupposing prior adherence to the religious community for which they are authoritative. Thus the question of confession or religious commitment is bracketed out of the inquiry without this meaning that the texts are simply relegated to the past of a receding epoch.

Now for such an investigation to be possible without being simply a violation of the integrity of the texts themselves it will have to be shown that the texts, or some of them, or some parts of some of them, really open themselves to this wider horizon of meaning. The texts were obviously produced with the issues of the religious community in view, and seem often to take for granted certain claims of religious exclusiveness. That is, the confessional appropriation of the texts seems to be superficially plausible, and to the extent that this is so then a humanistic interpretation will correspondingly seem implausible. If the texts are the texts of the Christian community then any determination of their meaningfulness or truth would seem to entail an acquiescence in the claims of that community.

But counting in favor of the possibility of a humanistic interpretation of these texts is the fact that early Christianity does not seem to have made a priori claims for the authority of its proclamation or basic texts. Rather it was necessary to make a case for the plausibility of Christian perspectives within and in terms of the canons of plausible argumentation of the first century. It is this attempt to make a plausible case for faith which offers the formal possibility of a humanistic interpretation—that is, one which deals with these documents not as the authoritative documents of a religious community but as attempts to make faith both intelligible and plausible within the wider context of Greco-Roman culture.

But if this produces the formal possibility for such an interpretation, then what of the material possibility, the content or subject matter of these texts? Are these texts primarily concerned with the making of metaphysical or mythological claims concerning the status of Jesus (christology) and so of disclosing a reality accessible only by adherence to such formulations, or are they concerned (by means of such language and conceptuality) to uncover the universal character of human existence in the world?

Traditional exegesis has proceeded on the assumption that NT texts are unanimous in focussing upon christological claims and so in bringing to expression a particularistic, confessional, and exclusivistic world view.

But this view depends, or seems to depend, on the notion that the unifying character of the NT is precisely this christological witness. However one of the features of an historical-critical investigation of these texts is to cast doubt on that supposition. The sheer diversity of christological concepts, the disjunction between many of them and what can with historical confidence be ascribed to Jesus' own mission, and the presence of non-christological or even anti-christological views in the NT make dubious the notion that the meaning of the NT may be reduced to this christological confession. But if it is not so reducible then there is an opening to a non-christological and so a non-confessional appropriation of the texts.

A sense of the progression of this opening may be given in terms of a quick survey of the steps by which this program comes to expression in the work of Boers. His dissertation was concerned precisely with the historical-critical investigation of NT christological conceptions which demonstrates both their diversity and the impossibility of anchoring specifically christological confessions in the ministry of Jesus. This then leads to an exegetical study of those NT texts which do not presuppose, even at the surface level, a christological or confessional restriction. This project then raises the question of a non (or pre-) confessional "theology of the NT." Meanwhile it becomes clear that such a non-confessional interpretation will concentrate on the theme of the meaning of human existence (Bultmann, Braun) without however reducing the texts to the concern for the individual but attempting to take into account and positively appropriate, apocalyptic (Käsemann) and mythological categories. If this can be done then it will be possible to engage in humanistic interpretation not restricted to those passages which superficially license such a reading but to include those which seem to entail christology in the narrowest sense.

Boers then seeks to anchor such a humanism in the ministry of Jesus himself and to demonstrate the character of this humanism in the Jesus traditions and in the texts of Paul and John.

But he also looks for a method which will permit the humanistic interpretation even of mythological language and categories. It is this which spawns his interest in linguistics, then in the structuralist analysis of myth, and, most recently, in the clarification of generative grammar (coming to fruition in the study of John 4.)

It will be apparent that a humanistic interpretation of the NT is one which is grounded in the historical-critical investigation of the texts, one which views these texts rigorously within their own historical, social and religious environment. But though it is based in such an investigation it also wants to ask about how the texts mean in order to get at the question of their meaning also for us, for us not specifically as Christians but, more generally, as human beings.

Now this last question does not preclude a confessional reading of the texts as well. That is, the aim of a humanistic reading is not the reduction of the texts to that which is non-religious but the exposure of that of the texts which is non-confessional. In so far as this project is a continuation of the reformation project of separating the text from the ecclesial tradition so that the latter may be criticized on the basis of the former then the task of confessional theology remains an open possibility. Thus many of those represented in this volume would consider themselves to be confessing Christians who however recognize that the text must first be clarified on its own terms before being made the subject of a dogmatic or confessional theological appropriation.

But this is not to say that a humanistic interpretation of these texts is not without profound consequences for a specifically Christian theology. Thus, for example, if it is the case that the confession of Jesus as Lord is less important for these texts than a commitment to an excluded and suffering humanity, then christological claims will need to be suitably altered so as not to obscure this meaning of the texts as normative for the confessing community. And if faith is a form of existence open to all regardless of the views which one may or not have concerning the identity of Jesus (as in the case of Abraham in Romans 4) then this will mean a fundamental revision of the doctrine of faith. Thus, while a humanistic interpretation does not preclude a confessional appropriation, it may make clear that certain kinds of confessional appropriation are distortions from the point of view of the very texts earlier taken to license such views.

But the most immediate significance of a humanistic interpretation is that it places the study of the NT squarely in the humanities without reducing it to the study of antiquities.

We may now turn to a consideration of the way in which the essays in this volume treat of various dimensions of a humanistic interpretation of the NT.

An initial set of essays deals with general, even philosophical issues of concern to a humanistic interpretation. The essay by Dieter Lührmann opens the question of the difference between an historical (religionsgeschichtliche) and a theological (existential) interpretation as this difference comes to expression in the thought of Rudolf Bultmann. William Beardslee argues for a more inclusive ethical perspective than the deontology which has been presupposed by so much NT scholarship, as a means of appreciating the diversity of NT conceptions and their openness to dialogue with other points of view. Willem Vorster explores the question of the pragmatic function of language as a means of interpreting metaphoric and apocalyptic imagery in the teaching ascribed to Jesus.

The question of the use of language is addressed by the second group of essays which employ rhetorical and structural methodologies for this analysis. Steven Kraftchick argues for attention to Paul's attempts to persuade his readers in Galatians while calling attention to the dangers of methodological captivity in the new appreciation of rhetorical criticism. Daniel Patte argues for the importance of a semiotic analysis of Matthew as a way of addressing the issue of Matthew's alleged anti-Judaism. The essay by Wayne Merritt demonstrates a structuralist approach to the birth narratives of Luke. David Hellholm offers a formal structural analysis of the prologue to the Apocalypse of John.

A third group of essays explores general theological issues which bear upon the question of a humanistic interpretation. Bernard Lategan shows how a question of anthropology of critical importance for contemporary political discussion is addressed in Hebrews and Luise Schottroff offers a reconsideration of the Pauline view of sin which may escape the anti-semitic, anti-feminist and anti-liberationist character of more traditional readings. Lars Hartman examines the question of the centrality of the cross in NT theology.

A fourth group of essays challenges the self-evidence of christological claims which typically serve as a barrier to this openness. Hans Dieter Betz demonstrates the absence of a christology in the sermon on the mount and develops, from Adolf Schlatter, a way of understanding the function of such a view. Hans Weder shows that the authority of Jesus' pronouncements in the same text do not derive from some ex officio status but from the self-evidence of the sayings themselves. Jennings claims that the martyrdom of the son of man in Mark does not establish Jesus' unique identity but is instead a program of action shared with John the Baptist and the disciples.

A fifth group of essays explores exegetical questions which bear on the question of the translation and transformation of the NT message. Robert Tannehill illustrates the ambiguity of inter-religious conflict and cooperation in Acts as the message of the apostles crossed over into diverse settings. J. C. Beker shows the way in which the transmission of Paul's thought to a new generation results in the transformation of that thought in the pastoral letters. Jean Delorme shows from Mark 1:15 that the gospel has a definite structure which permits a variety of semantic contents without simply being lost in this variety—thus making trans-cultural translation possible. Dorothee Sölle argues for an overcoming of the division in spheres of activity (religion, art, politics) so as to open ourselves not only to human aspiration but also to human suffering.

The reader will notice a number of intersecting themes and concerns which prevent any ordering or grouping of these essays from having an exclusive claim. Some of the essays emphasize rhetorical and semiotic methodologies (Vorster, Kraftchick, Hellholm, Merritt, Lategan, Patte, Delorme). Others stress the ethical dimension of the texts, including their political significance (Beardslee, Sölle, Schottroff, Lategan). Several demonstrate a concern to combat the sort of religious exclusiveness that leads to anti-semitism (Patte, Tannehill, Schottroff). Some deal primarily with NT texts (Betz, Weder, Delorme) while others engage the theological tradition of recent scholarship (Beardslee, Lührmann, Hartman, Betz, Kraftchick).

These essays do not represent a single school of thought. Rather they give expression to the diversity and fruitfulness of issues raised by the question of a humanistic interpretation of NT texts. These essays place the question of NT interpretation within the wider horizon of humanistic inquiry and philosophical reflection. In them we seek to demonstrate the ways in which the study of the NT exceeds the boundaries of an ecclesial interest and confessional circumference. We are concerned with a reflection on the NT which aims at disclosing the truth, not for a tribe or a sect, but for humankind. In Boers' phrase then we are concerned to discover a NT "theology out of the ghetto"—out of the ghettos of creed and institution, of narrow specialization and restricted fields of discourse. We hope these essays will not only illuminate this concern but also provoke it in the reader.

It is not often that a systematic theologian in North America has the opportunity to work so closely with NT scholars. I wish therefore to express my gratitude to all who have so willingly participated in this project. Some who desired to do so were prevented by events beyond their control from contributing essays, yet their encouragement was itself an impetus to the completion of the volume. The patience and generosity of the contributors has made the work of bringing these essays together a pleasure. Special thanks are due to James N. Creech who translated the essay by Delorme and to Wayne Merritt who translated Schottroff's essay.

Finally I must express my gratitude to those who assisted in the editorial work, to David Hellholm, who first recognized the possibilty of such a project, to Ida Boers who made several valuable suggestions, to Steve Kraftchick who provided help at several points and, especially, to Will Beardslee without whose wise counsel and unflagging support this project would have been but a dream.

The efforts of all who have participated in this project are a token and sign of our gratitude for the work of Hendrikus W. Boers whose scrupulous attention to the texts of the NT, relentless questioning of our institutional and disciplinary presuppositions, and unflagging quest for the truth lure us into the adventure of thought.

Theodore W. Jennings, Jr.

I
THEORETICAL ISSUES

RUDOLF BULTMANN AND
THE HISTORY OF RELIGION SCHOOL
Dieter Lührmann, *University of Marburg*

In *What is New Testament Theology?* Hendrikus Boers described the history of this problem from Johann Philipp Gabler to Rudolf Bultmann and Herbert Braun. He sees the relationship between Bultmann and the History of Religion School as hard alternatives: "As the object of historical-critical scrutiny in the Religionsgeschichtliche school ... the New Testament was surrendered to the past. ... If the New Testament writings were to have relevance also for the present, the question of what the New Testament writings meant in their own time would have had to be followed by another [question], namely, what was meaningful in them for more than just their own time. ... An attempt to carry out that task was made by Bultmann with his program of subject-oriented interpretation, in which he tried to distinguish between what was said and what was meant."[1] With that Boers recognizes the historical relationship between the History of Religion School and Bultmann, but correctly maintains that Bultmann should be understood as a theologian whose attempt was to write "a theology based on Paul:" not a reconstruction of the history of primitive Christian religion but a systematic theology, oriented to Paul, which addresses the present situation.

Helmut Koester, on the other hand, in his address at the 100th birthday of Rudolf Bultmann at the centenary at Wellesley wants to correct the image of Bultmann the theologian in favor of appreciation him as historian of religion.[2] He points out that of Bultmann's works

---

[1] Hendrikus Boers, *What is New Testament Theology?* (Philadelphia: Fortress, 1979), 86.
[2] Helmut Koester, "Early Christianity from the Perspective of the History of Religion: Rudolf Bultmann's Contribution," in Edward C. Hobbs (ed.), *Bultmann, Retrospect and Prospect* (Philadelphia: Fortress, 1985), 59-74.

his *Theology of the New Testament* and *Commentary on the Gospel of John* became known to the English-speaking world first, and only subsequently the *History of the Synoptic Tradition* and just a few essays that were oriented religious historically.³ These, however, as Koester correctly remarks, are not included in the volumes of *Glauben und Verstehen* and their English translations. These collections are predominantly systematic-theological in character. We do not know who made this selection, but it was surely not made without Bultmann's approval. Therefore, the conclusion is warranted that, with the appearance of *Glauben und Verstehen I* in 1933, Bultmann wanted to appear as a systematic theologian rather than as a historian of religion. This presumption is supported, not only by the fact that until then he did indeed write systematic-theological essays, but by the selection of the essays that were published at that point in *Glauben und Verstehen I*.

The question of Bultmann's relationship to the History of Religion School nevertheless remains an important theme, which should be supported by more biographical details and, especially, even more differentiated observations than are possible for me here. Rudolf Bultmann was a New Testament scholar from the History of Religion School, and it was from this background that he gained significance for theology in general. I would like to formulate this significance as follows: Bultmann practiced exegesis of the New Testament not as a pure historical reconstruction, but as a theological discipline.

Rudolf Bultmann, born in 1884, studied in Tübingen, Berlin and Marburg in 1903-1907.[4] In 1910 he received his doctorate in Marburg on the theme, *Der Stil der paulinischen Predigt und die kynisch-stoische Diatribe*.[5] His real Doktorvater was Johannes Weiß, who left for Heidelberg in 1908, and was succeeded by Wilhelm Heitmüller. In 1912 Bultmann was "habilitiert" with a work on *Die Exegese des*

---

[3]Bultmann's first publication in English is "The New Approach to the Synoptic Problem," *Journal of Religion* 6 (1926), 337-62, a presentation of the form critical approach.

[4]For the biography, see the autobiographic remarks in C.W. Kegley (ed.), *The Theology of Rudolf Bultmann* (New York: Harper & Row, 1966), XIXXXV; for the early period, Martin Evang, *Rudolf Bultmann in seiner Frühzeit* (Tübingen: J.C.B. Mohr [Paul Siebeck], 1988), 5-100, and 341-347; also Supplements to Bultmann's bibliography in *Rudolf Bultmann, Exegetica* (ed. by Erich Dinkler, Tübingen: J.C.B. Mohr [Paul Siebeck], 1967), 483-507.

[5]*FRLANT* 13 (Göttingen: Vandenhoeck & Ruprecht 1910, repr. 1984).

Theodor von Mopsuestia[6] (a Church Father of the 4th and 5th centuries) under Adolf Jülicher also in Marburg. With that and a few articles his required academic responsibilities were fulfilled. On the basis of his theological background and interests Bultmann could only be considered as a representative of the "History of Religion School." That made a call to a university in Prussia difficult, and equally so a chair in a conservative school.[7]

The first flourishing of modern exegesis in the 19th century took place under the motto of "historical critical theology." Theology took up a bond with historicism in order to protect itself from Hegel and the results that emerged from him: truth could be truth only when it can show itself to be historical. Understood in this way, however, historical truth was a criticism of all "speculation", whether early church speculative theology or idealistic speculation, in an inversion of a thoroughly positive conception in Hegelian philosophy. So historical criticism could, on the one hand, carry out a negative critical dispute with received traditions; on the other, it provided a positive tool to define and legitimate historically the truth of Christianity. Not speculative Christological dogma, but the historical Jesus, was the foundation of Christianity. A late, but characteristic document for what such a historical theology could achieve was Harnack's lectures on *Das Wesen des Christentums* (1899/1900)[8]—in reality a presentation of the historical Jesus which met the questions of the turn of the century in a remarkable way.

The presupposition that the genuine and essential could be only what proves to be historically true was shared—the individual theological directions distinguished themselves by the degree of historical criticism: either the historical Jesus against christological dogma ; or was it not after all possible to legitimate the dogmas through the historical Jesus?

---

[6]Edited by Helmut Feld and Karl Hermann Schelke from the handwritten manuscript of 1912 (Stuttgart: Kohlhammer, 1984).

[7]There is not yet a comprehensive presentation of the History of Religion School; see, however, Werner Klatt, Hermann Gunkel, *FRLANT* 100 (Göttingen: Vandenhoeck & Ruprecht, 1969): Antonie F. Verheule, *Wilhelm Bousset* (Amsterdam: Ton Bolland, 1973); Gerd Lüdemann and Martin Schröder, *Die Religionsgeschichtliche Schule in Göttingen* (Göttingen: Vandenhoeck & Ruprecht, 1987).

[8]ET, *What is Christianity?* ³1904.

Criticism against such historical theology arose from its own circles. For one thing, Albert Schweitzer[9] and Bultmann's teacher Johannes Weiß[10] recognized the meaning of apocalypticism for the historical Jesus, an apocalypticism which no longer proclaimed the value of culture, but announced a catastrophe for the world in the near future. It became clear that this historical Jesus was a historical figure who hardly belonged in the 20th century, but was at home in an alien world and a time that had passed.

On the other hand, and this was the danger of the "History of Religion School," it was discovered that a historical reconstruction was no longer able to substantiate the superiority of Christianity.[11] On closer scrutiny there remained almost nothing that could be claimed for Christianity: Jesus an apocalypticist like others; baptism and eucharist rites were shared with many other religions of the period; the death and resurrection analogous with the dying and rising deities of the mystery religions. Primitive Christianity appeared as nothing other than a special case of the general phenomenon of gnosticism, which in its many manifestations was the religion of Hellenistic times.

Such theses shocked the ecclesiastic and cultural public, especially since this kind of theology aligned itself politically with the cosmopolitically inclined left wing of German liberalism, whereas the majority of the liberal theologians were still affiliated with a national liberalism from which the spectrum among the theologians extended to the far right, where the *Magog* of John's Revelation was identified with the *Demagogs* of the revolution of 1848. It was only after the end of the German "Kaiserreich" that Bultmann received a chair in Gießen in 1920 and in Marburg in 1921 as the successor of Wilhelm Heitmüller. He continued teaching in Marburg until his retirement in 1951 and died there in 1976.

---

[9]*Von Reimarus zu Wrede* (Tübingen: J.C.B. Mohr [Paul Siebeck]), 1906, 2nd ed. *Geschichte der Leben-Jesu-Forschung*, 1913. ET, *The Quest of the Historical Jesus*, (by W. Montague, London: A. & C. Black), 1910, now as Macmillan Paperback 55, since the 1968 edition with the introduction by James M. Robinson.

[10]*Die Predigt Jesu vom Reiche Gottes*, (Göttingen: Vandenhoeck & Ruprecht), 1892, 3rd ed. by Ferdinand Hahn, 1964. ET, *Jesus' Proclamation of the Kingdom of God*, (translated, edited and with an introduction by Richard Hyde Hiers and David Larrimore Holland, Philadelphia: Fortress Press), 1971.

[11]See especially Ernst Troeltsch, "Über historische und dogmatische Methode in der Theologie," *Gesammelte Schriften* 2 (Tübingen: JC.B. Mohr [Paul Siebeck]), 1913, 729-53.

How closely Bultmann was associated with the History of Religion School is shown by the following three points which pervade his exegetical work:

1. Form criticism. His first better known work was the *Geschichte der synoptischen Tradition* which appeared in 1921; reprinted after the 3rd edition of 1931, it remains a standard work for the interpretation of the synoptic gospels into the present.[12] In this work he applies the form critical method developed by his Berlin teacher Hermann Gunkel to the Jesus tradition. Whereas the Gospels were previously interpreted literary critically with the question, what could be gained from them for the historical Jesus? — form criticism was concerned with the use and function of the Jesus tradition in the early Christian church. The method no longer provided the basis for asking the question concerning the historical Jesus, and also did not want to. Where Bultmann nevertheless does ask this question, he uses different criteria.

2. The understanding of history. The motto for liberal theology was: "Jesus, not Paul;" Jesus: the simple proclamation of a new morality; Paul: christological speculation and dogmatics that is alien to life, indeed even mythical. In the History of Religions School William Wrede achieved a cautious recovery of the theology of Paul, not to be sure, the doctrine of justification, but rather Paul's piety.[13] What is interesting about Paul in this investigation is not the individual theologian, but the representative of Hellenistic Christianity. In this way a new picture of the history of early Christianity emerges: Jesus—the primitive Palestinian church—the Hellenistic church with its representatives Paul and John—the early church.[14] Bultmann already used this picture of history in the *Geschichte der synoptischen Tradition*, and then as the foundation in his *Theologie des Neuen Testaments*; in the meantime it has become the almost unquestioned model for New Testament exegesis of every kind. Determinative for it was

---

[12]ET, *The History of the Synoptic Tradition*, (by John March, New York: Harper & Row), 1963.

[13]William Wrede, *Paulus* (Halle: Gebauer-Schwetsche), 1904; reprinted in: Karl Heinrich Rengstorf (ed.), *Das Paulusbild in der neueren deutschen Forschung* (Darmstadt: Wissenschaftliche Buchgesellschaft), 1964, 1-97.

[14]This was developed programmatically by Wilhelm Heitmüller, "Zum Problem Paulus und Jesus," *Zeitschrift für neutestamentliche Wissenschaft* 13 (1912), 320-37; reprinted in *Das Paulusbild in der neueren deutschen Forschung*, 124-43.

William Wrede's article on the theology of the New Testament,[15] which proposed such a presentation over and against one based on dogmatic concepts.

3. Gnosticism. This Hellenistic primitive Christianity is, according to the History of Religion School, the real Christianity, and it is this as a part of gnosticism.[16] This gnosis is defined by the so-called "myth of salvation," which comprises briefly the following elements: In the beginning the world was unspoiled until a part of this wholesome world of light fell into chaos, this lower world. In order to lead the fallen sparks of light back to their home, a savior comes from the world of light, gathers the dispersed sparks of light and leads them back above. The Christology of John or Paul is then, in the opinion of the History of Religion School, only a special formulation of this general myth. Bultmann held on to this model of interpretation: in his commentary on John's gospel (1941),[17] in the *Theology of the New Testament* (1953),[18] and in particular it is the presupposition for his program of demythologizing of 1941.[19]

These three points show how strongly Bultmann's exegetical work belongs with the "History of Religion School" and to what degree he promoted the results, but also the premises, of the School. Criticism of a theology that was defined as purely historical critical

---

[15]ET in Robert Morgan, "The Task and Methods of New Testament Theology," *The Nature of New Testament Theology*, (London: SCM Press/Naperville, Ill: Alec R. Richardson), 1973, 68-116. The original German title refers to the "so-called" theology of the New Testament. Bultmann must have had that formulation in mind when, in his article on "Das Problem einer theologischen Exegese des Neuen Testaments," *Zwischen den Zeiten* 3 (1925), 334-56, reprinted in Georg Strecker (ed.), *Das Problem der Theologie des Neuen Testaments* (Darmstadt: Wissenschaftliche Buchgesellschaft), 1975, 240-77, he writes that the main task of exegetical theology is formulted "quite correctly" as New Testament theology (274).

[16]See especially Wilhelm Bousset, Hauptprobleme der Gnosis, FRLANT 10 (Göttingen: Vandenhoeck & Ruprecht), 1907; Richard Reitzenstein, *Die hellenistischen Mysterienreligionen nach ihren Grundgedanken und Wirkungen* (Stuttgart: Verlag B.G. Teubner, 1910; reprint of the 3rd ed. of 1927, Darmstadt: Wissenschaftliche Buchgesellschaft), 1956. ET, Hellenistic Mystery *Religions: Their Basic Ideas and Significance*, by John E. Steely (Pittsburgh: Pickwick Press), 1978.

[17]ET, *The Gospel of John: A Commentary* (from the 1964 printing of *Das Evangelium des Johannes*, with the Supplement of 1966, Philadelphia: Westminster Press), 1971.

[18]ET, *Theology of the New Testament* (by Kendrick Grobel, New York: Scribners), Vol. I, 1951; Vol. II, 1955.

[19]"Neues Testament und Mythologie," reprinted in: Hans-Werner Bartsch (ed.), *Kerygma und Mythos* I (Hamburg: Herbert Reich), 1948, 15-48; ET, *Kerygma and Myth* I (by Reginald H. Fuller, London: SPCK), 1953, 1-44.

was already in place in the History of Religion School, but not yet achieved was a theological exegesis. Indeed what had been lost was nothing less than theology itself;[20] in its place came religion or, in its anthropological counterpart, a piety which no longer could be interpreted as still relevant for the present.

Thus it should be considered surprising that Bultmann took Karl Barth's *Römerbrief* in the edition of 1921 seriously as a theological commentary and did not understand it as merely "innovative practical scriptural interpretation."[21] And it is surprising that after the First World War Bultmann came out decisively on the side of dialectic theology, even if from the beginning with an idiosyncratic interpretation of what the expression meant.[22] For the representatives of the old historical critical theology this was seen as only the disastrous result of the "History of Religion School;" for the "historians of religion" it was seen as a flight back to dogmatics.

Bultmann took note of this criticism in his address on "Die Bedeutung der 'dialektische Theologie' für die neutestamentliche Wissenschaft"[23] in 1927 at the "Deutschen Theologentag," the congress of all German professors of theology. He opposes a misrepresentation of

---

[20]See Boers, *What is New Testament Theology?* 86.

[21]"Karl Barths' Römerbrief in zweiter Auflage," reprinted in Jürgen Moltmann (ed.), *Anfänge der dialektischen Theologie* I, Theologische Bücherei, 17 (Munich: Chr. Kaiser), 1962, 119-42; ET, "Karl Barth's Epistle to the Romans in its Second Edition," (by Keith R. Crim), in *The Beginnings of Dialectical Theology*, (ed. by James M. Robinson, Richmond, Virginia: John Knox Press, 1968), pp. 100-120. For a contrary understanding, see the reviews of Adolf Jülicher, "Ein moderner Paulusausleger," *Anfänge der dialektischen Theologie* I, 87-98; ET, "A Modern Interpreter of Paul," *The Beginnings of Dialectical Theology*, 72-81, and Adolf Schlatter, "Karl Barths' Römerbrief,'" *Anfänge der dialektischen Theologie* I, 142-47; ET, "Karl Barth's Epistle to the Romans," *The Beginnings of Dialectical Theology*, 121-25.

[22]See in retrospect Bultmann's letter of September 15, 1964 (reproduced in Lüdemann and Schröder *Die Religionsgeschichtliche Schule in Göttingen*, 20) to the publisher Ruprecht, who had congratulated him on his 80th birthday: "You recall names of old that not only remain in lively memory for me like Gunkel, Joh. Weiss, Bousset and Heitmüller , but for which the occasion to remember with gratitude is given by the octogenarian's reflections. I tried to remain true to the tradition represented by such names and to carry it further in my work. I think I can say that, precisely because I also incorporated motifs from the so-called dialectical theology in my work, I helped the old tradition of historical critical research retain its validity in theology." Bultmann alludes to the discussion concerning his program of demythologizing; note the similar remark with regard to the confessing church in the autobiographic notes (see above, note 4).

[23]*Theologische Blätter* 3 (1924), 73-86, reprinted in *Glauben und Verstehen* I (Tübingen: J.C.B. Mohr [Paul Siebeck], 1933), 1-25; ET, in *Faith and Understanding*, (by L.P. Smith, New York: Harper and Row), 1969.

dialectical theology as a new exegetical method; the existing exegetical method was not replaced, but was deepened, because it was no longer a case of historical reconstruction of history in the New Testament, but of understanding the texts.

In the article which appeared at more or less the same time, "Das Problem einer theologischen Exegese des Neuen Testaments,"[24] Bultmann expressed this difference with the formula: "Historical (zeitgeschichtliche) exegesis asks: What was said? and instead of that we ask: What was meant?" Here the interpreter is no longer in the role of distanced, unbiased spectator and critic. Understanding now means that one is involved and therefore knows what is meant when one translates the Greek word chara with "joy." It is the point at which anthropology becomes the key to exegesis for Bultmann, because in his view theological pronouncements could be meaningful only when they could be understood in this sense out of personal experience. At this time Bultmann could go so far as to say that the "misery of theology" after Ferdinand Christian Baur was owing to the fact that it no longer proceeded from anthropology—and unfortunately Baur had a wrong anthropology.[25]

Exegesis does not become theological for Bultmann through a specific method which is applied to these texts, but through its subject matter, the New Testament; but since in such an exegesis the interpretation can no longer be separated from the self-interpretation of the exegete, "theology and exegesis, or systematic and historical theology, coincide."[26]

This makes understandable the fascination for the exegesis of Bultmann and his followers, and explains the attraction of exegesis of this kind for students of the past decades; what could be read and heard here was not the interpretation of texts in the sense of the historical reconstruction of the beginnings of Christianity, but the simultaneous interpretation of texts and of oneself. In such interpretation one could find oneself again in the texts.

---

[24]*Zwischen den Zeiten* 3 (1925), 334-56, reprinted in Georg Strecker (ed.), *Das Problem der Theologie des Neuen Testaments*, 240-77.

[25]"Zur Geschichte der Paulus-Forschung," *Theologische Rundschau* N.F. 1 (1929), 26-59; reprinted in *Das Paulusbild in der neueren deutschen Forschung*, 304-37, specifically, 310.

[26]Das Problem einer theologischen Exegese des Neuen Testaments," in Strecker (ed.), *Das Problem der Theologie des Neuen Testaments*, 272.

Such a new starting point for exegesis could also have been understood differently; one could be shocked by the essay on demythologizing, misinterpreting it as a return to liberal theology, as Dietrich Bonhoeffer had done.[27] Overlooked was that Bultmann was never involved in a rejection of classical exegesis, but in deepening it. That was, in his understanding, what the theme of demythologizing was about: an old problem which liberal theology did not solve because it was engaged in historical reconstruction and not in an understanding of the text of early Christianity.

The way in which Bultmann reoriented all exegesis as theological exegesis can be shown by once more taking up the three earlier points in which Bultmann's origins in the History of Religion School became most clear.

1. Form criticism. Bultmann does not attempt a formal classification of the proclamation of Jesus as parables, beatitudes, etc., but sought after the motivating power of the Jesus tradition. According to him this was not to be found in the historical Jesus, but in the kerygma as something that was indeed present in the texts, but not only in them. Early Christianity did not appropriate the sayings of Jesus because they were sayings of Jesus, but because it wanted to proclaim Jesus as the Lord who was present in the congregation. Not the historical Jesus was the origin and essence of Christianity, as in Harnack, but the kerygma which had an impact on persons then as it does now, and gave them the ability to understand and interpret themselves in a new way. The historical Jesus is a figure of the past, at home in an alien land and time—the kerygma as a present expression and a present appeal allows the temporal difference to disappear.[28] In this way from criticism is more than just another exegetical method among others; for Bultmann it was part of a theological understanding.

2. The understanding of history. What has just been said explains the stubbornness with which Bultmann maintained his position that the historical Jesus was a presupposition for the New Testament, not

---

[27]For a general discussion, see Günther Bornkamm, "Die Theologie Bultmanns in der neueren Diskussion," *Theologische Rundschau*, NF 29 (1963) 33-141.

[28]Bultmann's Jesus book of 1926 (ET, by Louise Pettibone Smith: *Jesus and the Word* (New York: Scribners, 1934) describes such an alien Jesus, but in the German cultural context of that time it was a Jesus who could have been taken to be the real Jesus.

a part of it.²⁹ Theology comes into play for him only when, in the Hellenistic church in Paul and John, an explication of the newness of the self-understanding of faith, made possible by the kerygma, is present.³⁰ In this way the understanding of history which he took over from the History of Religion School was no longer a mere abstract model of thought, but was of fundamental significance for the understanding of theology in every respect. The old motto, "Jesus, not Paul," was now completely abandoned in favor of a new one, "The kerygma, not Jesus." And over against the History of Religion School it no longer involved a reconstruction of early Christian piety as part of the general religious atmosphere of that time, but an understanding of theology, and with that theological understanding.³¹ The doctrine of justification by faith once more becomes the key to the understanding of Paul, and of the entire New Testament: Justification by faith interpreted now as the appropriation of the new self-understanding made possible by the kerygma.³²

3. Gnosticism. If the objective of the History of Religion School was to place early Christianity with the framework of the history of the religion of that period, Bultmann also in this case went a step fur-

---

[29] Note especially his discussion of the research in *Das Verhältnis der urchristlichen Christus–botschaft zum historischen Jesus*, (Heidelberg: Carl Winter), 1961; reprinted in *Exegetica*, 445-469. ET, "The Primitive Christian Kerygma and the Historical Jesus," *The Historical Jesus and the Kerygmatic Christ: Essays on the New Quest of the Historical Jesus*, (by Carl E. Braaten and Roy A. Harrisville [ed.s], New York/Nashville: Abingdon), 1964, pp. 54-68.

[30] See Bultmann's definition of theology: "Theology is the conceptual presentation of human existence as something that is determined by God" ("Das Problem einer theologischen Exegese des Neuen Testaments," in Georg Strecker [ed.], *Das Problem der Theologie des Neuen Testaments*, 272.). The foundation of this definition is Bultmann's reaffirmation of Paul as a theologian against the understanding of the History of Religion School, and, at the same time, his understanding of theology as something which evolves in concepts, even if not in the sense of a dogmatics. This understanding of theology relates to Bultmann's contributions to the *Theologisches Wörterbuch zum Neuen Testament*.

[31] See, contrary to the idea of development in the History of Religion School: "That means that when it is a question of a real understanding of history we have to give up the idea of development." ("Das Problem einer theologischen Exegese des Neuen Testaments," in Georg Strecker [ed.], *Das Problem der Theologie des Neuen Testaments* [Darmstadt: Wissenschaftliche Buchgesellschaft], 1975, 266).

[32] The tradition in which Bultmann stood is in this regard complicated. The History of Religion School was formed in controversy with the theology of Albrecht Ritschl, to whom all the members had been dedicated since their student days. Reaching back over them, Bultmann now took over, in a completely new way, Ritschl's theme of "justification."

ther. The history of religion, and especially of gnosticism, did not reveal to him what all people had as common religious pronouncements, but what they had as common questions. The religious historical parts, for example, of the commentary on John serve to bring to expression these questions concerning truth and life which hounded people through the ages.[33] The Jesus of John's gospel is therefore not one among other redemptive figures who also promises the way, truth and life, but the single answer to the question concerning the way, truth and life. Similar to the understanding of history one could say here too: Gnosticism is not only a particular model in the history of religion but a part of the foundations of theology as the articulation of the questions and longings of human beings.

It is thus confirmed that Bultmann practiced historical exegesis of the New Testament as a theological discipline. In doing so he did not desert historical research, but methodologically he did give it a new orientation. He was still able to incorporate the edition of the Mandean texts of the twenties in his interpretation of John's gospel.[34] But he showed little interest in the newly discovered apocryphal gospels, even though he directed Mayeda's dissertation on PEgerton.[35] He hardly took note of the post World War II discoveries of the texts from Qumran and Nag Hammadi.[36] At this time he was too heavily involved in the controversies concerning demythologizing as a systematic problem in theology.

What remains of Bultmann's work is the claim of grounding Christianity in the writings collected in the New Testament. Over against this there are today not only very different attempts at such a

---

[33]This understanding is developed methodologically most consistently in the little 1929 volume, *Der Begriff der Offenbarung im Neuen Testament*, reprinted in *Glauben und Verstehen* III, 1-34.

[34]See the article on "Die Bedeutung der neuerschlossenen mandäischen und manichäischen Quellen für das Verständnis des Johannesevangeliums," *ZNW* 24 (1925), 100-146, reprinted in *Exegetica*, 55-104, as well as the commentary on John.

[35]This dissertation was accepted in the philosophical, not the theological, school of the University of Marburg. In the *Ergänzungsheft* to the *Geschichte der synoptischen Tradition* of 1958 Bultmann refers to this dissertation only on a few occasions, and always contrary to Mayeda's view by interpreting PEgerton as dependent on the synoptic gospels.

[36]Note the "Vorwort" to the 3rd edition of his *Theologie des Neuen Testaments* (1958; not in the English translation): The texts from Qumran "confirm what scholars like W. Bousset recognized long ago." As far as I can determine, there is no reference to the Nag-Hamadi texts that were edited only since the end of the fifties.

grounding of Christianity, but also the abandonment by New Testament scholarship of such a claim. The two dangers of an exegesis of the New Testament post Bultmann appears to me to be that it either withdraws to a historical reconstruction or that it is practiced as a kind of "amateur dogmatics." In neither case does it remain on the narrow path on which Bultmann trod. Criticism of, on the one hand, the historical foundations of the gnostic model or, on the other hand, of the binding to the philosophy of Heidegger, does not affect this conception of a theological exegesis. What is called for would be a new form of exegesis which does not have to rework anew the three issues mentioned, form criticism, the understanding of history, and gnosticism.

What is at stake in accepting the exegetical work of Rudolf Bultmann is the mandate to answer for theological pronouncements historically, and that means precisely religious historically. It is still a question of "a pure biblical theology,"[37] which means, at the same time, in accepting the theology of Rudolf Bultmann, to answer for a theology which is oriented both to the New Testament and to the contemporary situation.

---

[37]See Hendrikus Boers, *What is New Testament Theology*, 86.

ETHICS AND HERMENEUTICS

William A. Beardslee, *Center for Process and Faith, Claremont*

0. Ethical Presuppositions in Hermeneutics

The focus of New Testament hermeneutics on the conditions of understanding has meant that the ethical presuppositions of interpretation have usually not been closely examined. But as one reads recent New Testament interpretation, one cannot avoid being struck by the contrast between the ethical vision that shaped the earlier and still largely dominant styles of hermeneutics, and the very different understanding, or understandings, of ethics that more recent work presupposes.

In hermeneutics, ethical presuppositions function both in the process of interpretation and in the pattern of meaning that the interpreter finds in the text. To clarify these ethical dimensions of hermeneutics, we shall begin with the familiar distinction between deontological ethics, the ethics of the irreducible "ought," and teleological ethics, the ethics of action to achieve a goal. In the course of our study we shall try to show that this traditional classification used in philosophical ethics is inadequate, despite its great influence on hermeneutics.

The emphasis of this paper will be on ethical patterns discerned in New Testament texts, although the two aspects of hermeneutics, the process and the result, deeply interact. This theme is chosen in part because Elisabeth Schüssler Fiorenza has recently reopened the question of ethics in the process of interpretation with a forceful questioning of scholarly detachment as the central ethical criterion for methodology.[1]

---

[1] Schüssler Fiorenza, "The Ethics of Interpretation."

1. From Deontological to Teleological Ethics

Most older New Testament interpretation viewed the texts and culture of the past with the assumption that the human person is called to respond with a sense of obligation in a universe in which general moral (and religious) rules set a firm framework for choice. This view is classically illustrated by Adolf Jülicher's great work on the parables of Jesus.[2] Indeed, the ethical presuppositions which have dominated New Testament hermeneutics until recently have had a predominantly Kantian cast—assuming (1) that an irreducible sense of obligation is the distinctively human trait, and (2) that the sense of obligation can be clarified and applied by following consistently that aspect of it which leads toward generalizing or universalizing the claims in which it is expressed. Though responsibility was of course exercised in a social setting which defined most of the problems of choice, the clarification of ethical choices led toward principles rather than toward reflection about the social constitution of the self. And because principles were usually formulated in terms of the individual choosing self, the notion of social justice which lay behind the sense of obligation received little scrutiny.

If these ethical presuppositions have been little discussed, that is because most parties to the debates about biblical hermeneutics shared this kind of perspective. The New Testament texts were read with an eye to how grace transformed obligation, and to the question how one set the limits to the "acceptable" expressions of responsibility/faith within the diversity of early Christianity. As one moves from the time of Jülicher to the work of his successors in the early twentieth century, confidence in the existence of an ethical framework within which one exercised choices was steadily eroded, but the structure of human existence as responding to a sense of obligation was seldom questioned.

In more recent work, the ethical universalism presupposed in earlier hermeneutic discussion has been thrown into question by the increasing recognition that we must deal much more seriously with the pluralism of early Christianity than the older hermeneutics used to do, at the same time working in the setting of the pluralism of the societies in which the interpreters live. This change has meant that scholars have begun to question the adequacy of the central criterion

---

[2] Adolf Jülicher, *Die Gleichnisreden Jesu*.

of how believers responded to the "ought" and its transformation in faith. Other ways of setting ethical questions, often clearly focused on fulfillment rather than on obligation, are being reexamined as "acceptable" aspects of early Christianity. Equally important for the relation between ethics and hermeneutics has been a shift from an emphasis on obligation to an emphasis on aesthetic perception as the distinctive trait which is in focus as the interpreter works with New Testament texts. This shift was expressed in the lively movement of New Testament literary criticism. But the aesthetic clue to interpretation is in turn being superseded, or at least supplemented, by a return to strongly ethical interpretation of early Christian texts, but now with much more attention to the variety of their ethical claims, and to the social network within which these claims are developed and expressed. The aims and goals of the various groups in early Christianity are taken as central interpretive clues. Simply put, we see a shift from deontological to teleological ethics in New Testament interpretation. To examine this shift is the purpose of this paper.

2. Ethics of Decision: Bultmann's Hermeneutics

Bultmann's hermeneutics can serve as a starting point for this discussion, since Bultmann's work displays the deontological presuppositions of traditional hermeneutics so clearly, and since his work has been so widely influential.

Bultmann gave renewed life to the rigor of historical method by joining it to a phenomenological analysis of human existence. Historical study presupposes an unbroken chain of causation. But the historian must also "translate" to his or her own culture the existential meaning of the lives of the actors in history.[3] Neither aspect of the interpreter's methodology has any place for divine action, but it is clear that the faith which sees the described event (say, the resurrection of Jesus) as an act of God is understood as a transformation of the act of decision which was originally shaped by a deontological ethical vision.[4]

This "dialectical" hermeneutics, in which a given event both is and is not a witness to the divine presence, proved liberating to scholars, who were able to pursue the rigor of both historical and phenomenological research while reserving the question of divine

---

[3]Bultmann, "Is Exegesis Without Presuppositions Possible?", 291-93.
[4]Bultmann, "The Meaning of God as Acting."

action for faith. It has been a lasting tradition. Much attention has been given to the freedom for faith which was seen to result from this move. Less obvious, but more important for our purpose, is the strong sense of obligation to the rules of scholarly research, the strong deontological component in the rigorous separation between research and faith. In this way the ethics of the "ought" has had a strong community-creating function. Scholars of widely-differing commitments join in the common task of research. We shall see later that this apparently universalizing ethical thrust of scholarly distanciation has recently been challenged as unconsciously ideological.

The conviction that a transformation of the "ought" is at the center of Christian existence is fundamental for Bultmann's New Testament interpretation. On the one hand, this model makes intelligible the break with the "law" of Judaism, as well as casting light on the degeneration of Christianity into legalism in the post-apostolic period.[5] On the other hand, it serves as a criterion for excluding forms of self-understanding, such as gnosticism, which did not take seriously the decisional nature of human existence.[6]

We may note that Bultmann explicitly rejects a teleological ethic as a suitable framework for New Testament interpretation; specifically he had in mind an idealistic form of teleological ethics, rather than the utilitarian form of this ethic which has been so prominent in Anglo-American thought. Utilitarianism would no doubt have seemed to him even less appropriate.[7]

While the whole concept of "the imperative" that, in interplay with the indicative, is so constitutive of Bultmann's New Testament theology, is indeed drawn from New Testament texts, classically those of Paul, the imperative that Bultmann heard was a very Kantian one, as is shown by the universalizing tendency that goes hand in hand with the imperative's concreteness of call to decision. This tendency is shown in the implication that there is only one form of authentic existence.[8] At the same time, the insistence that what is significant is an individual person's decision means that political decisions can only be of second rank. Despite his insistence that biblical texts are to be interpreted in the same way as any other literature,[9] these

---

[5]Bultmann, *Theology of the New Testament*, I, 259-69; II, 218-31.
[6]Ibid., I, 345-51.
[7]Bultmann, "Das christliche Gebot der Nächstenliebe," 232-33.
[8]Bultmann, "The Historicity of Man and Faith."
[9]Bultmann, "The Problem of Hermeneutics," 256.

texts are to be interpreted in terms of their proper understanding of existence, and as this interpretation proceeds, it discloses a normative center which is given by the transformation of the "ought" by grace.

Thus, though Bultmann recognized the path into interpretation through aesthetic perception,[10] the deepest key is the serious encounter with a style of existence, and this means serious choice. An aesthetic approach seemed too much a matter of "looking on," while the aesthetic elements tended to appear as decorative details.[11] There was little place in Bultmann's hermeneutics for the entry into interpretation through "play" that appears, for instance, in Gadamer.

Bultmann's ethical clues to interpretation, then, arise from deontological ethics, but the basis of this ethics in social life (rules that make the common life possible) is strongly deemphasized. Even when the person is led into encounter with another, in *agape*, this relation does not arise out of internal relations with the other, but out of love's own spontaneity. A presupposition which lies behind the "ought" of this vision is a very traditional view of distributive justice—"rendering to each his or her due." The assumption is that there is a fixed quantity to be distributed. Though this definition comes from the Greek tradition, with its strong teleological thrust, it was also used to interpret the imperative of the "law." The understanding of justice as the giving of appropriate shares to separate individuals has a strongly patriarchal cast. Someone is dealing out to individual persons what they deserve. Such a patriarchal and individualistic view of justice has deeply affected the whole Protestant view of justice under the law. It is precisely the rigidity of this concept of justice which requires the transformation of the "ought" in faith and love, but the transformation only grudgingly makes room, if at all, for the teleological, goal-oriented aspects of life, or for an intrinsic relationality of beings.

3. Transition: Gadamer's Hermeneutics

The hermeneutics of Hans-Georg Gadamer can serve to illustrate a transition in approach that has also taken place beyond the explicit influence of his work. His hermeneutics is often treated as a further development along lines pioneered by Bultmann.[12] This is not incor-

---

[10]Ibid., 248-50.
[11]Tannehill, *The Sword of His Mouth*, 8.
[12]As by Richard E. Palmer, *Hermeneutics*, 48-52.

rect, but the ethical implications of interpretation are very different in Gadamer. It would not be wrong to regard the move from Bultmann to Gadamer as an instance of a very widespread shift in twentieth-century sensibility which can be described as a transition from a situation in which Kant's second critique defined the problems to be wrestled with, to one where the problems are set by the third critique.[13]

Gadamer notes that before the modern period, "common sense" did indeed imply a common moral context for decision-making, and he calls attention to the persistence of this theme in some religious hermeneutics; but he also shows how the mainstream of European thought moved away from this presupposition in the direction of a rationalistic individualism.[14] But he does not attempt to reconstitute an ethical basis for hermeneutics, turning instead to base his work squarely on the aesthetic dimension which Bultmann had skirted. His perceptive discussion of "common sense" is immediately followed by a treatment of (aesthetic) "judgment" (*Urteilskraft*).[15]

The contrast with Bultmann can be seen in Gadamer's taking "play" as a central hermeneutical clue.[16] Here we deal with the construction of a possible world, or, better, the construction of a variety of worlds, and the role of self-presentation in play contrasts with the self-in-decision model of Bultmann. Gadamer's central image of "fusion of horizons" also cuts very differently from Bultmann's hermeneutics. Although the latter was indeed a skilled interpreter of a wide variety of styles of existence, Bultmann's decisional emphasis tended to develop an interpretation in which one pattern excluded another. The goal of fusion of horizons, on the contrary, implies expansion of vision, and contrasting tensions within the fused horizons, rather than decision among competing options. The strong emphasis on "application" in Gadamer does not contradict this thrust of his work; it is precisely in applying the broader humanistic understanding that the expansion of vision will take place. Finally, we may note how Gadamer, virtually at the end of his great work, explicates the universal aspect of hermeneutics with a reference to Plato's vision in

---

[13]The emphasis on decision in Heidegger's *Sein und Zeit*, which is reflected in Bultmann's work, contrasts similarly with the focus on poetry and aesthetics in the later Heidegger, whose work was important for Gadamer.
[14]Gadamer, *Truth and Method*, 19-29.
[15]Ibid., 29-33.
[16]Ibid., 91-99.

which the key concept is beauty, and the beautiful is "fused" with the highest good.[17]

Gadamer's work is paradigmatic of a widespread focus on aesthetic vision in hermeneutics, including New Testament hermeneutics. Much of the vigorous work in New Testament literary criticism, whether or not is has been carried out specifically with reference to Gadamer, is consonant with the emphases noted above. In this style of interpretation the intention is to be open to as wide a range of options as possible, including ethical options. The implication is that there is a wide range of authentic forms of human existence, in which quite varied ethical patterns function. Gadamer's work has been criticized as still too narrowly focused on the Western tradition to carry out this intention.[18] Nevertheless, the direction of his interpretation, and of this type of interpretation generally, is to encompass, to use Gadamer's term, by fusion of horizons, multiple possibilities of being human. The action-oriented ethics of transformation, to which we shall shortly turn, is often impatient with this aesthetic turn in hermeneutics, but it has none the less played an important role in turning away from a universalizing deontological ethic toward the recognition of multiple aims for an ethics of goal-oriented action.

Further, this hermeneutics takes more seriously the human person and society as creative, as actors. Gadamer's use of Plato shows that his style of interpretation will be far more open to a positive evaluation of *eros* than was the hermeneutics which preceded it. As against a view of love which starts with disconnected realities and understands *agape* as the unilateral creation of a relationship, the perspective from which Gadamer works supposes that already existing relations and impulses provide a basis from which understanding can grow.

Ethical reflection is not highlighted in Gadamer's work. Nevertheless, we can note several implications of his perspective for the place of ethics in hermeneutics. In the first place, aesthetic perception is the central category, and ethics, however it is understood, will be drawn closer to aesthetics. Further, it will be easier to make the move from aesthetics to ethics if a teleological ethics, perhaps emphasizing the "fitting," is the framework, rather than the traditional ethics of the "ought."

---

[17]Ibid., 435-447.
[18]May, *Meaning in Buddhist-Christian Communication*, 255.

Second, Gadamer's model of dialogical interchange among a variety of positions is open toward a greater pluralism of ethical positions than was the case with Bultmann's hermeneutics. It is true that, though there is no "center" in Gadamer's vision, he does work within what he understands to be a connected flow of the Western tradition. His position has been criticized for its inability to offer a critical perspective on the present.[19] In this latter point we see the claim of ethics in hermeneutics reasserting itself. There is validity in this criticism, yet the greater openness of what is here termed an aesthetic hermeneutics has been, both specifically in the case of Gadamer, and more broadly in literary interpretation generally, a significant step toward a reopening of the question of ethical variety in early Christianity.

Finally, though the issue of justice is also not a focal one in Gadamer's work, the implication of his image of the fusion of horizons for justice is that of breaking away from the "zero sum game" model of rendering to each her or his due. A truly fused horizon is an enlarged world of new possibilities. We shall see that in the field of justice precisely this sort of new vision is needed. The aesthetic hermeneutical perspective itself did not develop into a hermeneutics of transformation, but it has provided a setting in which dialog between traditional hermeneutics and that kind of interpretation is more easily possible.

4. Ethics of Transformation:
The Hermeneutics of Elisabeth Schüssler Fiorenza

Hermeneutics of action has not been unknown in earlier New Testament interpretation.[20] Resistance to action-oriented interpretation which advanced the specific dogmatic or social aims of the institutional church generated the scholarly distanciation which characterized nineteenth-century historiography, and which is still a strong element in contemporary hermeneutics. The resistance to action-oriented interpretation is still strong. But the hermeneutics of transformation is pressing the point that the seeming neutrality of this traditional scholarly posture conceals its ideological function of supporting an establishment, and fails in its objective of sustaining a

---

[19]Schüssler Fiorenza, *Bread not Stone*, 132-35.
[20]For instance, a large part of Walter Rauschenbusch's *Christianity and the Social Crisis* consists of biblical exegesis.

community of scholars, since it excludes those who work from other perspectives.

On this point there is much convergence among Latin American, Afro-American, and feminist theologies. These theologies also move in the direction (though not all draw this conclusion) of reversing the assumption of traditional biblical interpretation, that the primary locus of divine action is to be seen in the biblical past. They affirm that divine action in the present, in the struggle for the liberation of the oppressed, is the starting-point for biblical interpretation. From the point of view of traditional hermeneutics, this starting-point can be seen as a particular preunderstanding. But the claim is a still stronger one than that. For the faith that, if divine action is significant anywhere, it must be so in the actual struggle of the oppressed, is incompatible with dialectical theology's closed world of historical causation. The claim entails reopening the question of the way in which God acts in the world, and demands the development of scholarly tools which can bring together the two worlds, the world of faith which sees God at work, and the world of social analysis which studies how human societies behave. It is because one can speak of God's action in the present that one can go back to the Bible and reread it as a book of liberation.[21]

We shall explore the hermeneutics of liberation through the work of Elisabeth Schüssler Fiorenza, since she has addressed the issue of interpretation theory explicitly. The positions noted above are explicit in her work.[22] She rejects the "neo-orthodox" attempt to find a way of "divorcing the language and text of the Bible from its patriarchal conditions,"[23] that is, of finding a general theological statement which would transcend the androcentric character of the actual Bible. Though she is more sympathetic to the "sociology of knowledge" model of Mary Daly, she holds that Daly has not sufficiently taken account of the historical character of human existence, which requires that women join themselves with the women, oppressed as they

---

[21]To say this is not to overlook the very positive response of many dialectical theologians to various forms of liberation theology. But it is to affirm that a theology will be crippled which both affirms the present action of the divine, and rigorously separates that action from scholarly analysis.

[22]Schüssler Fiorenza, *In Memory of Her*; *Bread Not Stone*; "The Ethics of Interpretation."

[23]*In Memory of Her*, 21.

usually were, of the Bible. What is required is to reclaim this past, by subverting the history which conceals it.[24]

Her aim is a critical hermeneutics of emancipation. "Liberation theologians must abandon the hermeneutic-contextual paradigm of biblical interpretation, and construct within the context of a critical theology of liberation a new interpretive paradigm that has as its aim emancipatory praxis."[25] This critical hermeneutics, which is critical both of traditional readings of the Bible and of its own presuppositions, arises from a concrete social location, the community of women engaged in the struggle for liberation. One of its central aims is re-reading of New Testament texts to recover the teleological ethic, the aims at the creation of community, of the almost-forgotten early Christian women.[26]

Such a hermeneutics squarely puts the final emphasis on engagement rather than on scholarly distance. Scholarly distance still has its place, in the "ethics of historical reading," which doubly relativizes the ancient text and the present situation of the reader.[27] In this way the "modern" achievements of "scientific" historiography are incorporated into the "postmodern" relational and transformational vision of the author. But in its final stage, interpretation is a battle against established powers. Schüssler Fiorenza observes, "Feminist biblical scholarship has its roots not in the academy but in the social movements for the emancipation of slaves and of freeborn women."[28] The "ethics of accountability" is a political ethic which is aware of the pragmatic impact of one's work, and aims for responsible social effects. The conflictual imagery must not deflect our attention from the strong emphasis on relatedness. An authentic style of existence cannot be described by showing how a self is structured, or how it confronts reality, but must focus on social relations, however perverted these may be. The social, related character of human existence is a basic presupposition. And the consequence for ethics is a strong emphasis on teleological ethics. The ends for which action is undertaken are what is to be judged ethically.

A struggle against injustice could be conceived in terms of traditional distributive justice, as a claim for a share in what has been de-

---

[24]Ibid., 31.
[25]Schüssler Fiorenza, *Bread Not Stone*, 63.
[26]Schüssler Fiorenza, *In Memory of Her*, passim.
[27]Schüssler Fiorenza, "The Ethics of Interpretation," 14.
[28]Ibid., 7.

nied. This is certainly a motif in most liberation theologies including that of Elisabeth Schüssler Fiorenza. But it is important to note that her interpretation also implies a far more relational and reconstructive image of justice. It is by no means implied that if women win men will always lose. And though the actual present circumstances compel a thorough commitment to the ecclesia of women, from this vantage point one can also see the church of women and men, not as a utopian ideal but as an actual reality which can emerge as the androcentric character of the church is overcome.[29]

5. Ethics and Hermeneutics

At the risk of some oversimplification, we have sketched a shift from the widespread presupposition of New Testament hermeneutics that ethics is rooted in an irreducible "ought," to a goal-oriented, transformative ethic of political responsibility. Acceptance in the guild of the latter is far from wholehearted, but there are many signs that this is the creative direction in the ethical aspect of interpretation. But the new direction would be terribly impoverished if it were taken to imply the abandonment of either rigorous historical discipline or a dialogical, contextual hermeneutics. All three forms of interpretation are required, if the New Testament is to recover its ability to speak to the issues which the community of the church and also the wider human community bring to it.

If interpreters of the New Testament give a somewhat uncertain sound about the shape of their ethical commitment, that is a reflection of a very widespread confusion in ethical thinking today. We cannot here survey the field of ethics (even if the present author were competent to do so), but we shall try to offer some directions toward greater clarity, and sketch a proposal which should make it easier for different points to view to communicate. Among the issues we can note the following. The connection between ethics and faith is problematic, not only because ethical standards are seen to be relative to particular social settings, but also because many hold that moral action is so inextricably connected with the use of power that it cannot be a gateway to the ultimate mystery. Thus Peter Sloterdijk closes his exhaustive *Critique of Cynical Reason* with the slender hope for a basis for life in "another reason than the activist one."[30] Perception of the

---

[29]Schüssler Fiorenza, *Bread Not Stone*, chap. 1.
[30]Peter Sloterdijk, *Kritik der zynischen Vernunft*, 2, 952.

use of ethical standards as expressions of power has placed a question over the whole project of traditional reasoning about ethics.[31] The erosion of an ethical consensus, which may seem dismaying to representatives of traditional positions, is often welcomed by those who speak for excluded groups, that have found traditional ethics repressive.[32] Another factor in the decline of established ethical traditions is the conviction among many professional ethicists that ethical statements are non-cognitive. Some claim that ethical discourse consists of a group of non-communicating language games.[33] In spite of these daunting problems, there still is profound ethical commitment on the part of many who have no way of making it intelligible.

To sort out these issues would carry us far beyond the scope of this paper. We can, however, seek to sketch a framework in which the original cleft between deontological and teleological ethical styles can be more adequately bridged. This can serve as an approach to some of the wider questions.

Deontology does not offer the self-evident claim that it used to do, or at least was thought to make. And the "ought" is so often perceived as a power claim that many are sceptical about universal ethical claims. Yet the ethics of the "ought" is far from exhausted. Despite our classifying the ethics of liberation as teleological, marked deontological elements do appear in it, especially in the claim of loyalty for the group. And the radical pluralist Jean-François Lyotard closes his conversation on ethics with an outright deontological command: [Justice]...prohibits terror, that is, the blackmail of death toward one's partners...".[34] We will expect that the claim of response to an "ought" will continue to be a part of the language of ethics.

This paper has shown the vitality of teleological ethics in theologies of liberation. This type of ethics suffers from the opposite difficulty from deontology. The ethical claim of a goal all too easily becomes the interest of a particular party. We need to recognize that a universal position is never available to us, and to take seriously the situatedness of any ethical formulation, but along with that particularism there needs to be a reach toward a wider situatedness, and a

---

[31]This issue is discussed by Jürgen Habermas, "The Genealogical Writing of History."
[32]Schüssler Fiorenza, *Bread Not Stone*, chap. 4
[33]Jean-François Lyotard, *Just Gaming*.
[34]Ibid., 100.

willingness to allow one's position to be transformed toward a deeper recognition of other claims.

An important resource for reconstructing ethical discourse is found in the work of H. Richard Niebuhr, who proposed that both of the classical approaches be subsumed in a more comprehensive ethical image—that of the "responsible self."[35] Niebuhr showed how the concrete image of responsibility can function more comprehensively than either of the traditional alternatives. It implies an interactive, related person and humanity; all action is response; it is interpreted response; and it takes place in a situation of social solidarity.[36] Without examining Niebuhr's book in detail, we can note how the ethics of interpreted response in social solidarity frees one from the abstractness of rules in the ethics of "ought," while at the same time the aspect of social relatedness serves as a constraint to the choice of limited goals.[37]

Niebuhr's model recognizes the pluralistic, non-centered ethical world in which we find ourselves. It is coherent with the view that values are not simply imputed to objects by the human mind, but are inherent in reality—an issue too complex to unfold here. At the same time, through its monotheism, it maintains that there is an inclusive standpoint, even though this is never fully available to us. Such an affirmation of pluralism as well as an ultimate inclusive standpoint will be a powerful tool in interpreting New Testament texts. Catherine Keller has sharply criticized Niebuhr for that aspect of his monotheism in which he presents the self as unified only by its relation to a unilateral divine influence which establishes unity in the flux of life. She calls for a "multiple integrity."[38] We agree with Keller that we encounter the divine in and not in opposition to the multiple and often conflicting strands of relationship which elicit our commitment. But that even stronger emphasis on pluralism does not negate the role of a unifying standpoint toward which we can, at least sometimes, in real measure approximate. Keller's caveat is an important

---

[35]H. Richard Niebuhr, *The Responsible Self*.
[36]Ibid., 61-66.
[37]Niebuhr's ethical thought is highly compatible with the ethics that arises from Whiteheadian or process thought, which can serve as a general framework in which to develop ethics. See Daniel W. Metzler, *Essay on Whiteheadian Ethics*, esp. 311-17.
[38]Catherine Keller, *From a Broken Web*, 181.

reminder that this approximation is not the only goal of ethical reflection.

If it be objected that this language is too private, too dependent on a particular commitment, the response is that public discourse always consists in conversation from particular standpoints. The image of the responsible self-in-relation, acting always in a particular social context, yet related to a universal standpoint, the standpoint of God, can very fruitfully enter in conversation with those who do not understand themselves as relating ethics to faith, through the affinity of the Niebuhr-process model to the model of the ethics of the ideal observer, a well-established ethical tradition which itself recognizes the difficulty of simple universals.[39]

Those of us who were trained in the universalism of deontological ethics may readily suppose that the goal of conversation among ethical positions is to find elements in common, convergences toward which a consensus can be built. This move is a valid one, but it is not the only one, and often is not the most important one, in an ethics of response in social relatedness. Equally important is the recognition of enduring differences, and the search for ways of respecting these. The deeper goal, not always to be attained, but to be striven for, is not the uncovering of commonalities but the transformation of conversing positions so that each may hold in tension its initial insights with elements at first perceived as incompatible, from the other position.

It is especially at this point that aesthetic hermeneutics and hermeneutics of liberation can fruitfully interact. For both work to understand and release the creative possibilities of the human. Each can easily be impatient with the other, since one emphasizes sympathetic understanding, and the other action. While each posture is a fully justified one, neither is self-sufficient. We noted above that those who speak for excluded groups are suspicious of overall ethical perspectives, because these support established powers. Similarly, the aesthetic hermeneutics of the humanistic tradition is suspicious of what appears to be the too limited perspective of the ethics of action. But both appreciate human creativity or *eros* in ways that the older hermeneutics did not, and this common, though differently developed, ground gives them both a stake in a continuing conversation.[40]

---

[39]See Metzler, *Essay on Whiteheadian Ethics*, 309-10; 321-23.

[40]The interplay of these styles of essentially humanistic interpretation points to the shared concerns of this essay with the work of my honored colleague, Hendrikus Boers.

This dialog will show that while the desire to use power does shape ethical discourse, it can be transcended since it does not totally control such discourse, and it will also show that a deeper humanistic understanding is unfinished if it does not lead to action.

The ethical framework here proposed will honor human creativeness more fully than much traditional ethics has done. A theme in New Testament interpretation in which this emphasis will be apparent is the understanding of love. Most treatments of love in the New Testament are suspicious of *eros*, and see *agape* to be the legitimate New Testament form of love. There is good reason in the texts for this tradition. But a fuller consideration of the dynamics of the New Testament communities calls for a wider view. Charles Reynolds remarks, "A full and robust theory of love...needs the attractive, luring, binding indeterminate and driving vitality of eros together with the steadfast, determinate, and equal-regarding characteristics of agape."[41] An interpretation of New Testament texts about love which recognizes the interaction and, often, struggle, out of which the texts arose can do justice to the centrality of both of these styles of love in early Christianity.

Finally, we have noted above that a fresh vision of justice is a major need in ethical thinking, and that recent moves in hermeneutics are places where one can see a new way of thinking about justice emerging. Particularly in the tradition of the ethics of the "ought," a distributive conception of justice has been the rule, and this view has all too often implied that justice consists simply in some authority dividing up a given amount of what is desired. This starting-point has heightened the incompatibility of justice and love, as well as increasing the interpreter's suspicion of human creative capacities, which so easily deform the rules of justice. We have shown that both Gadamer's dialogical hermeneutics and the feminist hermeneutics of Schüssler Fiorenza open the way to a more relational understanding of justice. In this kind of justice, participation and consideration of aim function not only in distribution but in the whole network of social relations, and the creation of new possibilities can be an aspect of justice. A commentator on *Economic Justice for All*, the Pastoral Letter of the Roman Catholic Bishops of the United States on the economy, interprets their view in this way: "Participation at all levels must be improved before justice in terms of both individual freedom and so-

---

[41]Charles H. Reynolds, "Somatic Ethics," 120.

cial equity can be realized."[42] An important distinction is that participatory justice can consider rearranging the structures so the social issue will not always be the distribution of an already fixed amount. Further exploration of a relational, participatory view of justice will be a central task of ethical thinking about the New Testament, for at important points New Testament texts point toward just this concept of justice, and where they do not, they can more fruitfully be criticized from this point of view than by working from traditional distributive justice.

Behind the ethical uncertainties which we noted above lies the intractable, disruptive terror of our time. The deeper issue is not the technicalities of ethical theory, but the question whether any ethical framework can enable women and men to live with moral integrity in our disordered world. The preceding reflections are not offered as easy solutions, but as a proposal for freeing the resources of the New Testament so that they may more fully be available to contribute to that task. The path sketched above envisages not a single uniform community of interpreters, but conversation among communities: uninstructed readers and scholars, humanists and activists. In such conversation the rigidities of each position can be questioned, yet each can speak, and frankly. This path will move away from the rigid image of hermeneutics as "translation," which presupposes a fixed element to be re-expressed. It will contribute to the formation of a hermeneutics that can fully recognize the strangeness of the text, which offers no "pure" disclosure, and yet can release the ethical power that successive generations have found in an encounter with the New Testament.

---

[42]Carol Johnston, "Learning Reformed Theology from the Roman Catholics." I am also indebted to an unpublished paper of Carol Johnston for analysis of the contrast between distributive and participatory justice.

WORKS CONSULTED

Bultmann, Rudolf, *Theology of the New Testament*. 2 vols. Trans. Kendrick Grobel (New York: Charles Scribner's Sons, 1951-55.)

———. "The Problem of Hermeneutics." Pp. 234-61 in *Essays Philosophical and Theological*. Trans. James C. G. Grieg (London: SCM Press, 1951).

———. "The Meaning of God as Acting." Pp. 60-85 in *Jesus Christ and Mythology* (New York: Charles Scribner's Sons, 1958).

———. "Das christliche Gebot der Nächstenliebe." Pp. 222-41 in *Glauben und Verstehen*, Vol I (Tübingen: J. C. B. Mohr, 1958).

———. "The Historicity of Man and Faith." Pp. 92-110 in *Existence and Faith: Shorter Writings of Rudolf Bultmann*. Trans Schubert M. Ogden (New York: Living Age Books, 1960).

———. "Is Exegesis Without Presuppositions Possible?" Pp. 289-96 in *Existence and Faith: Shorter Writings of Rudolf Bultmann*. Trans. Schubert M. Ogden (New York: Living Age Books, 1960).

Fiorenza, Elisabeth Schüssler, *In Memory of Her: A Feminist Theological Reconstruction of Christian Origins* (New York: Crossroad, 1983).

———. *Bread Not Stone: The Challenge of Feminist Biblical Interpretation* (Boston, Beacon Press, 1984).

———. "The Ethics of Interpretation," *Journal of Biblical Literature* 107 (1988), 3-17.

Gadamer, Hans-Georg, *Truth and Method*. Trans. Garrett Barden and John Cumming (New York: The Seabury Press, 1975).

Habermas, Jurgen, "The Genealogical Writing of History: On Some Aporias in Foucault's Theory of Power," *Canadian Journal of Political and Social Theory/Revue canadienne de théorie politique et sociale*, 10 (1986), 1-9.

Johnston, Carol, "Learning Reformed Theology from the Roman Catholics: The U. S. Pastoral Letter on the Economy." To appear in *Reformed Theology and Economics*. Ed. Robert L. Stivers (Lanham, MD: University Presses of America, forthcoming).

Jülicher, Adolf, *Die Gleichnisreden Jesu*. 2 vols. Tübingen: J. C. B. Mohr, 1899).

Lyotard, Jean-François, and Jean-Loup Thébaud, *Just Gaming*. Trans. Wlad Godzich. Afterword by Samuel Weber. Trans. Brian Massumi (Minneapolis: University of Minnesota Press, 1985).

May, John D'Arcy, *Meaning, Consensus, and Dialogue in Buddhist-Christian Communication: A Study in the Construction of Meaning* (Berne: Peter Lang, 1984).

Metzler, Daniel W., *Essay on Whiteheadian Ethics*. Ann Arbor: University Microfilms, 1988 (Dissertation, Emory University, 1987).

Niebuhr, H. Richard, *The Responsible Self: An Essay in Christian Moral Philosophy* (San Francisco: Harper & Row, 1978).

Palmer, Richard E., *Hermeneutics: Interpretation Theory in Schleiermacher, Dilthey, Heidegger, and Gadamer* (Evanston: Northwestern University Press, 1969).

Rauschenbusch, Walter, *Christianity and the Social Crisis* (New York: The Macmillan Company, 1907).

Reynolds, Charles H., "Somatic Ethics: Joy and Adventure in the Embodied Moral Life." Pp. 116-132 in *John Cobb's Theology in Process*. Ed. David Ray Griffin and Thomas J. J. Altizer (Philadelphia: The Westminster Press, 1977).

Sloterdijk, Peter, *Kritik der zynischen Vernunft*. 2 vols. (Frankfurt: Suhrkamp Verlag, 1983).

Tannehill, Robert C., *The Sword of His Mouth: Forceful and Imaginative Language in Synoptic Sayings* (Philadelphia: Fortress Press and Missoula: Scholars Press, 1975).

THE FUNCTION OF METAPHORICAL AND APOCALYPTIC LANGUAGE ABOUT THE UNOBSERVABLE IN THE TEACHING OF JESUS

William S. Vorster, *University of South Africa*

In his book *Theology out of the Ghetto: A New Testament exegetical study concerning religious exclusiveness*, Hendrikus Boers has a short section on "the ontological grounding of the message of Jesus" in the chapter on "Jesus and the kingdom of God". Ever since I first read the manuscript — still then in unpublished form — this section has been of interest to me. Reflecting on Robert Funk's distinction between the "foundational language" of the parables of Jesus and the "primary reflective language" of Paul's letters, Boers observes that the fundamental problem is: "What are the phenomena to which the language of Jesus pointed? What were the ontological bearings of his language?".[1] Obviously this has been the million dollar question since the days of the early church when Christians had to defend Jesus' talk about the unobservable and their own theological language. This can be seen, for instance, in Irenaeus' apologetic in his *Adversus Haereses*, II, 25-28, but also in all subsequent discussions from the allegorical, fourfold, and literal interpretations of the New Testament, through Strauss' and Bultmann's attempts to deal with myth and demythologization until the present attempts to deal with interpretation of theological texts in terms of models and metaphors. The question is complicated by its epistemological dimensions. How can humanity know and talk about the unobservable? Why are myth, metaphor, and revelatory language so often used in religious texts when the unobservable is spoken about?

---

[1]Hendrikus Boers, *Theology out of the Ghetto: A New Testament Exegetical Study Concerning Religious Exclusivism* (Leiden: Brill, 1971), 44.

Almost two decades after the publication of the book by Boers, I would like to discuss an aspect of the problem of the status of the language of the New Testament about things that cannot be observed, to honor a friend and colleague and to share with others a small aspect of our common concern about religious talk. I will concentrate on the function of metaphorical and apocalyptic language from a socio-semiotic point of view in order to show that the problem of God-talk and talk about the unobservable has a functional side which complicates the ontological status of theological language in the New Testament, and that this has to be taken into account in any systematic discussion about theological discourse concerning the unobservable. I will develop my argument by first dealing with the problem of the pragmatic function of language with regard to metaphorical and apocalyptic statements in the gospel tradition and then by drawing some conclusions about the cognitive function of these statements in view of a few remarks about epistemological models.

I
Metaphoric and apocalyptic statements and their function Language conventions and the unobservable

The New Testament in general and the gospel tradition in particular abound with imagery and metaphors especially with respect to the unobservable. In addition to terms such as "kingdom of God" and "Son of man", shorter statements and units such as sayings of Jesus and parables are phrased in mythic, metaphoric or apocalyptic language. This is typical of the type of discourse which the people of the New Testament world used when they spoke about the unobservable.

Both in the Mediterranean world and the Near East prior to and after the New Testament period people spoke about the unobservable.[2] Myth, metaphor and revelatory language were the conventional vehicles for communication about things which cannot be observed. Oracles made it possible to reveal things which humans cannot see clearly or speak about without special capabilities, and so did

---

[2]Cf. David Hellholm, ed., *Apocalypticism in the Mediterranean World and the Near East: Proceedings of the International Colloquium on Apocalypticism, Uppsala, August 12-17, 1979* (Tübingen: Mohr, 1983).

visions, dreams and "flights of the mind" of the philosophers.[3] We are told of journeys to otherworldly places, and special functionaries and people with the ability to speak about the unobservable. Mediators with special insight communicated knowledge about the unobservable to the ordinary person. Generally speaking this is also the situation in the New Testament where Jesus, for instance, is portrayed as somebody who could speak with authority about the unobservable, and others, like the author of the Revelation of John claim to have had visions which enable them to speak about things which cannot be seen. That this situation continued into the period after the New Testament is clear from the extracanonical literature, especially early Christian apocalypses and gnostic literature, not to mention the vast amount of philosophical thought about matters of afterlife and so on. What is remarkable is that it is taken for granted that at least some people are able to speak about the unobservable by using certain language conventions such as myth, metaphor or revelatory techniques. When the problem of *how* it is possible to speak about the unobservable is addressed, it becomes quite another matter. A different discourse type is used, namely "reflective language", if we may use the term of Funk referred to above. Herodotus (*Hist.* 2.33.2) maintains that the unknown should be judged from the plain, that is by way of inference, and although the Empiricists relied on what was seen by one's own eyes, they also allowed for inductive reasoning from the known to the unknown.[4] But, is this type of discourse also applicable to theological matters which cannot be seen by the eye?

By the second century C E, it became apparent that it was not easy to speak about the unobservable in theological terms. In fact, one can even argue that in certain circles people were skeptical about the possibility of talking about the unobservable. It was simply regarded as speculation and also dismissed. In the passage of Irenaeus referred to above, he clearly maintains that men like Valentinus, Ptolemaeus and Basilides who claim that they have knowledge of the whole universe are in the wrong. They first have to explain the things *quae in manibus sunt, et ante pedes, et in oculis, et terrenis ...*, that is, the things that are in their hands, and at their feet, and before their eyes, and on

---

[3]Cf. Johan C. Thom, "The Journey Up and Down: Pythagoras in Two Greek Apologists," unpublished paper read at a meeting of the South African Society of Patristic and Byzantine Studies, October 1987.
[4]Cf. William R. Schoedel, "Theological Method in Irenaeus (Adversus Haereses 2. 25-28)," *The Journal of Theological Studies* 35 (April 1984):37.

the earth (*Adv. haer.* II.28.9).[5] Irenaeus argues that some things are known, others not,[6] and that it is better to know that God exists than how things came about.[7] The same anti-speculative tendency is also found in the Mishnah text Hagigah 2.1: "If anyone speculates about four things, it would have been merciful had he never come into the world — namely, what is above, what is below, what is before, and what is after".[8] It is obvious that we have two types of discourse here. In the case of mythological, metaphorical and revelatory material it is assumed that the only way to talk about the unobservable, is by using a special kind of discourse. As soon as one starts rationalizing about the unobservable, quite another kind of discourse is needed.

Let us return to the conventional way of speaking about the unobservable in New Testament texts and the function of statements about the unobservable. First of all we have to explain what is meant by "function" in this essay because the term is used in many different ways in New Testament scholarship.[9]

1.2 Function and the use of language

Function is used here to indicate the semantic, pragmatic and textual functions of utterances in the New Testament. The intentions of a speaker— that is the functions for which a speaker uses language— are of an *ideational, interpersonal,* and *textual* nature.[10] *Ideational* refers to relating of experiences, providing information (experiential), indicating the relationship between the events described in texts (logical), and the use of language to order thoughts (cognitive). *Interpersonal* refers to expression of feelings (expressive), changing of the emotional state of the hearer (emotive), changing the behaviour of the hearer (imperative, persuasive), establishing the speaker's status (egocentric), changing the status of the hearer ("Your

---

[5]Cf. W. C. van Unnik, "Theological Speculation and its Limits," in *Early Christian Literature and the Classical Intellectual Tradition: In Honorem Robert M. Grant*, eds. William R. Schoedel and Robert L. Wilken (Paris: Editions Beauchesne, 1979), 35-37 for an interesting discussion of the term *ante pedes*.

[6]Ibid., 43.

[7]Cf. Schoedel, "Theological Method," 31.

[8]Cf. Schoedel, "Theological Method," for a full discussion of the topic.

[9]Cf. Willem S. Vorster, "'Genre' and the Revelation of John: A Study in text, context and intertext," *Neotestamentica* 22 (1, 1988 forthcoming).

[10]Cf. Victor N. Webb, "Some Aspects of the Sociolinguistics of Bible Translation and Exegesis, and of Religious Language," in *Sociolinguistics and Communication*, ed. Johannes P. Louw (London: United Bible Societies), 51-52.

sins are forgiven" — performative) and establishing and maintaining contact (phatic). *Textual function* refers to the use of language to give a particular form to the message, for instance, to signal topic. All three types of function are of importance for our topic.

In the past the semantic and textual functions have received most attention from New Testament scholars. In search of the meaning of texts we have realized that certain texts function within certain *fields* of meaning.[11] The original use of *Sitz im Leben* as a sociological category points in this direction[12] where cultic, apologetic and other social settings indicated the field within which utterances have meaning. Unfortunately *Sitz im Leben* lost its original purpose, and became a means of speculation about a concrete historical situation or context within which a text could have functioned. Much attention has also been focused upon the textual function or *mode* of New Testament utterances. The study of forms and their functions have been of primary importance in Form Criticism, for instance. In addition to *Sitz im Leben*, the mode of writing of smaller and larger forms has been studied extensively, as can be seen from the literature on sayings of Jesus or that concerning the writing of letters in the world of the New Testament. It is the pragmatic function of the use of language which generally has not received the necessary interest in the past, mainly because of the fact that pragmatics is a relative late-comer to the scene.

It is not possible to overrate the importance of the pragmatic side of language when we talk about the function of the use of language in any communication. The emphasis on the fact that people do things with words (speech acts) when they communicate, is what I have in mind when I refer to function now. Communication is more than the exchange of words or ideas. Language acts can be informative, expressive, persuasive, aesthetical, social and so on, as we have seen above. That is why it is so important to distinguish between the various functions for which language can be used. One and the same utterance can have totally different functions as is clear from the sen-

---

[11]Cf. J. Frow, "Discourse Genres," *Journal of Literary Semantics* 9 (1980): 73-81 makes a useful distinction between field, mode and tenor. He argues that the semantic function of genres should be described by specifying the dominance of *field*, that is the type of activity in which the text has significant function, *tenor*, the status and role relationships involved (interpersonal functions) or *mode*, that is the symbolic mode and rhetorical channels or textual function.

[12]Cf. Rudolf Bultmann, *Die Geschichte der synoptischen Tradition*, 8th ed. (Göttingen: Vandenhoeck und Ruprecht, 1970), 4.

tence: The door is open. This utterance can function either as a statement of fact or as an imperative. This also has bearing on the ontological status of sentences or the use of language in the New Testament.

Let us briefly explain pragmatic function with reference to a text from the gospel tradition which is well known. The pragmatic function of the little apocalypse of Mark 13 has to do with the interpersonal level of persuasion. The author of the Gospel of Mark tried to convince the reader that the message of Jesus about future turmoil is authoritative and that the reader/hearer should be confident that his/her following of Jesus will not be in vain. There is no sign that the author wanted to give a concrete or logical description about the future by using the type of language where it is difficult to find out what the sentences are referring to in the real world (cf verse 14). The function of these sentences is to create a new symbolic universe for the reader in which the return of the Son of man is an important symbol. We will return to this text below.

Social factors also determine the construction of a message and the function of language relates to these factors. Communication between members of a subculture or some socioreligious, or sociopolitical group is determined by the symbols they share. This is reflected in the language they use.[13] In order to be meaningful a text like a Gospel or the "Revelation" of John presupposes a group of people who share a common system of meaning, closely knit together in a unit with a strong concern for the beliefs of the group.[14] To communicate they use certain language conventions which have certain functions. That is why there has recently been so much interest in the specific nature of theological discourse.[15]

Function can be a very helpful means to form a conceptual framework of the social context "... as the semiotic environment in which people exchange meanings".[16] Function, in other words, is not an empirical category but a theoretical device, and social context is

---

[13]Cf. Webb, "Some Aspects", 53-55.

[14]Bruce J. Malina, *Christian Origins and Cultural Anthropology: Practical Models for Biblical Interpretation* (Atlanta: John Knox, 1986), 13-15.

[15]Cf. John Macquarrie, *God-Talk: An Examination of the Language and Logic of Theology*, (London: SCM Press, 1967); Sallie McFague, *Metaphorical Theology: Models of God in Religious Language* (London: SCM Press, 1983); Janet M. Soskice, *Metaphor and Religious Language* (Oxford: Clarendon Press, 1985).

[16]M.A.K. Halliday, *Language as Social Semiotic: The Social Interpretation of Language and Meaning* (London: Edward Arnold, 1978).

not primarily a particular historical context. This argument has to be developed a little further.

The way in which the material is presented, both with regard to the presentational process (e.g., narrative) and the presented world (e.g. , narrative world created by the text) affects the reader and the ontological status of the utterances within a particular text. Ruthrof has made valuable observations in this connection.[17] He argues that in myth, where the narrator functions as an authority (who knows how to speak about the unobservable), the narrative world is presented as a dictate and the implied reader in the text as a minor. In a parable, where the narrator is a preacher, the world is presented as analogue and as teaching, and the implied reader functions as a believer, normally with limited faculties. In prophecy, the narrator is a prophet who presents the world as divine vision and the future truth to rebellious believers as implied readers. This underscores the fact that different kinds of discourse are used for different purposes and for different functions, each with its own ontological status. An illustration will clarify the point.

In his discussion of the oracle of Trophonius with regard to the so-called apocalyptic genre, Hans Dieter Betz deals with the concept of myth. He makes the following remark which is of importance for our discussion of function: "The genre of *mythos* can do what *logos* cannot do: *mythos* can speak in human words about things that go beyond the human words and language. While *logos* must be understood rationally *mythos* is to be believed".[18] This distinction between *mythos* and *logos* also illustrates the point that on the interpersonal level *mythos* is used to persuade, that is to establish faith. It is hardly possible to think in ontological terms about the things at which myths point in the extratextual real world. Because myths do not refer to extratextual realities, and because they serve the purpose of establishing faith, scholars often distinguish between the meaning and the significance of myths.[19] It is correct to maintain that: "David Friedrich Strauss took a great step forward in seeing myth as primarily a con-

---

[17]Cf. Horst Ruthrof. *The Reader's Construction of Narrative* (London: Routledge and Kegan, 1981) 138.

[18]Hans Dieter Betz, "The Problem of Apocalyptic Genre in Greek and Hellenistic Literature: The case of the Oracle of Trophonius," in Hellholm, *Apocalypticism*, 587-88.

[19]Cf. Trevor D. Verryn, ed., *Reflections on Religion*, (Pretoria: University of South Africa, 1987), 171-98.

struct of the believing community, whereby its faith found expression ...".[20] Perhaps these remarks about the function of myth can also help us get a clearer idea of the function of metaphoric language about the unobservable.

The function of metaphoric language in the teaching of Jesus

A few words about the use of the term "teaching of Jesus" in this essay will be in order. What I have in mind is simply to take examples and explain the problems we have in dealing with the function of metaphorical and apocalyptic language in the teaching of Jesus. I also have to leave aside any critical discussion about the possibility of reconstructing the *ipsissima vox* of Jesus. For the sake of my argument I simply have to accept some of the domain assumptions of critical scholarship and work with the results.

One of these domain assumptions which I take as certain is the fact that much of the teaching of Jesus has a metaphoric character. Jesus made use of metaphors to say meaningful things about the unobservable. I am referring here to metaphors such as "kingdom of God", "father", perhaps "Son of man", "heaven", and so on, and also to his parables which I regard as metaphoric teaching.[21] He obviously used metaphors in talking about observable things also: "You are like light for the whole world. A city built on a hill cannot be hidden" (Matt 5:14).[22] Even here the observable, namely light, has a reference beyond the realities which one can see.

Although there still is a great deal of confusion and unclarity about the exact nature of the parables of Jesus as metaphors within New Testament scholarship, as Kjärgaard has convincingly indicated,[23] it is nevertheless clear that there should be little doubt that the parables of Jesus are metaphoric stories, or extended metaphors.

---

[20]John Macquarrie, *God-Talk*, 170.

[21]Cf. Wolfgang Harnisch, "Die Metapher als heuristisches Prinzip. Neuerscheinungen zur Hermeneutik der Gleichnisrede Jesu," *Verkündigung und Forschung* 24 (1979): 153-88; also Mogens S. Kjärgaard, *Metaphor and Parable: A Systematic Analysis of the Specific Structure and Cognitive Function of the Synoptic Similies and Parables qua Metaphors* (Leiden: Brill, 1986).

[22]All quotations from *Good News Bible*. I am aware of the difference of opinion concerning the origin of Matthew 5:14a. Cf. Ulrich Luz, *Das Evangelium nach Matthäus (Mt 1-7)*, Evangelisch-Katholischer Kommentar I/1, (Neu kirchen: Benzinger Verlag, 1985), 220.

[23]Kjärgaard, *Metaphor*, 133-97.

Before we turn to the function of the metaphoric teaching of Jesus about the unobservable, a few remarks have to be made about metaphors in view of current research on the topic. It is generally accepted that metaphors are rather complicated utterances, especially with regard to predication. In his excellent treatment of the subject, Kjärgaard makes use of the findings of interaction theory and argues that the sentence "Man is a wolf" involves the following: (1) Linguistic-grammatically it is a subject-predicate sentence, while logical-grammatically it contains an explicit primary subject "man" and an explicit secondary subject "wolf", and an implicit secondary predicate "... which is linked to and represented by the secondary subject." "Man" as primary subject is used literally, whereas the secondary subject "wolf" is not used literally. (2) The secondary predicate is a complicated system. Logical-grammatically it can be described as a series (e.g., man is a wolf; man is a wolf who is the implicit secondary predicate; man is a wolf who is a, b, c, ... n). The individual elements of the series "... represent concepts, assumptions and ideas that are or can be derived from and are or can be linked to the secondary subject". (3) The metaphor "Man is a wolf" is also a performative or speech act. It invites the reader to project the elements of the secondary subject onto the primary subject: "Man is a wolf who is a, b, c, ...n". That is why in the end (4) the metaphor can be formulated as: "Man is a, b, c, ... n", since it creates a structural similarity between the primary subject of the metaphor and its secondary subject by modifying the understanding of the sense of the primary subject.[24]

For our purpose it is of vital importance to realize that metaphors are not only semantically complicated. They are speech acts that invite readers to react and to project the elements of the secondary subject onto the primary subject. In the case of the "kingdom parables", for instance, the reader is invited to understand the meaning of the story about the kingdom and project that meaning onto the "kingdom of God". That is why I will argue below that the metaphoric language of the parables of Jesus does not point to some reality outside the text which is unobservable. They invite readers to interpret the sense of the parable with reference to the "kingdom".

If we now turn to the parables of Jesus as extended metaphors, it becomes apparent that, as far as function is concerned, we have a very interesting situation. Semantically and textually it is clear that

---

[24]Ibid..

most of these stories function as narratives. They were told by Jesus as short stories within very concrete communication situations. Undoubtedly it is impossible to recover these historical communication situations from the extant canonical and extracanonical sources. Nevertheless it is obvious that Jesus used these metaphorical stories to do something. On the textual level it seems clear that most of these parabolic utterances are of a narrative character and also reveal the characteristics of narratives.[25] In other words they were told as stories, many of them being stories about the unobservable "kingdom of God". The question which remains in view of what we have said above about the metaphor, is what is the pragmatic function of metaphoric language in the parables of Jesus.

It is not difficult to apply the insights given above about metaphors to the parables of Jesus and his metaphoric language with regard to pragmatic function. Jesus obviously wanted to do something with words and stories. There may be differences of opinion about the perspective from which Jesus told his stories, that is whether the "kingdom of God" is a future kingdom, whether the term is used within the ambit of "wisdom" or "apocalyptic" theology,[26] but there can be little doubt about the fact that Jesus tried to create a new symbolic universe for people who were in despair. By telling metaphoric stories to the "underdogs" of society in Galilee, Jesus attempted to establish belief in a coming kingdom ruled by God. In such a manner he created new hopes and resocialized people who were at a total loss. He effectively used stories of a metaphorical nature such as the story of the Good Samaritan, the Sower, the Mustard Seed, the Rich Man and Lazarus, the Workers in the Vineyard, the Wicked Husbandman, the Doorkeeper, the Unjust Steward, the Pearl and many others, to change the conduct of people and to make it possible for his followers to get involved in situations which society did not allow. The content of Jesus' message was not all that new. But his message was aimed at having people think in certain ways and do things which fit the rule of God.

The fact that after centuries we New Testament scholars still try to reach a decision on what the "kingdom of God" refers to in the

---

[25]Cf. Willem S. Vorster, "Meaning and Reference: The Parables of Jesus in Mark 4," in Bernard C. Lategan and Willem S. Vorster, *Text and Reality: Aspects of Reference in Biblical Texts* (Philadelphia: Fortress Press, 1985), 27-65.

[26]Cf. Burton L. Mack, "The Kingdom Sayings in Mark," *Foundations & Facets Forum* 3(1, 1987):3-47.

teaching of Jesus,[27] is an indication of the metaphoric character of the notion. In short, the function of metaphorical language in the teaching of Jesus has to do with the pragmatic rather than the ontological, when ontological refers to the things at which the stories point in reality. Jesus told these metaphoric stories about the unobservable God, the kingdom and other phenomena to establish faith in the possibilities which the kingdom of God gives. The function is pragmatic!

The function of apocalyptic language in the teaching of Jesus

For almost a century scholars have believed that the teaching of Jesus, especially regarding the kingdom of God, was embedded in Jewish apocalyptic. In recent times this has been challenged[28] and attempts have been made to argue that the teaching of Jesus should be related to Jewish Wisdom. For this and other reasons such as the many ways in which the term "apocalyptic" is used I shall first make a few general remarks about apocalyptic as a theological perspective before I turn to a discussion of the function of apocalyptic language in the teaching of Jesus.

Following the research of Hanson[29] and others, apocalyptic in my view[30] refers to a phenomenon which arises in a crisis. Apocalyptic eschatology on the other hand, refers to a meaning system, a theological perspective on God, humanity, and the world. Apocalyptic usually arises when values and structures of a particular society lose their meaning for some minority group within that society and are replaced by a new symbolic meaning system. It is therefore at the same time a crisis phenomenon and an all-embracing approach to life in which the future determines the present. Apocalyptic is not concerned with the future only, and adherents of apocalyptic are not merely interested in the future. The contents of their visions and their revelations also have bearing on the present and the past. Because life is seen in relation to the future there is great emphasis on correct conduct and ethics. Eschatology is of paramount importance. The

---

[27]Ibid.. Cf. also Helmut Merklein, *Jesu Botschaft von der Gottes herrschaft: Eine Skizze*, 2nd ed. (Stuttgart: Verlag Katholisches Bibelwerk, 1984).

[28]Mack, "Kingdom Sayings."

[29]Paul D. Hanson, *The Dawn of Apocalyptic* (Philadelphia: Fortress Press, 1975).

[30]Willem S. Vorster, "Texts with an Apocalyptic Perspective," in *Words from Afar: The Literature of the Old Testament*, eds. Ferdinand E. Deist and Willem S. Vorster (Cape Town: Tafelberg Publishers, 1986), 166-85.

past, present and future are interpreted in terms of the expectation of a new future or age and a new world in which supernatural space (heaven) and figures play an important role.

It is within this frame of reference that I refer to the teaching of Jesus as apocalyptic. For our present purpose it does not seem necessary to elaborate further on the question whether the teaching of Jesus was of an apocalyptic or a wisdom nature. More important is to develop the argument about the function of the apocalyptic teaching on the unobservable. My first example is taken from the macarisms or beatitudes of Jesus.

> "Happy are you poor;
> the Kingdom of God is yours!
> Happy are you who are hungry now;
> you will be filled" (Luke 6:20b-21b).

In Matthew's version the sayings read as follows:

> "Happy are those who know they are spiritually poor;
> the Kingdom of heaven belongs to them!
> Happy are those whose greatest desire is to do what God requires;
> God will satisfy them fully" (Matt 5:3 & 6).

Both sayings probably originated from Jesus although the Lukan and Matthean versions differ considerably. Matthew and Luke both made use of Q in compiling the beatitudes and, as the Greek text indicates, there are close similarities between the two versions of the sayings. Matthew probably edited the Q version considerably by changing the "poor" to the "poor of spirit" and "those who are hungry" to "those who hunger and thirst for righteousness". It is probable that in the socioeconomic conditions of the followers of Jesus in Galilee, he would have used the terms "poor" and "hunger" with reference to economically poor and therefore hungry people. It is possible that originally the sayings were in the third person and not in the second as Luke has them.[31] Are these sayings apocalyptic sayings about the unobservable? To answer the question we will first have to deal with the different settings within which beatitudes occur in

---

[31]Cf. Luz, *Evangelium*, 201.

The Function of Metaphorical and Apocalyptic Language 45

Jewish literature in order to construct possible fields of communication.

Beatitudes are used in two totally different *Sitze im Leben* in Jewish literature of the Old Testament and the intertestamental period and therefore reflect two different usages.[32] In the Wisdom-cultic setting they are used as declarative statements about the well-being of the believers (Prov 8:34; Ps 2:11; Wis 3:13-14; Sir 14:1-2 and others). The second setting is future-oriented and is primarily found in apocalyptic writings (1 Enoch 103:5, 2 Bar 10:6-7). Although the last two examples are rather late the roots of this usage probably go back to Isaiah 30:18 and Daniel 12:12. There is quite a remarkable difference between the two usages:

> In the Wisdom-cultic setting, the beatitude is a declarative statement, whose implications border on a paraenetic exhortation. The statement of blessing becomes in turn a model to be emulated or a goal to be attained. An ethical tone prevails. In the prophetic-apocalyptic setting, the beatitude is a declarative statement of future vindication and reward. It comes as assurance and encouragement in the face of trouble. The eschatological tone prevails.[33]

To my mind there is little doubt that these sayings of Jesus are used in the second way, that is in a prophetic-apocalyptic manner. It is interesting to note that both sayings point to the observable as well as the unobservable. The poor and the hungry refer to real people in the sayings while the kingdom and "being satisfied" refer to unobservable realities in the future. What are the functions of these sayings?

Although Jesus did not say what it means that the kingdom belongs to the poor or that the hungry will be satisfied, he obviously tried to encourage the poor and the hungry by creating a symbolic universe which includes the future. In other words he encouraged the poor and hungry to rely on the God who rules and to whose kingdom they belong. The future is not described in concrete terms but simply referred to. It is the unobservable kingdom and place of relief which makes life (in the observable conditions of poverty and

---

[32]Robert A. Guelich, *The Sermon on the Mount: A Foundation for Under standing* (Waco: Word Books Publisher, 1982), 63-66 has a very useful survey of the problem.

[33]Ibid., 65.

hunger) bearable. The sayings have a performative function. They invite the poor and the hungry to rely on the future kingdom of God. As did the metaphoric teaching of Jesus the apocalyptic mode enabled him to encourage people and convince them of the power of a ruler who cannot be seen. He spoke about this ruler and his kingdom without a discussion of the exact detail or a description of what the kingdom is like in observable terms. The apocalyptic sayings of Jesus do not point to describable or observable realities; they function as speech acts which invite people to do things or stimulate them to have part in the kingdom. Let us now turn to Mark 13 from an apocalyptic perspective.

Obviously the speech related in Mark 13:5b-37 cannot be regarded as transmitting the exact words of Jesus. The speech has a very complicated history of growth.[34] In addition, scholars also do not agree about the apocalyptic character of our text. But I believe that there are good grounds to argue that Mark 13 is an apocalyptic text in the sense discussed above and that it contains a core of the apocalyptic teaching of Jesus which has been reworked by Mark to suit his own purpose. For the sake of our argument this text can be used as a larger unit containing apocalyptic and paraenetic teaching of Jesus.

The eschatological conflict and the return of the Son of man are two of the master symbols of a new symbolic universe which the text offers. These aspects make it totally different from the rest of Mark's Gospel. Mark 13:5-37 presupposes a new context of communication, and presupposes a different implied reader. While the previous sections of the story of Mark deal with the future mainly in terms of the death and resurrection of Jesus, Mark 13 focuses upon the end and the return of the Son of man. In Mark 13 conduct is determined by the coming of the end and not by the death and resurrection of Jesus. The end-time is described in images which are familiar to those who are acquainted with apocalyptic imagination and theology. How does this text refer and to what does it point? The history of interpretation of Mark 13 offers an interesting picture of guesswork in this connection not restricted to the *crux interpretum* in verse 14.[35]

It should be kept in mind that texts written from an apocalyptic perspective do not refer to extratextual realities in the first place. That

---

[34]Cf. Egon Brandenburger, *Markus 13 und die Apokalyptik* (Göttingen: Vandenhoeck und Ruprecht, 1984), 21-46.

[35]Ibid., 46, 49-54.

is not their primary function. The image of a future conflict, persecution, tribulation, cosmic changes and the unexpected coming of the Son of man are used in Mark 13 to persuade the four to whom the speech is directed (and also the hearers/readers of the text) to be on the alert and to live with a view to the sudden coming of the Son of man.[36] The text obviously bears the marks of the time and historical context from which it arose, but the individual items which cannot be seen, because they are still to come, do not refer to extratextual realities.

Mark 13 was written from an apocalyptic perspective, as was the Revelation of John, not to reveal or describe the unobservable, but to persuade and instruct readers about their conduct, and to reinforce their beliefs. The function of apocalyptic texts should therefore be seen in terms of what they do and not in terms of what they point to in the metaphysical world.

II
The cognitive function of the metaphorical and apocalyptic language of Jesus

I will be using "cognitive function" here in a restricted sense. Do metaphorical and apocalyptic statements of Jesus also help us to ontologically know the unobservable realities they refer to? Can we claim cognitive reference for the metaphorical and apocalyptic language of Jesus? This question will be dealt with briefly in view of current epistemologies, and not in terms of the language reality problem which I have discussed in another context.[37] The basic problem is obviously: What do metaphorical and apocalyptic statements refer to, and how do we obtain knowledge about the unobservable?

The starting point for our discussion of the cognitive function of the metaphorical and apocalyptic statements about the unobservable in the teaching of Jesus is the observation that in principle neither is to be understood literally. In other words there is no direct one-to-one relationship between what is said and what is referred to. The problem is furthermore complicated by the claims of realists that theological language -in some way or other- refers ontologically in spite of its non-literal character. A few remarks on different epistemo-

---

[36]Cf. Willem S Vorster, "Literary Reflections on Mark 13:5-37: A Narrated Speech of Jesus," *Neotestamentica* 21(1, 1987): 218.

[37]Cf. Lategan and Vorster, *Text and Reality*, 27-65 and 95-112.

logical positions are necessary to explain the different stances on cognitive function.

There are basically two incompatible epistemological positions concerning the cognitive function of language which range from instrumentalism on the one hand to naive realism, positivism and critical realism on the other. This can also be said in terms of non-constructivism versus constructivism. Let us start with the first.

> According to non-constructivism, language has no constitutive function in the cognition of reality. Language is an arbitrary system of symbols, and its essential function is to describe the reality objectively existing according to experience, having regard to the relations convention ally established between language's symbols and reality's objects.[38]

This is similar to the position held by instrumentalists as we will see below.

Constructivism on the other hand holds that language has a constitutive function in the cognition of reality. "Language contains terms for a system of categories and concepts and, by virtue of this, its essential function is a condition of the cognition of reality".[39]

The two positions are mutually exclusive. A short survey of four epistemological positions will clarify the problem.

Instrumentalists hold that theories are products of human creative imagination. Models are therefore useful fictions with heuristic functions. These models are not true or false. They are mental devices. That is why "... an instrumental(sic!) position would first and foremost imply a definite reluctance to make any ontological claim for the modes of doctrines of Christian faith",[40] or, for that matter, utterances about the unobservable, be they in metaphorical or apocalyptic language. In fact, instrumentalism is the exact opposite of a realist position as we shall see below.

According to an instrumentalist position models and metaphors in the Bible will therefore not be depicting reality. They will simply serve to open the possibility of discovering that which is spoken about in any given part of the Bible. As such no written text can pre-

---

[38] Kjärgaard, *Metaphor*, 106.
[39] Ibid., 107.
[40] Wentzel van Huyssteen, *The Realism of the Text: A Perspective on Biblical Authority*, ed. Pieter G.R. de Villiers (Pretoria: University of South Africa, 1987), 21.

tend to give an exact copy of any event or person, not to mention the unobservable. Language does not have the ability to copy reality.

The implications of the naive realist position, which is not used here in a pejorative sense of the word, is given in the following words of John Updike in a poem concerning the resurrection of Jesus:[41]

> Let us not mock God with metaphor,
> analogy, sidestepping, transcendence;
> making of the event a parable, a sign painted in the faded credulity of earlier ages:
> let us walk through the door.
>
> The stone is rolled back, not papier-mâché,
> not a stone in a story,
> but the vast rock of materiality that in slow grinding of time will eclipse
> for each of us
> the wide light of day.
>
> And if we will have an angel at the tomb,
> make it a real angel,
> weighty with Max Planck's quanta, vivid with hair, opaque in the dawn
> light, robed in real linen
> spun on a definite loom.

The naive realist position simply means that theories, including the use of language, are accurate descriptions or replicas of that to which they refer. In the interpretation of the New Testament this position leads to Fundamentalism. The biblical text is without the mediation of any theory. That is why we can pretend to walk through the door.

Positivism also poses the same problems since positivists hold that "... it is possible to go directly from observation to theory without the critical use of models ...".[42] Little attention is given to the fact that knowledge is theory-mediated and that in any interpretation theory plays an important role. Biblical texts are therefore regarded as "empirical data". This leads to biblical literalism.

---

[41] John Updike, "Seven Stanzas at Easter," in *Seventy Poems*, (Harmondsworth: Penguin Books, 1972), 28-9.
[42] Van Huyssteen, *Realism*, 21.

Unlike the instrumentalists, critical realists hold that their theories are representations of the world as reality, and that the models and metaphors which are used in the interpretation of the New Testament refer to reality, even if it is only indirectly by way of *redescription* of reality. Critical realists accept that knowledge about reality is mediated through theories, models and metaphors. The point is, however, that according to this position language has the ability of depicting reality.

> The metaphorical language of the Biblical text, as well as the dominant models we have formed from this, represent aspects of the reality of what Christians believe are in no way directly accessible to use .... As such they are to be taken seriously but not literally, for although they refer in an ontological or cognitive sense, they are always partial and inadequate.[43]

Undoubtedly this is just avoiding the issue. If one accepts the value of models and metaphors in science, one should not forget that the "is" in every metaphor or model in reality is not equal to an ontological "is". It remains "is" in the sense of "is like".[44] Brown correctly observes with regard to metaphor that "... although it should be taken seriously, it should not be taken literally. So e.g. mathematical theories about reality are metaphorical. When the scientist now believes that (sic!) world really *is* mathematically organized — they have turned the metaphor into a myth".[45]

The problem posed by the different positions which I have briefly introduced, is a problem which has been with us since the days of Plato and Aristotle. It is a mind boggling problem especially for those who would like to use rational devices to make firm statements about the things which cannot be seen by human eyes. This is not the place to discuss the advantages and disadvantages of the different epistemological positions referred to above. For our purpose it should be clear that no constructivist or realist position can explain how we can get from a text to the reality outside the text other than by making use of "is like" or "as if" — arguments. That is one reason among others

---

[43] Ibid., 25.
[44] Cf. Paul Ricoeur, "Biblical Hermeneutics," *Semeia* 4(1975):98.
[45] As quoted in M. Elaine Botha, *Metaforiese Perspektief en Fokus in die Wetenskap: Die Rol van Geloof, Mite en Taal in Wetenskaplike Teorievorming* (Potchefstroom: Potchefstroom University for CHE), 55.

The Function of Metaphorical and Apocalyptic Language 51

why an instrumentalist position is preferable to a critical realist position. Instrumentalists are reluctant to make ontological claims in this regard. Basic commitments to realities we cannot observe are faith commitments and therefore not commitments depicting reality in the realist sense of the word.

In the case of the unobservable, both in natural sciences and theology, we have to look for the best theories and hypotheses to explain problems. Not one epistemological position can guarantee that a particular text has cognitive reference. Neither can any epistemological position help the theologian to make claims about the transcendental in ontological terms.

By this time it should be clear that current epistemology cannot help us determine in an ontological sense the "phenomena to which the language of Jesus pointed" or explain the "ontological bearings" of the language of Jesus. The cognitive function of the metaphorical and apocalyptic utterances of Jesus is not a means of discovering the "real persons and the things" that cannot be observed. What we have learnt is that Jesus used metaphoric and apocalyptic language functionally. He did things with words. He tried to resocialize his hearers by offering them a new symbolic universe. In this sense modern theories about language and how it is being used in the Bible help theologians in their attempt to speak meaningfully about the God in whom they believe. That includes the making of new metaphors and the use of metaphorical language about the unobservable.

II
RHETORIC AND STRUCTURE

WHY DO THE RHETORICIANS RAGE?

Steven J. Kraftchick, *Princeton Theological Seminary*

Throughout his work Hendrikus Boers has always maintained a high respect for the material and thought he has studied. The subject of New Testament theology, the history of its interpretation, and, especially, the analysis of the texts of the New Testament in light of these interests have always been more important to him than the need to maintain the status of his own answers or methods. A review of his work shows that Boers has constantly stressed that the essence of good scholarship is the discernment of proper questions and, in a sense, the scholar's task is to provide clearer and better—formed versions of those questions. As a result, while Boers has used various means to analyze the texts of the New Testament throughout his career, he has not made the mistake of allowing the methods to have priority over the object of investigation. His desire in investigating a text has always been to read it in such a way that its voice is heard rather than the voice of the interpreter.[1]

---

[1] This is not to say that he is unaware of the bounded nature of all readings and that all of us are historically and culturally encompassed, indeed, it is just such realizations which have moved his work into the area of semiotics. More importantly, in the pursuit of valuable and clearer readings he has never given such conditions the privilege of providing us an excuse for simply reading a text with any methods which happened to be handy or in vogue. If Boers has been clear about anything in his career, it is that the New Testament critic studies the New Testament. Tools that help in that study are welcome, however, the tools are never celebrated in their own right. They are but instruments providing scaffolding or means to help us on the way to the explication of the text. When this is not recognized, the scaffolding is mistaken for the structure and the tools for their material. The result is that one no longer studies the New Testament, but simply manipulates it.

I. Introduction:

Recently rhetorical criticism of Paul's letters has moved into a more prominent place in Biblical studies. As H. D. Betz recognizes this is not a new exercise, but a rediscovered one.[2] But, as is the case with many newer or older—rediscovered approaches, there is always a period of initial excitement and promise. Since the method proves to have some merit and to be able to expose some features of Paul's arguments that had been neglected with prior approaches it is quickly pressed into service. But, as might be expected, with such excitement there is often excess, more often than not the practitioners get carried away with the new approach, finding sources where none existed, forms that no one had seen before, and multiple layers of redaction that were heretofore invisible. Eventually, more temperate voices are heard and some of the sources disappear, the forms evaporate, and the redactions are found to be more the product of the critic than the writers.

Rhetorical criticism has been no less susceptible to this combination of excitement and excess, with the result that, along with insightful essays, studies have come forth which use the method in less than helpful ways. Often the work moves in a wrong direction, because the interpreter confuses the task with its object. That is, in the desire to find rhetorical forms and genres among Paul's letters, the letters themselves are forgotten. Instead of allowing the texts their rightful shape, the letters are often fitted to the canons of rhetoric. Often this fit is not a neat one and as a result important parts of the text are misshaped or, worse, excised. The exercise makes a subtle shift from the study of Paul's documents by means of rhetorical tools, to the study of rhetoric using Paul's letters as quarries for test drillings.

This essay is an attempt to suggest some of the reasons this occurs and to suggest some directions which the discipline might travel in order to avoid such excesses. I believe that the use of insights gained from the study of ancient and modern rhetoric can prove of great value to the critic of Paul's letters, because such study reveals to us the differences and similarities between ancient forms of argumentation and those prevalent in the modern era. Recognizing this will allow us better access to Paul's manner of argument and enable us to

---

[2]H. D. Betz, "The Problem of Rhetoric and Theology According to the Apostle Paul," *L'Apôtre Paul* ed. A Vanhoye (Leuven: University Press, 1986) 16-18.

avoid the misstep of ignoring or denigrating forms of his argument simply because they are alien to our own.

To achieve these goals I want to review the debate about the genre of Galatians. Further, I want to suggest that Betz's own position is not arbitrary, but reflects certain aspects of Galatians. Having proposed this, I also want to suggest that the rhetorical genre of Galatians may not be as distinct as Betz or his critics maintain and that in sustaining such a position important features of Paul and rhetoric are overlooked. Finally, I will suggest that the debate over the genre of Galatians is misplaced effort and that our rhetorical analyses of the letter might be pursued more fruitfully if we concentrate more on the "rhetorical situation" of Galatians and Paul's means of argumentation.³

What I have in mind is a move away from what appears to be a new form of methodological captivity. The emphasis on the genre of this document could lead (as it appears to in the case of Hall) to an analysis fixated on genre, but which does not explain what is going on in the text itself. Further, if, as Olbricht suggests, Galatians does not fit these genre with the regularity that either Hall or Betz desires, than an insistence on fitting them to the genre does not help us understand the text and, worse, ruptures the real fabric of the argument since it is forced into a form Paul did not choose. Olbricht's own alternative, to considering a fourth category may in fact be correct. However, before such a genre can be defined it is necessary to proceed along the lines of description that Aristotle used and that means that we must first consider each form of religious rhetoric in its own right. Thus, before one can assign a new category its features should be discovered. To do this it appears to me that the descriptive proce-

---

³The reason for this is that the understanding of "rhetorical situation" allows us to exercise an even more critical understanding of the distance between the letter and the actual historical circumstances that were in place. Modern rhetoric has realized that the situation and the audience are in a real manner a construct of the author. Of course, the construction cannot be completely at odds with the historical situation if the argument is to be effective, nevertheless it is not identical with it. On the audience as a speaker construction see Chaim Perelman and L. Olbrechts-Tyteca, *The New Rhetoric. A Treatise on Argumentation* (Notre Dame: Notre Dame Press, 1969) 14-26 and Perelman, *The Realm of Rhetoric* (Notre Dame Press, 1982) 9-20. On the rhetorical situation see: Lloyd F. Bitzer, "The Rhetorical Situation," *Philosophy and Rhetoric* 1 (1968) 1-14, Scott Consigny, "Rhetoric and its Situations," *Philosophy and Rhetoric* 7 (1974) 175-86, and Alan Brinton, "Situation in the Theory of Rhetoric," *Philosophy and Rhetoric* 14 (1981) 234-48.

dure of Chaim Perelman and those involved with New Rhetoric is quite helpful.

II. The Rhetorical Approach to Galatians

A. Hans Dieter Betz

Recent attempts at interpreting Galatians have incorporated insights gained from viewing the epistle in the light of Greco-Roman rhetoric. Of these, because its insights are rich and generally helpful in explicating the text, Hans Dieter Betz's commentary has taken its place among the major modern works on Galatians. The commentary is extremely helpful in providing an understanding of the ideas in Galatians, not only in their individual meanings but also as they relate to each other, and it is hard to imagine any contemporary study of Galatians which does not refer to it.

According to Betz, the situation which prompts Paul to write the letter is the abandonment of Paul and his gospel by the Galatian Christians. It is Betz's contention that the Galatians have been attracted to a new group of teachers who consider Paul's gospel inadequate.[4] Afraid that they may remain "in the flesh", contrary to Paul's promise of a new spiritual life, the Galatians have adopted the teachings of this other group, hoping in that way to guarantee that their life will be free of the hindrances of the flesh. The new teachers suggested that by submitting to certain regulations of the Torah one could move from the fleshly to the spiritual sphere of existence. The movement into a new existence would have enabled such a person to inherit the benefits promised to a child of Abraham.

As Betz argues, Paul wrote the present letter to counter this position and defend the role of the Spirit in creating a spiritual existence. He concludes that the nature and substance of the issue can be understood best if the reader is aware that Paul's letter is a form of forensic apology.[5] Once this genre is recognized its different parts are

---

[4]Betz, *Galatians*, pp. 28-33, but the argument was first developed in a series of articles which preceded the commentary. See especially, "2 Corinthians 6:14-7:1 an Anti-Pauline Fragment?" *JBL* 92 (1973), pp. 88-108., "Spirit, Freedom, and Law: Paul's Message to the Galatian Churches," *SEA* 39 (1974), pp. 145-60., and "In Defense of the Spirit: Paul's Letter to the Galatians as a Document of Early Christian Apologetics," in Elizabeth Schüssler-Fiorenza (ed.), *Aspects of Religious Propaganda in Judaism and Early Christianity*, (Notre Dame: University Press, 1976), 99-114.

[5]*Galatians*, pp. 14-25.

identifiable and they can be understood as members of the various categories from which a legal argument is constructed.

Betz bases this conclusion on two major premises. First, as an example of classical oratory in a written form, Galatians follows specifically the forensic genre. Secondly, the apology takes this particular form because Paul was following the canon of arrangement as it applied to forensic speeches. Thus, any part of the epistle is recognizable as a part of a typical forensic speech.[6]

However, when they are taken together the two premises present a significant difficulty. According to Betz's hypothesis, if we start with the forensic genre and follow the canon of arrangement then a place for parenesis at the end of the proof section should naturally occur. However, as Betz realizes,[7] the typical forensic speech did not contain a parenetic section. This poses a problem for his thesis. Since he cannot find a formal place for parenesis in the arrangement of arguments in ancient rhetorical handbooks, Betz is constrained to point out once again the ingenuity and inventiveness of classical rhetors. However, by doing this he shows that the forensic form was not rigid and that *invention* could overrule *arrangement* and so he violates his second working premise, the commitment to *arrangement* as the controlling factor in the production of the letter.[8] Thus, although Betz wishes to depend on *arrangement* for his understanding of the structure of Galatians, in the final analysis it is *invention* which enables him to include chapters 5 and 6 in his structure.

David Aune's succinct comments demonstrate the difficulty which the hortatory section causes for the proposed forensic genre.

---

[6]Betz uses Quintilian, Aristotle, Plato and *Ad Herennium* as his primary sources for suggesting the canon of arrangement as being dominant in classical rhetoric. But he seems to vacillate on this point. He recognizes that these rules were fluid in practice and that a speech was determined more by its *causa* (a concern of invention) than by its disposition but he frequently applies the rhetoricians observations as if they were iron clad rules, never violated by ancient orators. Yet, when the writer of Galatians does not adhere to these suggestions Betz takes the position that a good rhetorician had to be flexible. His comments on chapters 3 and 4 admit that,"an analysis of these chapters in terms of rhetoric is extremely difficult. One may say that Paul has been very successful—as a skilled rhetorician would be expected to be—in disguising his argumentative strategy." p. 29.

[7]*Galatians*, p. 254.

[8]George Lyons's rather biting comment underscores the dilemma, "Betz himself is such a skillful rhetorician in his analysis of 5:1-6:10, at the same time admitting and dismissing the fact that parenesis has no place in an apologetic latter." Lyons, p. 175.

> Though the body of Galatians (1:6-6:10) is regarded by Betz as an apologetic speech, he assigns the anomalous designation *exhortatio* to the lengthy position of the body in 5:1-6:10. In Betz' general analysis of this section (153-155), the customary references to the ancient rhetorical handbooks are missing. Indeed, no real attempt is made to integrate this extensive *exhortatio* into the general scheme which he finds in the letter. The reason is simply that it cannot be done, for no discussion of *exhortatio* is to be found either in ancient rhetorical handbooks or in the modern synthetic presentations of ancient rhetorical theory...the relationship between the setting of the paraenesis, epistolary paraenesis and the parenetical sections of the Pauline letter remains a subject for investigations.[9]

In one sense Aune's comment is too strong: Betz does attempt to integrate the section with the rest of the epistle. But he is correct in that this is not done on the grounds of the canon of arrangement. The ancient rhetoricians do speak, however, of the role of parenesis in their discussions of *invention*, especially when they refer to proofs of the author's moral character or the development of the author/audience relationship.

Betz's first suggestion also presents some problems for his interpretation. He has followed Aristotle in recognizing three kinds of rhetoric: deliberative, forensic, and epideictic. As we have noted, he chose the forensic mode primarily basing his decision on the letter's defensive tone, especially in the first two chapters. But a reading of the epistle reveals that it also contains elements of the deliberative and epideictic speeches. In a sense then, Galatians represents a different mode, perhaps a hybrid, but still part of the species. What this means is that while classical rhetoric can help uncover the meaning of portions of Galatians, a slavish commitment to one of the three modes of speech leads to misinterpretation. In the end we no longer analyze Galatians but an artificial text of our own creation.[10]

---

[9]Aune, "Review of *Galatians*," RSR 7 (Oct. 1981), 323-24.

[10]Tom Olbricht emphasizes this difficulty in a review of Betz's book. "Rhetorical Criticism of the NT: Betz on Galatians," unpublished paper SBL Seminar, 1982. Olbricht notes that the major concern of both ancient and modern rhetorical critics has not been the second discipline of rhetoric, arrangement, but the first, invention. The primary focus of ancient rhetors was in making the argument effective. It is for that reason that forms of argument were so fluid and that rhetorical genres were not precisely delimited. Therefore forensic, delibera-

The existence of the rhetorical handbooks notwithstanding, it is well to remember that ancient rhetoric, in its rules as well as the manifestation of those rules, was extremely fluid. This being the case it is incorrect to restrict Paul to a single form, especially one for which no analogy can be found. In that sense, granting Betz full respect for his achievement, we must still modify the manner in which the commentary's rhetorical analysis proceeds. Betz's adherence to the canon of arrangement as the heuristic device for interpretation presents a problem because this canon describes set forms of argumentation, not their variation. When Betz points out the deviation from the normal forensic speech which the hortatory section of Galatians presents he shows that it is the first canon of rhetoric, *invention*, and not *arrangement* which ultimately controls the production of the arguments of Galatians. Therefore, instead of emphasizing the form of Galatians we should focus on how the individual pieces of the argument are used to create a persuasive whole.

---

tive, and epideictic speeches could each incorporate elements of the others, depending on the rhetorical situation being faced. Thus, in terms of Galatians we should not be restricted to interpreting the epistle as an example of a specific rhetorical genre. Instead we should allow the fluidity its full force. What we are after is how the arguments function; if an arrangement typical of an ancient rhetorical genre does not help in this we should not feel constrained to make Galatians fit such a mold.

Since then Olbricht has expanded this criticism and suggests that we would be truer to Aristotle's goals if we did not restrict ourselves to the three genres which Aristotle has suggested.

"How did Aristotle arrive at his principles of rhetoric? It is obvious first of all that he collected whatever rhetorical works were then available, just as he collected constitutions of the city-states so as to amass a body of data from which to generalize about political systems. From the extant rhetorics he incorporated insights, but weighed and sifted the conclusions, often creating new categories, or adding examples from speeches, literature, and observations. He did not claim to have exhausted the discipline. He made no effort to dissuade others from building on his foundations and methodologies. We are therefore most faithful to Aristotle when we add to his categories and observations, both in respect to commonalities and diversities. Any use of *The Rhetoric* which treats it as a frozen corpus, is not faithful to the presuppositions of its author. We are indebted to Aristotle, more for his methodology, than for the completeness of his categories or conclusions." Thomas Olbricht, "An Aristotelian Rhetorical Analysis of Galatians. Unpublished paper. See especially pp. 7-8

B. Robert Hall

Robert Hall has noted some of these difficulties in Betz's choice and has tried to address them in a recent article.[11] There Hall contends that Galatians can be better understood if it is read as a deliberative piece of rhetoric. Hall realizes that such identification is difficult because the topics used in ancient speeches were interchangeable. Still he is convinced that Galatians exhibits enough evidence to decide in favor of the deliberative genre.

Hall bases his arguments on evidence from rhetorical handbooks and on what he understands to have been Paul's purpose for writing to the Galatians. Arguing from his reading of the letter, Hall maintains that Paul is not trying to justify his past actions, nor defend himself, as Betz has suggested, but rather, "to persuade the Galatians to cleave to Paul and his gospel and to reject the opponents and their gospel (Gal 1:6-9, cf. 6:12-16)."[12] Paul does this because he believes that the Galatians are trying to decide between his position and that of his opponents. When he turns to the handbooks themselves Hall notes four characteristics of deliberative speeches which fit the tone and content of Galatians. First, noting that declamatory forms of deliberative rhetoric were often impetuous and over embellished in style, he argues that this is the case in Galatians as well, suggesting that passages such as 1:6-9, 5:7-12, 6:12-13 display a "wild exclamatory manner."[13] Second, Paul's use of the narrative section fits the deliberative genre better than the forensic because the facts introduced here are external to the case.[14] Third, deliberative oratory typically dealt with choices between options and Paul was seeking to move the Galatians by appealing to an option which was to their advantage. Finally, the letter contains exhortations and these are an especial characteristic of deliberative rhetoric.

Hall's procedure opens itself to criticism because of its form of comparison. Noting general features of deliberative rhetoric, as described in various handbooks and some general features of the style

---

[11] Hall, Robert, "The Rhetorical Outline for Galatians: A Reconsideration," *JBL* 106/2 (1987), 277-87.

[12] Hall. p.279

[13] Hall, pp. 280-81.

[14] Instead of commenting on facts about Paul's past action the facts presented show Paul's authoritative ethos, show that his gospel is from God, and argue against the doctrine of the opponents. Hall, p. 280

of Galatians causes Hall to conclude that the letter is deliberative argumentation. No doubt there is a desire for deliberation by the Galatians on Paul's part. However, Hall's procedure for classification relies too heavily on general similarities and ignores too quickly Paul's own initiative and creativity. Too frequently Hall notes some features of a passage and assumes that these features signify that the text is an instance of deliberative rhetoric. This is especially true of his understanding of the narrative section of the letter and his sense that the letter is "wildly exclamatory."[15] Such terminology is too loose to allow for specific examination and the result is that any time Paul expresses dismay, uses sarcasm, or displays an emotion, Paul is making a calculated rhetorical move. It appears to me that Hall confuses the expressions of the letter with their rhetorical functions and so attributes to Paul a sense of calculation which the letter does not display.

In this regard, Hall confuses a strategy involving Paul's ethos portrayal with the overall purpose of the letter. Repeatedly, Hall refers to the purpose of the letter as Paul getting the Galatians to cleave to him, but the question he does not address well is why Paul desired such a move? For Hall the choice is "to cleave to Paul or to cleave to his opponents." But this is too general a category, all speeches of both the judicial and deliberative genre have this in common. In either genre there will be attempts to create association with the speaker and away from the opposition. This can hardly be classified as the goal of the letter, rather it is one of the strategies involved in accomplishing the goal. That is, Hall has mistaken one of Paul's strategies, i.e., turning the Galatians' loyalty to himself, for the

---

[15]Another concrete instance of this is his quick treatment of the exhortations in chapters 5 and 6. Hall simply says that Paul tries to persuade or dissuade the Galatians from certain behaviors. However, he does not explain why or how Paul does this. Any helpful rhetorical analysis should be able to suggest how this persuasion/dissuasion is effected and for what reasons. The idea that Paul is offering something advantageous to the Galatians is insufficient since, as Paul admits in chapter 6 his opponents also claimed to give the Galatians an advantage in living the Christian life.

When Hall does work with the hortatory section of the letter he simply subsumes chapters 5 and 6 under the heading Proof and the sub-category further headings. However, he does very little to describe how this material functions as proof. He does mention that such arguments "support the proposition by disposing reason and emotion (logos and pathos) to heed the summons to cleave to Paul and his gospel and to repudiate his opponents." (Hall,p. 284) But, this does not go very far in explaining how they do this, or in giving much force to the inclusion of the material.

actual goal of the letter, namely, the reorientation of the Galatians in the true understanding of the Christ event, the restructuring of the community ethic, and so, returning their loyalty to God who called the community into existence.

While one might agree with Hall's conclusion that Galatians is deliberative rhetoric, his quick assessment leaves the polemic sense of Galatians unaccounted for. If the only matter at stake was the future action of the Galatians, then Paul would have been able to move much more quickly to the positive portion of the letter. Hall's analysis does not take the polemical thrust of the letter seriously enough given that a third of the epistle involves a type of defense by Paul of himself and the nature of his gospel.[16] It may not be entirely true that the letter is a pure form of judicial rhetoric, in terms of past charges, but one can hardly ignore the severe and defensive language Paul has used.

Finally, for all its sense of classical rhetoric, Hall's analysis does not demonstrate a proper sense of the theological nature of the letter. Whole sections drop out of Hall's reconstruction so that one can find little reason for Paul's inclusion of the arguments in chapter 2 and almost no reason for the convoluted argumentation of chapters 3 and 4. The letter's parts are given labels, but they are not considered as part of a working argument concerning religious convictions. But to neglect this is to neglect what is crucial in an analysis of a theological document. Without attention to these features one is not working on Galatians, but simply engaging in an exercise of description. A new form of parallelomania, as Sandmel would suggest; only this time the arena is rhetorical handbooks and not the Jewish/Hellenistic moral world. Hall's rhetorical analysis enables him to note Paul's desire for the Galatians' allegiance, but the narrow scope of the investigation causes him to overlook the theological motivation for this desire. In the end we have a form of rhetorical captivity which threatens to make Paul into a form of sophist or opportunist.

C. The New Captivity

In an overview of recent kinds of rhetorical criticism Wilhelm Wuellner noted that the use of rhetoric for analysis of New Testament texts had suffered through a long captivity caused by the emphasis on stylistics, because rhetoric was equated with, and reduced to, the

---

[16]So too Aune, *RSR*, 326.

discovery and identification of tropes.[17] Wuellner is happy that contemporary use of rhetoric has sought to avoid that detour and has focussed on the matters of the rhetorical unit, the identification of the rhetorical situation, the disposition of an argument, its style, and the sense of the sum of an argument being greater than its constituent parts.[18] Wuellner's position is correct and the movement away from considering rhetoric as a device tacked on to substantive argument is a welcome one. However, it appears to me that a new form of captivity is also possible and that aspects of it emerge in contemporary analyses.

In 1979 when Betz published his commentary on Galatians a significant breakthrough was made both for the use of rhetoric in Pauline studies and in light of the meaning of the Galatian letter itself.[19] This is not to say that Betz's commentary was met with quiet applause.[20] From the initial reviews Betz's contention that Galatians was an instance of forensic rhetoric was challenged. Since then scholars have noted difficulties with Betz's analysis and throughout the last decade important modifications of his work have been suggested.

This has had positive and negative results. Positively it has awakened us to the fact that rhetorical critical work is complicated and that genre determination is not as simple as Betz initially appears to suggest. Further, we are aware that Paul's letters are less susceptible to an analysis like Betz's because the forms of Paul's arguments do not

---

[17]Wilhelm Wuellner, "Where Is Rhetorical Criticism Taking Us?," *CBQ* 49 (1987) 448-63. So also "Epistolography and Rhetoric," A paper delivered to the I Corinthians seminar at the 1988 SNTS meeting. "Rhetorical criticism is hampered, if not downright sabotaged, by two powerful legacies in our exegetical tradition: (1) The hegemony of the historical critical paradigm which forces the rhetorical critic's concern to prioritize ... 'the historical argumentative situation' as the first and primary of several 'levels of communication.' And (2) the tradition of reducing rhetoric to style which has blighted literary hermeneutics increasingly since the late sixteenth century." SNTS Seminar paper, p. 12

[18]Wuellner, pp.455-58. Wuellner follows the program set forth by George Kennedy in *New Testament Interpretation Through Rhetorical Criticism* (Chapel Hill, NC: Univ. of NC Press, 1984)

[19]Hans Dieter Betz, *Galatians*, (Philadelphia: Fortress Press, 1979).

[20]The recognition of the significance of Betz's commentary did not prevent scholars from disagreeing with it profoundly in their reviews. C. K. Barrett and F. F. Bruce refer to it as a masterpiece, but the reviews of David Aune and Wayne Meeks are less favorable and George Lyons is even more extreme in his critique. He puzzles concerning Betz's working assumptions, "One wonders what evidence Betz would require as sufficient proof against his theory that Galatians is an apologetic letter.", Lyons, p. 75.

strictly follow the canons of rhetoric. But negatively there has been a fixation on the question of genre which has detracted from the analysis of the letter itself. Whatever Betz was after, one thing is clear, rhetoric was not an end in itself, he was after a reading of Paul's letters. Some of his critics have missed this point and have centered too heavily on the genre question never returning to see how this helps or hinders the exegesis of the letter itself. When this has occurred rhetorical criticism has found a new captivity for itself.[21]

The problem with such insistence on genres is that it unduly imposes upon Paul a structure which is neither demonstrable in terms of his habit of constructing arguments or in terms of classical rhetoric. Because it forces Paul and his letters into one of these molds, (even though our evidence suggests that while he was aware of rhetoric techniques and used various forms of argumentation he was not a professional rhetor nor did he work from the same beginning premises) this procedure denies to him the creativity that those reviewing epistolographic evidence have observed and further damages the argumentative integrity of the texts in their own right.[22] Paul uses forms found in ancient Greco-Roman letters, but he apparently

---

[21] An instance of this is the recent study produced by Robert Hall, who admits that assigning a speech to one of the three genre is a difficult task, but is still persuaded that he can do this with Galatians. "Since the special characteristics of each species (defense or accusation of judicial, exhortation of deliberative, praise or blame of epideictic) may serve as topics for persuasion, it is not unusual for a speech of one species to employ a topic associated with another, as when a judicial orator exhorts a judge to think only of justice or praises the good character of the defendant. This overlap between characteristics of the species and topics of persuasion can cause some initial confusion in classification. Occasionally. if a work lacks unity, it may be impossible to assign it fully to one of the three species of rhetoric. nevertheless, the classification works reasonably well for many speeches and should be abandoned only when the categories clearly do not fit. Since the three species of rhetoric can significantly clarify the purpose of the writer or speaker, they remain useful tools in the rhetorical analysis of a text." p. 278

[22] Paul Meyer's warning about Betz's excesses is equally valid when applied to Hall's work. "So there is a real danger of imposing upon the analysis of Galatians an ideal construct, a kind of literary or rhetorical parallel to the phantom of "the" Gnostic redeemer myth, or the product of hypostatizing a rhetorical phenomenon into a historical one. The search for hard classifications has been dubbed a 'cookie-cutter criticism.' The best safeguard against such abuses of method is still deliberately cultivated sensitivity to the text itself that is being analyzed, to sense where it resists the overlay of predetermined patterns, and a readiness to acknowledge that Paul has proven himself in other ways to be quite free to modify or adapt the forms to which he is heir, be they literary (as in the letter itself) or oral (as in credal or hymnic material)." *RSR* 7 (Oct. 1981) 319.

did not feel constrained by those conventions.[23] Is it not reasonable to assume that the same freedom is exercised in terms of rhetorical skill? That is, noting that rhetoric was itself open to a certain amount of fluidity and allowing for Paul to have some creativity, it appears that the way in which classical rhetoric can best help us to analyze Paul is not in the manner of ancient categories, but in the types of proofs exercised, forms of argument employed, and figures of language used. Thus, as Olbricht contends, there is perhaps a new form of rhetorical category at hand.[24] Rather than propose what this structure might look like, I will suggest that the newer conceptions of rhetoric can be equally helpful, if not more so, in helping us to determine Paul's purposes and the manner of arguments which he uses.[25]

III. New Conceptions of Argument

It seems that a more fruitful method of appropriating rhetoric for analyzing Paul's letters is to consider how the arguments and techniques function. The genre plays a role but it appears that Galatians will not lend itself to easy classification and so we should begin with the material itself instead of imposing an outside description upon it. A promising method is to follow Perelman's lead in asking what forms of arguments are being used and then we may suggest what role this played in the overall argument of Galatians.

In that regard I should like to briefly describe Perelman's main points concerning argumentation which seeks adherence to values by means of association and dissociation. This done I will suggest some instances of the techniques in Galatians and then suggest some reasons for these strategies based on the discussions of Sillars and Ganer.

A. Perelman

Perelman, like Olbricht, finds the Aristotelian division too restrictive to account for the arguments he has analyzed. However, unlike Olbricht, he does not propose a new genre, but rather expands the understanding of epideictic rhetoric.[26] Perelman is aware that his-

---

[23] See on Paul's freedom with the letter form, Stan Stowers, *Letter Writing in Greco-Roman Antiquity* (Philadelphia: Westminster, 1986) and John L. White, *Light From Ancient Letters* (Philadelphia: Fortress, 1986)

[24] Olbricht, "An Aristotelian Rhetorical Analysis," pp. 12-13.

[25] As Wuellner notes this approach "invites us to rethink the task of analyzing "types of persuasion" without the tedious taxonomies of the classical theoreticians." Wuellner, SNTS 1988, p.14 n.22

[26] Perelman, *New Rhetoric*, pp.47-51.

torically epideictic discourse has been identified with ornamentation and with the self glorification of its presenter. However, he maintains that the disrepute which epideictic discourse enjoys is more the result of a misconception of argument than an intrinsic flaw in this particular genre. Initially, according to Aristotle, epideictic speech dealt with matters of value, things praiseworthy and things dishonorable and it is this aspect of epideictic which Perelman wishes to recover. Thus, he wishes to reclaim the genre as a valuable and necessary form of argumentation.[27]

This is important to Perelman because in his view arguments seek adherence to a set of values and usually a course of action predicated upon those values. "In fact, the aim of argumentation is not, like demonstration, to prove the truth of the conclusion from premises, but to transfer to the conclusion the adherence accorded to the premises. Lest he fail in his mission, the speaker should depart from his premises only when he knows that they are adequately accepted; if they are not, the speaker's first concern should be to reinforce them with all the means at his disposal."[28] His major point is that the proper analysis of arguments is to consider how they function to persuade an audience to shift its adherence to value sets and the theses which result from them. Moreover, not bound by conventions of arrangement, but desirous of attaining his/her goal the rhetorician uses whatever types of argument will work. That is, the author may use arguments normally found in forensic or deliberative rhetoric. The point is not what elements of argument are used,[29] but how they are

---

[27] "...epideictic oratory has significance and importance for argumentation, because it strengthens the disposition towards action by increasing adherence to the values it lauds. It is because the speaker's reputation is not the exclusive end of epideictic discourse, but at most a consequence, that a funeral eulogy can be pronounced without lack of decency, beside an open grave, or a Lenten sermon can have a purpose other than the renown of the preacher." *New Rhetoric*, p. 50.

[28] Perelman, *The Realm of Rhetoric*, p. 21.

[29] "Unlike the demonstration of a geometrical theorem, which establishes once and for all a logical connection between speculative truth, the argumentation of epideictic discourse sets out to increase the intensity of adherence to certain values, which might not be contested when considered on their own but may nevertheless not prevail against other values that might come into conflict with them. The speaker tries to establish a sense of communion centered around particular values recognized by the audience, and to this end he uses the whole range of means available to the rhetorician for purposes of amplification and enhancement.

used. If this shift in adherence is the goal of argumentation then epideictic discourse is especially well suited for it because it is a discourse which discusses values and desires to bring forth stronger commitment to them.

Generally an argument proceeds from shared premises in gradual steps to the thesis proffered by the author.[30] The discourse follows a series of arguments based on the techniques of association and dissociation. One begins with such premises but in an argument the status of the elements which enter into it are set by the adherence of the audience to those elements. Thus facts and truths can be questioned, facts can be modified by forms of presentation, and so on.[31] Thus, "contrary to demonstration, which is developed in a well-defined system, argumentation most often draws upon a very ill defined corpus of premises, and the theses upon which it is based can be partially understood or implicit."[32] Therefore arguments are more or less

---

In epideictic oratory every device of literary art is appropriate, for it is a matter of combining all the factors that can promote this communion of the audience." Perelman, *New Rhetoric*, p.51.

[30]The starting points for a discourse are those which bear on reality, e.g., facts and truths, and those which bear on the preferable, e.g., values, hierarchies, and the loci of the preferable. Perelman uses these terms to distinguish the sorts of beginning points that an author can use to begin the argument. he realizes that even these are not always self evident and that the author must present them in such a way that they produce a sense of commonality between author and audience. In the case of Paul and the Galatians certain tenets of the faith serve these purposes, e.g., the deliverance of the Galatians by the Christ, the desire of God, etc. Not all of these expressions are equally understood and part of Paul's task is to gain adherence to similar definitions and understandings, but that the expressions are shared as part of the faith is agreed upon and this is sufficient to begin the discourse.

Perelman understands facts and truths to be those statements generally accepted by the group as such. They are not infallible unless they are from a deity. Should a fact or truth be challenged then the challenger must be disqualified as such by the orator before he or she can continue with the argument. How might this be done? Either by providing evidence which corroborates the fact, or by disqualifying the objector as someone who objects for wrong reasons or because he/she is an untrustworthy interpreter. This untrustworthiness could be the result of a number of factors, lack of expertise, lack of proper understanding, moral character flaw etc. Paul uses all of these topics in Galatians to disqualify his opponents as adequate interpreters. He provides corroborating evidence, but he also disqualifies his objectors. That is, the attacks on the Teachers does not need to follow from personal attack on Paul but from their position as interpreters.

[31]Perelman, *Realm*, p. 48.
[32]Perelman, *Realm*, pp. 48-49.

strong rather than deduced conclusions in the formal sense of demonstration.

To move from premises to a desired goal the author attempts various strategies of association[33] and dissociation.[34] Association

---

[33]Perelman specifies three forms of association or liaison:

1) quasi-logical: arguments classifed by comparing them to formal reasoning. They appear to be like formal reasoning in structure but the ambiguity of terms and the possibility of multiple interpreataion makes them quasi-logical. Although in contemporary speech we are leery of such ambiguity, Perelman shows that it is still part of our argumentation and warns that, "in antiquity, when the mathematical version of scientific thinking was less developed, recourse to quasi-logical arguments was more frequent. Today our first reaction is to emphasize the weakness of such arguments by comparing them with formal structures." Perelman, *Realm*, pp. 53-54. A full discussion is found in *New Rhetoric*, pp. 193-195, *Realm*, pp. 53-54.

2) structure of reality: Primarily there are two different ways of structuring reality, liaisons of succession and liaisons of coexistence. Liaisons of succession, which correlate phenomena of the same level include, search for causes, the determination of effects, evaluation of a fact by its consequences. The argument of 5:1-4 seems to be of this type where the consequences of circumcision are used to disqualify it as an appropriate behavior. Paul's argument, which Perelman would identify as a pragmatic argument, appraises a fact through its consequences. Actually, Paul is extending a pragmatic argument which the Teachers have used. They have maintained that circumcision is proper because of the end it procures, Paul goes farther and claims that the real end of circumcision is separation from Christ. He desires to show the incompleteness of the Teacher's view because further explanation shows that a negative result applies, separation from Christ.

Liaisons of coexistence, argumentation based on terms which represent material or actions of unequal levels, such as an essence and its manifestations, a person and his/her acts, is used throughout the letter when Paul states his own biography and when he characterizes the opponents. However, in chapter 5:7-12 and 6:12-14 they are portrayed as people who frighten and agitate the Galatians, persecute Paul and, in the end, exploit the Galatians for the sake of their own reputation. The implication is that the actions betray people who are themselves detrimental for the Galatians as is the teaching which they suggest will be good for the congregations. (On the Teachers see, J. L. Martyn, "A Law Observant Mission to the Gentiles," *Scottish Journal of Theology*, 38 (1985), 307-324). Full discussions of this type of argument is found in *New Rhetoric*, 261-263, *Realm*, p. 81.

3) Arguments which establish the structure of reality. These establish a rule or precedent produced by example, illustration and analogy. One moves from the specific to the rule, i.e., in an opposite direction from which one moves in the arguments based on the structure of reality. Paul's primary mode in chapters 5-6 is in arguments based on the structure of reality, but an instance of this form occurs in 4:21-31 where the allegory is used to establish the principle of freedom. See Perelman, *New Rhetoric*, p. 350.

[34]Dissociative arguments include those primarily based on the difference between appearance and reality and, differentiation by definition, and those prompted by paradox or incompatibilty. The strategy is to provide the *real* defini-

transfers the adherence of the audience from a premise to a specific conclusion, while dissociation attempts to separate elements of language or recognized tradition which have previously been held together. Paul's use of the Abraham motif helps to show the differences. In Romans the argument proceeds by means of association, but in Galatians it is dissociated from the law.

It would be too bold to argue that Galatians is a instance of epideictic rhetoric, especially in the Aristotelian sense. Nevertheless, from Perelman's expanded perspective there are elements of this genre present. It is clear that Paul wants to do more than win his case forensically or to have the Galatians deliberate about the course of action to take, he desires action based on the core values and beliefs of the gospel he has preached. Obviously he seeks the cessation of certain cultic practices, but more than this he seeks the expulsion of the teachers[35], and for the Galatians to have a community ethic which reflects mutual love for its members. (Cf. 5:1-4; 13-15; 6:1-5)

In letters such as Paul's this goal of epideictic discourse remains a primary one. Paul is not only interested in winning a case as a forensic genre might indicate, or in having his audience deliberate on a course of action, he desires them to be reoriented in terms of the Christian proclamation and to act accordingly. That is, based on the activity of God through Christ, Paul calls for a restructuring of an audience's values and for it to follow a course of action consonant with those values. Thus, by combining exhortations with kerygmatic proclamation, Paul argues that the appropriate and sufficient response to God is community action based on and caused by God's liberating action in Christ.

B. Sillars and Ganer

Malcolm Sillars and Patricia Ganer have suggested that, argumentation is functional in a conflict situation "when differences arise over beliefs and values but cooperative means of resolving those con-

---

tion as opposed to the pseudo-definition which is operative or to expose the real essence from the appearances which are available to the audience. This is done by showing incompatibilty or contradiction and using paradoxical language. *New Rhetoric*, pp. 411-415. Such a strategy is evident in Paul's explantion that adherence to cultic practice has the appearance of spiritual behavior but is in fact, fleshly, 4:8-10. This he turns into an argument of waste , a means/end strategy with his lament that he has labored in vain.

[35]See J. L. Martyn, "Apocalyptic Antinomies," p. 419.

flicts are essential...."³⁶ However, for cooperation to take place, the parties in the conflict must acknowledge that some common ground exists,and in this case accepted values of good and bad are the basis of that common ground.

Sillars and Ganer understand this matrix of values as threefold: beliefs, values and attitudes.³⁷ They consider a belief to be the smallest unit in a social value system and define it as "any simple proposition, conscious or unconscious, inferred from what a person says or does, capable of being preceded by the phrase 'I believe that...' The content of a belief may describe the object of belief as true or false, correct or incorrect; evaluate it as good or bad; or advocate a certain course of action or a certain state of existence as desirable or undesirable."³⁸ Values are understood as "a type of belief, centrally located within one's total belief system, about how one ought or ought not to behave, or about some end state of existence worth or not worth attaining." And attitudes are understood as "a relatively enduring organization of beliefs around an object or situation predisposing one to respond in some preferential manner."³⁹ As the common ground between arguer and listeners they serve as the backing for statements within the argument. Thus, while they may often remain below the surface of a discourse they are actually its focal point.

According to Sillars and Ganer, argumentation is an attempt to modify the value system of one party by the other. But since people do not readily shift their value systems the arguer is faced with a difficult task. First, he or she must determine which values can be used to support the argument and which can be used to criticize the position of the opponents. Next the arguer must choose the approach to value modification he/she will use.

---

³⁶Malcolm O. Sillars and Patricia Ganer, "Values and Beliefs: A Systematic Basis for Argumentation," in *Advances in Argumentation Theory and Research*. eds. J. Robert Cox and Charles Arthur Willard. (Southern Illinois University Press, Carbondale and Edwardsville, 1982), p. 189.

³⁷Sillars and Ganer conclude that, "In argumentation, then, values form warrants for arguments, support beliefs that warrant arguments, and underlie choices that have to be made about a host of argumentation decisions such as evidence, style reason, and presumption." p. 198. Further, they maintain that, "Values, whether extrinsic or intrinsic, are the most pervasive factor in the argumentative situation. They serve as the underpinnings to all the process of general argumentation." p. 199.

³⁸They follow M. Rokeach in this definition and the definitions of values and attitudes. *Beliefs, Attitudes, and Values*. (Jossey-Bass, 1970), p. 113.

³⁹Sillars and Ganer, p. 186.

Sillars and Ganer suggest five possible options for the arguer: 1) value acquisition and abandonment 2) value redistribution—the value becomes more or less widely distributed within the society, 3) value re-scaling—causing a change in its relative importance, 4) value re-employment—changing the range of the value's applicability, and 5) value re-standardization—raising or lowering how a particular value becomes established in a specific belief.[40] Thus, values play a major role in an argument because the degree to which they can be shifted is directly related to the degree of the argument's success.[41] This suggests that the investigation of the parenetic materials which make up Galatians 5 and 6 clarifies the values which Paul sought to shift in order to create his argument.

IV. The Argumentative Strategy of Galatians

A. The Argumentative Use of the Hortatory Section

It is evident that these definitions of values and beliefs can easily be used to describe the content and function of parenetic materials. By his use of maxims, proverbs, and metaphors Paul, perhaps here more than anywhere else in the epistle, reflects the common value system which underpins the argument. Galatians 5:25-6:10 could play this important role in the letter because it reflects the values and beliefs which were held in common by Paul and his readers. Clearly Paul reconstructs this material in light of the "New Creation". Nevertheless, this reconstructed material can still serve as a common ground between Paul and the Galatians

Paul maintains this in two ways. First he attempts to show that he shares a common understanding and appreciation of the value system in which the Galatians function. As Sillars and Ganer point out, "A speaker seeking adherence from a specific audience that has a specific point of view predicated upon specific beliefs will be more effective when he or she can identify with those audience beliefs. To the extent that such specificity of beliefs cannot be determined or found, more general identification with audience values would be most ef-

---

[40]Sillars and Ganer, 191. The reference is to M. Rescher, "The study of value change." in *Value Theory in Philosophy and Social Science*. eds. E. Lazlo and J. B. Wilbur. (Gordon and Breech, 1973), pp. 14-16.

[41]It is interesting that Daniel Patte has suggested this in his book on Paul, but surprisingly, ignores the parenetic material, treating it in the standard way. *Paul's Faith and the Power of the Gospel*. (Philadelphia:Fortress, 1983), pp. 65-66, 334-335.

fective."[42] By incorporating the parenetic materials into the letter Paul attempts to identify himself as one who understands what these common grounds are.

Secondly, it is possible that Paul is faced with a consequence of the first option which creates a significant barrier for him in the argument. Because values are so formative for a community the attempts to shift or remove them are difficult and could result in emotional upheaval. Paul, faced with such a situation, utilizes the second, third, fourth, and fifth options to overcome this difficulty. Finally, because of the resistance to the abandonment of values Paul must assure his readers that they can acquire a value system which will be consonant with the gospel and, at the same time, fulfill their societal/communal needs if he wishes the Galatians to continue with him in the argument. As he moves through the argument Paul must provide this assurance, which he does by virtue a combination of logos, ethos and pathos appeals.

B. The Socio-emotional Context of Galatians 5-6.

It is evident that the Galatians were in a state of uncertainty due to their confusion over the right way in which to carry out the Christian life. It is also clear that they were faced with alternative claims, one from Paul and another from those whom he opposed. Even if Paul's view was that there was no real alternative, this is not the case with the Galatians. All the participants shared a common religious framework and there was definitely an interplay between an old and new set of beliefs. Further, the nature of the claims demanded a leap which was inferential and not demonstrable. Whatever else Paul was doing in this letter it is clear that he was trying to alleviate the uncertainty which the Galatians faced. Whether the leap be seen as an epistemological one (as J. Louis Martyn suggests) or more in terms of the argument concerning the role of the law alongside Christ for life in the Spirit, the Galatians were still brought to a point of decision by Paul's letter. This automatically involved him in the process of persuasive argumentation, which, we have seen, is the basic impetus for the development of rhetoric.

At this point I would like to suggest an analysis of the "emotional/rhetorical situation of Paul's listeners. In this regard I think that it is worth noting the insights of contemporary sociology of

---

[42]Sillars and Ganer, p. 194.

religion because they may shed some light on what had been taking place between Paul and his readers. Peter Berger's comments in *The Sacred Canopy* are especially revealing when he speaks of sociologically marginal situations of destruction/construction of worlds. Berger maintains that religion as a human product is a construction that legitimizes a society's way of structuring the world.[43] As long as the structure is not questioned its very facticity suffices as its legitimation. However, when a challenge appears this facticity can no longer be assumed. This sort of challenge occurs on a number of levels for the Galatians. First in Paul's initial appearance in their midst when he introduces the gospel to them. Secondly in the dissonance between their lived experience and Paul's statements about the reality of the gospel's effects. Third, with the appearance of a new set of teachers who overturn the teaching brought by Paul. And, fourth the significant challenge to the new religious posture of his readers in the argument of Galatians. All of this forces them to reevaluate the legitimacy of their religious structure. If this is the case then it is fair to say that we meet a situation of world destruction/construction in Paul's letter to the Galatians.[44]

Berger also notes that every society defines itself in terms of the world that it builds. He refers to the principle of ordering, interestingly enough, as nomos. The nomos is composed of a pre-theoretical "knowledge" consisting of "interpretative schemas, moral maxims and collections of traditional wisdom that the man in the street frequently shares with the theoreticians."[45] Society, by providing this nomos, guards itself against the loss of order and meaning.

Clearly Paul was adamant in his anti-law position in the mainparts of the letter, especially chapters 3 and 4 and the beginnings of chapter 5. Regardless of whether he intended it or not, it is conceivable that this anti-nomos argument was perceived (perhaps it is better to suggest that it was apprehended almost at an unreflective level of the corporate conscience) by the readers as a total elimination of

---

[43] Peter Berger, *The Sacred Canopy*. (New York:Doubleday, 1969.)

[44] This is all the more true if Martyn's construction of the argument in Galatians is correct. Martyn maintains that Paul has completely undercut the manner in which the Galatians and the teachers understood the world and their place in it. Although Martyn takes this to be the thrust of chapter 5 as well, it still is the case that the exhortations have another role of providing a new kind of structure for the community to live in. See Martyn, "Apocalyptic Antinomies," pp. 414, 420.

[45] Berger, p. 21-22.

their world ordering principles, the principles that satisfied their need for security. Thus, if they accepted Paul's thesis, it would have meant the rejection of the only way of structuring experience which they knew. However, the loss of this structuring would bring into stark relief the possibility of chaos, the loss of meaning, regardless of Paul's insistence on the control brought by the new creative actions of God.[46] Thus, even if, on a theological level, Paul was defeating the teachers, it is not clear that his arguments would overcome the resistance of the Galatians on the basis of their logical force alone.

The appeal of the other religion/other gospel, produced by the Teachers, was that it provided a new security. By performing certain tasks the events of the universe make sense and the individual's place is assured in it. Accepting Paul's thesis meant losing this security. This loss could act as a hindrance to the acceptance of Paul's position by the Galatians. Even if they could agree cognitively with his thesis, they may still have found it impossible to do so emotionally.

Again, the value, argumentatively, of the opposing position was its demonstrability. There was a certain "concreteness" to it which gave it more persuasive force than Paul's unseen promises. As I mentioned, Paul's only means of verification up to this point in the argument was a purely subjective one, i.e., the experience of the Spirit. However, the other side could point to tangible results of activity which the Galatians themselves could do (e.g.,circumcision, or following dietary laws etc.), results which could be seen or experienced concretely, and therefore had a stronger sense of reality and persuasiveness about them. In terms of making his argument acceptable and not losing the adherence of his readers it was incumbent on Paul to provide a counter argument to this strength of the opposition.

To be persuasive Paul must also display his own actions and good character. The position which he argues is not, in itself, demonstrable, that is, it calls for an element of belief.[47] If Paul can argue that circumcision is a fleshly activity his adversaries could just as well argue logically that it is spiritual. Both arguments could appear equally

---

[46]Berger, p. 21.

[47]Since the arguments which Paul used were not externally verifiable, i.e., his evidence was not tangible but experiential or inferential, they demanded a response based on belief from the readers. We should recall Aristotle once more; with evidence of this type "logical" syllogisms or enthymemes are not sufficient for persuasion. Both sides can argue convincingly for the logical nature of their position. As Aristotle recognized, in such situations the use of logical appeals alone would not accomplish the author's goal.

reasonable logically, which means that their outcome swings on the presentation of appeals other than logic, namely, appeals to the emotions. Faced with a decision which cannot be made dialectically the Galatians are influenced by their understanding of the wisdom and trustworthiness of the presenter of the argument. Paul could not depend on logic alone to prove that he was correct any more than he could that he was the apostle to the gentiles. He had to make use of other appeals to make his position persuasive.

This would have been complicated under ideal conditions; here it was even more difficult because Paul had to take into consideration the possibility that the position taken by the "opponents" already appeared no less viable or credible to his readers than the position he was advocating. The sheer existence of the letter makes this clear; if Paul had not viewed the alternative position as a real threat the reason for writing the letter would not have existed. The letter suggests, despite his protestations, that the "other gospel" did not appear as undeniably false to the Galatians.[48] The lack of demonstrability of his position, coupled with the viability of his opponents' position, required a different argumentative tack.

Furthermore, Paul's opponents had an advantage on him because they could point to distinct ways for measuring faithfulness to the gospel, the requirements of the law mentioned by Paul in the letter. The observance of circumcision, or feast days, or dietary restrictions could be recognized by anybody. Paul could not present such evidence; if he proposed a specific moral code to counteract theirs he would have reenacted the very position he opposed.

Paul's recourse to hard evidence is severely hampered by this restriction. He is limited to the scriptures, which were also at the disposal of his adversaries, and were, in fact, part of the debate. Since he had no inartificial proof material with which he could show the incorrectness of his opponents' position, and, faced with no visible means of demonstrating the correctness of his own, Paul responded by moving the discussion to reliance on artificial proofs, such as, inferences, reference to his own character, and the experience of his readers. In keeping with classical argumentative strategy Paul used these ethos and pathos appeals in support of his claim for a true understanding of the gospel and its implications.

---

[48]The letter makes this clear because in at least six places: (1:6, 3:1-5, 4:8-11, 4:21, 5:1-5, and 6:11). Paul seems to be admitting that some of the Galatians were following or about to follow the new form of teaching.

It is for this reason that he includes 5:25-6:10 in the parenetic section. By doing so he provides the Galatians with a way of structuring the world in a concrete form—recognizable, attractive and acceptable to the readers. The threat of anomy is alleviated, paving the way to the acceptance of his thesis. Thus the parenetic section acts as an emotional buffer; it becomes an extended appeal in light of the possible negative emotional response to the preceding forms of the argument. In the destruction of the opposing schema Paul created a state of disequilibrium for his readers, which, if left unattended, would have become intolerable for them. Because of its lack of originality and its traditional nature, parenesis materials provide a known set of values which serve as a means to re-create equilibrium in the readers, thus making the acceptance of Paul's thesis less threatening and therefore increasing its chances of being adopted and acted upon.

IV. Conclusion

I have not tried to provide a complete analysis of Galatians in this manner, although one could be done. Rather, I have suggested that certain argumentative strategies like those described by Perelman are present in the letter. Moreover, recognizing that Paul is after adherence to a set of values and the theses which can be developed on their basis is a better way to use the insights of rhetorical analysis than to debate the existence of a rhetorical genre. The procedures which Perelman outlines help us to ascertain more thoroughly what Paul desired for they tie goals and strategies together more specifically then the general categories of classical rhetoric do. Thus, new rhetoric, as Perelman describes it, can play an important role in clarifying how Paul proceeds in the production of his letters and why certain expressions are used to attain his goals.

A movement away from the formal categories of ancient classical rhetoric to the functionally oriented categories of modern rhetoric facilitates our investigation of Galatians. First, it does justice to the rhetorical aspects and strategies of the letter, allowing us to recognize and appreciate more of the facets of Paul's argument. Second, the recognition of these strategies helps us to refrain from stressing various parts of the letter at the expense of others. The possibility of misinterpreting the writer's intentions is therefore lessened. Third, given the nature of "rhetorical situation" we may better assess the "authoritative function" of the letter in present rhetorical situations. Fourth, in investigating the techniques of argument which are based on shared premises and, especially, shared values we may be able to utilize these arguments to discover what those initial premises were for Paul and with that set of premises begin to discern what the relationship among them is. If this is the case then we will be moving closer to finding out what Paul's initial starting points were and hence, to those things which were essential for the development of his arguments. In other words we will be moving closer to the core convictions of his thought.

"Love your Enemies"—"Woe to You, Scribes and Pharisees"
The Need for a Semiotic Approach in New Testament Studies
Daniel Patte, *Vanderbilt University*

One of Hendrikus Boers' many contributions is the development of semiotic approaches (more specifically, Greimas's structural semiotics) in New Testament studies. At the recent meeting of the SNTS at Cambridge University (August 1988), he commented on the difficulty in convincing our colleagues to perceive the potential contributions that such an approach can make, while expressing his confidence that they will progressively do so. The present essay is an attempt to take one more step in that direction by arguing that a semio-structural approach can help us address certain exegetical problems raised by the Gospel according to Matthew — problems that readily appear when the following texts are juxtaposed:

> "Love your enemies and pray for those who persecute you, so that you may be children of your Father who is in heaven" (Matt. 5:44-45). "Woe to you scribes and Pharisees, hypocrites..." (Matt. 23:13, 15, 16, 23, 25, 27, 29) ..."upon you may come all the righteous blood shed on earth" (Matt. 23: 35).

The juxtaposition of these two statements, put in the mouth of Jesus by Matthew, highlights the ambivalence of the message of his Gospel and raises questions for the exegetes. One could wonder if this message is not self-contradictory, and if it is not so fundamentally anti-Jewish that the Gospel according to Matthew cannot but convey some subtle or not so subtle form of anti-Semitism to its readers. In order to address these problems, a semio-structural approach asks the question: *What is, for the readers of the Gospel according to Matthew, the meaning-effect of polemics against the Jews addressed to disciples who are supposed to love their enemies?* By taking this example, I propose (1) to show the importance of seeing the study of the "meaning-effect" of a text as a part of our exegetical task, and (2) to explain the shift in emphasis that raising such a question brings about in our exegesis.

Studying the Meaning-Effect of a Text as a Part of the Exegetical Task

Asking "what is the meaning-effect of the Gospel of Matthew?" (or of any other text) raises a question that is suspect, if not nonsensical, for other exegetes. Yet it is necessary to raise it so that our exegesis will set up the possibility of addressing important hermeneutical problems posed by Matthew.[1] When this is perceived, one can recognize that this question is not as extravagant as it may appear at first, but rather that it is in continuity with the questions raised by other exegetical methods.

Raising such a question is adopting a semio-structural approach. For structural semiotics[2] (the theory upon which structural exegesis is based), the meaning of a text is its "meaning-effect" upon readers, because *any text is the partial representation of a discourse*.[3] A discourse (1) addresses an intended audience in a specific situation, (2) aims at transforming the audience's views (and thus also the situation), and (3) affects in certain ways the intended audience as well as other hearers, that is, it has a certain "meaning-effect" for them.[4]

---

[1] As Fiorenza emphasized in her presidential address to the Society of Biblical Literature, it is our ethical responsibility as exegetes to make sure that our exegeses study biblical texts in such a way that they open the possibility of addressing the hermeneutical problems raised by the texts. See Elisabeth Schüssler Fiorenza, "The Ethics of Interpretation: De-Centering Biblical Scholarship," *JBL*, 107, 1, 1988, pp. 3-17.

[2] The semiotic theory about the generation of meaning by A. J. Greimas, as found in A. J. Greimas and J. Courtés, *Semiotics and Language. An Analytical Dictionary*. Trans. by L. Crist, D. Patte, et al., Bloomington: Indiana University Press, 1982.

[3] In a text, the "discourse" represented is not complete; it is a discourse with an imagined reader, the implied reader or enunciatee. Yet it lacks the dialogical reactions of actual readers/hearers.

[4] The text as a partial represented discourse sets *constraints* for the realizations of the discourse in and through readings. As such, it produces a certain "meaning-effect" that is appropriated in different ways by different readers in different cultural, social, and/or existential situations. Note that in this technical sense *"meaning-effect" refers to the characteristic constraints* that a text sets for any potential reader, and not to the many different possible appropriations of the text by actual readers (that could be viewed as a multiplicity of "meaning- effects," in another sense of that phrase).

Exegesis usually strives to provide a critical assessment of the first two steps of this process by interpreting a text (1) in terms of the situation it addresses and refers to, and (2) in terms of the intended transformation it aims at achieving. Structural exegesis goes one step further by attempting (3) to provide a critical assessment of the effect of the text's discourse upon the intended audience as well as upon other readers. Thus, together with literary and rhetorical criticism, structural exegesis is in continuity with traditional exegesis. Yet, by focusing upon the meaning-effect of the text, structural exegesis prolongs the exegetical quest beyond its traditional limits.

Why a Study of the Meaning-Effect of a Text?

What kind of exegetical results are we to expect? And, why do we need to raise questions regarding the "meaning-effect" of the Gospel according to Matthew?

Since structural exegesis aims at studying a fleeting reality, an "effect" rather than a stable object (e.g., the set message of a text), and since it insists that this effect is generated through the interaction of several meaning-producing dimensions of a discourse, structural exegesis can be a very abstract analytical exercise. Yet, it can also propose much more concrete results. Understandably, one can be sceptical. Because a text's meaning-effect is so fleeting a reality, it seems nebulous. Does it not defy any exegetical study? Will not the study of such a nebulous reality be as nebulous as that reality itself? This is forgetting that a text's meaning-effect, even though it is fleeting, is *a reality with very concrete consequences.*

The need for the study of a biblical text's meaning-effect appears most clearly when its consequences are so unwelcome that we cannot afford to ignore them; we need to address the hermeneutical problem raised by these unwelcome consequences. This is the case when readers *repeatedly* draw the same conclusions from a text, and when these are in tension (or even contradictory) either with our scholarly conclusions regarding the message of that text, or with our understanding of the Christian faith that is grounded in the New Testament texts. Because this is a repeated occurrence, one cannot simply put the blame for such interpretations upon certain irresponsible readers; one has to suspect that they result from a part of the text's meaning-effect upon readers. Starting with such a concrete hermeneutical problem, one seeks to elucidate the text's features that might have generated it. For this, one must reexamine the text so as to elucidate how this represented discourse affects readers.

The Anti-Jewish Meaning-Effect of Matthew

These general remarks become clear as soon as we consider the case of one of the hermeneutical issues raised by the interpretations of Matthew's Gospel. It is a problem that is most unwelcome because of its concrete consequences. Yet it is also a problem directly related to the central issue of Matthean scholarship. I refer to the hermeneutical difficulty arising from the painful fact that, through the centuries, as well as in our recent past (and even today), the Gospel according to Matthew has been used by Christians to justify anti-Semitism. Of course, I assume that anti-Semitism and its horrors are an evil that is contradictory with the Christian faith (an assumption that does not need to be justified after the Holocaust). Consequently, the fact that Matthew has been perceived as conveying anti-Semitism (or at least, as supporting anti-Semitic views) is highly disturbing.

We readily reject such anti-Semitic readings of Matthew as illegitimate and unwarranted. Nothing in Matthew justifies pogroms and the Holocaust! But the issue becomes more complex as soon as we acknowledge that anti-Semitic acts and attitudes are rooted in a mindset involving *the rejection of the Jews simply because they are Jews*, whether they are identified in terms of their race (the narrow definition of anti-Semitism) or in terms of their religion. This mindset, that can take the form of an anti-Judaism (religion), is already a latent anti-Semitism (race) that, when aroused by social or cultural factors, too easily becomes a virulent anti-Semitism. Thus, painfully, we have to acknowledge that the anti-Semitic interpretations show that there is a strong possibility that the Gospel according to Matthew might have the effect of conveying a latent anti-Semitism in the form of an anti-Judaism. This possibility becomes a certitude when one notes that our Jewish brothers and sisters strongly resent the Gospel according Matthew, because, for them, it definitely conveys an overarching anti-Jewish stance.[5]

---

[5]Michael Cook, in an assessment of Jewish perspectives on the New Testament, underscores what he calls Matthew's "overarching anti-Jewish stance" to which the so-called "pro-Jewish passages" also contribute. See Michael J. Cook, "Confronting New Testament Attitudes on Jews and Judaism: Four Jewish Perspectives," *The Chicago Theological Seminary Register*, LXXVIII, 1, 1988, p. 21, and "Interpreting `Pro-Jewish' Passages in Matthew," *Hebrew Union College Annual*

The hermeneutical problem raised by the explicitly anti-Semitic interpretations of Matthew cannot be resolved by simply rejecting these interpretations (although they should be rejected). Through its numerous polemics against the Jews, Matthew seems to have the more insidious effect of conveying to its readers a latent anti-Semitism by promoting an anti-Jewish stance.

The Ambivalence of Matthew's Statements about the Jews as the Source of Its Anti-Jewish Effect

This emotionally charged issue needs to be set in the proper context. To begin with, note that I spoke of the "effect" of Matthew. I did not say that the Gospel according to Matthew *is* anti-Jewish. Actually, its statements against the Jews are quite ambivalent, in the sense that their meaning-effects depend upon the perspective from which they are perceived. Consequently, we have to expect that they might have different meaning-effects when perceived from the perspective of the author, from the perspective of the implied audience (the audience imagined by the author and implied by the text), and from the perspective of actual readers in various situations.

As Matthean scholarship suggests,[6] this ambivalence of the polemics against the Jews comes from the recognition that the rejection of Judaism in the process of affirming another faith, the Christian faith, does not necessarily involve an anti-Judaism (as latent anti-Semitism). There is a big difference between the affirmation that the Christian faith is *not like the Jewish faith* (Christianity is not Judaism), and the affirmation that the Christian faith demands a *total rejection of Judaism* (Christianity is an anti-Judaism that involves a latent anti-Semitism). In the former case, the Christian faith would define itself by comparison and contrast with Judaism; one acknowledges a certain continuity between Judaism and Christianity, even though one might want to emphasize the discontinuity. In the latter case, the Christian faith would involve the rejection of all that is Jewish, and thus of the Jews themselves "simply because they are Jews." Yet, ob-

---

54, 1983, pp. 143ff, and the bibliographies in footnotes. See also Samuel Sandmel, *Anti-Semitism in the New Testament?* Philadelphia: Fortress Press, 1978.

[6]The following distinction is used by many scholars, whether or not they make it explicit. For its direct expression, see, for instance, S. Légasse, "L'antijudaïsme dans l'Evangile selon Matthieu," in M. Didier, ed., *L'Evangile selon Matthieu. Rédaction et théologie*, Bibliotheca Ephemeridum Theologicarum Lovaniensium 29, Gembloux, 1972, pp. 417-428.

viously, it is all too easy to pass from the former view to the latter. According to the perspective one adopts, the same statement can be understood either as an affirmation of a Christian faith in basic continuity with Judaism, or as an expression of anti-Judaism (as latent anti-Semitism).

This ambivalence is frequent in Matthew. For instance, how should one understand the suggestion that the Christian community is separated from the Synagogue (cf., for instance, the references to "*their* synagogues," 4:23, 9:35, 10:17, 12:9, 13:54)? This separation may be understood as implying an affirmation of the distinctiveness of the Christian faith, that does not necessarily involve a systematic anti-Jewish stance.[7] Yet, it may also be perceived as one of the expressions of an overarching anti-Jewish stance.[8] Similarly, the view that the Christian faith is the true form of Judaism, and therefore that the Church is the true Chosen People[9] (suggested, for instance, in the interpretation of the parable of the vineyard, 22:43), could be read as demanding an anti-Jewish stance; the Christian faith replaces Judaism and demands a total rejection of Judaism and of the Jews.[10]

---

[7]This is the case for the interpretations that emphasize the Jewishness of the Gospel (Matthew as a Jewish Christian Gospel). These interpretations include those which view the controversy with Judaism as "*intra muros*," when the community is essentially viewed as a Jewish Christian community (as it is viewed by G. D. Kilpatrick, *The Origins Of the Gospel According to St. Matthew*. Oxford, 1946, and following him, e.g., by R. Hummel, *Die Auseinandersetzung zwischen Kirche und Judentum im Matthäusevangelium*, Munich, 2nd ed. 1966, and by W. D. Davies, *The Setting of the Sermon on the Mount*, Cambridge, 1966). This is also the case of the interpretations that view the controversy with Judaism as "*extra-muros*," when the community is viewed as "in sharp contrast to the Jewish community," although one can still speak of "a far smoother transition from Judaism to Christianity that we usually suppose" (as K. Stendahl proposes in *The School of St. Matthew and its Use of the Old Testament*, 2nd ed. Philadelphia, 1968; see also E. Schweizer, *Matthäus und seine Gemeinde*, Stuttgart, 1974, and C. F. D. Moule, *St. Matthew's Gospel: Some Neglected Features*, Berlin, 1964).

[8]This possibility appears when Matthew is no longer viewed as a Jewish Christian Gospel; the redaction, by contrast with the traditions it uses, involves strong Gentile Christian emphases. Therefore, Matthew involves a rejection of the Jewishness of the gospel. See P. Nepper-Christensen, *Das Matthäusevangelium: ein Judenchristliches Evangelium?* Aarhus, 1958; G. Strecker, *Der Weg der Gerechtigkeit*, 3rd ed. Göttingen, 1971; and W. Trilling, *Das Wahre Israel*, 3rd ed. Munich, 1964. Such studies that reject the traditional understanding of Matthew as a Jewish Christian Gospel open the possibility (but not the necessity) to interpret the separation from the synagogue and the polemics against the Jews as expressions of an overarching anti-Jewish stance.

[9]As emphasized by Trilling, *Das Wahre Israel*.

Yet, it can also be understood as an affirmation of the Christian faith as distinct from, but *in continuity* with, Judaism, that is, as an affirmation of the fundamental Jewishness of the Christian faith.[11] This would mean that the Christian faith fulfills the most basic features of the Jewish faith, that the Jews themselves should also fulfill, and will hopefully fulfill one day (a possible interpretation of 23:39). A similar ambivalence can be perceived in most statements in Matthew about the Jews and Judaism, including in the "pro-Jewish" statements.[12]

The Traditional Solution: Overcoming the Text's Ambivalence

Whatever our exegetical methodology might be, we can all agree that the hermeneutical problem raised by anti-Semitic interpretations of Matthew can be traced to the ambivalence of Matthew's statements about Judaism. Yet, a basic difference between our methodologies appears in the ways in which we propose to deal with this ambivalence and the hermeneutical problem it engenders. Following traditional exegetical methodologies (including redaction criticism), the majority of exegetes sees this ambivalence of the text as an obstacle to be overcome. By contrast, from the perspective of the new exegetical methodologies (including rhetorical and literary criticisms as well as sociological approaches and structural exegesis),[13] this ambivalence is an intrinsic part of the text as discourse. Rather than attempting to overcome it, one should acknowledge that this ambivalence participates in the production of the text's meaning-effect.

Traditional Matthean scholarship seeks to overcome this ambivalence. It does so by showing what Matthew *meant to say*, i.e., how the

---

[10] When chosenness is transferred from Israel to another people, the rejection of Israel is "final and complete," as D. R. A. Hare argues in *The Theme of Jewish Persecution of Christians in the Gospel According to St. Matthew*, Cambridge, 1967. See also Hare and D. J. Harrington, "'Make Disciples of all the Gentiles' (Mt. 28.19)," *CBQ*, 37, 1975, pp. 359-69.

[11] For instance, Trilling's interpretation (in *Das Wahre Israel*), according to which the perception of the community as "true Israel" involves a recognition of continuity with the "false" Israel. The polemical statements are then viewed as reflecting the tension between two communities making claim to the election for themselves. See also S. Légasse, "L'antijudaïsme dans l'Evangile selon Matthieu."

[12] As M. Cook emphasizes in his essay "Interpreting 'Pro-Jewish' Passages in Matthew."

[13] All these methodologies have in common the view of meaning as "relational and multidimensional meaning-effect." Yet, when these approaches are used in conjunction with traditional methods, they are often used as an additional tool for overcoming the text's ambivalence.

text is to be understood from the author's perspective. The meaning of the text is "what the author meant to say." From this perspective, if the exegesis determines that Matthew's intended message is not anti-Jewish (and thus does not involve a latent anti-Semitism), the so-called hermeneutical problem is resolved; any anti-Jewish interpretation of Matthew is wrong. Actually, there is no real hermeneutical problem. By contrast, if the exegesis determines that Matthew's intended message is anti-Jewish, there is a "real" hermeneutical problem that theologians and church authorities will have to address. For instance, they will have to struggle with the question: What should Christians do with an anti-Jewish text in their Scripture?

From the perspective of the new methodologies, this exegetical strategy makes it impossible to address the actual hermeneutical problem, because it fails to make a critical assessment of the ways in which a discourse conveys meaning. Beyond the critical assessments of the historical situations that presided over the generation of the text proposed by source criticism, form-criticism, tradition-criticism, and redaction-criticism, one needs to proceed to a critical assessment of the discourse process viewed in terms of its effects — an assessment that could be called a "discourse criticism," and which the new methodologies make possible.

The issue is not that traditional Matthean scholarship does not take into account that the text is a discourse. It does. Indeed, in order to discover the author's perspective, exegetes strive to elucidate the "discoursive" situation that Matthew addressed. Matthew's relationship with Judaism (whether or not he is of Jewish origin), his community's relationship with Judaism (whether or not it is a Jewish Christian community, and the extent to which it is separated from Judaism), and Matthew's goals in writing the Gospel (the specific ways in which he attempts to transform his audience's views) are studied to assess the perspective from which Matthew intended his own statements and their purpose.[14] No one can deny the importance and the value of such studies. Actually, as we shall further discuss below, they are most convincing because they respect what Matthew's Gospel as a discourse strives to accomplish. Indeed, any discourse strives to be as clear as possible by emphasizing its unity and by smoothing out any possible ambivalence. Following this thrust of the

---

[14]For an excellent survey of the scholarship on these issues, see Graham Stanton, "The Origin and Purpose of Matthew's Gospel: Matthean Scholarship from 1945 to 1980," *ANRW* 25, 3, 1985, pp. 1906-21.

discourse toward semantic unity (toward univocity), Matthean scholarship strives to overcome any ambiguity of the text by unifying the text around what appears to be its core, namely, "what the author meant to say."

Yet, this strength of Matthean scholarship is also a potential weakness. From the perspective of the new methodologies, such studies respect so much what the discourse strives to do that they have been trapped by the discoursive strategy of the text. They have failed to adopt a critical attitude toward the discoursive process and the way a discourse affects readers, including exegetes. Such studies fail to perceive that the unity the discourse strives to project toward its audience is an effort to hide its lack of semantic unity, rooted in its discoursive strategy, and attested by the various ways in which the discourse affects readers. Identifying the meaning of the text as "what the author meant to say" is submitting to the power of the discourse, rather than critically assessing it. This flattens out the text's meaning, viewing it as a "one-dimensional" entity, rather than viewing it as a "multidimensional meaning-effect" — as one has to do when one critically evaluates the discourse's effect upon readers.

For example, saying, with many exegetes, that Matthew is not anti-Jewish, and thus that anti-Jewish interpretations are wrong, fails to recognize that the intentional message of the text is merely one dimension of its meaning-effect. It ignores the other dimension(s) of its meaning-effect that convey(s) an anti-Jewish stance. It acts as if these other dimensions of the meaning-effect do not exist, as if they do not participate in the overall meaning-effect of Matthew's Gospel. It also deprives oneself of the possibility of truly addressing the hermeneutical problem raised by anti-Semitic readings. According to this example, by saying that anti-Jewish interpretations are wrong, we have decreed that this hermeneutical problem does not really exist; consequently, we have deprived ourselves of the possibility of critically examining the features of the text that have the insidious effect of conveying to readers an anti-Jewish stance, as our Jewish brothers and sisters readily perceive. The situation is similar in the opposite case, i.e., when the exegesis concludes that Matthew's intended message is anti-Jewish. By reducing the meaning-effect of the text to its intended message, we deprive ourselves of the possibility of considering the features of the text that opened the possibility of the many readings of Matthew that do not involve an anti-Jewish stance. Then our exegesis leaves theologians and the Church with a single alternative; either resolving the hermeneutical problem by radically rejecting Matthew, or not rejecting Matthew and accepting that anti-Judaism is an intrinsic part of the Christian message. But this is a false dilemma, since there are readings of Matthew that do not involve an anti-Jewish stance.

From the perspective of traditional exegetical methodologies, these suggestions are certainly puzzling and even suspect. For those who have concluded that Matthew is not anti-Jewish, this unnecessarily muddles an issue which is already resolved. But, Jewish scholars remind us that it is not resolved that easily. For those who have concluded that Matthew is anti-Jewish, this approach is suspect of trying to avoid confronting the reality of the situation. Both these potential criticisms are rooted in the deep suspicion against the suggestion that meaning is to be viewed as a multidimensional meaning-effect. We need, therefore, to clarify this point.

Toward an Understanding of a Text's Meaning as
a Multi-Dimensional Meaning-Effect

First, let me emphasize that by saying that traditional exegetical methodologies view the text's meaning as a "one-dimensional entity," I do not deny that they view the text's meaning as multifaceted. The text's complexity is constantly underscored, for instance, by elucidating all the possible connotations of each of the key terms, and by showing the interaction of sources, traditions, and redaction. Yet, this investigation of the complexity of the text is aimed at clarifying its meaning (singular), that is, "what the author meant to say." We are so used to this way of considering the text that it appears to be nonsense to suggest that the text might also have other meanings — or more precisely, other meaning-effects — which are as intrinsic to the text as "what the author meant to say." Indeed, this suggestion seems to go against our common experience. In order to try to overcome this suspicion, the best is to discuss briefly our common experience as speakers. In so doing, we will simultaneously clarify the distinction between two dimensions of the text's meaning-effect that need to play a central role in our study of New Testament texts.

As speakers or writers, we see ourselves as being in control of the meaning of our discourses. If there is any doubt or question, we are the ultimate referees concerning their meaning, because we know what we meant to say. We are in a position to remove any ambiguity, something we already strive to do as we utter our discourse. And we reject as wrong any interpretation that does not coincide with what we meant to say. But, the very fact that we have to clarify our discourses and to defend them against misinterpretations shows that our discourses often do not convey exactly what we meant to say. The nature of this discrepancy appears when one notes that we can say in a few sentences what we meant to say by a long discourse. In other words, our discourses often convey more than what we meant to say.[15]

The surplus of meaning conveyed by our discourses can be illustrated by a common experience for contemporary English-speaking male speakers. We have learned to recognize that our discourses are often resented by women as sex-exclusive or even as sexist when we use masculine pronouns to designate human beings in general. Our intentional message (our topic) might have absolutely nothing to do with this issue. Furthermore, we did not intend to exclude women; for us, the use of masculine pronouns was "inclusive." But, as feminist critics have taught us, our discourses nevertheless conveyed androcentric and often patriarchal views. What do we do? We correct our "language," using a sex-inclusive language, so that our discourse will no longer have a sexist meaning-effect, and so that "what we mean to say" will be more readily acceptable to readers or hearers with strong convictions about sex-inclusive views. Assuming we have been successful,[16] what is the outcome? Our intentional message is more readily accepted. Yet, this does not mean that our discourse does not have a surplus of meaning. The only difference is that, now, this surplus of meaning is a sex-inclusive point of view — which still has nothing to do with the point we wanted to make (our topic).

---

[15]This is *always* the case with "figurative discourses" (including all religious discourses), by contrast with "purely informational discourses" (such as scientific discourses) that can eventually be limited to what we mean to say. I allude to the distinction between "plain speech" (or informational speech) and "symbolic speech" (figurative speech) that Robert Tannehill discusses in *The Sword of His Mouth*. Philadelphia: Fortress Press, 1975, pp. 1-37. Most discourses expressed in "natural languages" are somewhat figurative. I exclude from the following discussion scientific (and scholarly) discourses that strive to avoid this ambivalence by using precise technical language. The more technical the language is, the less ambivalent the message is. The ultimate technical language is the mathematical language; a mathematical discourse (e.g., a string of formula) is theoretically without surplus of meaning.

[16]Transforming an androcentric or patriarchal discourse into a truly sex-inclusive discourse involves, of course, much more than changing personal pronouns!

What have we learned from this brief illustration? First, that in order to communicate a point, we cannot simply state what we mean to say. Let us review our situation as speakers. We want to communicate a point to an audience. This means that this point will be somewhat new for our audience; otherwise our discourse would be pointless. Accepting this new point demands that the audience set aside some of its own ideas and views, or at least be receptive to new ones. Thus, our audience needs to be convinced that what we say is true and/or valuable. For this purpose, it is imperative that we show our audience that we and our message are reliable — reliable from the point of view of the audience, of course. The only possible way to do this is to enter into dialogue with our audience by presenting ourselves and our message *in terms of what our audience values and views as truthful*. In sum, in order to convince our audience to accept the new view that we want to communicate to them, we need to express this new view in terms of other views that our audience holds and that we can affirm. We need to express our intended message in such a way as to make clear that it is in continuity with our audience's own views. Thus, the explanations, the illustrations, the symbolism, indeed the entire figurativization of our discourses, are "audience specific" in the sense that they attempt to express a given message in terms of the views of a given audience; we change them when we want to convey the same message to a different audience.[17]

These brief remarks about the complex process of "discoursivization"[18] are enough to understand that ambivalences in a text reflect the fact that a discourse always expresses two points of view: the author's point of view (what he or she meant to say) and the intended audience's point of view (in terms of which the author attempts to express his or her intentional message). The intended audience's point of view is inscribed in the text, as much as the author's point of view is. Thus, together with literary critics, we call them, respectively, the implied reader and the implied author. We can also understand that these two points of view are closely interwoven, with the hope that the intended audience will perceive them

---

[17]Of course, this intended audience is often a complex audience, that we imagine to include people with different points of view. Consequently, a discourse might involve several implied readers. To simplify the discussion to follow, we speak of a single implied reader.

[18]For a more complete discussion of these issues see my forth-coming book *Greimas's Structural Semiotics and Biblical Exegesis*, ch. 3.

"Love your Enemies"—"Woe to You, Scribes and Pharisees" 93

as a single one. Actually, this is an essential feature of the strategy of any discourse. So that the intended audience might accept the new points that constitute the intentional message, this audience must be led to perceive these new points as consistent with its own point of view. For this purpose, the discourse blurs the differences between the two points of view, so that they *appear* to be a single point of view. The discourse strives to create the illusion that the point of view of the implied author and that of the implied reader are coextensive, even though they are necessarily different, because the intentional message demands from the intended audience that it abandon at least some of its own views. Actual readers are enticed by the discourse to perceive the text's meaning as one-dimensional, and thus to play the role of an ideal reader by resolving (overcoming) the ambiguities of the text, even when they cannot identify themselves with the implied reader.

It is this ideal reading situation (readers reacting exactly as the author expected them to behave) that we often presuppose in our critical historical investigations. We strive to be objective by putting ourselves in the position of the original audience, an audience belonging to a distant historical, social, and cultural milieu. This is actually a strength of our studies. Because our exegetical discourses conform to the text's thrust toward unity, they avail themselves of the convincing power of the text by making clear that they submit themselves to the text. Our exegetical conclusions are convincing precisely in that we can readily show that they conform to the text.[19]

Let me emphasize this. Such exegetical conclusions are quite valuable and responsible, insofar as we are aware of the fact that in interpreting the text as we do we submit to the discoursive strategy of the text. This is an essential condition. We must acknowledge that we are merely dealing with one dimension of the multidimensional meaning-effect of the text as a represented discourse. Without such an acknowledgment, we deprive ourselves of any possibility of making a critical assessment of the discourse as discourse. Then, it be-

---

[19]More precisely, they simultaneously conform to the thrust of the text toward semantic unity, and to the demand of the critical discourse which has as implied reader a critic of one sort or another, for instance, a historian, a redaction-critic, or a structural exegete. Note that I voluntarily listed among these examples the structural exegete. Indeed, even though from the perspective of structural exegesis one emphasizes the multidimensional character of the text's meaning-effect, one must also acknowledge the importance of the study of "that which gives unity to the text," that is performed by historico-critical methods.

comes impossible to account for the diversity of meaning-effects upon readers through a critical study of the discursive process represented by the text. As a consequence, we are led to make undue totalitarian claims for our exegeses,[20] and thus to deprive ourselves of the possibility of proposing an exegesis which will allow us to address the hermeneutical problems raised by the diversity of meaning-effects that the text has for readers.[21] In sum, historico-critical exegetical approaches should acknowledge the need for other methods that aim at accounting for the multiplicity of meaning-effects of a text, as semio-structural exegetical approaches must acknowledge (as I just did) the need for historico-critical exegeses that account for the meaning of a text as one-dimensional.

Some Suggestions For the Study of Matthew's Anti-Jewish Meaning-Effect

We need to adopt a semio-structural approach in order to address the issues concerning the meaning-effect of the Gospel according to Matthew, especially of its polemics against the Jews as juxtaposed to a teaching calling disciples to love their enemies. This demands that we take into account that it is the interaction of several dimensions of meaning that produces this meaning-effect. For the purposes of this essay, we limit our comments to the interaction of the two broad dimensions of meaning that represent the views of the implied author and of the implied reader.

We noted that, because of the ambivalence of the text, the Gospel of Matthew was perceived by certain people (including Jewish scholars) as conveying an overarching anti-Jewish stance, and by others as not conveying such a stance. In light of the preceding discussion, we can suspect that what happens is that these two views are present in

---

[20] And this, even though we carefully underscore that our conclusions are relative by following the principles that govern historiography, such as those proposed by Troeltsch. See Ernst Troeltsch, *Gesammelte Schriften*, Tübingen: J. C. B. Mohr, 1913, II, pp. 729-753; and Van Harvey, *The Historian and the Believer*. New York: Macmillan, 1966, pp. 14-15.

[21] Of course, the reverse is also true. A new methodology which would make the totalitarian claim that studies of the discursive process alone account for the text's meaning would result in the same impasse. They deprive themselves of the possibility of availing themselves of the convincing power of the text. This is, unfortunately, the impression that many structuralist, semiotic, and post-structuralist studies of texts give. They deconstruct the text; yet, their analyses have lost the ability of conveying the power of the text. Such analyses are essential as methodological and theoretical research, but are not exegeses that open the possibility of an hermeneutic.

the text; one being the view of the implied author, and the other being the view of the implied reader. The different readings would then result from the identification of one or the other of these points of view (or their combinations) as "the meaning" of the text, and this according to the position that the readers occupy vis-à-vis the text. Semio-structural approaches, and structural exegesis, makes it its task to elucidate each of these dimensions of meaning, by developing criteria allowing us to distinguish them. Thus, on the basis of the theoretical identification of the relations between narrative/argumentative syntax (e.g., the plot of a story, the logic of an argument and their polemical character) and deep semantics (that expresses the author's convictions), structural exegesis can elucidate the point of view of the implied author by following well defined procedures. This is what I have done in *The Gospel According to Matthew: A Structural Commentary*.[22] Yet, this work only deals with one dimension of the meaning-effect of this Gospel; many things in the text were bracketed out. Indeed, elucidating the point of view of the implied reader demands a quite different strategy, for a close study of the figurative aspects of the text as discourse.

I have not yet completed this latter study. Thus, I cannot propose definite conclusions regarding these two dimensions of meaning in Matthew, and how they affect the question regarding the anti-Jewish character of the Gospel according to Matthew. I will nevertheless make some tentative suggestions so as to provide a concrete example for a concluding remark

To begin with, Matthew's intentional message is not anti-Jewish. On the contrary, it advocates a return to a more Jewish understanding of the gospel in general, and more particularly of Christ and of discipleship. The audience that he envisions, and that is in dire need of such a message, is a church that is totally separated from Judaism, views itself as the "true Israel," and radically rejects any continuity with the Jews and their Judaism, a false Israel. In brief, the implied reader has an overarching anti-Jewish stance. This is not the primary concern of Matthew; for him, the problem is that in the process they have lost (or are losing) what he views as essential aspects of the gospel. Thus, in order to convince them to adopt his "Jewish" views (convictions) about Christ and discipleship, in his figurative descriptions he contrasts Jesus and the disciples with people that he knows

---

[22]Philadelphia: Fortress Press, 1987.

his readers will view as the archetypical villains, namely Jewish leaders, Pharisees, scribes, and priests. In other words, he uses their anti-Judaism and their caricatures of Jewish leaders in his attempt to lead them to adopt a more Jewish understanding of the gospel.

These very sketchy comments are enough to allow me to ask a last question. Let us suppose for the sake of argument that these conclusions have been established. Since Matthew's intentional message is not antiJewish, should we further conclude that the Gospel according to Matthew does not convey anti-Judaism? It is clear by now that this would be a wrong conclusion. Indeed, Matthew did not convey anti-Judaism to the audience that he envisioned! How could he! They already had such a stance. Actually, his discourse might have had the effect of turning them away from this point of view by leading them to discover the continuity between Jesus and Judaism. But, for all the readers who do not share the anti-Jewish views of the implied reader, the effect of Matthew's discourse is to communicate this anti-Jewish stance to them, or, at the very least, to justify for them a subtle form of anti-Judaism. Thus, even though we have discovered (according to these tentative conclusions) that Matthew did not intend to convey anti-Judaism, it remains that the meaning-effect of his discourse includes such a latent anti-Semitism. Then, the specificity of the hermeneutical problem is clarified, and hopefully can be addressed as Matthew's text is re-read, taught, and/or preached.

The Angel's Announcement:
A Structuralist Study
H. Wayne Merritt, *Interdenominational Theological Center*

Literary critical analysis of Luke-Acts has long recognized that the author constructs his narrative according to the principles of parallelism.[1] While this observation has proved fruitful, producing numerous insights at the narrative, syntagmatic level of the text, a central question remains. Borrowing an observation from C. Lévi-Strauss, the question may be formulated according to the following; namely, "What is the 'meaning of the 'meaning' of this literary, compositional technique that is presently, sufficiently established."[2] Since the quest for the 'meaning of the meaning' is the characteristic feature of the career of Hendrikus Boers as an interpreter of texts, it seems appropriate to raise such a question at the present.

While it is not possible to answer this broadly focused question in one essay, a point of departure for doing so may be found in the parallelism that exists at the outset of Luke-Acts in the narratives announcing the births of John and Jesus (Lk 1:5-56). Again, while the parallelism in these two narratives is recognized generally,[3] its significance is not. Two quotations illustrate the point well. "Luke 1-2," according to C. Kraeling, "is a combination of two series of parallel episodes held together by material basically unrelated to the thread of either series."[4] R. A. Spivey, on the other hand, offers an intriguing

---

[1] Cf. Charles H. Talbert, *Literary Patterns, Theological Themes And The Genre Of Luke-Acts*, SBLMS, 20 (Missoula, Montana: Scholars Press, 1974).

[2] C. Levi-Strauss, "The Meeting of Myth and Science," *Myth and Meaning* (New York: Schocken Books, 1979), p. 12; According to Levi-Strauss, "There is something very curious in semantics, that the word 'meaning' is probably, in the whole language, the word the meaning of which is the most difficult to find. What does 'to mean' mean?"

[3] Talbert, for example, identifies no less than "two seven-part cycles comparing John and Jesus" in Luke 1-2; (Talbert) *Literary Patterns*, pp. 44-45.

[4] Carl Kraeling, *John the Baptist*, (New York: Scribner, 1959), p. 16.

proposal based on an earlier suggestion from E. R. Leach that may well point toward a resolution of this dilemma. According to Spivey, the parallelism between John and Jesus, found not only in Luke but in early Christian tradition in general, may be perceived along the lines of the binary opposition 'nature-culture' central to Lévi-Strauss analysis of mythology.[5] From this perspective, Jesus stands within culture as a city dweller, son of a carpenter, who goes into the wilderness only to be tempted of Satan, while John, the prophet, presents the contrast of nature by living in the wilderness, eating nature's food (wild honey and locusts), wearing nature's clothing (the skins of animals) and encountering God precisely within the context of the wilderness.[6] Our question, therefore, is how does the binary opposition 'nature-culture' inform our understanding of the parallelism of John and Jesus present at the outset of Luke's gospel.

To answer this question, our procedure will be as follows. First, we shall describe as briefly as possible the syntagmatic/narrative structure of the Lukan accounts of the announcements of the births of John and Jesus (Lk 1:5-56). Secondly, we shall place the constitutive elements of these narratives in relation to each other; and, thirdly, we shall seek to decipher the larger paradigmatic significance of these narratives by a reading of the material that holds the two in tension. In the latter instance, Lévi-Strauss' formula for the analysis of myth will be pressed into service.

Syntagmatically, both narratives are composed around three *foci*: 1) an introduction and description of the main characters; 2) an angelic annunciation of the respective births — each framed by a setting and a reflection on the human situation posed by the annunciation; and 3) a conclusion/transition in the framework of the larger narrative in which the problems posed by the announcements are resolved. In the first syntagm, the main characters are the parents of John: Zechariah and his wife Elizabeth (Lk 1:5-7). The reader learns that Zechariah is a priest and his wife, Elizabeth, is a descendant of a priestly tribe (Lk 1:5). Additionally, both are described as persons who are righteous and keep all of God's commandments and ordinances (Lk 1:6). Finally, the reader learns that the couple is childless due to Elizabeth's sterility and their advanced age (1:7). Although

---

[5] Robert A. Spivey, "Structuralism and Biblical Studies: The Uninvited Guest," *Int* 27 (1974), p. 139. The suggestion originated with Leach but the formulation is Spivey's.

[6] Ibid.

brief, this characterization is central to the remainder of the syntagm and is not substantially further developed.[7]

The second of the *foci* presents the angelic announcement of the John's birth (Lk 1:8-25). It is framed, on one side, by a temple setting (Lk 1:8-10) and, on the other, by a reflection on the human situation which characterizes the announced birth as miraculous (Lk 1:18-20). In the narrative, an angel appears to Zechariah in the midst of his temple duties and announces the impending birth of a child to the couple. The child that is to be born is described as an ascetic, filled with the Holy Spirit from conception, who will prepare Israel for God's activity by turning the nation to God (Lk 1:15-18). The character and function of the prophesied child, therefore, are clearly in line with Israel's prophetic tradition.

The reaction evoked by the announcement is one of surprise, mystification and unbelief in light of the problems posed by the human situation; namely, sterility on the part of the wife and the advanced age of the couple (Lk 1:18). Zechariah is chastened for his unbelief (Lk 1:20) and loses his power of speech until the fulfillment of the prophecy (Lk 1:63-64).

Upon the conclusion of his duties, Zechariah leaves the temple and returns home. In so doing, the people outside the temple note his dumbness and attribute it to a vision (Lk 1:22-23). The reader of the story learns by this that the fulfillment of the prophecy is already in process despite Zechariah's initial resistance. Subsequently, we are told that the problems posed by the human situation are overcome. Elizabeth conceives a child and hid herself according to custom (Lk 1:24-25).

Similarly, the second narrative (Lk 1:26-38) introduces the main characters, Mary and Joseph, with a brief description of these characters. Mary lives in the city of Nazareth and is a virgin betrothed to Joseph — a descendant of the royal house of David (Lk 1:26-28). As in the above, this brief characterization, although not as developed as the first, is central to the remainder of the narrative and is only minimally further developed. Only, in Focus II, for example, does the reader learn that Mary and Elizabeth are blood relations (Lk 1:36).

---

[7]One is inclined to regard the characters in both syntagmas as exceedingly 'flat.' Cf. E. M. Forster, *Aspects of the Novel* (New York: Penguin Books, 1962), p. 73 and Robert Scholes and Robert Kellogg, *The Nature of Narrative*, (New York: Oxford University Press, 1966), p. 169.

The second focus, The Annunciation (Lk 1:28-38), is framed also by a setting and a reflection on the human situation. The setting in this instance is a city and the problem posed by the human situation is that, although betrothed, Mary presently lacks a sexual, reproductive partner (Lk 1:34). The child that is to be born is described as the Son of the Most High, who will sit upon the throne of his father David and rule over the nation in an unending kingdom (Lk 1:31-33). The child, according to character and function, is presented as a king.

Noticeably, Mary's mystification is not chastened but reciprocated by additional information concerning the child and Elizabeth's pregnancy. Here Mary learns the manner in which the child is to be conceived and the significance of this conception; namely, the child is considered holy and will be called the Son of God (Lk 1:35).

The resolution and conclusion of the narrative, indeed, the point at which the two are explicitly interwoven, occurs with Mary's visit to Elizabeth (Lk 1:39-56) — Focus III. At this time the reader learns of Mary's pregnancy.

To further clarify the relationship between these narratives, the syntagmatic structure of the two can be reduced to the following diagram:

SYNTAGM X

adv. age	sterile		
righteous	adv. age		
priest	righteous	prophet	
	desc. of Aaron	Temple-Sterility	John
Zechariah-Elizabeth		John	Elizabeth's Pregnancy
I		II	III
(Characters and Characterization)		(Setting Annunciation Reflection)	(Conclusion: Mary's Visit Elizabeth)

SYNTAGM Y

Mary——Joseph	Jesus	Mary's Pregnancy
City-dweller desc. of David	City-Lack of	Jesus
Nazareth desc. of David	sexual partner	
betrothed betrothed	king	
virgin		

From the diagram, Kraeling's reference to the narratives as parallel episodes held together by material 'unrelated' to either series is clear. The 'unrelated material' is nothing other than the syntagmatic material read 'diachronically.' On the other hand, the diagram also shows that at the paradigmatic level the narratives are anything other than 'unrelated.' In fact, they are very related and it is the deciphering of this relationship that is the primary task of the interpretive process.

To illustrate the above, the principle of binary opposition noted at the outset of the essay is of valuable service. Indeed, the diagram already hints that each narrative fundamentally represents the inverse of the other. The diachronic tension of Male-Female (Zechariah-Elizabeth) of Syntagm X, for example, is reproduced inversely (Female-Male; Mary-Joseph) in the diachronic structure of Syntagm Y and paradigmatically when the two narratives are juxtaposed and read top to bottom. Here Zechariah, the first character introduced in Syntagm X, and the recipient of the angelic announcement, is opposite Mary, the first character introduced in Syntagm Y, who is also the recipient of the angelic announcement.

Moreover, at the level of characterization it is significant to note that the descriptions are given in the form of oppositions. The non-explicit paradigmatic opposition of priest-city-dweller becomes evident in the diachronic oppositions of the individual syntagmas. Syntagm X contrasts Zechariah (priest) and Elizabeth (descendants of priests) or religious functionary and religious non-functionary as Syntagm Y juxtaposes Mary (city-dweller) and Joseph (descendant of city/nation-rulers) or secular non-functionary and 'potential' secular functionary. These diachronic tensions are maintained in the paradigmatic structure in the oppositions Zechariah-Mary (male/religious functionary/ruler-female/secular non-functionary/ruled) and Elizabeth-Joseph (female/religious non-functionary/ruled-male/'potential' secular functionary/ruler).

Further, when the central characters are viewed diagonally in the diagram, the paradigmatic structure is brought into even sharper focus. Here the religious functionary (priest) is opposite the 'potential' secular functionary (king) in the opposition of Zechariah-Joseph. Similarly, the opposition of the females furthers this by opposing 'ruled' members of varying sociological systems; namely, religious (Elizabeth) and secular (Mary).

Additionally, in Syntagm X, Elizabeth (as well as Zechariah) is specifically characterized as beyond childbearing age (old), whereas Mary is implicitly acknowledged as childbearing age (young) as the description 'betrothed' indicates. Finally, Elizabeth, who is barren, is specifically characterized as sterile and, thus, the metaphorical opposition sterility- fertility emerges clearly in association with the virginal description of Mary. The larger paradigmatic structure of Focus I, therefore, can be graphically represented as follows:

	Barren/Sterile
Beyond Child Bearing/Old	Beyond Child Bearing/Old
Religious Functionary/Ruler	Religious non-functionary/Ruled
Male/Priest	Female/descendant of Priests
ZECHARIAH	**ELIZABETH**
MARY	**JOSEPH**
Female/City-Dweller	Male/Descendant of Kings
Secular Non-Functionary/Ruled	Secular Functionary/Ruler
Child Bearing Age/Young	Child Bearing Age/Young
Virgin/Fertile	

Focus II produces similar observations. The settings are related paradigmatically in that the angel's announcement in Syntagm X occurs within the temple and in Syntagm Y in the city. Moreover, the city-temple opposition is reflective of oppositions developed in the birth announcement itself. On the one hand, John, is described as a ascetic prophet,[8] and, Jesus is described as a king. The oppositions, therefore, are clear in that temple = city as prophet = king.

---

[8]The prophecy states that John shall neither drink wine nor strong drink (1:15, cf., 7:33). Subsequently, wilderness, desert, and 'hill country' mythemes are significantly present in descriptions of John. To be sure, Zechariah and Elizabeth also live in a 'city' but it is a city in the 'hill country' of Judah (1:39). The news of John's birth is spread throughout the 'hill country' (1:65). Following birth, John remains secluded in the desert until his appearance to Israel (1:80). His ministry is inaugurated by the word of the Lord coming to him in the wilderness (3:2). Above all he is the Isaianic voice, crying in the wilderness (3:4). Curiously, Luke alone of the Synoptic evangelists omits the description of John's distinctive apparel and wilderness diet (cf. Lk 3:1-6 and para.).

The functions of the two prophesied children are also presented as oppositions. The function of John as prophet is to return Israel to God but Jesus is to sit upon the throne of his father David and rule over a kingdom that knows no end. The oppositions in function, therefore, are appropriately described by the terms subjugator-dominator.

Further, the reflection on the human situation evoked by the angelic announcement is structured in terms of binary oppositions. The problem of Syntagm X is that both prospective parents are beyond childbearing age and the female is specifically characterized as sterile. The problem of Syntagm Y, rather, is neither 'age' nor 'sterility.' As far as the narrative is concerned, both characters are of childbearing age and, as we have seen, the virginal description of the female suggests fertility. The problem in Syntagm Y is that the female is sexually inactive and lacks a sexual reproductive partner insofar as the culture's sexual mores are concerned. On this point, it is also important to note that there is no suggestion anywhere in Syntagm X that the conception of John will take place outside of the normal reproductive cycle. The abrogation of the normal reproductive cycle, however, is explicit in Syntagm Y. These oppositions, therefore, may be appropriately presented as the opposition of abnormal age, normal sexuality-normal age, abnormal sexuality.

Finally, it should be noted that the announcement in Syntagm X is met with 'unbelief' (Zechariah) and reciprocated by the infliction of a malady (blindness) that is relieved only after the fulfillment of the prophecy. In Syntagm Y, 'belief' and 'acceptance' are the responses to the mandate of the announcement and these are reciprocated by the giving of additional information concerning the child and even Elizabeth's pregnancy. The following diagram illustrates the resulting oppositions of Focus II:

Unbelief
Normal Sexuality/Abnormal Age
Prophet/Subjugator
Temple

John

Jesus

City
King/Dominator
Abnormal Sexuality/Normal Age
Acceptance

Focus III, Mary's Visit to Elizabeth, is a significant point in the narrative. First, it is the vehicle for the conclusion- resolution of Syntagm Y. Here one learns that Mary is pregnant. The problems evoked by the annunciation have been resolved and the syntagm begun with the announcement of the birth is complete and ends appropriately with an exclamation of praise (Lk 1:46-54).

Secondly, the paradigmatic code receives further detail through the juxtaposition of the two women central to the narratives of the respective syntagmas. In Focus III, both women are brought face to face. Both are pregnant. The human problems and the circumstances inherent in the two narratives are resolved. In a real sense the two children who are later to face each other at the baptismal waters of the Jordan are here proleptically juxtaposed. In doing so, the final paradigmatic opposition is posed and transformed in the respective responses of Elizabeth and Mary. In the former, Elizabeth's response to Mary (Lk 1:39-45), an act of deference occurs on the part of Elizabeth, and, as the simultaneous leap of the babe in her womb suggests (Lk 1:41), the deference expressed receives the concurrence of John — her as yet unborn child.[9] In turn, the speech of Mary, The Magnificat (Lk 1:46-55), acknowledges this and fully exhibits Mary's understanding of her and her child's place of preference before God. Thus, the central opposition of Focus III, deference-dominance, is transformed and the tensions between the two narratives are brought to conclusion by the acceptance of a divinely appointed relationship (inferior-superior) between the two women and their children.

At this point it is possible to inventory the paradigmatic structure of the two narratives and formulate a judgment concerning the significance of the binary opposition 'nature-culture' for elucidating the relationship between John and Jesus as presented in our test case. In terms of Syntagm X, the signifiers are: priest, descendant of priests,

---

[9] On the leap of the unborn child in the mother's womb as a sign of subordination, see Charles H. Talbert, *Literary Patterns*, pp. 104-05.

temple, beyond child bearing age, barren, normal reproductive partner, prophet and miraculous conception. At the metaphorical level these signifiers yield: religious functionary (ruler), religious non-functionary (ruled), old, sterile, sacred/cult, ascetic, subjugator, subordinate and inferior.

In Syntagm Y the signifiers are: Nazareth, child bearing age, virgin, descendant of a king, city, lack of normal reproductive partner, king, miraculous conception. Metaphorically, we have seen that these signifiers mean: secular non-functionary (ruled), secular functionary (ruler), young, fertile, secular, dominator and superior. The binary opposition 'nature-culture,' therefore, attains prominence in the paradigmatic structure through the association of signifiers which attribute ascetic and prophetic mythemes to John in contrast to the more general 'secular' mythemes attributed to Jesus. As such, the binary opposition 'nature-culture' attains a recognizable prominence in the paradigmatic structure of the announcements of the births only insofar as the narratives sharpen the focus between John and Jesus with respect to their status and function. One must concur, therefore, with the suggestion that the opposition posed between John and Jesus in our test case, and, presumably, in early Christian tradition, is recognizable from the standpoint of the binary opposition 'nature-culture,' but, at the same time one must state that the opposition is not overtly stressed in the 'Lukan' narratives announcing their births.

The primary or initial opposition posed by Luke's narratives, in the absence of the sharpened focus between John and Jesus, is more clearly recognizable as a 'sacred-secular' binary. Stated differently, the opposition posed by the two prophesied children in Luke's narrative ('nature-culture') must be regarded as a transformation of a prior opposition posed by their respective parents as representatives of two opposing and competing socio-cultural systems. Syntagm X, for example, presents a viable pattern of cultural organization based on a synthesis of the Israelite priestly and prophetic systems with the temple/cult as its center, or, as we have seen, religious functionary and cult (Zechariah-Elizabeth). Syntagm X, however, presents a competing pattern. This pattern elevates the role of city-dweller and potential secular functionary to the center stage (Mary-Joseph). Thus, while one can concur with Spivey and Leach, one must also state that the nature-culture opposition posed by John and Jesus in Luke's narrative represents an attempt to transform one opposition by a secondary opposition that is perceived to be of the same character;

namely, the paradigmatic opposition 'nature-culture' is proposed as a means of overcoming the equally paradigmatic opposition of sacred-secular.

The parallelism of Luke's narrative of the announcement of the miraculous births of John and Jesus, thus, yields the structure and process outlined for mythology by C. Lévi-Strauss in his classic article "The Structural Study of Myth."[10] Here, the formula Fx(a) : Fy(b) :: Fx(b) : Fa-1(y) amply clarifies what has been observed earlier in our analysis.[11] In the Lukan narrative of the births of John and Jesus, Zechariah, a priest (a) and religious functionary (mediator between God and man (Fx) [= Fx(a)]) is the polar opposite of Joseph, a potential king (b) and secular functionary (subjugator of men to the rule of man (Fy) [= Fy(b)]) :: Jesus, the Davidic king (b) and Son of the Most High/Son of God (Fx) [= Fx(b)] : John, a prophet (Fa-1) and subjugator of man to the rule of God (y) [= Fa-1(y)]. Here one sees clearly that state 'b' of the initial polar opposition (potential king) is attributed to Jesus in the secondary 'nature-culture' opposition insofar as Jesus is designated as the legitimate heir of the Davidic throne.

Similarly, the religious function of mediation between God and man signified by Zechariah's priestly status (Fx), in the initial polar opposition, is carried over to the secondary binary insofar as Jesus is prophesied as the "Son of the Most High/Son of God." In fact, this aspect of the myth is only more strongly emphasized when other variants of an angelic announcement of the birth of Jesus are taken into account in Luke and elsewhere. In contrast to the emphasis upon

---

[10]C. Lévi-Strauss, "The Structural Study of Myth," *Structural Anthropology*, translated by Claire Jacobson and Brooke Grundfest Schoepf (New York: Basic Books, Inc., Publishers, 1963), pp. 206-231. The purpose of myth, according to Lévi-Strauss, "is to provide a logical model capable of overcoming a contradiction (an impossible achievement if, as it happens, the contradiction is real) ..." (Ibid., p. 229). It accomplishes this in its mythical structure "by the progressive mediation of a fundamental opposition through a series of secondary oppositions which admit a mediator" (Daniel Patte, *What is Structuralism?* GTBS (Philadelphia: Fortress Press, 1976), pp. 57-58).

[11]Ibid., p. 228; In Lévi-Strauss' description, the formula is read "with two terms, 'a' and 'b', being given as well as two functions, 'x' and 'y,' of these terms, it is assumed that a relation of equivalence exists between two situations defined respectively by an inversion of 'terms' and 'relations,' under two conditions: (1) that one term be replaced by its opposite (in the above formula, 'a' and 'a-1'); (2) that an inversion be made between the 'function value' and the 'term value' of two elements (above, 'y' and 'a'). For a discussion of the formula see, Daniel Patte, *What is Structural Exegesis?* pp. 55-58, 76-77 and the bibliography cited there.

the role of Jesus as Davidic king, the angelic announcement to the shepherds in Lk 2:8-14 stresses only more strongly the religious function of Jesus through the titles "Saviour," "Christ," "Lord" (Lk 2:11).[12] Jesus, therefore, is the mediating term of the initial polar opposition in that he embodies within himself both aspects of the sacred-secular binary; namely, Jesus is both king/secular functionary and Son of God/religious functionary.

Elements of the initial polar opposition 'sacred-secular' are carried over to the secondary nature-culture opposition with respect to John as well and in the manner specified by Lévi-Strauss.[13] Thus, in the announcement of John's birth the term/state value 'a' (priest) of the initial opposition is signified inversely by John's function as prophet (= non-priest; Fa-1). Interestingly, the status of priest is never attributed directly to John in Luke, or, in the early Christian tradition in general, despite the fact that this office is dynastically transferred in Israel according to the rules of the cultural code.[14] Moreover, function y follows a similar course. Whereas the function of the king [= Fy(b)] was to 'subjugate' humankind to the rule of man, the angelic announcement describes John's prophetic state as one that 'subjugates' the nation to God. This in effect, is accomplished in two ways. Considered from the viewpoint of John alone, the announcement can only mean that John is to subject Israel to the theocratic rule of God. In the Lukan narrative this status is fulfilled insofar as John — as forerunner of the Messianic King — announces the in-breaking reign of God that comes to expression in the person of Jesus.

We may conclude with two final observations. First, the transformation and inversion of the semantic elements of the sacred-secular opposition, accomplished by the binary 'nature-culture,' signifies the secondary character of the latter in our test case. What is at stake in the parallelism of Luke's narrative is the attempt to resolve an irresolvable tension (sacred-secular) by means of an opposition, that is perceived as semantically equivalent (nature-culture), but, unlike the former, admits mediation.

---

[12]Similarly in the angel's announcement of the birth of Jesus in Matt 1:18-25. Here the name 'Jesus' is interpreted to mean one who will 'save' his people from their sins (1:21); cf. also 1:23 ('Immanuel').

[13]See above footnote # 11.

[14]I am indebted to my colleague Prof. Randall Bailey for this observation. Prototypes in Israel for prophets who are also priests and descendants of priestly families are found in Jeremiah and Ezekiel.

Secondly, insofar as the semantic features of the initial opposition are embodied in Jesus' status and function ([Jesus = Fx(b)]), the underlying mythic dilemma of the binary is clear. Since the angel announces that Jesus is both 'divine' (Son of God) and 'mortal' (Davidic king/child of the 'presumed' parents Mary and Joseph)[15], the fundamental opposition signified by the binary 'sacred-secular' is none other than the opposition posed by the terms 'God-Man.' Although this tension may be resolved in various ways, depending upon the particularity of a given culture's cultural script, Luke resolves the tension, *via* a variation on the Hellenistic myth of the miraculous birth of the divine-man who embodies primary socio-political and religious status and function in himself.

---

[15]Cf. Luke's genealogy (3:23-38); especially 3:23, 38. See also 2:41, 48-51 and 4:22.

THE VISIONS HE SAW OR: TO ENCODE THE FUTURE IN WRITING

An Analysis of the Prologue of John's Apocalyptic Letter*

David Hellholm, *University of Bergen*

In the following investigation of the prologue to John's Apocalyptic Letter I will first carry out a formal compositional analysis delimiting this first sub-text of the entire text, i.e., the Apocalypse of John, into further formal subtexts. Following upon the formal analysis I will bring a functional commentary taking text-internal as well as text-external aspects into consideration.

1. The Formal Delimitation of The Prologue into Text-sequences on Nil-grades.

When delimiting the prologue of the Apocalypse of John, the following markers and their abbreviations will be used.

1.1. Abbreviations of notations used in the analysis

CF^{1-n} = change in literary forms of various intensional and extensional ranges.
CSW^{1-n} = change in set of worlds of various intensional and extensional ranges.[1]
DP(set) = dramatis personae: change in grouping of agents and their *verbal* status: OE (speaker), ⟦OE⟧ (quoted speaker), ŌE (listener addressed), ŌE (listener not addressed), ŌE (in discourse not participating not-I), (OE) (reference to in discourse not participating not-I), ŌE (in discourse not participating not-I being indirectly addressed), OE (not addressed en-

---

*For computer drawings and technical advice I am obliged to my son, Christer D. Hellholm.
[1]For the differentiation of the marker "Changes in set of Worlds", see D. Hellholm 1980, 87-91, idem 1986, 40f.

coder), [OE] (implied speaker);[2] change in grouping of agents and their *non-verbal* status: agens, patiens.

DP(ind) = dramatis personae: change in individual agents and their *verbal* and *non-verbal* status according to the same specification as under DP(set) above.

F = literary form.

MNE^{1-n} = meta-narrative expression: a combination of MS and SM of various intensional and extensional ranges.[3]

MNT^{1-n} = meta-narrative text standing in *suppositio materialis* vis à vis the following narrative text.[4]

MS^{1-n} = meta-communicative sentences of various intensional and extensional ranges. In this text the MS$^{1-2}$ designate meta-communicative sentences and/or verbs on the text- external level, i.e., between author and receiver while MS^{3-n} designate meta-communicative sentences and/or verbs on the text-internal level, i.e., between various dramatis personae acting within the text itself.

SM^{1-n} = substitution on meta-level of various intensional and extensional ranges.

TP = change in tense.

1.2. Text-delimitation of the Prologue of John's Apocalypse

^{00}ST [ΑΠΟΚΑΛΥΨΙΣ ΙΩΑΝΝΟΥ] (*inscriptio*)
[F: "name label"; SM^1]

^{0}ST Prologue [*incipit*] (1:1-3)
[CF^1: *inscriptio* as "name label" —*incipit* as title; MNE^1?; MNT^1]

^{01}ST^1 Titulus proprius (1:1-2)
[F: title; DP(set): supernatural senders: agens; human recipients: patiens; TP: aorist]

^{02}ST^{11} Title- and Genre-designation with account of revealer (1:1a)
 [DP(ind): Jesus Christ: agens]

^{02}ST^{12} First account of hierarchic revelation embedment (1:1b)
[DP(ind): God: agens; Christ: patiens^1; Servants: patiens^2]

^{03}ST^{121} Statement of hierarchical embedment (1:1bα)

^{03}ST^{122} Statement of content: ἃ δεῖ γενέσθαι ἐν τάχει (1:1bβ)

^{02}ST^{13} Second continued account of hierarchic embedment (1:1c)
[DP(ind): Christ: agens; angelus interpres: patiens^1; John: patiens^2]

^{02}ST^{14} Qualifying accounts about the transmitters written encodement (1:2)

---

[2]For the differentiation of *dramatis personae*, see Kl. Heger 1976, 228.

[3]For this combination, see E. Gülich 1976, 242 note 35.

[4]Gülich ibid., 237: "Der Erzähltext auf der 1. Ebene der Kommunikation steht – als Erzähltext über das Erzählen einer bestimmten Geschichte – im Verhältnis zum eingebetteten Erzähltext auf einer Meta-Ebene, ist also ein *meta-narrativer Text*..." (italics mine).

[DP(ind): John: agens]
03ST141 Statement about encodement: ὃς ἐμαρτύρησεν (1:2a)
03ST142 The qualifying statements (1:2b)
04ST1421 First qualifying statement: τὸν λόγον τοῦ θεοῦ (1:2bα)
04ST1422 Second qualifying statement: τὴν μαρτυρίαν Ἰησοῦ Χριστοῦ (1:2bβ)
03ST143 Statement about form of content of encodement: ὅσα εἶδεν (1:2c)
[Gram. form: relative clause]
01ST2 Macarism with performative and prescriptive functions (1:3)
[CF2:titulus proprius ∇ macarism; CSW1: supernatural ∇ natural; DP(set): human recipients: agens; TP: present]
02ST21 The macarism proper (1:3a-b)
03ST211 Apodosis: *performative* promise of blessing (1:3a)
[DP(ind): receiving agents: patiens]
03ST212 Protasis: *prescriptive* condition for fulfillment of promise (1:3b)
[DP(ind): receiving agents: agens]
02ST22 Eschatological justification (1:3c)
[CF3: macarism ∇ motivation; causal conj.: γάρ]

2. Functional Commentary on the Analysis of the Prologue

The functional aspects of texts can be viewed to refer (a) either *text-internally* to the textual context/co-text or (b) *text-externally* to the social or situative con-text/presuppositions, or (c) to a combination of both.[5]

2.1. Text-internal Functional Aspects

The text-internal function can – as I have shown elsewhere[6] – be divided into two groups: (1) the function of text-sequences within a given context on the level of *parole,* and (2) the function of *linguemes*[7] of the rank Rn ±1 on the level of *langue*. In this connection I will confine myself essentially to the level of *parole*.

The macro-syntagmatic delimitation of the beginning of the Apocalypse of John shows the following hierarchical structure of sub-texts on different levels:

---

[5]See Hellholm 1989b, § 3.3.3.2.; Kl. Brinker 1983.
[6]Ibid.
[7]*Linguemes* are defined as "units on the level of langue", see Heger 1976, 28-30.

00ST The sub-text on *double-nil grade* consists of a secondary "name label":[8] Ἀποκάλυψις Ἰωάννου, which, however, is found already in the uncials ℵ* and A.

This *inscriptio* which also serves as a genre-designation[9] stands in contrast to the subsequent prologue (1:1-3), which begins with the emphatic title- and genre-designation Ἀποκάλυψις Ἰησοῦ Χριστοῦ.[10]

Important in this connection is the parallel change from a secondary 00ST *inscriptio* to a likewise emphatic 0ST *incipit* with title and genre-designation in the Didache:[11] Διδαχὴ τῶν δώδεκα ἀποστόλων (00ST) vs. Διδαχὴ κυρίου διὰ τῶν δώδεκα ἀποστόλων τοῖς ἔθνεσιν (0ST).[12]

In both instances there is a change in the adnominal genitive constructions from John or the Twelve Apostles as revealer or originator to Jesus Christ or the Lord respectively. Furthermore, the two agents occupy-ing the function of transmitters in the 0ST-*incipits* of both prologues (i.e., John and the Twelve Apostles) are given the functions of revealer or origina-tor respectively in the 00ST *inscriptiones*.[13]

From a historic-diachronic point of view the tendency seems to go in the direction of changing the status of the transmitter in the

---

[8]W. Bousset 1906, 180; R.H. Charles 1920, 5; Ph. Vielhauer 1975, 486. The titles of 2 and 3 Baruch are perhaps not original but may have originated under the influence of Christian usage of the title, so Vielhauer ibid., and 1965, 582.

[9]See, e.g., Justin Martyr, Dial. 81:' Ἰωάννης ἐν ἀποκαλύψει γενομένῃ αὐτῷ...; Canon Muratori (lines 71f.): *Scripta apocalypse(s) etiam johanis et petri tantum recipimus*. H. Kraft 1974, 17; P. Prigent 1981, 9; U.B. Müller 1984, 65 and M. Karrer 1986, 17-22 do not recognize this reference to be a reference to a text-manifestation or a genre-designation. The formulation as an abbreviated adaptation of the *titulus proprius* (γενομένῃ αὐτῷ), however, without any doubt reflects a reference to a *written* text. ἐν ἀποκαλύψει thus cannot refer to the revelatory visions/auditions prior to the written encodement. For the understanding of the expression as a genre-designation, see below ad note 22, and notes 57 and 60.

[10]See below note 74.

[11]Text according to Codex Hierosolymitanus 54.

[12]This parallelism is a strong argument for the originality of the 0ST text in the Didache: contra J.-P. Audet 1958, 91-203, Vielhauer 1975, 722-725, W. Rordorf/A. Tuilier 1978, 13-17 and K. Wengst 1984, 14f. and now K. Niederwimmer 1989, 81f. and in agreement with A. Harnack 1884 (Prolegomena), 24: "Von ihnen (sc. den beiden Überschriften) ist natürlich die zweite, längere, die ältere". The question, if it is also original, is answered by Harnack, ibid. in the affirmative. So also K. Aland 1980, 133f. and Karrer 1986, 88f. and cf. the synopsis of a series of texts ibid. 94f.

[13]Parallels between the *dramatis personae* are discussed below.

primary ⁰ST-*incipit* into revealer or originator respectively in the secondary ⁰⁰ST-*inscriptio*. In addition, the short-form is handier and more manageable particularly when reference is made to these texts in other writings regardless of whether they are partially inserted or only referred to.[14] This is as good a reason as any for the "Titelverkürzung".[15]

The *inscriptiones* (⁰⁰ST-texts) function quite differently from the *inci-pits* (⁰ST-texts). The former are in fact no longer proper titles but merely names for identification purposes.[16] This distinction is so important, since a proper title as a matter of principle cannot be arbitrary, while the name label may very well be.[17] As a "name label"

---

[14]Cf. Eusebius: διδαχαὶ τῶν ἀποστόλων; Athanasius: διδαχὴ τῶν ἀποστόλων; Rufin: *doctrina apostolorum;* L: *(de) doctrina apostolorum.* It is important to notice that these designations all are "name labels" for identification purposes and do not constitute titles. For further evidence, see the editions by Audet 1958, Rordorf/Tuilier 1978, Wengst 1984 and now Niederwimmer 1989, 81, who fails to recognize the secondary character of the "name label" over against the original title.
With regard to "name labels" used in antiquity, see the remarks by R. French Strout: "It may be that the most significant contribution which the Greeks made to cataloging was the use of the author of a work for its entry. There is no doubt that our whole concept of author entry first came with the Greeks; it never once appeared in any work which has survived from the earlier civilizations of the East (1956, 257; I am indebted to Ms. Nancy Pickett, Chicago, for the reference to this art.). The opposite is the case with regard to titles, see French Straout, ibid.: "Even today in the Orient the traditional entry for a book is its title"; cf. also W.D. Davies/D.C. Allison 1988, 151f.; D. Fehling 1975, 61 and below ad note 128.

[15]Audet's argument that the short title must be given priority, since otherwise the reference to the Lord as originator would have been replaced with the less authoritative reference to the twelve apostles (1958, 99f.; so also Vielhauer 1975, 723, Rordorf/Tuilier 1978, 13-17 and Wengst 1984, 14f.) is in fact refutable in view of the *inscriptio* and *incipit* of the Apocalypse of John, since otherwise the *inscriptio* ⁰⁰ST-text of the Apc. would have to be regarded as having priority on the same grounds, a possibility not even mentioned – and rightly so – by Vielhauer when discussing the *inscriptio* and the *incipit* of the Apocalypse of John (idem 1975, 486). Disappointing in the recently published commentary on the Didache by K. Nieder wimmer 1989, 81f. is the absence of any actual analysis of the "name label" and the title per se.

[16]See Kraft 1974, 17f. Kraft, though, uses the designation titel for the ⁰⁰ST- *inscriptio,* which is highly misleading.

[17]Cf. P. Hellwig 1984, 8: "Daß Titel ihrem Wesen nach keine Namen sind, betone ich deshalb, weil dadurch der These ihrer prinzipiellen Willkürlichkeit der Boden entzogen wird". When Karrer 1986, 87 contra L. Hartman 1980, 132 states that "der Titulus der Apk war ja erst sekundär aus unserem Abschnitt zu gewinnen" (cf. ibid., 17-19 –DH) and in fact uses title for the *inscriptio* (⁰⁰ST) and labels the incipit (⁰ST) "Vortitulares Incipit von Offenbarungsschriften (ibid., 93), then

Ἀποκάλυψις Ἰωάννου could be arbitrary without making much of a difference,[18] and in a sense it is, since it does not identify the "author"[19] but only serves as a *differentia* vis à vis other books or letters by authors with other names. The "proper title", however, could not have been any other than Ἀποκάλυψις Ἰησοῦ Χριστοῦ without having entirely changed the descriptive, semantic as well as pragmatic understanding of the Apocalyptic letter itself.[20]

Yet there is reason to notice that the name label in the *inscriptio* lies in between the naming and the title[21] insofar as it picks up the genre-designation from the title in the prologue and thus curtails the possible arbitrariness by itself. The genre-designation in the *inscriptio* thus functions as a *differentia* vis à vis other books or letters by an author of the same name.[22]

0ST   The sub-text on *nil grade* consists of the prologue (1:1-3): Ἀποκάλυψις Ἰησοῦ Χριστοῦ κτλ.

As this prologue constitutes a brief opening sub-text with specific functions vis à vis the rest of the Apocalypse,[23] it must be analyzed in its totality, before the delimitation of the subsequent sub-texts can be carried out. This is the limited task of this paper.

Regarding the markers setting 0ST off from the rest of the Apocalypse, see the discussion in my essay "The Apocalyptic Genre: The Case of The Apocalypse of John"[24] ad 1ST[1].

---

his argument becomes invalid, as he evidently has not observed that Hartman uses title to designate not the 00ST *inscriptio* but the 0ST *incipit*.

[18]This is somewhat different in pseudonymous Jewish Apocalypses, since the names there are important for the authoritative claim of the Apocalypses. However, the choice of pseudonymous names (Enoch, Baruch etc.) of old may to a certain extent have been arbitrary.

[19]Even if at the time of the creation of the "name label", the author was identified, this knowledge soon vanished and as a matter of fact the identity of John still remains unknown.

[20]A title like ἀποκάλυψις τοῦ θεοῦ for instance would have deprived the prologue of its distinct Christian character and a title like προφητεία Ἰησοῦ Χριστοῦ or τοῦ θεοῦ is from a Christian and Jewish point of view resp. inconceivable.

[21]See the discussion in W. Raible 1972, 209 and cf. also Kraft 1974, 17.

[22]E.g., the Gospel of John or the Letters of John.

[23]So also Hartman 1980, 140 and Karrer 1986, 86-108.

[24]Hellholm 1989b.

(1) The sub-text on the *nil grade* is – as was stated above – *a prologue*, which is clearly divided into two parts or better: two sub-texts:[25]
01ST1 the *titulus proprius* (1:1-2) and
01ST2 the *macarism* (1:3).

The delimitation markers on the surface level that set the title off from the macarism are in hierarchical order:[26] (a) change in form (CF): from proper title to macarism; (b) change in set of worlds (CSW1):[27] from supernatural world to natural world, which is indicated by (c) a change in *set of agents* (DP:set):[28] from a set of supernatural senders to a set of human recipients; (d) change in set of grammatical subject:[29] from a set of senders (i.e., God, Christ [or John]) to a set of receivers (i.e., lector, audience); (e) change in tense (TP): from the aorist to the present (i.e., missing copula and participles).

01ST1. The first sub-text on the *nil-one grade,* i.e., the so called *titulus proprius* (1:1-2), divides into four sub-texts on the next higher grade:
1   Text- and Genre-designation with account of revealer: Jesus Christ (1:1a);
2   First account of hierarchic revelation embedment (1:1b);
3   Second account of hierarchic revelation embedment (1:1c);[30]
4   Qualifying statements about the transmitter's written encodement, either written by himself (as a fictive editor) or by someone else (as a real editor)[31] (1:2).

The markers on the surface level of the text that delimit the proper title into the above indicated sub-texts is constituted by changes in *individual agents* (DP:ind)[32] within the set of supernatural senders. In

---

[25]Cf. Hartman 1980, 132f.
[26]For the description and classification of hierarchically arranged delimitation markers, see Hellholm 1980, 78-95, idem 1986, 38-42, idem 1989b, § 3.2.1.3.
[27]See Hellholm 1980, 87-91, idem 1986, 40f., idem 1989b, § 3.2.1.3.2.
[28]For changes in groups of agents, see Hellholm, ibid.
[29]See Hartman 1980, 133.
[30]Christ, not God (so E. Lohmeyer 1953, 8), is the subject of ἐσήμανεν, see Bousset 1906, 182; Charles 1920, 6; Müller 1984, 68; partly differently Kraft 1974, 21.
[31]Regarding the alternatives "fictive or real editor", see the deliberations below.
[32]See above note 29.

this connection it is of vital importance that John occupies a middle position between the supernatural senders and the natural recipients: he is called δοῦλος[33] and his encoded writing directly obtains a double qualification as does he himself indirectly as the transmitter of the Apocalypse of Jesus Christ. John is the one who establishes the relationship between the two worlds, the super-natural and the natural world. The accessibility relation,[34] which is so constitutive for establishing connections between different worlds, is thus provided for even in the very structure of the prologue. The change in active agents (*agens*)[35] can be described as follows:

(a) from Jesus Christ in 02ST1.1 to God in 02ST1.2;
(b) from God in 02ST1.2 to Jesus Christ in 02ST1.3;
(c) from Jesus Christ in 02ST1.3 to John in 02ST1.4.

These changes in active agents here coincide with the changes in grammatical subject. The passive agents in the sub-texts concerned, however, vary. This fact justifies the usage of the changes in *active* agents as a delimitation marker on this grade.

01ST2. The second sub-text on the *nil-one grade,* i.e., the so called *macarism* (1:3), divides into two sub-texts on the next higher grade:

1 The macarism proper (1:3a-b);
2 Eschatological justification for the macarism (1:3c).

The marker setting the proper macarism off from the eschatological justification is the change in form (CF[1]) from a macarism to its motivation indicated by the causal conjunction γάρ.

02ST2.1. The first sub-text on the *second nil-two grade,* i.e., the so called macarism proper (1:3a-b) divides into two sub-texts on the next higher grade:[36]
1 Apodosis: *performative* promise of blessing (1:3a);
2 Protasis: *prescriptive* condition for the fulfillment of the promise (1:3b).

---

[33]See the discussion of the title δοῦλος below page 130 and 134.
[34]See Hellholm 1980, 91, idem 1989b, § 3.2.1.3.2. note 265.
[35]See below note 37.
[36]For the distinction between *theoretical* and *practical* functions on the one hand and various practical functions on the other, see Hellholm 1980, 57f. and idem 1989c, 30f.

The marker on the surface level of the text dividing the apodosis-element from the protasis-element is a change *in the status* of the receiving agents:[37] from *patiens* (ἀναγινώσκων and ἀκούοντες) to *agens* (τηροῦντες).

2.2. Text-external Functional Aspects

In addition to text-internal functions texts also have several text-external functions interrelated with one another.[38] The three semiotic functions mentioned below will serve as a paradigm for the analysis not only of the prologue but also of the rest of the Apocalypse:

(1) The *sigmatic, referential* or *extensional* function:[39] this type of function is dependent on the classical *"aliquid stat pro aliquo"* concept with regard to *external* objects ("Gegenstände"), and state of affairs ("Sachverhalte"), text-classes, texts or sub-texts[40] with the *signemes*[41] standing in *suppositio formalis;* or further with regard to *internal* text-classes, texts or sub-texts with the signemes standing in *suppositio materialis*.[42] This can be illustrated by the following figure:[43]

---

[37]Concerning agents, see A.J. Greimas/J. Courtés 1982, 5f. s.v. Actant; Greimas 1983, 147f.; J. Lyons 1973, 300ff., 346ff., 357ff., as well as the reference to Heger 1976 above ad note 2.

[38]See Hellholm 1989b, § 3.3.3.2.

[39]See Hellholm 1980, 22 and 32 with further references, esp. to G. Klaus 1973, 67ff.; Heger 1976, 33f. and F. von Kutschera 1975, 19-58.

[40]See Hellholm 1989a, 7 note 39: "In diesem Falle, wenn das Zeichen sich außerhalb des Textes selbst befindet und nicht ein Teil davon ausmacht, ist die Referenz auf einen Text nicht substitutionell, sondern reell; es handelt sich in solchen Fällen also nicht um materiale, sondern um formale Supposition".

[41]*Signemes* are defined as "significative units of all ranks", see Heger 1976, 40 and K. Bal-dinger 1980, 262.

[42]For the distinction between these two concepts, see below note 48.

[43]The following fig. describing in detail the lower right side of Heger's semantic trapezium (Heger 1976, 58; Baldinger 1980, 260) is an adaptation from H. Kubczak 1975, 69 and idem 1978, 34. To the objects on the level of *suppositio formalis* I have with regard to "Things" added "Text-classes, Texts, Sub-texts", and in addition I have also added the entire *suppositio materialis* section. Kubczak's specification of the *"aliquo"* qua *suppositio formalis* coincides partly with Aristotle's understanding of πράγματα, which "sich auf alle Entitäten, die im Rahmen der aristotelischen Ontologie vorkommen können...also nicht nur auf räumlich ausgedehnte, sinnlich wahrnehmbare *Gegenstände*, sondern auch auf *Sachverhalte, Handlungen, Eigenschaften, Klassen (Gattungen und Arten), Klassenmerkmale etc.* (beziehen)" (Kl. Oehler 1986, 256; italics mine); cf. also J.L. Ackrill, who in his interpretation of *de. inv.* 16b 19 remarks: "The word here (and elsewhere) [sc. ...τοῦ πράγματος... – DH] translated by 'actual thing' applies to *deeds, facts, states of affairs, &c.,* as well as to *objects*" (1963, 122; italics mine). For a detailed discussion of the trapezium, see Hellholm 1989a, 12-16.

THE ALIQUO OF THE CLASSICAL ALIQUID STAT PRO ALIQUO

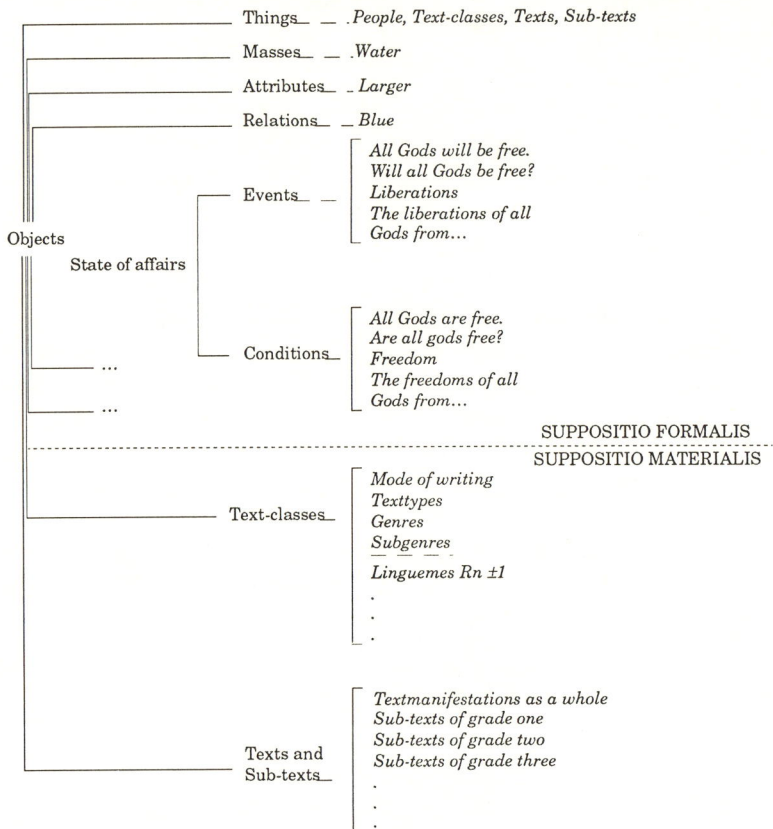

(2) The *semantic* or *intensional* function: this type of function is dependent on the stoic-scholastic concept that *"verba significant res mediantibus conceptibus"*,[44] in which *res* – as within the sigmatic function – encompasses objects, state of affairs,[45] text-classes, texts and sub-texts.

(3) the *pragmatic-communication* or *sense* function: this type of function concerns the interaction between sender(s) and receiver(s)

---

[44]See E. Coseriu 1973, 1f.
[45]See Hellholm 1980, 52-61 and idem 1989b, § 3.2.1.3.2., § 2.1., and § 2.2.3.2. #(a) with references; idem 1989a, 16; further Coseriu 1981, 48-50.

with regard to, inter alia, illocutionary, perlocutionary (J.L. Austin)[46] and evocative (E. Coseriu) aspects.[47]

2.3. Functional Analysis of the Prologue

In order to establish the overall function of the prologue as a whole its, on text-internal grounds, hierarchically delimited sub-texts have to be analyzed according to the semiotic paradigm of text-external functions just displayed.

2.3.1. The *sigmatic, referential* or *extensional function* of the prologue and its sub-texts

As I have tried to show elsewhere, it is pertinent to distinguish between text-external and text-internal reference or extension, i.e., between reference to analoga outside of the text, to objects or state of affairs on the one hand and texts or sub-texts within the text itself on the other; in other words between *suppositio formalis* and *suppositio materialis*.[48]

Three components are usually entailed in a prologue:[49] (1) author(s)/ sender(s) and addressee(s)/receiver(s); (2) summary of content of the writing; (3) information about the purpose of the writing. All three are represented in Apc. 1:1-3. One point of uncertainty, however, concerns the identity of the author of the prologue, a problem I will return to below.

In the *titulus proprius* the *senders* are not only mentioned by names or by appelativa but their hierarchical status is also indicated: God as originator, Jesus Christ as revealer, an *angelus interpres* as mediator and John as the this-worldly transmitter and encoder of the written text of the other-worldly revelation.[50]

---

[46] See J.L. Austin 1975 and cf. Hellholm 1980, 52-61.

[47] See Coseriu 1981, 73ff., 77ff.; von Kutschera 1975, 16-24, 132-51.

[48] Hellholm 1986-87, 80-89, and more detailed in idem 1989a, § 2.1.

[49] Cf. Hellwig 1984, 1f.: "...1) Der Titel informiert über den pragmatischen Stellenwert des Ko-Textes. 2) Der Titel informiert über den Inhalt des Ko-Textes. 3) Der Titel kann eine Interpretationshilfe zum Ko-Text darstellen. 4) Der Titel grenzt den Ko-Text äußerlich von anderen ab. 5) Abschnitts- und Kapiteltitel markieren Gliederungseinheiten eines längeren Textes. 6) Durch Setzen als Überschrift wird der Titel dem Ko-Text zugeordnet"; see further ibid. 5-8. Cf., e.g., Hos. 1:1; Amos 1:1; Jes. 1:1; 1Enoch 1:1-2; Luke 1:1-4; Didache: *inscriptio* and *incipit*; Gospel of Thomas CG II, 32,10-12, Apocryphon of John CG II, 1,1-4. See esp. Fehling 1975, 69-71; Hartman 1980, 132.

[50] See Hellholm 1989b, § 4.2.2.1.2. #(2)(c) with note 290; cf. also Müller 1984, 66.

In the following *macarism*, however, the *receivers*, i.e., the lector and the audience, are mentioned anonymously which, as we will see below, is of great significance for determining the overall function of the prologue.⁵¹ By means of distribution of senders and receivers onto separate sub-texts, i.e., onto the proper title and the macarism, the prologue – although on a higher meta-level – in fact corresponds to the division of the epistolary prescript into *superscript* and *adscript* which follows immediately upon the prologue (1:4: Ἰωάννες ταῖς ἑπτὰ ἐκκλησίαις ἐν τῇ Ἀσίᾳ...).⁵²

The parallelism between the "name labels" and the "titles" of the Apocalypse and the Didache respectively – as we have seen above – is remarkable. Equally striking though is the parallelism in function of the *dramatis personae* (originator–transmitter–receivers) within the prologues of each text as the following diagram will try to show:

(1)	Genre-designation	Ἀποκάλυψις	Διδαχή
(2)	Revealer	Ιησοῦ Χριστοῦ	–
(3)	Originator	ἣν ἔδωκεν αὐτῷ ὁ θεὸς...	κυρίου
(4)	Mediator	...διὰ τοῦ ἀγγέλου...	–
(5)	Transmitter	ὅς (sc. Ἰωάννης) ἐμαρτύρησεν...	διὰ τῶν δώδεκα ἀποστόλων
(6)	Lector	...ὁ ἀναγινώσκων καὶ	–
(7)	Audience	οἱ ἀκούοντες...καὶ τηροῦντες...	τοῖς ἔθνεσις

This striking parallelism displays at the same time, however, the evident difference: as expected there are more mediating agents in the prologue introducing the Apocalypse, which undoubtedly is due to the difference in generic form as already the genre-designations indicate: Ἀποκάλυψις versus Διδαχή.

All agents mentioned in the prologue of the Apocalypse have text-external analoga, to which they refer. Thus the agents in the prologue *all* stand in *suppositio formalis* referring extensionally to 'realities' outside the text itself. Thereby it does not matter whether these are real or fictive extra-textual personal objects.⁵³ With regard to the question of the agents' *suppositio materials* status, however, there is a difference between the senders and the receivers: (a) The *senders* in the *titulus proprius*, – contrary to the *receivers* in the *macarism* – have a text-internal function, since they are *all* referred to as active agents in the Apocalypse itself as well (this also applies to God himself in 21:5-

---

⁵¹See below 137ff.
⁵²See the analysis of the prescript in Hellholm 1989b.
⁵³See Hellholm 1986, 13f. note 1.

8!). Thus, the senders at the same time stand also in *suppositio materialis* referring extensionally to 'realities' or personal objects inside the text that follows, i.e, on the *text-internal meta-level*. (b) This text-internal meta-function on the other hand does not apply to the addressees, since in the macarism they are not referred to as active agents in the Apocalyptic Letter itself, but rather their function is set in relation to the already encoded written document as an existing text-manifestation, i.e., John's Apocalyptic Letter, which the lector shall read and the audience decode, i.e., on the *text-external meta-level*.[54] Also in the epilogue they are addressed as persons standing on a text-*external* meta-level vis à vis the text of John's Apocalyptic Letter. References in the Apocalyptic letter itself on the other hand are made exclusively to text-external analoga and in no instance, either explicitly or implicitly, to text-internal *dramatis personae*. Thus, already from the mere analysis of the function of the *dramatis personae* as agens or patiens in the prologue one can only arrive at the conclusion that the entire prologue stands in *suppositio materialis* and is meta-narrative in character.[55]

I shall now present further arguments for my thesis that the *entire* prologue and not only the proper title stands in a meta-relationship vis à vis the rest of the Apocalypse, i.e., the Apocalyptic Letter of John:[56]

(1) The genre designation ἀποκάλυψις[57] with its emphatic position at the very beginning of the *titulus proprius* does not refer directly

---

[54]For the distinction between text-*internal* and text-*external* meta-levels in connection with the medieval practice of writing liturgical instructions (so called rubrics) in handbooks, see Hellholm 1989a, 5 with reference to A. Menne 1980, 64.

[55]Cf. Hartman 1980, 134: "Vv. 1-2 were characterized as meta-communicative clauses. Also the macarism of v. 3 certainly stands on a meta-level as compared to the following text. If vv. 1-2 take into account the *text* of Rev. one may say that v. 3 also does so, but in addition, and above all, it does so with regard to the *actual communicative act* in which the text is made to work, i.e. the reading in the community" (italics mine).

[56]Cf. Hellwig 1984, 7: "...daß bei der Erwähnung eines Textes mithilfe des Titels in Wirklichkeit eine elliptisch verkürzte Kennzeichnung vorliegt, die in etwa lautet: *der Kotext mit dem Titel 'x'*. Dabei ist 'x' ein Zitat – oder theoretischer: 'x' steht in materieller Supposition".

[57]See Hellwig ibid., 5: "Der Titel über einem Textstück, das der Leser selbst vor sich hat, informiert zunächst darüber, als was für ein *Sprechakt* der Ko-text zu gelten hat. Dies kann dadurch geschehen, daß im Titel bzw. Untertitel die *Illokution* oder das *Genre* des Kotextes direkt bezeichnet wirt..." (italics mine). That

to a visionary experience outside the text,[58] but rather — as the τὰ ἐν αὐτῇ γεγραμμένα at the very end of the prologue (by means of *inclusio*[59]) indicates — to the written text that follows, to which the first three verses serve as a prologue.[60] This is all the more likely, since genre designations function as "names of texts" or perhaps even bet-

---

ἀποκάλυψις constitutes a genre-designation is almost certain (contra, e.g., Karrer 1986, 17-22), because of its emphatic position at the beginning of the *titulus proprius* forming the first part of the prologue, which is standing on a meta-level over against the Apocalyptic Letter itself (cf. the parallel phenomenon in the Didache). See further below note 60. Should αὐτή (in v. 3b) indeed refer to ἀποκάλυψις, which I think is highly probable, then it still is connected to the senders, since τὰ γεγραμμένα is the result of the encodement by John as the transmitter of the Apocalypse. Even more important than the nominal definition "Apocalypse" is the real definition a fact which has been accentuated explicitly by Vielhauer 1975, 486, when he with regard to Apocalypses in general writes: "Die als 'Apokalypsen' charakterisierten Werke haben von Haus aus keine einheitliche und manchmal gar keine Selbstbezeichnung. Ihre nachträgliche Benennung nach dem Titel der christlichen Johannesapokalypse *ist gleichwohl berechtigt, weil diese und jene zur gleichen Gattung gehören*" (italics mine).

[58]Contra, e.g., Kraft 1974, 22.

[59]The question of, whether ἐν αὐτῇ refers to ἡ προφητεία or ἡ ἀποκάλυψις is problematic to answer. W. Bauer 1988, 1625 s.v. τηρέω 5 takes αὐτή to refer to prophecy: τὰ ἐν τῇ προφητείᾳ γεγραμμένα. Even so there seems to be no contradictions between the Letter being designated as an apocalypse and at the same time as a prophecy, both being historical genre manifestations of the ahistoric 'type of text' named Revelatory writings (see Hellholm 1986, 20 and 30). This is evident from the fact that the two designations each from different perspectives are ascribed by the author to each part of the prologue: ἀποκάλυψις to the title and its double encodement by the senders; προφητεία to the macarism and its double decodement by the addressees.

[60]The very fact that the emphatic designation Ἀποκάλυψις Ἰησοῦ Χριστοῦ stands in a *suppositio materialis* position vis à vis the Apocalyptic Letter that follows is a decisive argument for taking the *signeme* ἀποκάλυψις to be not only a title but at the same time a genre-designation, see the quotation from Hellwig above note 57; Regarding titles and their relationship to subsequent texts, see Hellwig ibid., 7ff., 16f.: "Die Relation Metatext zu Objekttext liegt vor, wenn ersterer über letzteren handelt. Titel sind Metatexte, da sie auf einen Ko-Text Bezug nehmen und ihn nach Art und Inhalt charakterisieren" (p. 16); cf. also Hartman 1987, 63. Regarding the functional relationship between titles as names of texts and as genre-designations, see Raible 1972, 211: "Der Eigenname des Textes und der Gattungsname des Textes stehen nicht auf derselben Ebene. Beide Arten...liefern jedoch eine zusätzliche Information über den Inhalt des Textes, der eine auf direktem Wege, der andre auf dem Umweg über die Gattung, zu welcher der Text gehört". For the title as genre-designation, see also 2 Bar., 3 Bar., Didache (cf., however, above note 8). See now also with regard to Matt. 1:1 Davies/ Allison 1988, 151: "The question of whether 1.1 is a general title should take into account this consideration: it was a custom in the prophetic, didactic, and apocalyptic writings of Judaism to open with an independent titular sentence announcing the content of the work".

The Visions He Saw or: To Encode the Future in Writing 123

ter as meta-texts. As a genre designation ἀποκάλυψις thus stands in *suppositio materialis* vis à vis the letter which John had written to the seven churches in Asia Minor beginning in 1:4 with an epistolary prescript and ending in 22:21 with an epistolary benediction.[61]

(2) The two qualifying statements about the transmitter's written encodement each contains a reference to the following text of the Apocalypse.

At first this interpretation seems untenable: the usage of ὁ λόγος τοῦ θεοῦ[62] and ἡ μαρτυρία Ἰησοῦ Χριστοῦ[63] as standing in *material supposition* in the prologue would deviate from its usage in 1:9 and 6:9: διὰ τὸν λόγον τοῦ θεοῦ[64] καὶ τὴν μαρτυρίαν (Ἰησοῦ [Χριστοῦ][65]), where both signemes clearly stand in *formal supposition* referring to 'realities' (i.e., oral or written preaching) outside the present text:[66] in 1:9 with regard to John, in 6:9 with regard to αἱ ψυχαὶ τῶν ἐσφαγμένων. In 1:9 the event is indeed related to John but precedes the present writing ("διά denotes the ground and not the purpose in this Book"[67]). In 6:9 reference is made to an event or even events, which neither can be defined in time nor are related directly to John.[68]

---

[61]Regarding the Apocalypse as letter, see Karrer 1986 and J. Roloff 1984.

[62]The genitive is here a *genitivus subiectivus*, see Charles 1920, 7.

[63]The genitive is here a *genitivus subiectivus*, see Bousset 1906, 183; so also Charles, ibid. Methodologically unsatisfactory is the procedure in H.P. Jörns 1971, 114 note 33, when he without distinguishing between meta- and object-levels presupposes that the adnominal genitive construction has to be interpreted as a *genitivus obiectivus* in all instances, where it occurs in the Apocalypse. Correct however: A. Satake 1966, 111f.; hesitant T. Holtz 1962, 23 note 1.

[64]The genitive τοῦ θεοῦ is in both instances a *genitivus obiectivus* or in the first case possibly a *genitivus qualitatis*, and not as in 1:2 a *genitivus subiectivus*, Charles 1920, 21; Holtz, ibid., 23; Satake, ibid., 111.

[65]The genitive Ἰησοῦ [Χριστοῦ] in 1:9 is a *genitivus obiectivus* (Charles, ibid.; Holtz, ibid.) and a qualification of ἡ μαρτυρία in 6:9 is missing altogether. In 1:2 the genitive is as we have already seen a *genitivus subiectivus*.

[66]Cf. also Charles statement that "the phrase τ. λόγον τ. θεοῦ καὶ τ. μαρτυρί-'αν 'I. here give the contents of his preaching whereas in 2 they describe the apocalypse itself: cf. ὅσα εἶδεν" (ibid., 21). Otherwise Vielhauer 1975, 501 due to his misinterpretation of 1:2 as *suppositio formalis*.

[67]Charles 1920, 22; so also recently A.Yarbro Collins 1984, 102-104 and Roloff 1984, 39.

[68]Cf. however the author's statement in 1:9: ἐγὼ Ἰωάννης ὁ ἀδελφὸς ὑμῶν καὶ συγκοινωνὸς ἐν τῇ θλίψει, καὶ βασιλείᾳ καὶ ὑπομονῇ ἐν Ἰησοῦ.... Should 6:9 refer also to John's θλίψεις in 1:9, those would under all circumstances precede his revelation on the island of Patmos.

That the qualifying statements in the prologue, on the other hand, could refer to John's μαρτυρεῖν *prior* to his revelation on Patmos — as is the case in 1:9 (and possibly in 6:9) —, and thus to a text-external state of affairs, is excluded by the text itself by means of a subsequent relative clause: ὅσα εἶδεν. There is nothing in the text that could lead us to interpret the relative clause as referring to another revelation than the one narrated in the rest of the book.

However, could not ὅσα εἶδεν refer *directly* to the reality of the visionary experience that logically and temporarily preceded the text, i.e., to the text-external realm to which the present text bears witness?[69] This is not to be excluded altogether but is highly improbable as the following deliberations will try to show:

(a) The first qualifying statement ($03ST^{1.4.1.}$): ὃς ἐμαρτύρησεν τὸν λόγον τοῦ θεοῦ by all likelihood does not refer to John's testimony of the word of God outside the present text but rather refers to the text itself as τὸν λόγον τοῦ θεοῦ.[70] If the aorist ἐμαρτύρησεν is epistolary as most commentators take it to be,[71] then it is certainly a direct indication of John's encodement of the Apocalypse in written form. This is clearly the case in view of the usage of the verb μαρτυρεῖν and the substantivized participle ὁ μαρτυρῶν in the epilogue, where both, in connection with *substitutions on abstraction level* (ταῦτα 22:16 and 20), explicitly refer to John's Apocalyptic Letter regardless of whether the subject is the angel (v. 16), John (? v. 18) or Jesus Christ (v. 20). This interpretation of μαρτυρεῖν τὸν λόγον τοῦ θεοῦ is further substantiated by its correspondence to the statement about God as the origina-

---

[69] Notice that it is the *direct* reference in the prologue that is at stake here. I am here *not* discussing the *indirect* reference, which lies behind the direct one in the prologue, neither am I here discussing the *direct* reference to text-external analoga within the following text, i.e., within the Apocalyptic Letter itself.

[70] Cf. Satake 1966, 111: "An dieser Stelle bezieht sich μαρτυρέω auf den Dienst des Verfassers selbst. Daß in 3 eine Seligpreisung für den Vorleser des Buches und seine Zuhörer folgt, zeigt, daß der Verfasser mit μαρτυρέω *faktisch die Abfassung des Buches* meint. Die Form ἐμαρτύρησεν ist als brieflicher Aorist zu verstehen" (italics mine). See also the quotation from Roloff 1984, 29 below ad note 79.

[71] See, e.g., Bousset 1906, 183: "Der Aor. ist gewählt, weil der Schreiber sich auf den Stand-punkt seiner Leser versetzt"; Charles 1920, 7: "The aorist ἐμαρτύρησεν is epistolary: the author transports himself to the stand-point of his readers". See also the quotations from Satake in the previous note and from Roloff 1984, 29 below ad note 79.

tor of the Apocalypse in 1:1, where the text reads: ἥν (sc. ἀποκάλυψιν) ἔδωκεν αὐτῷ (sc. Ἰησοῦ Χριστῷ) ὁ θεός.[72]

(b) Likewise the second qualifying statement ($03_{ST}1.4.2.$): καὶ τὴν μαρτυρίαν Ἰησοῦ Χριστοῦ ὅσα εἶδεν does not refer to Jesus' testimony outside the text but to his "self-testimony" within the text.[73] Already in the genre designation Jesus Christ is depicted as the revealer: ἀποκάλυψις Ἰησοῦ Χριστοῦ.[74] Μαρτυρία in the meaning of testimony of scripture or proof text is also attested in patristic texts.[75] This parallelism in interpretation of the two qualifying statements about John's written encodement is a decisive support for the *suppositio materialis* interpretation of the entire prologue.

(c) How important the distinction between *formal* and *material supposition* in fact is, becomes evident, when we have to translate the text. The Revised Standard Version translates v. 2 as follows: "who bore witness to the word of God and the testimony of Jesus Christ, even to all that he saw." The relative pronoun ὅσα is here translated with "even to all", which presupposes a distinction between the "Word of God" and the "Testimony of Jesus Christ" on the one hand and the "Visions of John" on the other. This translation is determined by the interpretation of the qualifying statements as *suppositio formalis*, while the relative clause is interpreted as *suppositio materialis*. This, however, is an unacceptable rendering of the Greek, since it requires a καί before or after the pronoun ὅσα. This interpretation is also favoured by Heinrich Kraft in his commentary from 1974 when he, with reference to 1 John (sic!), states: "Daraus folgt, daß ὅσα εἶδεν nicht bloß auf den Inhalt der Apokalypse bezogen werden kann".[76] Here the consequences of the form critical observation of vv. 1-3 as a prologue being meta-narrative in character are ignored with regard to the interpretation of the text, which shows, how important the formal analysis of a text in fact is for its correct interpretation.

---

[72]Cf. the analysis of the chiastic structure of the proper title below 16.

[73]Similarly Bauer 1988, 1000, s.v. μαρτυρία 2dβ.

[74]The genitive is a *genitivus subiectivus* "doch nicht Gen. des Besitzers, sondern des Urhebers in der nachfolgenden Beschränkung" (Bousset 1906, 181), thus better: *genitivus auctoris*, so Kraft 1974, 19f.; Müller 1984, 66; Roloff 1984, 28 and Karrer 1986, 86.

[75]This usage of μαρτυρία for scripture, proof texts etc. is found, e.g., in Justin Martyr, *Dial.* 67:3: μετὰ μαρτυρίας τῶν γραφῶν; Clemens Alexandrinus, *Paed.* 1:9: μετὰ μαρτυρίας προφητικῆς, see Lampe 1968, 828 s.v. μαρτυρία 3 with further examples.

[76]Kraft 1974, 22.

Pierre Prigent in his commentary of 1981, on the other hand, translates: "...qui (sc. Jean) a rendu temoignage de Jesu Christ: tout ce qu'il a vu".⁷⁷ By putting a colon after Christ Prigent indicates that he takes ὅσα εἶδεν as referring to the λόγος τοῦ θεοῦ and to the μαρτυρία Ἰησοῦ Χριστοῦ. Further, in his commentary on the passage he explicitly spells out that he understands the relative clause as standing in *suppositio materialis,* when commenting upon the ὅσα εἶδεν, he writes: "C'est de la vision, c'est-a-dire de l'Apocalypse, qu'il s'agit".⁷⁸ The same interpretation is also to be found in Jürgen Roloff's recent commentary from 1984, in which the author in his translation likewise put a colon after Christ, and in his commentary on the passage writes: "Er (sc. Johannes) hat alles, was er schaute, und was seinem Wesen nach Wort Gottes und Zeugnis Jesu Christi war, vollständig und ohne davon etwas zu verschweigen, bezeugt, so daß sein Zeugnis nun in verschrifteter Gestalt den Gemeinden vorliegt".⁷⁹ So already Wilhelm Bousset in his KEK-commentary from 1906: "Hier wird der allgemeine Ausdruck durch das folgende ὅσα εἶδεν näher bestimmt als die speziell in diesem Buch vorliegende Offenbarung".⁸⁰ ὅσα εἶδεν is then translated: "so viel er schaute". Also R.H. Charles deliberations in his ICC-commentary from 1920 go in the same direction: "...in the present passage the expression (sc. τὸν λόγον τοῦ θεοῦ καὶ τὴν μαρτυρίαν Ἰησοῦ Χριστοῦ) is limited by the words that follow ὅσα εἶδεν – to the revelation made in this Book".⁸¹

(d) A final indication for the appropriateness of the *suppositio materialis* interpretation of the two qualifying statements is the chiastic

---

⁷⁷Prigent 1981, 9.
⁷⁸Ibid. 13.
⁷⁹Roloff 1984, 29.
⁸⁰Bousset 1906, 183.
⁸¹Charles 1920, 7. Charles' interpretation, though, is not crystal clear, since a few lines later he states: "The λόγος τοῦ θεοῦ is not to be limited in our text to the OT. It embraces the entire revelation of God which now in its fullness is attested by Christ". This seems to indicate that all of a sudden Charles takes λόγος τοῦ θεοῦ to stand in formal supposition. A benevolent interpretation of the seemingly contradictory statements would be to suppose that Charles without noticing it switches from an *extensional* to an *intensional* description, i.e., from a sigmatic to a semantic interpretation. There is, however, one problem with this favorable interpretation of Charles' text: he is explicitly referring to the OT as text, which raises some doubts as to his 'unintentional' move from extension to intension.The least that can be said is that Charles' text is unclear on this point.

structure within the *titulus proprius* between the genre-definition and the qualifying statements:[82]

(A) Ἀποκάλυψις Ἰησοῦ Χριστοῦ
(B) ἣν ἔδωκεν αὐτῷ ὁ θεός...
(B') ...τὸν λόγον τοῦ θεοῦ
(A') καὶ τὴν μαρτυρίαν Ἰησοῦ Χριστοῦ.

(3) In the following sub-text (0_1ST^2), i.e., the *macarism*, the reference to the subsequent text is so evident that we need only to point it out without further comments: τοὺς λόγους τῆς προφητείας can as τὰ ἐν αὐτῇ γεγραμμένα shows only refer to the Apocalyptic Letter of John. This becomes absolutely certain in view of the parallel expression in the epilogue 22:18: μαρτυρῶ ἐγὼ παντὶ τῷ ἀκούοντι τοὺς λόγους τῆς προφητείας τοῦ βιβλίου τούτου κτλ.[83] These prophetic words are to be read aloud to the audience (plural) by a lector (singular):[84] μακάριοι ὁ ἀναγινώσκων καὶ οἱ ἀκούοντες.

(4) In conclusion of our sigmatic-extensional analysis we have good reasons to suggest that the entire prologue refers extensionally to the following text and this interpretation is of utmost importance for the semantic-intensional as well as for the pragmatic-illocutionary function of 1:1-3 as a prologue for the subsequent Apocalyptic Letter.

2.3.2. The *semantic* or *intensional function of the prologue and its sub-texts*

If, as we have just tried to demonstrate, the prologue as a whole stands in *suppositio materialis*, i.e., on a meta-level, vis à vis the rest of the writing (1:4-22:21), the intensional interpretation of the entire prologue and its sub-texts will have decisive consequences for its semantic understanding of John's Apocalyptic Letter.

(1) A semantic-intensional analysis of the four most important *lexemes* and/or *syntagmata* – already discussed in connection with the

---

[82] This form of chiasm constitutes what H. Lausberg has called the "Groß-Chiasmus" and which he has defined as the "Überkreuzung semantisch aufeinander bezogener (Haupt- oder Neben-) Sätze innerhalb einer Satzgruppe oder einer Periode" (1976, 130 [§ 392 II]).

[83] Cf. already 22:7 and 22:10.

[84] Bousset 1906, 183: "Der 'Lesende' ist der Vorleser im öffentlichen Gottesdienst..."; so also Charles 1920, 7. See Justin Martyr, *Apol*. I, 67: τὰ ἀπομνημονεύματα τῶν ἀποστόλων ἢ τὰ συγγράμματα τῶν προφητῶν ἀναγινώσκεται. See further below 132 with note 101.

sigmatic-extensional analysis – shows a remarkable hierarchic structure:

(a) In the *titulus proprius* (^{01}ST^1) John's Apocalyptic Letter is semantically qualified first of all as a generic text, more precisely as an apocalypse by means of a genre-designation,[85] which, however, contrary to the *inscriptio* does not say Apocalypse of John but rather Ἀποκάλυψις Ἰησοῦ Χριστοῦ;[86] further, it is claimed to be not any word but rather a *divine* Word: ὁ λόγος τοῦ θεοῦ;[87] and finally, the testimony is not just anybody's but to the contrary the Testimony of *Jesus Christ*: ἡ μαρτυρία Ἰησοῦ Χριστοῦ.[88] Thus, all designations of the Apocalyptic Letter of John in the proper title are *semantically* qualified by adnominal *genitivus subjectivus* constructions, each serving as a specific *seme* of divine impact in its respective micro-syntagma.[89]

(b) In the subsequent *macarism* (^{01}ST^2) the claim is made that it is not merely general Christian words that have been encoded in writing but Prophetic Words: οἱ λόγοι τῆς προφητείας.[90] In this connection it is significant to notice that in the receiver-oriented sub-text the adnominal semantic qualification is not bound to a person (divine or human) but to a subject matter. The reason being that a person bound qualification would have made John, the transmitter, a prophet, which the redactor/author evidently wanted to prevent. This observation is congruent with the reluctance on the part of the redactor/author to attribute any title to John except δοῦλος,[91] and it should make us cautious to interpret this passage as well as the ones in the epilogue as claiming John's Apocalyptic Letter to be a prophetic book

---

[85]As in all instances where genre-designations are given no definition is provided, but rather presupposed, in general terms that is (this is true of modern as well as ancient literature). A list of *semes/noemes* or, as we might call them, semantic and distinctive characteristics for a *paradigmatic* definition of the generic concept Apocalypse has been assembled in Hellholm 1986, 22f. and idem 1989b, § 3.2. A list of *syntagmatic semes/noemes* is not yet within reach.

[86]See the discussion above 112ff. and further 121 with notes 56f.

[87]See above note 62. Cf. Müller 1984, 67: "Die Botschaft des Verfassers beansprucht »Wort Gottes« zu sein, weil sie in Gott ihrem Ursprung hat..."

[88]See above note 63. Cf. Müller, ibid.: "...und sie ist »Zeugnis Jesu Christi«, weil Christus selbst sie bezeugt (22,20)".

[89]For the pragmatic interpretation of the semantic qualifications, see 130f.

[90]The genitive is here a *genitivus qualitatis*.

[91]For the interpretation of δοῦλος, see below 130 and 134.

in the common sense,[92] viz., as opposite to an apocalypse on the same level of abstraction, i.e., as a Revelatory Writing.[93] Further, these words are explicitly referred to as having been transmitted to the receivers in written form: τὰ ἐν αὐτῇ γεγραμμένα.[94]

(2) When reflecting the distribution by the redactor/author of these semantic *semes* to the various sub-texts as they have been delimited above, we arrive at the following pattern:

01ST1 Titulus proprius [DP: *divine* senders; *divine* qualifying signemes underlined]

    02ST1.1 Genre-designation: ἀποκάλυψις Ἰησοῦ Χριστοῦ

    02ST1.2 First hierarchic statement: ἣν ἔδωκεν αὐτῷ ὁ θεός

    ⋮

    02ST1.4 Two qualifying statements: ὁ λόγος τοῦ θεοῦ

                                           ἡ μαρτυρία Ἰησοῦ Χριστοῦ

01ST2 Macarism [DP: *human* recipients; *humanly* qualifying signemes underlined]

    02ST2.1 Performative promise of blessing: οἱ λόγοι τῆς προφητείας

    02ST2.2 Prescriptive condition: ἐν αὐτῇ γεγραμμένα

Most significant in this connection is the series of intensional designations (dotted underlined) of John's Apocalyptic Letter from the perspective of the senders in the *titulus proprius:* (a) as an Apocalypse from Jesus Christ; (b) this Apocalypse has its origin in God; (c) as the Word of God and finally (d) as the Testimony by Jesus Christ;

From the perspective of the receivers in the *macarism* the two intensional designations are (a) the Prophetic Word and (b) the Apocalyptic-Prophetic (ἐν αὐτῇ[95]) Letter in written form. The two designations here are *directly* human and only *indirectly* divine, insofar as the prophetic words claim to have their origin in God (Jer. 1:1 דבר־יהוה אליו

---

[92]This seems to me to be an additional reason, why the *inscriptio* from the second century chose not to render the name label: Προφητεία Ἰωάννου but precisely Ἀποκάλυψις Ἰωάννου.

[93]For the distinction between various hierarchically arranged abstraction levels, see Hellholm 1986, 29f.

[94]See the discussion of this phrase above notes 57 and 59.

[95]See previous note.

דברי ירמיהו...אשר היה; Joel 1:1 דבר־יהוה אשר היה אל יואל; cf. also Hos. 1:1-2 and Amos 1:1-2).⁹⁶

Thus, the very structure of the prologue and the division of *semes* unto the two different sub-texts on grade one indicates that the intensional interpretation of John's Apocalyptic Letter is dialectical: *divine* with respect to its origin (ἀποκάλυψις), *human* and *divine* (οἱ λόγοι τῆς προφητείας) with respect to the accessibility of the divine message by means of the transmitter to the human addressees, i.e., the human lector and the the human audience.

(3) The only direct way in which the transmitter and author John is introduced is by means of the attribute ὁ δοῦλος, which does not constitute an official or dignitary designation,⁹⁷ but rather stipulates his relationship to Christ. Indirectly, however, John obtains his dignity by means of the direct qualifying statements about his message encoded in writing as ὁ λόγος τοῦ θεοῦ and ἡ μαρτυρία Ἰησοῦ Χριστοῦ and as it is stated programmatically at the very beginning and at the very end of the prologue: ἀποκάλυψις Ἰησοῦ Χριστοῦ respectively ἐν αὐτῇ (sc. ἀποκαλύψει?) γεγραμμένα. In addition, the very fact that he was chosen as the transmitter (...ἀποστείλας διὰ τοῦ ἀγγέλου αὐτοῦ τῷ δούλῳ αὐτῷ Ἰωάννῃ...) is a distinction in itself. In the prologue John does not bring a distinction with him, rather he obtains it (a) from his election and (b) from the dignity of his transmitted writing.

(4) It is also important to note, how little in fact is said in the prologue about the content of John's Apocalyptic Letter: once within the *titulus proprius* (⁰³ST1.2.3) in the formulation: ἃ δεῖ γενέσθαι ἐν τάχει⁹⁸ (1:1) and once within the macarism (⁰²ST2.2) in the formulation: ὁ γὰρ καιρὸς ἐγγύς (1:3).

(a) These two statements, however, are asymmetric in their functions, since the first clearly is referring only *indirectly* to the extra-textual events that are to come; *directly* it refers – as almost everything in this prologue – to the subsequent Apocalyptic Letter as the verb δεῖξαι proves. In addition one has to acknowledge that the succinct and abstract formulation is indeed appropriate for a statement of content on a meta-level vis à vis the Apocalyptic Letter itself.

---

⁹⁶See, e.g., J. Lindblom 1962, 108-122; H. Wildberger 1942.
⁹⁷Roloff 1984, 28; contra Bousset 1906, 182.
⁹⁸This phrase is derived from Dan 2:28; cf., e.g., Charles 1920, 6.

(b) The second statement of content: ὁ γὰρ καιρὸς ἐγγύς (1:3) does *not* refer *directly* to the text of the Apocalyptic Letter but as its syntagmatic function indicates to events outside of the text. As an "eschatological justification for the macarism", its promise and conditional threat, it *directly* refers to the fact that time is short. One has to observe that no reference whatsoever is given as to what is going to happen in the near future. What the reader encounters is only an urgent and yet vague time limit. The redactor's/author's affirmation that time is running short presupposes *indirectly* that this affirmation can and must be sustained by the content of the following Letter.

(4) In conclusion of our semantic-intensional analysis we have reasons to affirm that the intensional function essentially is concentrated upon as well as limited to disclosing the subsequent Apocalyptic Letter as the Word of God, the Testimony of Jesus Christ as far as its origin is concerned, and as Prophetic Words as far as its reception is concerned. Intensionally the prologue also discloses John as God's chosen transmitter and encoder of the Apocalypse of Jesus Christ.

2.3.3. The *pragmatic-communication* or *sense function* of the prologue and its sub-texts

If the *sigmatic suppositio-materialis*-interpretation of the prologue has an impact on the semantic interpretation, it – together with the *semantic* interpretation – certainly is of no less a consequence for the pragmatic interpretation not only of the prologue itself but esp. for its understanding of the following Apocalyptic Letter.

(1) The delimitation of the prologue into two parts:[99] one addressing the question of senders, the other that of the receivers is an obvious token of the thematization within the prologue itself of the communication situation. This interpretation can be substantiated by the following observations:

(a) Within the sub-text $01ST^1$, the *titulus proprius*, we encounter a programmatic *hierarchical embedment structure* as far as the senders of the revelation are concerned:[100] (α) from God: the originator, (β) to Jesus Christ: the revealer, (γ) to an angelic mediator: the *angelus interpres*, (δ) to John: the transmitter of the apocalyptic message from the other-world to this world in form of an Apocalyptic Letter.

---

[99] See above.
[100] See the diagram above 120.

Within the sub-text $01_{ST}2$, the *macarism*, we again encounter a *hierarchical embedment* with regard to the receivers: [(α) from John's encoded writing as implied in sub-text $02_{ST}1.4$ from the proper title], (β) to the ecclesiastical lector, (γ) who reads the text aloud to the audience:[101] This "gradation of authorities"[102] within both sub-texts of the prologue clearly shows the redactor's/author's concern for authorization of John's Apocalyptic Letter.

(b) As a connecting link between the senders and the receivers we find – as we already have seen above – the transmitter of the message, John with his written encodement of what was revealed to him.[103] Looking at the text from this point of view, we arrive at the following tripartition:

(1) *Titulus proprius* (a) What the senders encode by means of visions and auditions is named: *Apocalypse*;

(b) What John transmits by means of a written encodement is named: *God's Word* and the *Testimony of Jesus Christ*;

(2) *Macarism* (c) What the receivers decode is named: *Prophetic Words*.

That John as the transmitter of the message falls under the sender oriented *titulus proprius* is only logical, partly on account of the text-internal reference to his visionary experience: ὅσα εἶδεν, partly on account of his written encodement (μαρτυρῆσαι) of the senders' in hierarchical order encoded Apocalypse.

This is further confirmed by the fact that – as our synopsis above shows – the encoded written message in form of a Letter throughout has been attributed various qualifications in form of adnominal genitive constructions: as a qualification of God's, Jesus Christ's and the

---

[101] See above note 84. Cf. further Roloff 1984, 30: "Gegen Ende des 1. Jahrhunderts scheint die Praxis, neben Texten aus dem Alten Testament auch christliche Schriften im Gottesdienst zu verlesen, schon vielfach verbreitet gewesen zu sein (Kol. 4,16; Justin, Apol. 1,67,3)". Regarding the letters of Paul, see in general Hartman 1986 and further 1 Thess. 5:27 and for this passage cf. Holtz 1986, 273-75; regarding Col. see Hartman 1985, 193.

[102] Bousset 1906, 181.

[103] Cf. Roloff 1984, 29: "V.2 schlägt die Brücke von der Absender- zur Empfängerseite,...so daß sein (sc. Johannes) Zeugnis nun in verschrifteter Gestalt den Gemeinden vorliegt". Cf. the transformation of the auditory to the written, n.b., epistolary mode in Hermas 5:4 and 6:1-7:4 and see Hellholm 1980, 150-54.

interpreting angel's message it holds the title and genre-designation: Apocalypse from Jesus Christ; as a qualification of John's written testimony it holds the double designation: the Word of God and the Testimony of Jesus Christ. The last two designations could for obvious reasons not have been attributed to the encoded message of the divine senders, since it would have caused a tautology. These two qualifying designations together with the genre-designation obviously perform a legitimizing and authorizing function of John's written encodement of the divine message labeled Apocalypse in v. 1. As a qualification of the message recited by the lector and decoded by the audience it holds the indirect divine and direct human designation:[104] the Prophetic Words, which is a common designation not only on the level of Genre but also for Revelatory writings on the level of Type of texts. All these diverging designations with their qualifying adnominal constructions contribute to the enforcement of the illocution of authorization that already the gradation of authorities demonstrated.[105]

Also in view of the stipulated communication situation in the prologue as well as in the Apocalyptic Letter itself it is only consequent that John falls under the sender oriented *titulus proprius*, since he as the transmitter and encoder of the written text in no instance functions as a receiver, either as a lector, or as a part of the audience.[106]

If (a) from a *semantic-intensional* point of view the designations and their qualifications emphasize the *meaning*[107] of the Apocalyptic Letter, i.e., the semantic connotations of the text, (b) the *pragmatic-illo-*

---

[104]See above 128.

[105]See above 120 and 130f. Cf. also the pertinent comment on the recitement of the text in the congregation by E. Lohse 1960, 12: "Wenn der Verfasser eine so große Verheißung an die Verlesung und das Hören seines Buches knüpft, so zeigt er damit an, welche Autorität er beansprucht. Sein Wort soll nicht hinter dem der alttestamentlichen Propheten zurückstehen (22,18f.)." This authority, though, has its foundation not in John but to the contrary in its divine origin. Further Hartman 1980, 135: "...the macarism draws the reader into the text itself, and thus also confronts him personally with the authority that according to v.1f., is the origin of the revelation".

[106]John's rôle is in this respect different from that of Hermas, see Hermas 8:3d: σὺ δὲ ἀναγνώσῃ εἰς ταύτην τὴν πόλιν μετὰ τῶν πρεσβυτέρων προϊσταμένων τῆς ἐκκλησίας. See Hellholm 1980, 108 and 156.

[107]For the distinction between "function of meaning" and "function of sense", see Hellholm 1980, 56 fig. 8. Regrettably, however, I did not there differentiate between the extensional-sigmatic and the intensional-semantic functional aspects.

cutionary function serves the communicative purpose in accentuating the *sense*[108] of the text, i.e the illocutionary–evocative force of these semantic qualifications in their capacity of ascribing authority and legitimacy on the one hand and consolation, exhortation and even warning or threat on the other to John's written encodement in form of his Apocalyptic Letter. Here we encounter a clear example of the interaction between semantics and pragmatics: the prerequisite of semantics for pragmatics in the analysis on the one hand and the priority of pragmatics over semantics in the interpretation of texts on the other.[109]

(2) John's rôle in the prologue is that of a *patiens* as well as an *agens* insofar as he first receives the visionary and auditory revelation, which he then turns into written form and then in a first round[110] sends to the Seven Churches in Asia Minor in form of an Apocalyptic Letter.

In this connection it is important to notice that John is given (by a real redactor) or gives himself (as author and/or fictive redactor) no other designation (δοῦλος) than is given to the ultimate addressees in the *titulus proprius* (δοῦλοι).[111] If the appelativa in the first place[112] indicate the relationship with the servant(s) to God or Christ respectively, in the second place they reveal the mutual relationship based on equality between the transmitter and the receivers of the divine message.

From a *pragmatic* point of view this is a clear manifestation of the fact that the overall dominant illocutionary force of the Apocalyptic Letter in this prologue is of an other-worldly nature and not of an inner-worldly hierarchical structure.[113]

---

[108]While the "function of meaning" is explicitly formulated by means of inherently entailed *semes/noemes* in the *signemes* (e.g., Apocalypse, Testimony) or by qualifying adnominal constructions, the "sense function" is only implicitly present in the *signemes* and qualifiers. For this distinction, see the discussion in Hellholm 1980, 57.
[109]See Hellholm 1980, 32.
[110]See the discussion below.
[111]Cf. Holtz 1962, 43: "...schließlich werden offenbar alle Glieder der Gemeinde δοῦλοι θεοῦ genannt"; cf. also Lohmeyer 1953, 7: "δοῦλοι sind also die Gesamtgemeinde...".
[112]See above 130.
[113]Roloff 1984, 28: "Nimmt man dazu, daß das einzige Predikat, daß er (sc. Johannes) hier für sich in Anspruch nimmt, das des Knechtes Jesu Christi, kein anderes ist als jenes, das er allen Gliedern der Gemeinde beilegt, so nötigt sich

The Visions He Saw or: To Encode the Future in Writing 135

(3) The division of the prologue (a) into a *titulus proprius* relating exclusively to the hierarchical encodement of the text with respect to senders and trans-mitters, and essentially being descriptive[114] as far as its *explicit* illocutions[115] are concerned on the one hand, and (b) into a *conditional macarism* with respect to lector and audience, and essentially being non-descriptive[116] but almost exclusively performative and prescriptive[117] as far as its *explicit and implicit* illocutions are concerned on the other, is in fact a remarkable way of indicating the main purpose of the Apocalyptic Letter to its receivers, who in this way are directly addressed in the very prologue.[118]

The second part addressing the receivers explicitly is formulated *not* as a description or information of *how to read* or *listen* to its content, *but how to react* or *respond* to its message. Insofar the receivers are first comforted through a performative promise of blessing in the Apodosis and then admonished in the Protasis to keep not merely the particular exhortations in the letters to the Seven Churches in Asia Minor (e.g., 3:3, 8,10) but everything that is demanded of them in the entire Apocalyptic Letter, esp. as it is expressed in 14:12: ῟Ὧδε ἡ ὑπομονὴ τῶν ἁγίων ἐστίν οἱ τηροῦντες τὰς ἐντολὰς τοῦ θεοῦ καὶ τὴν πίστιν Ἰησοῦ.[119] What the τηρεῖν in fact is referring to here, is

---

der Schluß auf, daß Johannes bewußt und betont auf einen Autoritätsanspruch aufgrund seines Amtes oder seiner Stellung verzichtet, was seiner Botschaft Gehör verschaffen soll, ist allein der Umstand, daß Christus selbst durch sie zu Wort kommt". This is a congenial interpretation, perhaps with the exception of Roloff's presupposition that John in fact was in possession of a dignitary position in the Church. As far as our evidence goes this account cannot be substantiated, see Vielhauer 1975, 501: "Welche Stellung, Funktion oder Würde er (sc. Johannes) besessen hat, bleibt unklar".

[114]This is a *theoretical* function of language. For convincing arguments that the descriptive-informative function is at the same time an illocutionary one, see von Kutschera 1975, 178 and see the discussion in Hellholm 1980, 57f. with further references and see in addition also Coseriu 1981, 49f. and Kubczak 1984, 18ff.

[115]For the distinction between explicit and implicit illocutions see Hellholm 1980, 56-61, esp. 57.

[116]Regarding the descriptive function of $^{02}ST^{2.2}$, see the discussion below.

[117]These constitute *practical* or *non-theoretical* functions of language.

[118]See above 121f. with note 54.

[119]Cf. also 12:17: καὶ ὠργίσθη ὁ δράκων ἐπὶ τῇ γυναικὶ καὶ ἀπῆλθεν ποιῆσαι πόλεμον μετὰ τῶν λοιπῶν τοῦ σπέρματος αὐτῆς τῶν τηρούντων τὰς ἐντολὰς τοῦ θεοῦ καὶ ἐχόντων τὴν μαρτυρίαν Ἰησοῦ.

the endurance "in face of universal martyrdom",[120] whether imagined or real.[121]

The double illucotionary function of the macarism as a performative consolation and a prescriptive exhortation containing an implicit performative warning or even threat to those, who do not fulfil the prescriptive condition, has its precise counterpart in the most embedded texts of all, viz. in the summary of John's Apocalyptic Letter from the lips of the Supreme Divinity on the throne, which constitutes a performative promise to those who conquer that they shall live in unity with God in the New World and a performative threat to the unfaithful of ultimate separation form God and the faithful servants of his.[122]

The second sub-text (^{02}ST2.2) of the macarism has consequently to be interpreted as an "eschatological justification"[123] not only for the performative promise of blessing in the apodosis or for the prescriptive condition in the protasis but for the entire macarism with its two or three illocutionary functions.

ὁ γὰρ καιρός ἐγγυς "relate to the blessedness of those who are faithful in the present evil time, for they will not have long to wait; the season of their deliverance is at hand".[124] This is, however, – contra Charles – only one of two illocutionary aspects. The explicit exhortation to endure in times of θλίψεις[125] with its implicit threat to those who do not τηρεῖν τὰ ἐν αὐτῇ γεγραμμένα is equally important.

The informative or descriptive illocution is here as in the subsequent Letter only of subordinate significance.[126]

---

[120]Charles 1920, 8 and cf. 369f.
[121]Cf. Yarbro Collins 1984, *passim*.
[122]See Hellholm 1986, 44-46.
[123]Γάρ here expresses cause or reason.
[124]Charles 1920, 8.
[125]Bousset 1906, 183: "Die ganze Schrift will eine mächtige Mahnung an die Christen sein, in der letzten Zeit der bittersten Not und des heißen Kampfes getreu auszuharren".
[126]Cf. from a comparative point of view, Hartman 1975, 14: "...when the literary convention of different kinds of apocalyptic timetables was developed in Jewish apocalyptical literature, it had not primarily a theoretical, informative, and calculating function, but rather some practical one", and from an historical point of view with regard to the Apocalypse of John, Yarbro Collins 1984, *passim*.

(4) The pragmatic communication situation, as it can be deduced from the prologue, is a very complicated one as the following deliberations will show:

The Prescript of the Apocalyptic Letter names the addressees as ταῖς ἑπτὰ ἐκκλησίαις ἐν τῇ 'Ασίᾳ in the *adscriptio*, which indicates that the entire Letter was originally written for the Seven Churches mentioned in the so called Seven Letters in chapters 2 and 3. The prologue, however, widens the set of recipients from the Seven Churches in Asia Minor to an infinite set of anonymous receivers, when in the macarism ὁ ἀναγινώσκων καὶ οἱ ἀκούντες are called blessed.

The real redactor or the author himself as a fictive redactor in this way changed the status of the Apocalyptic Letter from being addressed to a specific group of churches in a specific situation to an Apocalyptic Letter or perhaps better: an Apocalypse addressed to a wider audience beyond the specific situation of the original Letter.

Whether this change actually ever happened or in fact constitutes a fictive generalization[127] of the addressees is in my opinion not easy to discern. The following options should be evaluated: (a) In case of a real redactor, he would be responsible for the generalization of the addressees at a later stage; (b) in case of a fictive redactor (being the author himself), either (α) the address to the Seven Churches is fictive and the letter form is in a sense fictive as well, (β) or he has turned an authentic letter of his to the original addressees into an "open letter" to a general audience without any specifications.

If understood as a redactional addition the aorist ἐμαρτύρησεν (v. 2) need not be interpreted as an epistolary aorist but as a (quasi) historical one pointing out what John by means of a written encodement had testified to in his Apocalyptic Letter. The viewpoint is that of an editor regardless of whether he is to be identified with John as the author or not.

If, however, the prologue only follows the ancient Greek and Oriental convention "nach der ein Author nur dann in erster Person von sich selbst sprechen kann, wenn ihm die Anfangsworte seines

---

[127]Cf. the generalizations in Hermas, which, however, are carried out in quite different ways within the text itself and not, as is the case in Apc., on a meta-level in the prologue, see, e.g., Hellholm 1980, 100 ad 1:9, 105 ad 6:4, 106 ad 7:2, 110 ad 9:9 and ad 10:2.

Werkes gewissermaßen das Wort erteilt haben",[128] then the aorist must be regarded as epistolary and John is indeed the author also of the prologue and the prologue is not only a "meta-narrative text"[129] but also a "meta-narrative expression", which entails both a "substitution on meta-level" and a "meta-communicative sentence".[130] In this case one must at least ask the question, whether the address to the Seven Churches is in fact not fictional. This question must be raised, in view of the generalization of the addressees in the prologue as well as in view of the "generalization and specification formulas" ending each of the seven messages to the Seven Churches in Asia Minor: Ὁ ἔχων οὖς ἀκουσάτω τί τὸ πνεῦμα λέγει ταῖς ἐκκλησίαις.[131] The Apocalyptic Letter was then never intended – at least not exclusively – for the Seven Churches in Asia Minor.

Or is there still a possibility? Granted that the last option, i.e., the analogy with ancient Greek and Oriental conventions, is correct, could the seemingly anonymous addressees (ὁ ἀναγινώσκων καὶ οἱ ἀκούοντες) not merely refer to lectors and listeners in the Churches of Asia Minor presupposed in the *adscriptio* of the prescript of the Apocalytic Letter? This solution, however attractive, does not explain, though, the generalization formula at the end of each of the seven letters just referred to![132]

---

[128]Fehling 1975, 61. Of spec. interest is the "messenger formulas" of the Prologue to each of the seven 'letters', to which F. Hahn (1971, 366) has drawn attention to the prophetic כה אמר יהוה = LXX οὕτως λέγει κύριος. As Fehling, ibid., 63 has shown these oriental *exordia* are also to be found in Greek texts: "Wie uns orientalisierende Inschriften Parallelen für die dritte Person brachten, so bringen uns orientalisierende Briefanfänge bei griechischen Autoren die nächsten Parallelen für das den Sprecher einführende Proömium." Ἄμασις Πολυκράτει ὧδε λέγει Hdt. 3,40,1; ὧδε λέγει βασιλεὺς Παυσανίᾳ Thuc. 1,129, 3; Στρυαγγαῖος Ζαρινᾴα οὕτω λέγει Ctes. Pap. Ox. 2330 (= frg. 8b Jacoby). Es ist gewiß kein Zufall, daß Thukydides für die Briefe des Themistokles und Pausanias nicht dieselbe Form wählt. Die Form ist tatsächlich orientalisch, und die engste Parallele liefert gerade der Perserkönig: ...כה אמר כורש מלך פרס [LXX: οὕτως εἶπεν Κῦρος βασιλεὺς Περσῶν...–DH]. 'So spricht Cyrus, der König von Persien' [2] Esdra 1, 2 = 2. chron. 36, 23". Cf. also Hartman 1980, 132.

[129]See above note 4.

[130]For the distinction between these two delimitation markers and their combination in "meta-narrative expressions", see above § 1.1.

[131]Bousset 1906, 207: "Zum Schluß erfolgt in allen Briefen eine Wendung von der einzelnen Gemeinde zur gesamten Christenheit. Da das Buch als ganzes schon von vorherein zur Vorlesung im öffentlichen Gottesdienst bestimmt war, so ist eine solche Wendung an und für sich begreiflich".

[132]Bousset, though, is of the opinion that the Apocalypse from the beginning was addressed to the entire Christian community, see previous note.

Before we can answer the above posted alternatives one way or the other firstly the epilogue of the Letter itself has to be examined in detail with regard to, among other things, its authenticity, and secondly the Greek style of the prologue (and of the epilogue) has to be investigated in relation to the style of the Apocalyptic Letter as such. These tasks, however, go beyond the scope of this essay. What can be said already now, however, is that whoever wrote the prologue thereby recommended the following Apocalyptic Letter "in feierlicher Weise als heiliges prophetisches Vorlesungsbuch".[133]

---

[133]Bousset 1906, 183.

Bibliography

I. Texteditions and Lexica

Audet, J.-P.
1958   *La Didachè. Instructions des apôtres* (Études bibliques), Paris: Gabalda 1958.

Nestel, E./Aland, K.
1979   *Novum Testamentum Graece*, 26. Aufl. Stuttgart: Deutsche Bibel-stiftung 1979.

Rordorf, W./Tuilier, A.
1978   La Doctrine des douze apôtres (Didache). Introduction, Texte, Traduction, Notes, Appendice et Index (Sources chrétiennes 248), Paris: Les Éditions du Cerf.

Wengst, Klaus
1984   *Didache (Apostellehre), Barnabasbrief, Zweiter Klemensbrief, Schrift an Diognet* (Schriften des Urchristentums 2), Darmstadt: Wissenschaftliche Buchgesellschaft.

Bauer, Walter
1988   Griechisch-deutsches Wörterbuch zu den Schriften des Neuen Testaments und der frühchristlichen Literatur, hrsg. von Kurt Aland und Barbara Aland, 6. Aufl., Berlin/New York: de Gruyter.

Lampe, G.W.H.
1968   A Patristic Greek Lexicon, Oxford: Clarendon.

II. Exegetical and historical works

Aland, Kurt
1980   "Noch einmal: Das Problem der Anonymität und Pseudonymität in der christlichen Literatur der ersten beiden Jahrhunderte", in: E. Dassmann/K.S. Frank: Pietas. FS Bernhard Kötting (Jahrbuch für Antike und Christentum. Ergänzungsband 8), Münster/Westf.: Aschendorff, 121-139.

Bousset, Wilhelm
1906 Die Offenbarung Johannis (Kritisch-Exegetischer Kommentar 16), 2. Aufl., Göttingen: Vandenhoeck & Ruprecht [reprint 1966].

Charles, R.H.
1920 The Revelation of St. John (The International Critical Commentary), Edinburgh: T. & T. Clark.

Davies, W.D./Allison, D.C.
1988 The Gospel According to Saint Matthew (The International Critical Commentary), Vol. I, Edinburgh: T. & T. Clark 1988.

Fehling, Detlev
1975 "Zur Funktion und Formgeschichte des Proömiums in der ältesten griechischen Prosa" in: ΔΩPHMA. Dauer und Überleben des antiken Geistes. FS Hans Diller (Griechische Humanistische Gesellschaft. Internationales Zentrum für klassisch-humanistische Forschungen. Zweite Reihe: Studien und Untersu- chungen 27), Athen, 61-75.

French Strout, Ruth
1956 "The Development of the Catalog and Cataloging Codes", in: Library Quarterly 7, 254-75.

Hahn, Ferdinand
1971 "Die Sendschreiben der Johannesapokalypse", in: H.W. Kuhn/H. Stegemann (edd.): Tradition und Glaube. Das frühe Christentum in seiner Umwelt. FS K.G. Kuhn, Göttingen: Vandenhoeck & Ruprecht, 357-94.

Harnack, Adolf
1884 Lehre der zwölf Apostel nebst Untersuchungen zur ältesten Geschichte der Kirchenverfassung und des Kirchenrechts (Texte und Untersuchungen 2,1.2), Leipzig: Hinrichs.

Hartman, Lars
1975 "The Function of Some so-called Apocalyptic Timetables", in: New Testament Studies 22, 1-14.

1980 "Form and Message. A Preliminary Discussion of «Partial Texts» in Rev 1-3 and 22,6ff", in: Jan Lambrecht (ed.): L'Apocalypse johannique et l'Apoca- lyptique dans le Nouveau Testament (Bibliotheca Ephemeridum Theologicarum Lovaniensium 53), Leuven: University Press, 129-49.

1985 Kolosserbrevet (Kommentar till Nya testamentet 12), Uppsala: EFS-förlaget.

1986 "On Reading Others' Letters", in: G.W.E. Nickelsburg/G.W. Mac Rae: Christians Among Jews and Gentiles. FS Krister Stendahl, Philadelphia, PA: Fortress, 137-46.

1987 "Vad säger Sibyllan? Byggnad och budskap i de sibyllinska oraklens fjärde bok", in: P.W. Bøckman/R.E. Kristiansen (edd.): Context. Essays n Honour of P.J. Borgen (»Relieff« 24), Trondheim: Tapir, 61-74.

Hellholm, David

1980 Das Visionenbuch des Hermas als Apokalypse. Formgeschichtliche und texttheoretische Studien zu einer literarichen Gattung. I: Methodologische Vorüberlegungen und makrostrukturelle Textnalayse (Coniectanea Biblica 13:1), Lund: Gleerup.

1986 "The Problem of Apocalyptic Genre and the Apocalypse of John", in: Adela Yarbro Collins (ed.): Early Christian Apocalypticism: Genre and Social Setting (Semeia 36), Atlanta, GA: Scholars Press, 13-64.

1986-87 "En textgrammatisk konstruktion i Matteusevangeliet", in: Svensk Exegetisk Årsbok 51-52, 80-9.

1989a Probleme und Bedeutung substitutioneller Gliederungsmerkmale für die Komposition des Matthäusevangeliums (Manuscript in preparation for publication, Bergen).

1989b The Apocalyptic Genre: The Case of the Apocalypse of John (Manuscript in preparation for publication, Bergen).

1989c Bergspredikans saligprisningar som inverterade makarismer (Manuscript in preparation for publication, Bergen).

Holtz, Traugott

1962 Die Christologie der Apokalypse des Johannes (Texte und Untersuchungen 85), Berlin: Akademie-Verlag.

1986 Der Erste Brief an die Thessalonicher (Evangelisch-Katholischer Kommentar zum Neuen Testament 13), Zürich/Neukirchen-Vluyn: Benziger/ Neukirchener.

Jörns, K.-P.

1971 Das hymnische Evangelium. Untersuchungen zu Aufbau, Funktion und Herkunft der hymnischen Stücke in der Johannesoffenbarung (Studien zum Neuen Testament 5), Gütersloh: Gerd Mohn.

Karrer, Martin
1986   Die Johannesoffenbarung als Brief. Studien zu ihrem literarischen, historischen und theologischen Ort (Forschungen zur Religion und Literatur des Alten und Neuen Testaments 140), Göttingen: Vandenhoeck & Ruprecht.

Kraft, Heinrich
1974   Die Offenbarung des Johannes (Handbuch zum Neuen Testament 16a), Tübingen: J.C.B. Mohr (Paul Siebeck).

Lindblom, Johannes
1962   Prophecy in Ancient Israel, Philadelphia, PA: Fortress.

Lohmeyer, Ernst
1953   Die Offenbarung des Johannes (Handbuch zum Neuen Testament 16), 3. Aufl., Tübingen: J.C.B. Mohr (Paul Siebeck).

Lohse, Eduard
1960   Die Offenbarung des Johannes (Das Neue Testament Deutsch 11), Göttingen: Vandenhoeck & Ruprecht.

Müller, Ulrich B.
1984   Die Offenbarung des Johannes (Ökumenischer Taschenbuchkommentar zum Neuen Testament 19), Gütersloh/Würzburg: Gerd Mohn/Echter.

Niederwimmer, Kurt
1989   Die Didache (Kommentar zu den Apostolischen Vätern 1), Göttingen: Vandenhoeck & Ruprecht.

Prigent, Pierre
1981   L'Apocalypse de Saint Jean (Commentaire du Nouveau Testament 14), Genève : Labor et Fides.

Roloff, Jürgen
1984   Die Offenbarung des Johannes (Zürcher Bibelkommentare NT 18), Zürich: Theologischer Verlag.

Satake, Akira
1966   Die Gemeindeordnung in der Johannesapokalypse (Wissenschaftliche Monographien zum Alten und Neuen Testament 21), Neukirchen-Vluyn: Neukirchener.

Vielhauer, Philipp
1965 "Introduction" (to Apocalypses and Related Subjects), in: E. Hennecke/W. Schneemelcher (edd.): New Testament Apocrypha (Eng. translation ed. R. McL. Wilson), Vol. II, Philadelphia, PA: Fortress, 581-607.

Vielhauer, Philipp
1975 Geschichte der Urchristlichen Literatur (de Gruyter Lehrbuch), Berlin/New York: de Gruyter.

Wildberger, Hans
1942 Jahvewort und prophetische Rede bei Jeremia, Zürich: Zwingli.

Yarbro Collins, Adela
1984 Crisis & Catharsis. The Power of the Apocalypse, Philadelphia, PA: Westminster.

III. Philosophical and linguistic works

Ackrill, J.L.
1963 Aristotle's Categories and De Interpretatione. Translated with Notes (Clarendon Aristotle Series), Oxford: Clarendon Press.

Austin, J.L.
1975 How to Do Things with Words, 2nd ed., Cambridge, MA: Harvard.

Baldinger, Kurt
1980 Semantic Theory. Towards a Modern Semantics, Oxford/New York: Blackwell/St. Martin.

Brinker, Klaus
1983 "Textfunktionen. Ansätze zu ihrer Beschreibung", in: Zeitschrift für germanistische Linguistik 11, 127-48.

Coseriu, Eugenio
1981 Textlinguistik. Eine Einführung (Tübinger Beiträge zur Linguistik 109), Tübingen: Narr.

1973 Probleme der strukturellen Semantik (Tübinger Beiträge zur Linguistik 40), Tübingen: Narr.

Greimas, A.J.
1983 Structural Semantics. An Attempt at a Method, Lincoln/London: University of Nebraska Press.

Greimas, A.J./Courtés, J.
1982   Semiotics and Language. An Analytical Dictionary, Bloomington, IN.

Gühlich, Elisabeth
1976   "Ansätze zu einer kommunikationsorientierten Erzähltextanalyse (am Beispiel mündlicher und schriftlicher Erzähltexte", in: W. Haubrichs (ed.): Erzählforschung (Zeitschrift für Literaturwissenschaft und Linguistik [LiLi], Beiheft 4), Göttingen: Vandenhoeck & Ruprecht, 224-56.

Heger, Klaus
1976   Monem, Wort, Satz und Text (Konzepte der Sprach- und Literaturwissenschaft 8), 2. Aufl., Tübingen: Niemeyer.

Hellwig, Peter
1984   "Titulus oder über den Zusammenhang von Titeln und Texten. Titel sind ein Schlüssel zur Textkonstitution", in: Zeitschrift für germanistische Lin- guistik 12, 1-20.

Klaus, Georg
1973   Semiotik und Erkenntnistheorie, 4. Aufl., München: Fink.

Kubczak, Hartmut
1975   Das Verhältnis von Intension und Extension als sprachwissenschaftliches Problem (Forschungsberichte des Instituts für deutsche Sprache 23), Tübingen: Narr.

1978   Die Metapher. Beiträge zur Interpretation und semantischen Struktur der Metapher auf der Basis einer referentialen Bedeutungsdefinition, Heidelberg: Winter.

1984   "Bühlers 'Symptomfunktion'", in: Zeitschrift für romanische Philologie 100, 1-25.

Lausberg, Heinrich
1976   Elemente der literarischen Rhetorik., 5. Aufl., München: Hueber.

Lyons, John
1973   Einführung in die moderne Linguistik, 3. Aufl., München: Beck.

Menne, Albert
1980   Einführung in die Methodologie. Elementare allgemeine wissenschaftliche Denkmethoden im Überblick (Die

Philosophie), Darmstadt: Wissenschaftliche Buchgesellschaft.

Oehler, Klaus
1986 Aristoteles Kategorien. Übersetzt und erläutert (Aristoteles Werke in deutscher Übersetzung I/1), 2. Aufl., Berlin/Darmstadt: Akademie-Verlag/Wis- senschaftliche Buchgesellschaft.

Raible, Wolfgang.
1972 Satz und Text. Untersuchungen zu vier romanischen Sprachen (Beihefte zur Zeitschrift für romanische Philologie 132), Tübingen: Niemeyer.

von Kutschera, Franz
1975 Sprachphilosophie (Uni-Taschenbücher 80), 2.Aufl., München: Fink.

III
THEOLOGICAL THEMES

SOME IMPLICATIONS OF HEBREWS 2:5-18 FOR A CONTEXTUAL ANTHROPOLOGY
Bernard C. Lategan, *University of Stellenbosch*

1. Introduction

The involvement of Hendrikus Boers with New Testament literature has been motivated by strong personal concerns. Of these, three have been especially prominent: his insistence that theology should break through its own confines and become an active participant in the wider arena of humanistic inquiry and philosophical reflection; his spirited defense of what he understands as the best of the humanistic tradition and his life-long involvement with New Testament texts in a sustained effort to interpret them on their own terms.

This essay is an attempt to respond to aspects of all three of these concerns from a Third World perspective, or at least from one segment of that perspective. In the first section some features of "theologies out of the ghetto" which have developed in a Third World context, are discussed. In a second section the anthropological significance of these developments is briefly indicated and in a last section tentative pointers for a more contextual anthropology will be drawn from an analysis of Hebrews 2:5-18.

2. Contextual theology as a theology out of the ghetto

A remarkable feature of theological reflection during the past two decades is the emergence of various forms of contextual theology, especially in the Third World. The development of liberation theology, of black theology, of feminist theology, of different versions of "peoples' theologies," not only attests to the vitality of theological reflection in these areas, but also presents a challenge to more traditional ways of doing theology. It is not the intention of the present study to give a survey of these developments, nor to assess their relative strengths and weaknesses in comparison to existing theological systems.[1] What interests us are the motifs and features which would qualify them as theologies "out of the ghetto," in the sense that Boers uses this concept.[2] Although he did not have these theologies in mind when originally developing the idea, they do display important characteristics of what he had in mind.

Contextual theology forms part of a much wider movement towards what may be called pragmatics. This movement is noticeable on many levels and includes such developments as sociological, socio-lingusitic or materialistic exegesis, reception theory, speech act analysis, and others.[3] The common concern which binds these diverse phenomena together, is the interest in the *effect* of interpreting biblical material, of its *implications* for actual conditions of human existence. The underlying assumption is that exegetical and theological reflection have consequences for much more than their own fields of study and that they have an important contribution to make to the interaction of social processes. It is indeed an attempt to take the world seriously as a partner in dialogue.[4]

Unlike the situation in the First World, where secularization has become a permanent feature and the influence of theology on social processes often has been marginalized, religion in the Third World and especially Africa is a central concern which has a marked effect on the shaping of the social environment. Religion is one of the "givens" of life with unavoidable social consequences. This awareness has drawn theology into the open and forced it to reflect on its social role in a new way. It also means that theology had to take cognizance of what was happening in other disciplines, and had to enter into dialogue with other social sciences on an equal footing. In some cases, as in Latin America, this has led to some unusual alliances, which was not without controversy and which has lent a new dimension to, for example, the Christian-Marxist debate.

Contextual theology, therefore, presupposes an interaction with its social environment which precludes any possibility of theology as

---

[1]For the hermeneutical implications of these developments cf e.g. Norman Gottwald, *The Bible and Liberation: Political and Social Hermeneutics* (New York: Orbis, 1984); Mark Branson and Rene Padilla, *Conflict and Context. Hermeneutics in the Americas* (Grand Rapids: Eerdmans, 1986).

[2]Hendrikus Boers, *Theology out of the Ghetto* (Leiden: Brill, 1971).

[3]Cf Bernard Lategan, "Current issues in the hermeneutical debate," *Neotestamentica* 18 (1984), 5-12.

[4]Cf Boers, *Theology out of the Ghetto*, 1.

an isolated activity. But it also has implications for the way in which theology is done. Instead of generalizations and universal solutions, the focus is on the specific situation and its needs. Social analysis often precedes theological reflection. At the same time, the movement is from the bottom upwards, not from the top downwards. Two consequences flow from this: theological "solutions" cannot be imported so easily from other contexts - what is needed has to be decided in situ. Conversely, this means that not all theological themes have the same relevance at a given time. What may be considered as a solved problem in one context, may still be very much alive in another.

This pertains, in a specific sense, to theological anthropology. What may be considered to be a solved problem in a context where the protection of human rights is a presupposition in society and a bill of human rights forms part of the constitution, is very much still a problem in a context where human rights are formally and materially in jeopardy. It may even be that the new context brings to light new aspects of the problem which were not so evident in a "human rights" environment. In order to illustrate what is meant by this, let us look at a specific context where theological anthropology has a critical role to play.

3. Social order and its anthropological underpinnings in a South African context

"Ideas have consequences." In a South African context, it would be more correct to say that *theological* ideas have consequences. In a country where 77% of the total population consider themselves to be part of the Christian tradition,[5] this shared religious heritage, in fact, constitutes the largest common denominator among all its inhabitants. It would, therefore, not be unreasonable to expect the Christian tradition to serve as a strong uniting force in society, despite the diversity which exists on almost all other levels. But the opposite is true - religion is one of the most divisive factors in this society contributing to tension and leading to what, in the perception of many, appears to be a classical confrontation between church and state.

There are many reasons why religion does not have a unifying influence in the present situation, which cannot be discussed here at

---

[5]G. C. Oosthuizen *et al*, *Religion Intergroup Relations and Social Change in* South Africa (Westport: Greenwood Press, 1988), 19.

any length.⁶ Suffice to say that much depends on the peoples' perceptions and expectations of the role of religion in society: whether it should serve as a conserving force or as an agent for change, whether it should cater for individual or communal needs, whether it should be directly involved in political processes or whether it should provide a neutral ground where people of different political persuasions could meet.

The important point for our discussion, is that theological reflection in this context never is merely a theoretical exercise. Theological presuppositions have a direct influence on the way society is structured. It is, therefore, not surprising that the seeds of contextual theology found very fertile soil in a South African environment, producing a full spectrum, ranging from white theology to different varieties of liberation, black and African theology.⁷ These have been articulated in a series of documents, of which the *Belhar Confession* and the *Kairos Document* are perhaps the best known outside South Africa, but which also have their counterparts in other church communities..⁸

By far the most incisive and sustained effort to order South African society according to an underlying value system, was the emergence of an *apartheid* state in the course of the last forty years. The way in which theological arguments and presuppositions were used to support its establishment, has by now been well documented and provides the best counter-example of a contextual theology.⁹ The fiercest and most bitter debate in recent years was focused on this theological justification of *apartheid*, which eventually led to the rejec-

---

⁶For a fuller discussion, cf H. C. Marais *et al*, *The South African Society: Realities and Future Prospects* (Westport: Greenwood Press, 1987), 65-74.

⁷Cf. Johann Kinghorn, "Wit teologie"?, *Scriptura* 12 (1983), 54-73; Richard J Stevens, "An orientation to Black Theology as a hermeneutic of suffering," *Scriptura* 24 (1988), 17-26.

⁸Cf. *The Kairos Document* (Grand Rapids: Eerdmans, 2nd edition 1986); Daan Cloete and Dirkie Smit, *A Moment of Truth* (Grand Rapids: Eerdmans, 1984); *Church and Society* (Pretoria: Dutch Reformed Church, 1987); *Geloof en Protes* (Pretoria: Voortsettingskomitee, 1987).

⁹Cf Johann Kinghorn (ed), *Die NG Kerk en Apartheid*, (Johannesburg: Macmillan, 1986); John de Gruchy, *The Church Struggle in South Africa* (Cape Town: David Philip, 1979).

tion of *apartheid* as a heresy by churches both inside and outside South Africa.[10]

The transition to an open, inclusive, democratic and just society in South Africa will not be an easy task. In the perception of many, this is no longer possible via peaceful means, leading to the consideration of other alternatives. But whatever the outcome of this process, it is clear is that in the struggle for a future dispensation, theology has a vital role to play. Exegetes and theologians can no longer withhold their participation in developing a value system which would not only make the creation of a democratic society possible, but which would sustain and foster the growth of a wider democratic culture. Ending the era of *apartheid* will not automatically lead to a more humane and peaceful society. It is all too easy to rid the house of one devil and to have seven take its place. Therefore, it is of the greatest importance to raise the question of the eventual outcome of the process of transformation during the process itself.

In accepting this task, exegetes should also understand their specific role. They are not called upon to supply yet another theological justification for an alternative political system, but to re-examine the values underlying the Christian tradition, and to articulate them in such a way that an open, free and democratic society becomes possible. Their responsibility is of a much more fundamental nature, much less visible, but not less important.

Once the commitment to a post-apartheid society is accepted, the important question is: Is there a broad enough basis of shared values to sustain such a society and what are the values needed to achieve this? At this point the potential inherent in a shared religious tradition referred to above, becomes important. Initial research has indicated that, although dormant, the appeal to and reconsideration of this tradition could provide the framework for moving towards a sustained, participatory, inclusive democracy in a just society.[11]

To illustrate what kind of exegetical and theological input is required in this process, we shall concentrate in the remainder of this contribution on one aspect, namely the implications which anthropo-

---

[10]Cf Daan Cloete and Dirkie Smit, *Moment of Truth;* John de Gruchy and Charles Villa-Vicencio (edd), *Apartheid is a Heresy* (Cape Town: David Philip, 1983).

[11]Bernard Lategan, Johann Kinghorn, Lourens du Plessis and Etienne de Villiers, *The Option for Inclusive Democracy. A theological-ethical study of appropriate social values for South Africa* (Stellenbosch: Centre for Contextual Hermeneutics, 1987).

logical concepts have on the development of social values and the promotion of human rights. This will also enable us to link up with Boers's defense of humanism and his plea for the liberation of theology.

Racism as a social phenomenon is the product of a combination of psychological, sociological and philosophical factors. In its institutionalized form, as is the case in an apartheid society, these factors are often reinforced by theological considerations. At the heart of these considerations lies a specific understanding of humanity which can be described as a group-based, exclusivist and pessimistic anthropology.[12] It is group-based in the sense that people are primarily seen not as individuals, but as part of a group. Group affiliation is understood in ontological, not in functional terms. It is inherited, not achieved. This perception carries with it all kinds of consequences. Firstly, the concept of freedom is affected. Freedom of choice and freedom of association comes under pressure, which conversely means that freedom to accept responsibility is likewise curtailed. Secondly, the basic tendency is towards exclusivism, not inclusivism. When society is understood as consisting primarily of dIfferent (conflicting) groups, boundaries become important and the individual is defined in terms of the own group at the cost of excluding others. Thirdly, the concepts of democracy and participation develop a very restricted connotation. Inside the group a democratic culture is cultivated, but this does not apply to the relationship between groups. Fourthly, in this anthropological model it is possible to uphold the ideal of equality, but only because equality is defined in terms of an external factor or on a group basis. People are equal in so far as they share a common fate, in so far as they belong to humankind, or because they do not belong to a certain group. This "formal" or "status" equality remains abstract and does not refer to the relationship between people in real life situations. Very revealing in this context is the preference for the term "equal worth" (*gelykwaardigheid*) instead of "equality" (*gelykheid*). A further consequence is that a shift takes place from anthropology to ecclesiology. The church becomes the primary sphere of existence, which leads to greater isolation from the wider society.

---

[12]Cf Johann Kinghorn, "Teologie en sosiaal-antropologie," *Scriptura* 27 (1988), 8-25.

All these elements combine to form a quite formidable interlocking system which provides the anthropological basis for an *apartheid* society. We are dealing with a mindset which will not be changed by merely appealing to moral criteria or by an indignant reference to the imago Dei motif of the biblical tradition. Not only is an incisive critique of this system called for, but also the development of an alternative anthropology. The latter is even more urgent because explicit theological arguments are used to support this discriminatory system. These arguments are based on what may be called a "low" biblical anthropology. What is meant by this term?

In the biblical tradition of both testaments, at least two lines of the anthropological thinking can be traced - a "high" and a "low" anthropology. The "high" tradition is exemplified by the *imago Dei* motif of the creation stories. This line reaches a high point in the exalted anthropology of Psalm 8. In the New Testament it is continued in the exaltation predicates of the Son of Man. This line is countered by a "low" anthropology, which finds its expression in Psalm 22 and Romans 3. The first line articulates the almost limitless potential of human beings, the second takes its point of departure in the stark reality of human failure. Both lines accept the basic equality of people - the one in the universal destiny of all mankind, the other in the universal need for salvation. Once again, this equality is understood in a formal sense, referring to the status of people and not to equality in real life situations.

The theological support system which undergirds the *apartheid* mind set is based on a "low" anthropology. This anthropology is reinforced by other theological motifs. The sinfulness of people becomes an important element, which discourages people to think too highly of themselves. The emphasis on grace alone is interpreted to mean that people should accept the position they are in and not try to change the (social) system by their own efforts. Added to this is the pietistic notion that the focus of the believer should be on the next world, while the present should be endured. A combination of all these factors means that a low anthropology not only seriously inhibits social change, but that it precludes the development of a positive self-image and self-understanding by believers.

It does not come as a surprise that a strong resistance to the concept of human rights exists in these circles. The human rights movement is often rejected as a misguided humanistic enterprise, based on a false *hubris* which does not take the sinful nature of humanity seriously.

In this way, a deficient theological anthropology opens the door for the emergence of an anti-human frame of mind, with serious consequences for the positive selfunderstanding of people and with the concrete result that the belief in and possibilities for positive social change is severely restricted.

This brings us right back to the question which Boers posed in *Theology out of the Ghetto*, namely whether the human being has the possibility, only in principle to realize authentic existence or whether this is also an actual or practical possibility.[13] Stated otherwise: Does reality have priority over possibility or does possibility have the priority, thereby making the change of reality possible?[14]

The situation explained above cannot be countered by a shallow optimistic anthropology which grudgingly accepts the fact that people are sinners, but still thinks that basically they are okay. It can also not be countered by a superior attitude that discrimination is a problem that has already been disposed of and it should not be a subject to be raised in decent company.

What is called for is an alternative contextual anthropology which accepts on the one hand the devastating effect of sin, but on the other hand opens the way to self-respect and fundamental social change.

4. Hebrews 2:5-18 and its implications for a contextual anthropology

The remainder of this article will be an attempt to take a few tentative steps in this direction. I intend to do so by looking at a very interesting passage, namely Hebrews 2:5-18, where both "high" and "low" anthropology meet, leading to a fundamental reinterpretation of the anthropology of Psalm 8.

Our remarks are based on a linguistic analysis of the *colon* structure of Hebrews 2:5-18.[15] This technique deals with only *one* level of textual analysis, which could (and should) be supplemented by other

---

[13]Hendrikus Boers, *Theology out of the Ghetto*, 2.

[14]Cf Eberhard Jungel, "Die Welt als Möglichkeit und Wirklichkeit: Zum ontologischen Ansatz der Rechtfertigungslehre," *EvTh* 29 (1969), 417-442. Cf also his discussion of important features of theological anthropology in Eberhard Jungel, *Entsprechungen: Gott-Wahrheit-Mensch* (München: Kaiser), 290-317.

[15]Cf Johannes Louw, *Semantics of New Testament Greek* (Philadelphia: Fortress, 1982) for an explanation of this technique. Cf also *Neotestamentica* 11(1977) and 15 (1982).

procedures. We also leave aside the historical aspects for a moment, as our focus will be exclusively on the argumentative logic of the author's reinterpretation of Ps 8.

Before we deal with the argument as such, some observations on the original *scopus* of Ps 8 are in order. This psalm (according to some, a "nature psalm") praises God's greatness and his kindness to humanity, as revealed in nature. Already Delitzsch[16] referred to it as a lyric poem, in which echoes of the creation story can be heard. On a clear night in the mountains of Judea, under a star-studded sky, the poet is overawed by the majesty of God. The amazing, the overwhelming of it all, is that God, in his majesty, bestows so much glory on *human beings*. They are almost divine. All the usual attributes of the oriental monarch are transferred to humanity as such. The anthropology of Ps 8 can be interpreted as a call to sovereignty - even to *cosmic* sovereignty. Here we see the human race at the breathtaking zenith of its possibilities - created and destined to reign over the cosmos.

When looking at the formal aspsects of Hebrews 2:5-18 (cf the appendix), it becomes clear that the passage is framed by *cola* 1 and 9-10 - *cola* 11 and 12 are an extension of *colon* 8 and do not form, strictly speaking, part of the passage. *Cola* 1 and 9 are the outer boundaries of a circular composition which finds its pivotal point in *colon* 3. This pivotal point (more precisely in 3a) is indicated by the way in which the quotation of Ps 8 and its reinterpretation are centered around 3a.

The passage is structured around three statements - *cola* 1, 3 and 9/10, which are separated by the two longer sections Y (2) and Z (5-8). In Y the quotation from Ps 8 is prepared, while Z explains why the statement in *colon* 1 can be maintained in the light of the reinterpretation.

The heart of the passage is section B, where the christological reinterpretation of Ps 8 takes place. What prompts this reinterpretation is not immediately clear. A possible reason is the occurrence of υἱος ἀνθρωπου (*v* 5) in the Greek translation of the *LXX*. *Michel*[17] is of the opinion that we are dealing with a wider christological tradition, because Ps 110 and 2 are also commented on by the author of this letter.

---

[16]Franz Delitzsch, *Commentary on the Epistle to the Hebrews* (Edinburgh: Clark, 1868), 104.

[17]Otto Michel, *Der Brief an die Hebräer* (Göttingen: Vandenhoeck, 1966, 12. Aufl), 138.

When we trace the development of the argument in this passage, it is clear that an expansion of the original *scopus* of Ps 8 is taking place by means of the exegetical commentary which the author offers on the psalm. We can follow his line of thought by taking our cue from the key phrase "angels" which occurs four times in the passage and which is arranged in a chiastic pattern:

1.   Humanity more, the angels less
2c. The angels more, humanity less
4.   The angels more, the Human (Jesus) less
9.   Humanity more, the angels less

The initial statement, that the world to come will be subjected not to angels (but to humanity), is apparently supported by the quotation from Ps 8 (where the privileged position of humanity is described). The expression "little less than the angels/as a divine being" is clearly meant as indicative of a "high" anthropology. But in this commentary, the author argues that it should be understood as referring to a "low" anthropology. People have clearly not realized their lofty potential *(colon 3)*. In a remarkable way, the "lowness" predicate is related to Jesus' *humiliation.* This opens the way for human beings to transcend their own failures and to fulfil their high calling. In this way, the initial statement of *colon* 1 is confirmed by *cola 9* and 10.

This argumentative strategy of initial statement - apparent denial of the statement using the denial as the premise of a new argument - transference of the new possibility on the initial statement and thereby confirming it, is indeed a remarkable rhetorical feat.

When analyzing the content of the argument in more detail, it is clear that *cola* 2a-f (section Y) is used to prepare the scene for the christological reinterpretation of Ps 8. First the high calling of humankind is recalled (2x-f), to be followed by a sharp criticism from reality (3): At this point, we see no evidence that this potential has been realized. To the contrary. The comment may be meant to be ironic: For all the idealism of Ps 8, real life offers no evidence to support it. Would that imply that humans only have the possibility *in principle* to realize their authentic existence?

But then the christological reinterpretation follows in *colon* 4. Rightly understood, the ἄνθροωπος of Ps 8 is in fact Jesus. But the fulfillment of his high calling - and that is what believers have to understand - is achieved through *suffering,* even death *(colon 45).* The paradoxical truth that honor and glory is only to be gained through service and suffering is mirrored by the chiastic construction of *colon* 4.

The view that Hebrews 2 should be interpreted christologically already from verse 5 onwards, that is, the view that *colon* 1 refers to the reign of *Jesus* in "the world to come," which is at the moment not realized, but will be so at the end of time, fails to explain the strong anthropological focus throughout this passage.[18] Such an exegesis requires that the αὐτῷ of *colon* 3 be identified with the Ἰησοῦν of *colon* 4, which ignores the implied contrast between the two. But then the following argument: in *cola* 5-8 becomes inexplicable, because this section deals with the way in which the broken relationship between God and *humanity* is restored. The strongest argument against a christological interpretation from 2:5 onwards is to be found in *colon* 9-10 where the angels are contrasted with the "seed of Abraham" that is, with humankind. No doubt, the constrast between the superior glory of Jesus in comparison with the glory of the angels constitutes an important theme in Hebrews, but this does not preclude the development of specific anthropological perspectives.

The "high" anthropology of Ps 8 is, therefore, not merely an idealistic dream. It is a concrete possibility, to be realized in real life. It is remarkable to note how time categories are introduced in the reinterpretation of Ps 8. The unlogical combination of the past (ὑπέταξεν) with the future (τήν μέλλουσαν) in *colon* 1 alerts us to the fact that the "world to come" is understood as the already existing time of faith. But the most famous shift is the replacement of a status qualification (little less than the angels) with a time phrase (for a short while) in *colon* 4. This transition is made possible because the βραχύ τι of the Septuagint (as translation of the Hebrew m^{c}t) can indicate both status and time. The placing of the reinterpetation of Ps 8 in the context of *history is* continued in *colon* 3a, which forms the *crux* of the argument. The time indicators are doubled: νῦν/οὔπω - *Now* we still do not see ... νῦν as the first marker is placed at the beginning of the sentence for emphasis, while οὔπω dominates both the following imbedded sentences S$_1$ and S$_2$ as a structural diagram of the *colon* shows:

---

[18]Contra Michel, *Hebräer*, 136; with Hugh Montefiore, *The Epistle to the Hebrews* (London: Black, 1964), 56-57; Robert Jewett, *Letter to Pilgrims* (New York: Pilgrim Press, 1981), 42-43.

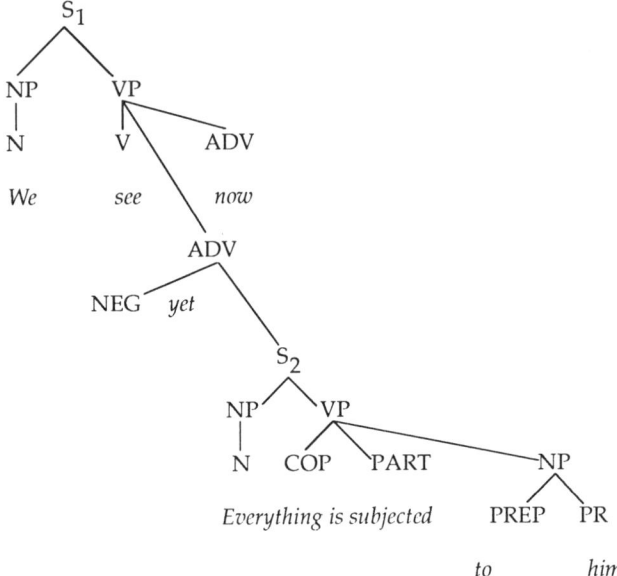

The reinterpretation of Ps 8 in terms of time categories places its anthropological statements within the context of *history* - firstly the history of Jesus, but also the history of humans, for Jesus' identification with them was an identification with real humans as part of real human life *(colon 8)*.

The "high" anthropology of Ps 8 is, therefore, not an idealistic dream, nor need humans be trapped in a "low" anthropology which render them submissive and apathetic. Humans have the possibility to realize their authentic existence *in fact*, in the course of history and as part of real life. When humans strive to fulfil their existence, it is not through ignorance of the possibility of failure but indeed *despite* the reality of failure. It is not without reason that contextual theologies are linked to the hermeneutic of suffering.[19] Suffering does not cancel out the potential for achievement, but opens the way to it. God is indeed not worried about angels, but about the seed of Abraham.

To live life to the full, to realize all its potential is indeed a way to thank and to honor God. And every stumbling block in the way to achieve this, must be removed Therefore, it is the responsibility of believers to keep these avenues open, to uphold human rights, to be-

---

[19]Richard Stevens, "Black Theology," 17.

come active again in this field which for too long has been left to the "humanists."

Boers should, therefore, be supported in his call for a theology out of the ghetto and for his appreciation of a true humanism. Nonetheless, his contention that the christological interpretation of human existence necessarily leads to Christian exclusiveness, restricting the scope of God's operation and isolating believers from the fellow-human[20] can be questioned on the basis of our exegesis of Hebrews 2. Our analysis shows that the christological reinterpretation of Ps 8 has an *inclusive,* not an exclusive purpose: Jesus' suffering was aimed at *broadening* the base (πολλοὺς υἱους *colon* 5) of those participating in the discovery of full humanity. At the same time, this interpretation does not restrict Jesus in any sense, but leads to the recognition of people as ἀδελπφοί and παιδία *(cola* 6-8), with whom he shares their full and true humanity, which opens the way to their complete acceptance as fellow-humans.

In this way, rethinking and rediscovering the richness and fullness of the anthropological perspective of the biblical tradition can lead to a strengthening and deepening of the human fabric of society, especially in a context where humanity is severely threatened in both an ideological and concrete sense. This may be one of the important contributions which a contextual theology has to offer. But it can also be a strong impetus to open doors to a restored humanity and to realize the Godgiven potential of people.

---

[20]Cf Boers, *Theology out of the Ghetto,* 105.

ΠΡΟΣ ΕΒΡΑΙΟΥΣ 2:5-18

A. The text of Hebrews 2:5-18 arranged by *cola*.

(v. 5) 1. Οὐ γὰρ ἀγγέλοις ὑπέταξεν τὴν οἰκουμένην τὴν μέλλουσαν,
περὶ ἧς λαλοῦμεν.

(v. 6) 2. διεμαρτύρατο δέ πού τις λέγων,
    a. Τί ἐστιν ἄνθρωπος ὅτι μιμνήσκῃ αὐτοῦ,
    b. ἢ (τί ἐστιν) υἱὸς ἀνθρώπου ὅτι ἐπισκέπτῃ αὐτόν;
(v. 7)   c. ἠλάττωσας αὐτὸν βραχύ τι παρ ἀγγέλους,
    d. δόξῃ καὶ τιμῇ ἐστεφάνωσας αὐτόν,
(v. 8a)   e. πάντα ὑπέταξας ὑποκάτω τῶν ποδῶν αὐτοῦ.
    f. ἐν τῷ γὰρ ὑποτάξαι αὐτῷ τὰ πάντα οὐδὲν ἀφῆκεν αὐτῷ
ἀνυπότακτον.

(v, 8b) 3. νῦν δὲ οὔπω ὁρῶμεν αὐτῷ τὰ πάντα ὑποτεταγμένα.

(v. 9) 4.* τὸν δὲ βραχύ τι παρ ἀγγέλους ἠλαττωμένον βλέπομεν Ἰησοῦν
διὰ τὸ πάθημα τοῦ θανάτου δόξῃ καὶ τιμῇ ἐστεφανωμένον,

ὅπως χάριτι θεοῦ ὑπὲρ παντὸς γεύσεται θανάτου.

(v. 10) 5.* ἔπρεπεν γὰρ αὐτῷ, δι᾽ ὃν τὰ πάντα καὶ δι᾽ οὗ τὰ πάντα,
πολλοὺς υἱοὺς εἰς δόξαν ἀγαγόντα τὸν ἀρχηγὸν τῆς σωτηρίας
αὐτῶν διὰ παθημάτων τελειῶσαι.

(v. 11) 6. ὅ τε γὰρ ἁγιάζων καὶ οἱ ἁγιαζόμενοι ἐξ ἑνὸς πάντες
δι᾽ ἣν αἰτίαν οὐκ ἐπαισχύνεται ἀδελφοὺς αὐτοὺς καλεῖν,

(v. 12) 7. λέγων
    a. Ἀπαγγελῶ τὸ ὄνομά σου τοῖς ἀδελφοῖς μου,
    b. ἐν μέσῳ ἐκκλησίας ὑμνήσω σε.
(v. 13)   c. καὶ πάλιν, Ἐγὼ ἔσομαι πεποιθὼς ἐπ᾽ αὐτῷ.
    d. καὶ πάλιν, Ἰδοὺ ἐγὼ καὶ τὰ παιδία ἅ μοι ἔδωκεν ὁ θεός.

(v. 14) 8.* ἐπεὶ οὖν τὰ παιδία κεκοινώνηκεν αἵματος καὶ σαρκός, καὶ
αὐτὸς παραπλησίως μετέσχεν τῶν αὐτῶν, ἵνα διὰ τοῦ θανάτου
καταργήσῃ τὸν τὸ κράτος ἔχοντα τοῦ θανάτου, τοῦτ᾽ ἔστιν
(v. 15) τὸν διάβολον, καὶ ἀπαλλάξῃ τούτους, ὅσοι φόβῳ θανάτου διὰ
παντὸς τοῦ ζῆν ἔνοχοι ἦσαν δουλείας.

(v. 16a) 9. οὐ γὰρ δήπου ἀγγέλων ἐπιλαμβάνεται,
(v. 16b) 10. ἀλλὰ σπέρματος Ἀβραὰμ ἐπιλαμβάνεται.

(v. 17) 11.* ὅθεν ὤφειλεν κατὰ πάντα τοῖς ἀδελφοῖς ὁμοιωθῆναι, ἵνα
ἐλεήμων γένηται καὶ πιστὸς ἀρχιερεὺς τὰ πρὸς τὸν θεόν,
εἰς τὸ ἱλάσκεσθαι τὰς ἁμαρτίας τοῦ λαοῦ.

(v. 18) 12.* ἐν ᾧ γὰρ πέπονθεν αὐτὸς πειρασθείς, δύναται τοῖς
πειραζομένοις βοηθῆσαι.

Some Implications of Hebrews 2:5-18

B. The syntactic structure and key *cola* in more detail.

4.* βλέπωμεν Ἰησοῦν
├── ἠλαττωμένον βραχύ τι ....
└── ἐστεφανωμένον διὰ τὸ πάθημα ....
   └── ὅπως γεύσηται ....

5.* ἔπρεπεν αὐτῷ
├── δι ὃν ... τὰ πάντα
└── τελειῶσαι τὸν ἀρχηγὸν
   └── ἀγαγόντα πολλοὺς ... εἰς δόξαν

8.* ἐπεὶ ... κεκοινώνηκεν αἵματος καὶ σαρκός
μετέσχεν
└── ἵνα
   ├── καταργήσῃ τὸν ... ἔχοντα τὸ κράτος   τοῦτ ἔστιν τὸν διάβολον
   └── ἀπαλλάξῃ τούτους
      └── ὅσοι ... ἔνοχοι ἦσαν δουλείας

11.* ὤφειλεν
└── ὁμοιωθῆναι
   └── ἵνα γένηται
      ├── ἐλεήμων
      ├── πιστὸς ἀρχιερεὺς
      └── εἰς τὸ ἱλάσκεσθαι τὰς ἁμαρτίας

12.* δύναται
├── ἐν ᾧ πέπονθεν
│   └── πειρασθείς
└── βοηθῆσαι τοῖς πειραζομένοις

THE SEDUCTION OF EVE AND ADAM'S SIN
Social Historical Feminist Interpretation of Paul's Understanding of Sin and Freedom*

Luise Schottroff, *Gesamthochschule, Universität Kassel*

I
The Situation In Paul

Paul states: All have sinned. Again and again Paul stresses this "all." In Rom. 3:9, he states "We previously raised the charge that all are under sin, both Jews and Greeks." Then Paul concludes with a moving accusation which is assembled from sentences of the Hebrew Bible: "No one is righteous, no, not one; no one understands; no one seeks after God . . ." (Rom. 3:10). The whole world is guilty before God (Rom. 3:20).

Paul states: Sin estranges me from my own life interests. In Rom. 7:13ff., Paul describes the estrangement and entanglement under sin. "For I do not do what I want, but I do the very thing I hate . . . So then it is no longer I that do it, but sin which dwells within me . . ." (Rom. 7:15-17). I am possessed by sin; imprisoned by it. "Wretched one that I am! Who will deliver me from this body of death" (Rom. 7:24)? The estrangement of the self here is between "willing" and "doing." In Rom. 7, sin does not directly pertain to the plane of the will — the aim of the heart — but, rather, to that of action. I do not do that which is right. I know the will of God. I even want to do it. I love the good but I act falsely.

Paul states: Sin came into the world through Adam (Rom. 5:12). Adam's transgression of God's will subjugated humanity under the power of sin. All have a part in Adam's sin because all sin. Adam, therefore, is a prototype of humanity. Here one should set aside later conceptions of original sin. Adam is in Paul a mythic figure.¹ In Adam's fate, the fate of all humanity is disclosed. Anthropology in the Jewish tradition proceeds on the basis of reflection on the creation story in Gen. 1-3 and not within the conceptual framework of philosophical speech. The collective fate of the whole of humanity is represented in Adam. Thereby, humanity is seen from the perspective of an adult Jewish man; "All," i.e., Jews and non-Jews, men and women, free and slave are here represented. Again the perspective is that of a Jewish man — "Adam." Eve's sin, woman's sin, is also indicated. Hence, we have to acknowledge here the phenomenon of "androcentrism."² Adam represents humanity and Eve is included within this. If one speaks of Eve then this concerns women only, whether this has to do with sin or any other theme. But in Paul, Eve is mentioned directly only once in 2 Cor 11:3 (indirectly in 1 Cor 11:2-16). In 2 Cor 11:3, the church is compared with a virgin bride whose bridegroom is Christ. Paul says, I feared that you — i.e., the community — have allowed yourself to be seduced. "I feared that as the serpent seduced Eve in his cunning" — so also you have allowed yourself to be seduced and are no longer chaste. This comparatively incidental remark about Eve points out that Paul knew the myth of feminine original sin. His remarks presuppose that the cunning seduction by the snake was a sexual one. The snake in Greek and Hebrew grammar has masculine gender. The snakelike-one, therefore, has sexually violated Eve and she has allowed herself to be sexually seduced. In Paul, this remark stands completely unconnected to his theology of sin. It appears here through verbal association with the seduction of the virgin bride.

Paul's theology of sin is thought out radically, collectively, and completely. Adam has transgressed God's command and all humanity has sinned. I am enslaved by sin. A particular sin of women, or Eve, is not present in Paul's Letter to the Romans. Two theories of sin, therefore, stand heterogeneously and unconnected one to the other in Paul. We shall return to the theory of feminine original sin which Paul mentions only marginally and which does not harmonize with his theology of sin.

---

*Translated by H. Wayne Merritt and Elizabeth A. Tourville
¹Cf. Luise Schottroff, *Der Glaubende und die feindliche Welt* (Neukirchen, 1970):115ff.
²On the "androcentrism" of the New Testament tradition see especially E. Schüssler Fiorenza, *In Memory of Her* (New York: Crossroad, 1983).

Paul states that sin even serves the Law, the Nomos, the will of God. God desires that we live. If we orient ourselves to God's will, we have life in its fullest. We, however, do not keep the law and, therefore, the will of God, and so are guilty and deserving of death. In the hand of sin, even God's law becomes an instrument of death. God's law — the essential means of life — is in the broad sense of the word holy, just and good (Rom. 7:12) but we do not keep it. All have sinned.

II
The Interpretation of Paul's Theology of Sin in Dominant Exegesis and Theology and the Necessary Criticism of this Interpretation

I refer in the following to the scientific interpretation of Paul of the present and preceding generations which, however, holds throughout as representative for the ecclesiastical proclamation of both large churches in our context — Protestant as well as Roman Catholic. Here, the basic thesis is: "sin is the arbitrary action of a person against God." As an initial example, I choose Rudolf Bultmann. The evidence demonstrates that Bultmann formulated a theological consensus which already had a long prior history. Even today in contemporary interpretation of Romans, this same conception of sin is championed. I give an assortment of key concepts which always mean the same thing. Sin is "to turn to one's own power," "self-motivated aspirations," "sinful-autocratic conduct," "humanity's confidence in itself," "striving for achievement." Representative for this arbitrary lust for power, in this view, is the "Jew" who wants to achieve salvation by means of the law.[3]

I leave this summary of contemporary ecclesiastical and scientific conception of sin (dependent on Bultmann's position) in this concise form since it is actually very uniformly advocated. As I see it, however, this theology of sin is undoubtedly deserving of criticism on numerous grounds. It is "anti-Jewish," "anti-female," "exegetically incorrect" and an "inadmissible generalization." I do not attack individuals with this. It would be grotesque to doubt Bultmann's political integrity at the time of National Socialism. Nevertheless, his interpretation of Paul is anti-Jewish. It comes to this; how can "we" with our theological tradition avoid this anti-Jewishness? Where do we extend

---

[3]Rudolf Bultmann, *Theology of the New Testament*, vol. 1 (New York: Scribner, 1951): 241-43 (par. 23.2).

it? Where do we develop it further? The anti-Jewishness of our theological tradition is not Bultmann's problem, but, "our" problem. What do we do if — much too late — we recognize this anti-Judaism in our theological tradition? Correspondingly, what do we do with it in feminist theology?

The dominant Pauline interpretation is anti-Jewish because of the theory that Judaism maintains the law as a self-sufficient way to salvation and that the Jew represents human self-sufficiency against God. The God of Jesus is a God of grace for the miserable sinner while the God of the "Old" Testament is a God of law and vengeance. But the law, the Torah, is in reality not to be understood as a self-reliant striving for achievement — neither according to the Old Testament nor according to post-biblical Jewish understanding. Instead God's mercy opens to human beings a living space in which they are able to act according to God's will. The Torah is law "and" gospel. The anti-Jewish conception of law, as a self-reliant means of salvation, is a Christian distortion of the Jewish religion which has nothing to do with Jewish self-understanding.

The theology of sin (in dominant theology) is anti-female in two respects. 1. Exaggerated self-confidence is not at present directly characteristic of the female situation and self-understanding. On the contrary, experiences of powerlessness are more typical of woman's reality. 2. The theory of sin in dominant theology is meant in an anti-emancipatory sense and also is used explicitly against the emancipatory efforts of women. The argument goes this way: a struggle for emancipation is self assertiveness which does not take fallenness in sin seriously. It attempts by its own power and possibilities to alter structures. In Ulrich Wilken's commentary on Romans this understanding of sin is indirectly used as criticism of liberation theologians of the "Third" world.[4] In the theses of the North Elbe bishops' response to feminist theology, this anti-emancipatory theory of sin emerges again. Feminist theology is caricatured as maintaining "humanity without sin" and "emancipation as self-liberation." Here we encounter the employment of the anti-emancipatory orientation of the theology of sin directed against feminist theology. This theol-

---

[4]Ulrich Wilckens, *Der Brief an die Römer*, EKK VI, Aufl. 1-3 (Zürich: Benziger Verlag, 1978, 1980, 1982)– passim; e.g., 1, 160 (against "self-realization tendencies").

ogy of sin thus provides a standard critique of Jews, the left and now feminists — of all who do not cover themselves with the traditional interpretation of sin.

This theology of sin is furthermore exegetically unfounded. Paul describes sin *not as arbitrary self reliance,* but, rather, as entanglement, subjection under death and *powerlessness.* Exegetes have to struggle in order to interpret Paul as maintaining that sin consists in the desire to fulfill the law (i.e., the anti-Jewish *Tendenz*), because Paul says that it consists in trespassing the law. See, for instance, interpretations of Rom. 7:11, where, according to the text, the issue revolves around Adam's *transgression* which can be understood only with difficulty as a use of the law as a means of salvation.

This theology of sin signifies an inadmissible generalization. There are human behaviors which are to be described, in fact, as self-assertion. In the Bible, royal hybris is described as in a way that corresponds to the dominant theology of sin. The dictatorial tyrant sits upon the throne and says: "I have the power and no one is over me" (e.g., Ezek. 28; Daniel). Thus, those who are subjugated criticize tyrannical power as self-assertion against God and as hybris. Here, *this special* form of sin has its place and here it must be called sin before God. That is, we no longer have the right on methodological grounds to speak of sin in a non-concrete and generalizing manner which lumps everything together as the same. One may agree that all are sinful but still maintain that their sin is very different. It is to be named concretely and contextually according to an exact analysis of power relations as the Bible does it. Sins of women, sins of slaves, sins of kings, sins of men, etc., all are to be seen in their context (i.e., in the social sense). The theology of sin, therefore, must also be nuanced in a social-historical sense. Paul speaks of the collectivity of sin, but, all the same, in a concrete social connection.

The anthropological generalization ("Man-kind"), and, lumping all people together as if they were all the same, is primarily to be seen as theological sin. In any case, it is to be seen as the theological sin of most theologians of the First World. Feminist theology, like Liberation theology, proceeds from concrete experiences in all their complexity. I personally endeavor to demonstrate that these experiences must be grasped together with social structures, and, therefore, must not be cursorily individualized or psychologized. The social and political context can not be eliminated.

I see a legitimate use of the presentation of sin in the dominant theology only where it is not turned against the powerless in society, but, rather, against those who shortsightedly and brutally pursue the greedy conquest for social power. They are rightly to be subjected to Ezek. 28, etc. They embody the hybris which delights in being able to trample on the powerless; the hybris of National Socialism and its modern descendants among the proper, upstanding, bourgeois.

III
The Seduction of Eve
The Origin of Female Guilt in Judaism, Christianity and Gnosticism

The rather incidental note in 2 Cor 11:3, concerning Eve's seduction by the snake (or better the snakelike one), is one of the earliest documentations of the myth of the sexual seduction of Eve. Around the same time, one encounters this myth also in Philo of Alexandria (b. 25 C.E.) in a greatly expanded form. The negative evaluation of sexuality and the definition of women in relation to sexuality is bound up with this myth from the beginning onwards. In Paul, this myth plays no particularly noteworthy role despite its significance only a generation later in Christianity according to the evidence of 1 Timothy. According to 1 Timothy:

> Let a woman learn in silence with all submissiveness. I permit no woman to teach or to have authority over men; she is to keep silent. For Adam was formed first, then Eve; and Adam was not deceived, but the woman was deceived and became a transgressor. Yet woman will be saved through bearing children, if she continues in faith and love and holiness, with modesty (1 Tim 2:11-15).

From the text it is clear that Eve's sin stands for "the nature and character of women as women" and,– from this basis, consequences for the reality of Christian women are derived. Further, Eve's seduction was a sexual seduction since childbearing appears as reparation for the (sexual) fault. It is even clear that this myth does not originate from Genesis 2-3 since the distinguishing traits of the myth are not found there — neither Eve's special guilt nor her sexual blunder.

It is especially important to recognize that the myth of feminine guilt has spread widely in the first century C.E., and has *nothing* to do with the so-called Old Testament and almost nothing to do with Judaism before the time of the Roman Caesars. 1 Tim 2:14 is not to be derived from the biblical creation stories.

The myth of the origin of feminine sin appears approximately at the same time in the first century in Jewish, Christian and Gnostic texts. Its history, up to the present time, is characterized by a series of triumphal marches in concert with the triumph of *Christianity*. It is unfounded, therefore, when the important feminist critique of this myth (as for instance in the case of Mary Daly) directs itself against the biblical creation stories and an allegedly patriarchal Judaism. The necessary feminist critique of this myth must direct itself instead against Christianity in the past and in the present.

This myth contains the following elements: a) the definition of women on the basis of their sexuality; b) the assertion of the sexual sin of the original mother (Eve or Sophia); and c) the derivation of the misery of the world on the basis of this original sin of woman. This myth can also connect itself with an ascetic lifestyle or with the maintenance of a rigorous patriarchal marriage and the bearing of children as reparation for women.

IV
A Social-Historical Clarification
of the Conception of Sin in Paul and in the Myth of Feminine Original Sin

Paul's theology of sin and the myth of feminine original sin originated at approximately the same time and both have a common social background. The two conceptions, however, are mutually exclusive. I can only say *either* all humanity is in bondage to sin through Adam, through Adam sin came into the world, *or*, the world is situated in deceit and Eve bears the guilt for that on account of her dangerous sexuality and her seduction. One excludes the other. I would like to try to order both conceptions in terms of their social history.

The theological analysis of Paul, according to which the whole of humanity is enslaved through sin, describes a universal world condition in categories of power and, especially, in terms of world power. Sin, as a world power, is described in Paul as a slaveholder and ruler of the world. According to Paul,

> Sin should not rule in your mortal bodies so that you obey its desires. Place not your members at the disposal of sin as instruments of injustice ... sin should not rule over you (Rom. 6:12-14).

Sin, as a world power, affects all people and it affects all people as whole beings in their bodies. There is no remainder. The word "body" in Paul describes humanity as a whole. The reign of sin stands against the power of God. I can place myself at God's disposal and with that take away sin's domination. Paul describes the universal power of sin as a critique of the *Pax Romana* describes the Roman Empire: as universal despotism.[5] There exists a connection between the Jewish experience of suffering in the Roman Empire and the Pauline theology of sin. This connection is especially clear to me in the Jewish writing 4 Ezra. The Roman Empire alienated Jewish people so greatly from their life relations that they no longer attempted to live according to the will of God. Their relation to their God was destroyed through the destruction of the basic realities of life: All have sinned, there is no justice any more — says the author of 4 Ezra.

Industrial society today shows a comparable process. The bonds in every day life are destroyed — those between people and those between people and God. What remains left over is the completely disposable individual: a body (in the Pauline sense) who is subjugated to the worldwide rule of injustice and death.

This far-reaching analysis of the world as slaves of sin, of death and injustice was possible for Paul only because he had set over and against this world power an experience of life and salvation. Through Christ's resurrection the power of sin is broken. In faith one can participate in the liberation and true life in Christ. This analysis of sin is itself a part of the process of liberation.

The myth of feminine original sin interprets the same despairing conditions of humanity in the world. Here also appear worldwide imprisonment and world domination. This myth, however, participates in a false analysis. It places blame on the wrong people; namely, on women. The social historical connection is the same in both cases. Both myths arise among the classes in the Roman Empire which not only did not participate in power and wealth but, rather, were ex-

---

[5]The historical material for this is found in Luise Schottroff, "Die Schreckensherrschaft der Sünde und die Befreiung durch Christus nach dem Römerbrief des Paulus," *Ev Theologie* 39 (1979): 497-510.

ceedingly oppressed economically and politically. There is a Jewish writing from this time (*The Life of Adam and Eve*), which describes clearly the social historical interpretation of the myth. There it is stated that Adam worked the earth and still did not prosper. In Gen. 3:17-19 Adam is a small farmer who works hard, but, nevertheless, can live off the earth. In *The Life of Adam and Eve*, Adam is restless, overworked, bitter and on a hopeless treadmill. Always, if things go especially bad for Adam, Eve accuses herself and says, "Adam, my lord, strike me dead since I am at fault because life goes so badly for you."

Neither Paul's theology of sin nor the myth of feminine original sin names the true cause; namely, the profiteers of the *Pax Romana*. The myth of Eve's sin interprets Adam's misery with a scapegoat theory of sin. On the other hand, the Pauline understanding of sin, despite its pre-political character, strikes deeper than many political analyses.

To speak concerning the myth of feminine original sin as a false analysis, however, is not to relegate it to the past. Even in our secular society, where often very little is left of the Christian tradition, this nonsense spread by Christianity is straightforwardly maintained and still alive. Women are still defined by their sexuality and very readily regarded as devilish if they don't fit into the structures. I speak from personal experience.

V
Theological Reflection On the Power of Sin and Liberation through Christ in Conversation with Paul

The Pauline analysis of sin as a world-power is immediately intelligible for many people today. Especially Rom. 7:14-24 and Rom. 3:10-18 express a description of the condition of humanity which I can directly reconstruct. It allows itself to be interpreted historically. The *Pax Romana* and the structures of the world-dominion of capitalism today resemble each other at decisive points. Paul was in a position to carry out his analysis because he knew and lived an alternative — liberation from the power of death through God's power. This liberation changed him from an instrument of death into a person who lived as one raised from the dead: "Present your members not at the disposal of sin as instruments of injustice, but, at God's disposal as one who has become alive from the dead" (Rom. 6:13). *The real basis of the claim of liberation through Christ was the praxis of the ekklesia.*

Because of this, the confession of Christ was not mere words. This praxis was the everyday attempt to place the members at God's disposal. Ought we to pay taxes or not? Ought we to eat meat sacrificed to idols or not? What does it mean for us not to fall into greediness? These were questions which were discussed at the time of Paul; thus, *the real basis of the claim of liberation through Christ was the daily praxis of the Christian community.* It is possible to live according to the will of God despite the power of sin. This experience of liberation through keeping the commandments was so great that Paul perceives it as resurrection from the dead.

The contemporary destruction of our obligations and the transformation of our existence into anonymous individuals is just as far reaching as the enslavement of the body through sin of which Paul writes. Powerful oppression under the forces of death, militarism, exploitation of nature, contempt for people is extensive. The "normal" attitude to this is resignation. Resignation, *consent to one's own powerlessness*, is the sin which Paul means. Here men are in a different situation from women. Men still have Eve under them. Of course Eve also participates in this sin. Eve's subjugation is even *doubled*. She is tied to Adam's powerlessness in his powerless consent to the forces of death and at the same time she is subject to Adam. Metaphor aside, the particular powerlessness of women is that they learn from infancy onwards that the questions of war and death are decided over their heads. I reconstruct Adam's desperate cry in Rom. 7:24 as the cry of the powerless, small man and the doubly powerless small women. But this cry contains already the conditions of rebellion in itself. *I am participating in sin*, but, therefore, this tyranny shall also end. I have possibilities to enact deeds which aim at justice and peace. These deeds, this praxis, is called at the time of Paul — living according to the will of God. Liberation is called Jesus Christ.

Remarks

*Abridged version of an abstract from a lecture series which was given for the Kassel Feminist Liberation Theology Summer University of 1987. The complete version is a contribution to a monograph which will appear in the Autumn of 1989, published by Kaiser-Verlag, Munich: Christian Schaumberger and Luise Schottroff, *Schuld und Macht aus der Perspektive einer Feministischen Befreiungstheologie.*

IS THE CRUCIFIED CHRIST THE CENTER OF A NEW TESTAMENT THEOLOGY?[1]

Lars Hartman, *University of Uppsala*

The Problem of the Center of the New Testament

The reader may rightly sense that the title of this contribution smacks of German. For several of our German colleagues have frequently posed the question, is there a center in the New Testament, *eine Mitte des Neuen Testaments,* or even *eine Mitte der Schrift*?[2] Almost always the response has been, "Yes, there is a center, viz., the cross, or Jesus' death on the cross." Such a response is frequently given by those influenced by the existentialist theology of Professor Bultmann and others, for whom the cross has a central position by virtue of its historical and thus non-mythical character. The cross is a scandal which

---

[1] A thoroughly revised version of a paper read at a conference arranged June 1987 in Oslo for the faculties of theology at the universities of Greifswald, Rostock, Kiel and of the Scandinavian countries.

[2] See the works of Ernst Käsemann, e.g., *Paulinische Perspektiven* (Tübingen: J.C.B. Mohr, 1972), 61-107; furthermore, e.g., Klappert, Bertold (ed.), *Diskussion um Kreuz und Auferstehung* (Wuppertal: Aussaat, 2nd ed. 1967); Werner Georg Kümmel, "Das Problem der 'Mitte des Neuen Testaments'", in *L'Évangile, hier et aujourd'hui. Mélanges offerts au Professeur Franz-J. Leenhardt* (Genève: Labor et fides, 1968), 71-85, reprinted in Idem, *Heilsgeschehen und Geschichte II* (Gesammelte Aufsätze) (Marburg: Elwert, 1978), 62-74; Ulrich Luz, "Theologia crucis als Mitte der Theologie im Neuen Testament," *Evangelische Theologie* 34(1974), 116-141; Wolfgang Schrage, "Die Frage nach der Mitte und dem Kanon im Kanon des Neuen Testaments in der neueren Diskussion," in J. Friedrich, W. Pöhlmann, P. Stuhlmacher (eds.), *Rechtfertigung. Festschrift für Ernst Käsemann* (Göttingen: J.C.B. Mohr, 1976), 415-442; Siegfried Schulz, *Die Mitte der Schrift. Der Frühkatholizismus im Neuen Testament als Herausforderung an den Protestantismus* (Stuttgart: Kreuz, 1976); Bernhard Ehler, *Die Herrschaft des Gekreuzigten. Ernst Käsemanns Frage nach der Mitte der Schrift* (Berlin, New York: de Gruyter, 1986), which also contains an extensive bibliography. Cf. Franz Mussner, "Die Mitte des Evangeliums in neutestamentlicher Sicht," *Catholica* 15 (1961), 271-292; René Kieffer, *Die Bibel deuten - das Leben deuten. Einführung in die Theologie des Neuen Testaments* (Regensburg: Pustet, 1987), 22 f.

must not be made less offensive, since it stands for an authentic faith, one without security for its trust in the God who demands faith without reserve.

Exegetes working at faculties which are connected to this or that denomination may find it easier than their colleagues to decide whether there is a center in NT theology, at least if they accept the theological tenets of the Church in question. But when I understand the title of this paper as an open question, I do so while loyal to my school: a faculty of divinity at a state university, studying theology as *Religionswissenschaft*.

Naturally our question immediately leads to another, which should be discussed first, viz., what do we mean by a NT theology?[3] Greater difficulties would have ensued, if the question had pertained to the center of *the* NT theology. In the worldwide exegetical community scholars like Hendrikus Boers have taught us how awkward this would have been.[4] We may, of course, talk of a certain unity of the NT, in so far as the documents which gradually came to compose the NT have several basic ideas in common. But the traditions and writers who are represented in this library hold opinions so diverse that a NT theology may only be achieved in one of three ways. First, by harmonizing: Paul with Matthew and James and John. In this case a dogmatic system guides the understanding of the biblical texts, while the theological profiles of their authors are blurred,[5] and the risk of wrongfully attributing opinions to them must be accepted. Or, second, one particular author is allowed to dominate, and his theology understood according to some canon within the canon, which, consciously or unconsciously, is determined by the reader's Church affiliation or private views on religious matters.[6] Finally, the road of abstraction may be followed more or less far. Assume, for example, that the different NT authors in reality wrestle with humanity's fun-

---

[3]See the material in Georg Strecker (ed.), *Das Problem der Theologie des Neuen Testaments* (Wege der Forschung 367; Darmstadt: Wissenschaftliche Buchgesellschaft, 1975), especially the editor's own introduction. Furthermore Hendrikus Boers, *What Is New Testament Theology? The Rise of Criticism and the Problem of a Theology of the New Testament* (Guides to Biblical Scholarship, N.T.Series; Philadelphia: Fortress, 1979), with an annotated bibliography.

[4]See the preceding note.

[5]Alan Richardson, *An Introduction to the Theology of the New Testament* (New York: Harper, 1958) comes close to this type of a New Testament theology.

[6]It is clear, for example, that Paul, and a rather Lutheran Paul at that, dominates E. Käsemann's theology.

damental existential problems,[7] and make their solutions more and more abstract, until you reach a level at which their answers can be reconciled. Thus, Herbert Braun finds that NT theology ultimately concerns our relationship to our neighbour. When the NT tells how a god and a son of a god relate to humankind, this is translated into a view, in which other persons, their existence and their problems, represent external demands on us but also gifts to us. Braun's point of departure is, he maintains, what he finds typical of, and peculiar to the NT as compared with its milieu.[8]

The question, what is NT theology, can also be put in this way: what do you do when you write a NT theology? A member of a *religionswissenschaftlich* faculty could obviously chose to reply in a way reminiscent of the classical History of Religions School, as represented by e.g., William Wrede.[9] For him NT theology was a presentation of the thought of different early Christian theologians. The task then pertains to the history of ideas and the history of religion. It is only natural that its scholarly context is the study of the religions in Antiquity, of which Christianity is one. The consequence of such a perspective is also that it becomes artificial to limit the study to the canonical NT.

As a rule, however, scholars seek a further objective when constructing a NT theology. They seek to lay the foundation of a reflection upon Christian faith and assign their NT theology a critical function vis-à-vis such a reflection. Whether consciously or not, the exegete's Church affiliation plays a role in this connection (or, in some cases, the exegete's negative attitude towards some denominational or theological point of view.)

One further point of principle concerns the problem of text and context. Our analytical and historical interest may lead us to spend as much energy on reconstructing sources and/or older layers of the

---

[7]For example, Rudolf Bultmann, *Theologie des Neuen Testaments* (Tübingen: J.C.B. Mohr, 6th ed. 1968), especially 586 f

[8]Herbert Braun, "Der Sinn der neutestamentlichen Christologie," *Zeitschrift für Theologie und Kirche* 54 (1957), 341-377, reprinted in Idem, *Gesammelte Studien zum Neuen Testament* (Tübingen: J.C.B. Mohr, 1962), 86-99; Idem, "Die Problematik einer Theologie des Neuen Testaments," *Zeitschrift für Theologie und Kirche* 58 (1961), 3-18, reprinted in *Gesammelte Studien*, 325-341, and in Strecker (ed.), *Das Problem* (above, note 3), 405-424.

[9]William Wrede, *Über Aufgabe und Methode der sogenannten neutestamentlichen Theologie* (Göttingen: Vandenhoeck & Ruprecht, 1897); pp. 7-80 reprinted in Strecker (ed.), *Das Problem* (note 3), 81-154.

texts as on the result of the efforts of the NT authors and redactors. So we are prepared to discuss the theology of, for example, the Logia-source,[10] but can also accept the idea of a theology of Matthew, although it differs from that of the source included in his text. The same holds true of the Gospel of John: many would differentiate neatly between the theology of the original evangelist and that of the final "ecclesiastical redactor",[11] but are nevertheless willing to discuss the theology of the fourth Gospel as we have it today.

The observations of the preceding paragraphs indicate that when we consider the work of authors and redactors it is as true as ever that texts lend themselves to several interpretations. When we think of the first readers/listeners, who encountered the texts without differentiating the sources from the redactor, they can be said to have done the same thing as we, when we write the theology of the same Gospel and forget about its tradition-history. Sources and redaction become attuned to each other, and particular original nuances or references of the former disappear or acquire new meanings.

But as, for example, the completed Gospel of Matthew has a prehistory which led to a situation in which traditions were used, revised and interpreted in a new context, viz., that of the present Gospel of Matthew, so the same Matthew was very soon embodied in a larger context, called the Gospel or the Four-fold Gospel. In other words, what the exegete cherishes as the particular message of Matthew is understood in the light of this context of the fourfold Gospel. With Paul it is the same. An exegete may ask whether Paul changed some of his views, say those on the Torah, from Galatians to Romans.[12] But once not only the undisputed letters, but also the deutero-and trito-Pauline epistles came to belong to the Pauline letter collection, the readers read the whole as expressing Paul's theology.

---

[10] E.g., Paul Hoffmann, *Studien zur Theologie der Logienquelle* (Neutestamentliche Abhandlungen N.F. 8; Munich: Aschendorff, 1972).

[11] Of course inspired by Rudolf Bultmann, *Das Evangelium des Johannes* (Kritisch-exegetischer Kommentar...; Göttingen: Vandenhoeck & Ruprecht, 10th ed. 1941).

[12] Hans Hübner, *Law in Paul's Thought*, trans. James C.G. Greig (Edinburgh: Clark 1984). Cp. E. P. Sanders, *Paul, the Law, and the Jewish People* (Philadelphia: Fortress, 1983); Heikki Räisänen, "Paul's Theological Difficulties with the Law," in E.A. Livingstone (ed.), *Studia Biblica 1978*, vol. 3: Papers on Paul and Other New Testament Authors (Journal for the Study of the New Testament, Supplement Series 3; Sheffield: JSOT Press, 1980), 301-320, reprinted in Idem, *The Torah and Christ* (Publications of the Finnish Exegetical Society 45; Helsinki 1986), 3-24.

Is the Crucified Christ the Center of a New Testament Theology?

We are anxious to separate the historical Paul from the Paul envisaged from Colossians, Ephesians and 2 Thessalonians, not to mention the Pastorals. But those who disseminated the collection gave us a Paul of the Church in the same way as the school of John gave us their John. Indeed, we may even say that in reality this Paul of the Church has been of greater importance throughout the centuries than the Paul we reconstruct from the authentic letters. Thus, there is one Pauline theology made up from the authentic letters and another, derived from the whole Pauline collection of the NT, the origin of which is not only a man but also a re-interpreting tradition and a Pauline school.

Thus, the more we regard the present texts from a reader's point of view, the closer we *can* come to a traditional Christian perspective, leaving aside the historical search for the opinions of individual NT authors or of their sources. I do not say we should do so, but we may do so and adduce some reasons for so doing.

The deliberations of the preceding paragraphs are not simply a few pirouettes on the ice of methodology but sketch a feature of the problematic background for a discussion of a NT theology and its possible center. In what follows, I shall start on a relatively low level of abstraction . Thus, by a "NT theology" I shall refer to the structured world of thought which we can reconstruct from the NT texts with the help of a particular author or a text- producing group. I first pose the question of this paper to the theology of Paul and to that of the fourth Gospel. Secondly I shall, albeit sketchily, widen the perspective and, on a higher level of abstraction, ask our question of a NT theology and its center.

But first one further modification. Often it happens that "the crucified Christ" is understood so broadly as to refer to suffering and death in general. But here I will focus on the crucifixion in the narrow sense of death on the cross as the specific form of Jesus' suffering and death.[13] The more general emphasis would lead us to speak of a "theology of Jesus' suffering and death" rather than a "theology of the cross" (*theologia crucis*).

When we consider the NT writings with this narrower significance of "the crucified Christ" in mind, we find that, although many of them mention Jesus' death on the cross, it is actually only with

---

[13]So does also Heinz-Wolfgang Kuhn, "Jesus als Gekreuzigter in der frühchristlichen Verkündigung bis zur Mitte des 2. Jahrhunderts," *Zeitschrift für Theologie und Kirche* 72 (1975), 1-46.

Paul and John that the cross *per se* is important. In other words, all theologians of the Early Church presumably sought an answer to the question of the meaning of Jesus' death, but to judge from our texts, not all have elaborated on the fact that it was on a cross that he died.

The Crucified Christ in Paul

But with Paul this is the case.[14] In the undisputed letters the motif is first encountered in a polemic against the divisions caused by the devotees of wisdom in Corinth (1 Cor 1-3). Against those who say "I belong to Paul" etc. (1:12), Paul's argument is: Christ is not divided (1:13), which he develops by saying that Paul was not crucified for them nor were they baptized in his name. Indeed, he has only baptized a few of them (1:14-16), since his mission is to preach the Gospel, though not with wisdom of words, lest the cross be made of no effect (1:17). Paul then develops the contrast between wisdom of words and Gospel preaching: the latter is folly to those who perish but the power of God to those who are saved (1:18). For, he says, through this foolish preaching of the crucified Christ, God, in His wisdom, saves the one who believes. A crucified Christ (or a crucified Messiah) is, of course, a stumbling-block to the Jews and a crucified saviour (a *soter* or a *kurios*) a folly to the Greeks, given the associations with crucifixion, the punishment of major, despicable criminals.

In this exercise of God's power the cross represents a principle of folly and weakness, the validity of which is then exemplified. First, it is proved in the social structure of the Corinthian Church, because its members came chiefly from the lower classes. Thus, everything comes from God, so that he who boasts can boast only in the Lord (1:31, quoting Jer 9:24). The next proof of the principle is Paul's own behaviour as an apostle: he refrained from speaking with wisdom and rhetorical elegance in order to know only Christ and Him crucified (2:1-4). Again he states: in human weakness God was powerful.

Furthermore, there is a contrast between Christ's being crucified for the Corinthians and their high esteem for men, which led to the

---

[14]See, e.g., Käsemann, *Paulinische Perspektiven* (note 2), 61-107; Ortkemper, Franz-Josef, *Das Kreuz in der Verkündigung des Apostels Paulus* (Stuttgarter Bibelstudien 24; Stuttgart: Katholisches Bibelwerk, 2nd ed. 1968); Wolfgang Schrage, "Leid, Kreuz und Eschaton. Die Peristasenkataloge als Merkmale paulinischer theologia crucis und Eschatologie," *Evangelische Theologie* 34 (1974), 141- 175; Peter Stuhlmacher, "Achtzehn Thesen zur paulinischen Kreuzestheologie," in *Rechtfertigung* (note 3), 509-525.

divisions Paul is attacking. His argument about crucifixion and baptism in 1:13 presupposes that in baptism Christ's death was related to the one baptized. Further, in order to prevail, the argument must assume that the consequence of baptism was that the Corinthians became Christ's property (see also 3:23). Then belonging to Christ in that way would be so overwhelming as to invalidate the all too human views that lay behind the divisions. But it is difficult to tell whether this belonging to Christ has anything to do with the crucifixion *per se*. Indirectly the Corinthians detest the shameful death on the cross through their veneration of men, and in other passages Paul expresses the idea that this belonging to Christ implies a life which is determined by the cross (Gal 2:19 f.; 5:24; 6:14). But here he does not develop such a thought.

In Galatians too Christ the crucified is contrasted with something more acceptable, less shameful, at least to the Jewish mind, namely circumcision. Paul is horrified at the fact that in obedience to the Law the Galatians can take up circumcision, these people before whose eyes Christ was set forth as crucified (3:1 f.). When this proclamation of Christ the crucified was received in faith, the Galatians were endowed with the Spirit, but now they seem to reject it in order to "end with the flesh" (3:3), which I take to denote the concrete fulfilment of the Torah commandment.

In this Galatians passage the crucified Christ is not only contained in the preaching to which people have listened in faith, but also adduced in the argument for the principle of justification by faith which follows. Thus, in 3:13 he cites Deuteronomy 21:23, "Cursed is everyone who hangs on a tree." This implies that "Christ redeemed us from the curse of the Law, becoming a curse for us" (3:13). The conclusion is that, when the curse is taken away, the way is clear for the Gentiles, so that they can inherit Abraham's blessing through faith (3:14).

Towards the end of Galatians the motif of the cross is taken up again. In contrast to the opponents, who "want to show fair in the flesh" (6:12, also 6:13, and cf. 3:3), i.e. through their persuading the Galatians to submit to circumcision, Paul will not glory in anything except in the cross of Christ "through which (or: through whom) the world has been crucified to me and I to the world" (6:14). Here the idea is not so much that of the proclamation of the crucifixion and its salvific consequences as of a continuing relationship to Christ based on this salvation (also 5:24). This relationship is entered through faith and baptism (2:19; 3:20-29), so that now, when we belong to Christ (3:29; 5:24), everything mundane, shame and the works of the Law included, is of no importance - Paul is crucified to the world.

Thus we have seen how in 1 Corinthians the preaching of the folly of the cross was opposed to human wisdom and distinction, and how in Galatians the "for us" of the death on the cross was developed in an exposition of an OT passage on the curse of a hanged person. In Galatians we also noted how the Christ- relationship, established through the application of the consequences of his death in baptism had sequels for the life of the Christian: it became determined by the cross, and conventional values were overthrown.

Since I am examining the position of the cross in a Pauline theology, it may be worthwhile to touch upon another aspect of our motif. Not only is the shameful fact of the crucifixion of importance to Paul, but also the person so executed. He and His cross belong, on the one hand, definitely to human history. On the other, this Christ is also the exalted Lord with whom Christians are united. Nonetheless he is always the crucified one - Paul uses the perfect tense (1 Cor 1:29; 2:2; Gal 3:1). Even the exalted Christ is ever one who has experienced the utmost human misery.

Is then the crucified Christ, understood in the narrow sense I defined above, the center of a NT theology, and, particularly, of a Pauline one? When, as a theologian of the *Religionswissenschaftliche* school, I am confronted by the question and attempt to deal with it in historical terms, I cannot help feeling a little uneasy. For certainly you can speak of things that are important or less important, e.g., in the thinking of Philo or in the theology of Rudolf Bultmann. But a center? One single, indispensable center of a circle? Or am I too rigid? From this unease a new question emerges: why ask for a center at all? Do theologians ask for an exclusive center because, fundamentally, they want to build a bridge between NT theology and Christian preaching and Christian life today? Or are they at least eager to systematize more than is needed for purely historical understanding?

There are more questions. My academic ego - in which there is also a pastor - reminds me that in these passages, in which we surmise a theology of the cross, caution is needed inasmuch as Paul is involved in a keen polemic. In a polemic you are often compelled to mark your profile, but as the opponent has decided the issue, both the counterattack and its target are determined by the position of the other. Thus, neither the cross nor the crucifixion is mentioned in

Romans, and from a historical point of view it seems to be a little difficult to answer in the affirmative to the question, whether Christ as crucified, and precisely as crucified, is the center of Pauline theology. *In* the center, yes, but hardly *the* center. That it belongs to the center is proved by the passages we discussed above, but this central area also encompasses the death of Jesus, His resurrection, the problem of Jews and Gentiles, the role of faith, etc.

So far I have posed our question to what we may call the undisputed Paul. I stated above that there is some reason also to deal with the transmitted Paul, whom we encounter in the collection in which the deutero- and trito-Pauline writings are included. Thus, in Col 1:15-20 the author speaks of the divine fullness, which, through the Son, reconciled everything on earth and in heaven with it (or: with Him) and made peace "by the blood of His cross" (v. 20). No issue is made of the fact that the death on the cross was offensive. That it effected reconciliation is of course Pauline, but we do not encounter the cosmic perspective in such a connection in the undisputed letters.

In Col 2:8-15 the author is involved in his controversy with the so-called philosophy. Taking as his point of departure that baptism meant remission of sins, he concludes that this remission also invalidates the demands which certain powers make through "philosophy". In v. 14 this is developed in a complicated image. I paraphrase the unusually entangled sentence: "Canceling our bond which concerned our duties over against the demands, He set it aside, nailing it to the cross." I suggest that the author makes use of two associations with crucifixion. One is that it was a shameful destruction of a despicable criminal; so God did with our guilt. The other intimates how this was done, viz., through Christ's death on the cross, with which the addressees were united in baptism.

The author of Colossians would then attach some importance to the fact that Jesus died precisely on a cross. But he does not use it for a theology of weakness, on the contrary: the crucified Lord is a cosmic victor, in whose victory the audience participates. Insofar as this Paulinist has learned from Paul, the crucified Christ certainly belongs to the center of his thinking, but with different shades of meaning. The shame falls on the powers, while the Christians are victors with Christ.

A short glance at Ephesians draws our attention to 2:16, where the author seems to repeat the thought of Col 1:18-22, applying it to the relationship between Jews and Gentiles: "He reconciled the two to God in one body through the cross." Here the cross "is only the place of the reconciliation, a topos of Christian preaching."[15]

We could wish the material were more reliable, but yet some conclusions can be drawn concerning the motif of the crucified Christ in a Pauline theology built on the whole Corpus Paulinum. In Paul's school they were certain as to the central importance of Christ's death on precisely the cross, and as well, as to the salvific effects of this death. That it was regarded as shameful should be self-evident because of current cultural conventions, but use is rarely made of this fact. Nor does the weakness aspect seem to play any role after First Corinthians, and the thought that the cross should determine the life of the Christian (as crucified to the world) does not occur in the deutero-Pauline letters.

Thus, the crucified Christ is *in* the theological center of the larger collection of Pauline writings, but it is not *the* center. Even if naturally the accents of the historical Paul have not disappeared, they have weakened, on the one hand, through the fact that First Corinthians and Galatians are no longer read in the light of the crises in Corinth and Galatia. On the other hand, they are also attenuated by the fact that now the deutero-Pauline writings belong to the Pauline context.

The Crucified Christ in John

In the Gospel of John the cross and the crucifixion are not mentioned more frequently than in the Synoptic Gospels. But the fourth Gospel has taken into account the crucifixion *per se* in a way the Synoptics do not.[16] This is done through the ambiguous term "lift up", "elevate". "The Son of Man must be lifted up, as Moses lifted up the serpent in the wilderness, that whoever believes in him may have eternal life" (3:14-15). The death on the cross belongs to the divine "must", i.e., to the work the Son had to fulfill. The verb "lift up",

---

[15]Rudolf Schnackenburg, *Der Brief an die Epheser* (Evangelisch-Katholischer Kommentar zum Neuen Testament 10; Zürich, Einsiedeln, Köln: Benziger, Neukirchen-Vluyn: Neukirchener, 1982), 117.

[16]See U.B. Müller, "Die Bedeutung des Kreuzestodes Jesu im Johannesevangelium. Erwägungen zur Kreuzestheologie im Neuen Testament," *Kerygma und Dogma* 21 (1975), 49-71; Peter von der Osten-Sacken, "Leistung und Grenze der johanneischen Kreuzestheologie," *Evangelische Theologie* 36 (1976), 154-176; Rudolph Schnackenburg, "Paulinische und johanneische Christologie. Ein Vergleich," in U. Luz, H. Weder (eds.), *Die Mitte des Neuen Testaments. Einheit und Vielfalt neutestamentlicher Theologie* (Festschrift für Eduard Schweizer) (Göttingen: Vandenhoeck & Ruprecht, 1983), 221-237.

refers on the one hand to the concrete lifting up of the criminal at crucifixion. But on the other, its meaning is close to that of the words on the glorification of Jesus: the passion and the death is the "hour" of his glorification (12:13; 13:31 f.; 17:1) and the hour of his going to the Father (13:3 etc.). Paradoxically the crucifixion reveals who the crucified Jesus really is and so also who the Father is.

The ambiguity of the term "lift up", "elevate", and the motif of departing, i.e., dying, and so going to the Father, justify us in saying that according to John Jesus dies to (or into) the Father on the cross. But yet the reader is not allowed to stop at such a statement. Mary Magdalene is not permitted to touch or hold Jesus for he has not yet ascended to the Father (20:17). In the sequence of the Johannine story the lifting up on the cross becomes but one element of the ascension to the Father, and the result is a tension between the two modes of reference to going to the Father.

This tension has caused some exegetical debates. The more a scholar (with, e.g., Bultmann) equates crucifixion and lifting up- ascension to the Father,[17] the more it can be claimed that in the humiliation of the incarnate Son the power of God is paradoxically at work. At the other end of the scale there are those who read John in the perspective of the Synoptic texts.

In John the offensiveness of crucifixion is not emphasized. Certainly precisely the crucified Jesus is the King of the Jews (19:19), whose Kingdom is not of this world (18:36). But all through the passion story he is also the unbroken One, who is the master of the situation until the work which the Father sent him to perform is completed (19:30).

Is this crucified Christ the center of a Johannine theology? I am convinced that the answer is: without any doubt he is in the center, but he is not *the* center. On the cross his work reached its culmination and was completed, and in the dialogue with Nicodemus this is presented as the final answer to the question how it is possible to enter the kingdom of God (3:3,5-8): the Son of Man must be "lifted up" (3:14). Moreover the divine revelation, which took place in the Son's incarnation and work debouches in the elevation and glorification in the passion. But nevertheless his death on precisely the cross is not the exclusive center of Johannine theology.

---

[17]Bultmann, *Das Evangelium des Johannes* (note 11), 324-332, 532 f.

Toward a NT Theology

So far I have stayed on a relatively low level of abstraction, dealing with two easily delimited areas of thought and using the NT authors' own modes of expression. But also an exegete working on a purely academic basis can legitimately try to understand in depth what authors of antiquity are saying. This can be achieved by penetration of modes of expression and concepts, and translation of forms of thinking, mythical language, etc. Of course such an undertaking always runs the risk that the interpreter's imagination brings him so far that the ties to the object of his study and its historical particularity are stretched beyond the breaking-point.

Such considerations bring us for a moment back to Paul and John. I have intimated that the resurrection of Jesus should also belong to the center of a Pauline theology. To one who heeds the opinion that the resurrection of Christ is tantamount to a renewal of the life of the disciples so that they were inspired to adopt the cause of Jesus, the resurrection hardly becomes as important as the offense of the cross. There are, however, other manners of speaking of the resurrection without resorting to neo-orthodox or objectifying language, in which resurrection and ascension are discussed as if they belonged to the same category as a bus ride from the campus into the city. Here the Johannine mode of reference to Jesus' death as an exaltation and a departure to the Father may be taken as a start. Above I reformulated this imagery by saying that Jesus died to (or into) the Father. But, as we noticed, in the fourth Gospel this imagery is combined with another, more narrative one, whereby what is held together in the exaltation language is distributed in a time sequence so that Jesus is first lifted up on the cross, and then ascends to the Father after He has spent three days in the tomb, risen, and appeared to some people. It is feasible to concentrate on the former, the "dying to the Father" language, and do so, not only in a "translated" Johannine, but also in a Pauline theology. Death and renewed transcendent existence with the Supreme Being would then be held together and, thus, cross and death become even more dominant in a Pauline theology, since they are included in his resurrection.

Attempts at such "translation" can be made also for a larger body of material than the texts written by two individual NT writers. Thus, we could try to present early Christian approaches to life, donning the same courage to simplify and generalize as when speaking of the view of life in Ancient Greece, of Buddhism, or of the philosophy of Romanticism - and running the same risks. And, I may add, we should do so, while prepared to discuss other perspectives and other evaluations of the data.

So our search for a NT theology proceeds on a higher level of abstraction, viz., one on which, in principle, use may be made of material from the whole NT. The reason for such an undertaking need not be only a Church interest, but should already be a generally humanistic one, since we learn to be more human through reflection on the humanity of others and their reflections thereon. No doubt such considerations lie behind several expositions of NT theology, not least such as are written by theologians who maintain that the cross is *the* very center of *the* NT theology. But even though I am convinced that the theologian makes too biased a selection of NT motifs who does not render some justice to the motif of the crucified Christ, I do not believe that this motif must be the absolute center, around which must revolve all attempts at a meaningful exposition for our time of early Christian faith as represented by the writings gathered in the NT. A meaningful exposition here means not only one which is intellectually honest but also one that really engages the human subject .

We could as well imagine the construction of a NT theology around the concept of the Kingdom of God. It was central to the proclamation of Jesus; he engaged in this Kingdom through a radical devotion to God and neighbours. From such a center we could also deduce certain principles of Christian ethics. Nonetheless the concept of the Kingdom of God would not be *the* very center but an important idea possibly belonging to the central area.

Or, could we not, with the same reservations, write a NT theology of hope, or one of humanity or human fellowship? Briefly, however much it may be maintained that a particular NT theology is based on the indisputable "center of the NT", I am afraid that the criteria must always remain too subjective to allow us to claim that we have found such an absolute, obligatory center for a NT theology. The world is not so simple, nor the diversified world of the thought of NT writers. This does not mean that we have to surrender to an uninhibited subjectivism. So, like many others, I am convinced that the theme of the crucified Christ, and precisely the crucified one, is important to any NT theology. But how important and in what way - these questions must be answered with the help of other criteria, which can differ, depending on the context in which, and the presuppositions from which, a NT theology is devised. That is why we can formulate the theme of this paper as a question, the answer to which is ultimately determined by the one who gives it.

IV
Critique of Christology

THE PROBLEM OF CHRISTOLOGY IN THE SERMON ON THE MOUNT

Hans Dieter Betz, *University of Chicago*

The strange absence of clearly stated christological affirmations in the Sermon on the Mount (Matt 5:3-7:27) has always been a source of consternation. The fact is that Jesus delivers this first programmatic speech without mentioning his death and resurrection, without claiming any christological titles, and with scarce reference to himself apart from his role as the teacher. This lack of christology is peculiar whether or not Matthew was the author of the Sermon on the Mount (henceforth abbreviated SM). If Matthew did compose it, why did he not make his christological views clear, as he did elsewhere? On the other hand, if, as I assume, he took the SM over as a source[1], then for reasons to be explored that source did not make christological statements. Matthew, of course, "corrected" this deficiency, or what may have appeared to him to be a deficiency, by placing the SM within the framework of his entire Gospel, where the highly developed christology[2] of the latter could compensate for what the former lacked. Matthew could further tolerate this incorporation of the SM by historicizing and thus relativizing it. To him it indicated that Jesus had initially refrained from christological self-explanations, whereas more and more information concerning his person was let out as the events

---

[1] See my *Essays on the Sermon on the Mount* (Philadelphia: Fortress Press, 1985), esp. 92, 93-95, 151-54.

[2] I agree here with Christoph Burchard's review of my *Essays* in *Theologische Literaturzeitung* 112 (1987): 508-09: "Auch wenn Matthäus sie (sc. die Bergpredigt) wörtlich abgeschrieben hat, ist sie jetzt ein Teil seines Evangeliums. Vieles, was Betz für seine Epitome bestreitet, wird für Mt 5-7 immer noch richtig sein und umgekehrt." Indeed, one must distinguish between the SM and its interpretation by Matthew. See also Burchard's article "Bergpredigt," *Evangelisches Kirchenlexikon* 1 ([2]1985):433-36.

unfolded. The full self-disclosure finally occurs only in Matt 26:63-64, when the high priest confronts Jesus with a solemn oath:

"The high priest then said, 'By the living God I adjure you so that you tell us: Are you the Messiah, the Son of God?' Jesus replied to him: 'You said it. And I tell you: From now on you shall see the Son of Man sitting at the right side of the Power and coming on the clouds of the heavens.'"

When Matthew's reader bears this and other passages (e.g., 14:33; 16:16; 28:18-20) in mind, there is no question from the beginning as to who it is that opens his mouth to pronounce the great Sermon (5:1).

While Matthew was apparently not bothered by the lack of christology in the SM, later authors were. Marcion, e.g., senses that the SM was Jewish, not Christian[3]. In a different way, St. Augustine in his commentary *De sermone Domini in monte* combined the seven beatitudes with the tradition of the seven gifts of the holy spirit, thereby supplementing the text with a soteriology which in turn would presuppose a christology.[4] In modern times, some theologians welcomed the absence of christology in the SM because they favored a plain message of Jesus free from heavy dogmatic language.[5] Others felt the

---

[3]See Theodor Zahn, *Geschichte des neutestamentlichen Kanons*, 2 vols. (Erlangen: Deichert, 1888-1892), I:2, pp. 666-72; Adolf von Harnack, *Marcion. Das Evangelium vom fremden Gott* (Leipzig: Hinrichs, ²1924; reprinted Darmstadt: Wissenschaftliche Buchgesellschaft, 1960), *191-*95, *249-*52.

[4]See Almut Mutzenbecher, ed., *Sancti Aurelii Augustini De sermone Domini in monte libros duos*, Corpus Christianorum, series latina 35 (Turnholti:Brepols, 1967), pp. XI-XVII.

[5]The issue at stake was clearly understood by Julius Wellhausen in his *Einleitung in die drei ersten Evangelien* (Berlin: Reimer, ²1911), 102-104. When speaking of "the impact" Jesus had upon his disciples ("der Eindruck seiner Person"), the question is, what was more decisive, the Jewishness (and particularity) of his message, or his humanity (and universality)? Wellhausen remained undecided. On the one hand he says (102): "Jesus war kein Christ, sondern Jude." On the other hand (103): "Man darf das Nichtjüdische in ihm, das Menschliche, für charakteristischer halten, als das Jüdische." Building on Wellhausen, Adolf Harnack's preference for the source Q as the main source for the message of Jesus has its reason here as well; see his *Sprüche und Reden Jesu. Die zweite Quelle des Matthäus und Lukas*, in his *Beiträge zur Einleitung in das Neue Testament*, 2 (Leipzig: Hinrichs, 1907), 173: "Vor allem wird die übertreibung des apokalyptisch-eschatologischen Elements in der Verkündigung Jesu und die Zurückstellung der rein religiösen und moralischen Momente hinter jenes immer wieder ihre Widerlegung durch die Spruchsammlung finden. Sie bietet die Gewähr für das, was in der Verkündigung Jesu die Hauptsache gewesen ist: die Gotteserkenntnis und die Moral zu Busse und Glauben, zum Verzicht auf die Welt und zum Gewinn des Himmels - nichts anderes." See also the programmatic statements in his *Das*

need to speak of the SM as having an "implicit" christology,[6] while again others simply interpret the evangelist Matthew's christology into the SM.

The aim of this paper, however, is not to trace the whole history of the problem. Instead we shall confine ourselves to the evidence in the texts themselves and the options available to interpret them (Part I). Then (Part II) we shall examine an interesting hypothesis by the renowned scholar Adolf Schlatter which he published in a rather obscure publication and which deserves to be rescued from oblivion. Part III will offer some conclusions.

- I -

As far as the text of the SM is concerned, the absence of christological affirmations should be obvious. As we have already indicated, there is no reference to Jesus' crucifixion and resurrection. No christological titles are affirmed, and there is no specifically Christian soteriology, no doctrine of the holy spirit, no reference to church, baptism, or imitation of Christ. Instead of these points of doctrine the important observation to be made about Jesus throughout the discourse is that he is the speaker, as indicated by the frequent phrase "(but) I say unto you"[7] or simply the first person singular.[8] But there is nothing extraordinary about these frequent self-references, for they merely conform to Jesus' role as a teacher.[9] Still, there are some passages

---

Wesen des Christentums (Leipzig: Hinrichs, 1900), esp. 10-11, 13 (cited according to the reedition by Rudolf Bultmann [Stuttgart: Klotz, 1950]). Harnack's position can be traced back at least to Erasmus; see Paul Wernle, *Renaissance und Reformation* (Tübingen: J.C.B. Mohr [Paul Siebeck], 1912), 69, 114-15; Friedhelm Krüger, *Humanistische Evangelienauslegung. Desiderius Erasmus von Rotterdam als Ausleger der Evangelien in seinen Paraphrasen*, Beiträge zur historischen Theologie, 68 (Tübingen: J.C.B. Mohr [Paul Siebeck], 1986), 201-04.

[6]"Implicit" christology means that texts may refer to a christology not explicitly stated. The implicitness may be a matter of presupposition or consequence. See also Rudolf Bultmann, *Theologie des Neuen Testaments* (Tübingen: J.C.B. Mohr [Paul Siebeck], [9]1984), 1-2, 46, 586-89; Herbert Braun, *Gesammelte Schriften zum Neuen Testament und seiner Umwelt* (Tübingen: J.C.B. Mohr [Paul Siebeck], [3]1971), 341.

[7]See Matt 5:18, 22, 26, 28, 32, 34, 39, 44; 6:2, 5, 16, 25, 29, 31; 7:21.

[8]See 5:11, 22, 28, 32, 34, 39, 44; 7:21, 23, 24, 26.

[9]These self-references express Jesus' self-consciousness as a teacher teaching the right doctrine in opposition to other teachers (cf. the phrase "you have heard that it was said" in 5:21, 27, 33, 38, 43), singling out the scribes and Pharisees

which have been taken to imply a christology of some sort, and we need to examine these passages briefly.

(1) The beatitude in Matt 5:11 contains a description of three possible situations of harrassment of the disciples:

"Blessed are you, if they revile you, persecute you and speak all kinds of evil against you [provided they are lying] because of me." Numerous textual variants indicate that the text has been tampered with, but if we accept Nestle-Aland (26th edition) as the original text, the question is, what kind of christology could be implied in it? The statement is a factual description of three situations of harrassment. It is the persecutors who are said to turn against the disciples "because of Jesus." In other words, Jesus is the pretext and motivation for the opponents to persecute the disciples. The phrase "because of me" characterizes their prejudice, not a christological affirmation. This passage is, therefore, not to be seen at the same level as its parallels, especially in Matt 10:17-18, 39, or those expanding "because of me" into "because of me and the gospel" (Mark 8:35; 10:29).[10] While the phrase "because of me" does not motivate the disciples to endure the harrassment, Matt 5:12 does: As persecuted the disciples stand in the tradition of the persecution of the prophets of old. As these received their reward, so can the disciples if they suffer the same persecutions. It is simply a matter of equal justice. This motivation is Jewish, a fact

---

(5:20). Jesus' authority for doing this is not, we think, based on a special commission as messiah, but on the "will of God" and the "righteousness of God" (6:10, 33; 7:21), guiding the interpretation of the Torah (5:17-20; 7:12) and its proper observance.

In contrast Matthew's framework and interpretation assume that as a teacher Jesus was endowed with a special personal authority (5:1-2; 7:28-29), which is identical with Matthew's christology (see 3:13-17; 4:1-11; 9:6, 8; 10:1; 21:23-27; 28:18-20). This christology must not be read back into the SM as is often done; see, e.g., Eduard Schweizer, "Jesus Christus I. Im Neuen Testament," TRE 16 (1987):671-726, 701, lines 23-24: "Jesus ist in gewisser Weise das Gesetz selbst, also sein Lehrer in nicht mehr überbietbarer Weise." Similarly 723, line 43 on Jesus as "der Mann, der alle Schemata sprengt." Rather, that Jesus' authority is the Torah can also be seen from the fact that Christian teachers who disregard it (5:19; 7:21-23) are subsumed under the category of false prophets (7:15-20).

[10]Differently Graham N. Stanton, "The Origin and Purpose of Matthew's Sermon on the Mount," in: *Tradition and Interpretation in the New Testament. Essays in Honor of E. Earle Ellis for his 60th Birthday,* ed. Gerald F. Hawthorne with Otto Betz (Grand Rapids: Eerdmans, 1987), 181-92, 187: "5:11 presupposes that disciples will have been persecuted on account of their commitment to the person of Jesus (ἕνεκεν ἐμοῦ)." Stanton takes this to imply a christology. See also his review of my *Essays* in *JThS* 37 (1986): 521-23. Cf. Schlatter's interpretation, cited below, n. 31.

that is evident in comparison with its parallel in 1 Thess 2:14-16, where the persecution of Jesus is also mentioned, so that persecuted Christians appear as imitators of the prophets as well as of Jesus. By contrast Matt 5:11-12 has no reference to Jesus' persecution. Consequently, there is neither an implied christology nor room for one.

(2) Another passage which is believed to contain an implied christology is Matt 5:17-20. In this passage Jesus is seen to "fulfill" the law by setting aside, abolishing or "breaking with" the law of Moses. Such claims would indeed imply a christology of messianic authority. This interpretation has, however, been shown to be wrong.[11] We must assume, rather, that opponents have accused Jesus of abolishing the Torah and that the SM tried to clear Jesus of such an accusation. From this perspective the section 5:17-48 is apologetic and attempts to prove that Jesus' interpretation was "orthodox" in Jewish terms. If Jesus interpreted the Torah according to its intent and not in literal terms, this interpretation cannot be misconstrued as abolishing the Torah.[12] As the so-called "antitheses" demonstrate in six cases (5:21-48), God's intent in the Torah is to make it serve his superior justice

---

[11] See my *Essays*, 37-53, and in greater detail my commentary on the SM and the Sermon on the Plain (presently in preparation). I am in agreement here with Burchard, "Bergpredigt," 433: "Jesus selber kam, um Gesetz und Propheten zu erfüllen, nämlich ohne Abstrich oder Zutat zu tun und zu lehren (nicht: zu vollenden oder zu überbieten)." Differently Otto Betz, "Bergpredigt und Sinaitradition. Zur Gliederung und zum Hintergrund von Matthäus 5 7," in his *Jesus der Messias Israels. Aufsätze zur biblischen Theologie* (Tübingen: J.C.B. Mohr [Paul Siebeck], 1987), 333-84. For Betz the SM is the authentic teaching of the messiah Jesus who fulfills the Torah of the eschatological Son of Man as predicted in Isa 56:1. Jesus is more than an ordinary teacher and even exceeds Moses on Mount Sinai; he reveals himself as the messiah and Son of Man. Similar, but somewhat different is the view of Martin Hengel, "Zur matthäischen Bergpredigt und ihrem jüdischen Hintergrund," *ThR* 52 (1987): 327-400. For Hengel, Matthew is a Jewish-Christian scribe, the composer of the SM, for whom Jesus is the Messiah and Son of God revealing the will of God and figuring as the antitype of Moses's revelation of the Torah on Mt. Sinai. In order to portray Jesus in this way, Matthew has used numerous traditions going back to Jesus himself. For Hengel, therefore, Jesus' self-understanding and Matthew's christology are basically the same, and all of it is within the pluralistic Judaism of the first century.

[12] Differently Stanton, "The Origin," 187-88; Charles E. Carlston, "Betz on the Sermon on the Mount - A Critique," *CBQ* 50 (1988):47-57, esp. 53-55. Both critics, however, simply insist on the traditional viewpoint which they take to be that of Ernst Käsemann, "The Problem of the Historical Jesus," in his *Essays on New Testament Themes*, SBT 41 (London: SCM, 1964), 15-47, esp. 37-38. See also Ulrich Luz, *Das Evangelium nach Matthäus*, vol. 1 (Neukirchen-Vluyn: Neukirchener Verlag; Zürich: Benziger Verlag, 1985), 230-36.

(5:20), not merely a lower justice of compliance with the letter. This debate of interpretation by intent versus literal interpretation must be seen against the background of legal debates current at the time.[13] There is no need to resort to a christology at this point. Rather it has always been the task of teachers of the law to see to it that justice prevails in the application of the law (5:21-48), the performance of the cult (6:1-18), and general morality (6:19-7:12). Refutations of inadequate interpretations of the law must not be confused with abolishing the law, although there is a long line of such confusion.[14] John Calvin, a lawyer himself, understood very well that the SM simply discussed the doctrine of the law and the facilitation of justice.[15]

(3) Christological implications have also been seen in the Lord's Prayer (6:9b-13). Joachim Jeremias,[16] in particular, maintained that Jesus' address of God as Father implies his self-understanding as God's son. His invocation of God as *abba*, according to Jeremias, expresses a uniquely intimate relationship with his Father which gave rise to the Son of God christology.[17]

---

[13] Again I must refer to my commentary for the evidence in detail.

[14] The same issues are at stake in the accusations against Paul. Even though Paul in effect says that Christ is the end of the law (Gal 3:23-25; Rom 10:4), this does not make him an antinomian (cf. Gal 2:17; 1 Cor 9:19-23; Rom 3:5-8; 6:1-2; Acts 15:2; 21:28; 23:7, 10; 24:5-6; etc.). Paul claims merely to have a better interpretation of the Torah than he had as a Pharisee (cf. Gal 5:3; 2:19a); his present interpretation supposedly agrees with Jesus (Gal 5:14; 6:2; Rom 13:8-10). Also Paul affirms the Torah (Rom 7:12, 14-16), but in quite different terms as compared with the SM.

[15] See Heinrich Julius Holtzmann, *Die synoptischen Evangelien, ihr Ursprung und geschichtlicher Charakter* (Leipzig: Engelmann, 1863), 174; Dieter Schellong, *Das evangelische Gesetz in der Auslegung Calvins*, ThExH 152 (München: Kaiser, 1968); idem, *Calvins Auslegung der synoptischen Evangelien*, Forschungen zur Geschichte und Lehre des Protestantismus, 10:38 (München: Kaiser, 1969). Cf. on Luther's interpretation Gerhard Ebeling, *Evangelische Evangelienauslegung. Eine Untersuchung zu Luthers Hermeneutik*, Forschungen zur Geschichte und Lehre des Protestantismus, 10:1 (München: Lempp [Kaiser], 1942), 261-69.

[16] Joachim Jeremias, *Abba. Studien zur neutestamentlichen Christologie und Zeitgeschichte* (Göttingen: Vandenhoeck & Ruprecht, 1966), 15-67, esp. 63-67; idem, *Neutestamentliche Theologie*, Teil I: *Die Verkündigung Jesu* (Gütersloh: Mohn, 2^{1973}), 67-73. On Jeremias see James Barr, " Abba Isn't 'Daddy,'" *JThS* 39 (1988):28-47. See also Ulrich Luz, *Das Evangelium nach Matthäus*, 1.339-41.

[17] See also Carsten Colpe, "Gottessohn," *RAC* 12 (1983):19-58, esp. 41-42; Hans Dieter Betz, "Gottmensch II (Griechisch-römische Antike und Urchristentum)," *RAC* 12 (1983):234-312, esp. 288-90.

The problem is, however, that the Lord's Prayer in the SM does not use *abba*,[18] but the Greek "Our Father."[19] This address, interpreted in conjunction with the frequent phrase "your father who is in the heavens" assumes that God is the Father of all human beings, including Jesus himself. Only once (7:21) does Jesus speak of God as "my Father who is in the heavens."[20] In the SM at least Jesus includes himself as equal with his disciples when he refers to them as "sons of God."[21] The SM, therefore, emphasizes the inclusiveness, not the exclusiveness of the Father-son relationship. This relationship is also different from Paul, for whom Christian sonship is a derivative of Christ's sonship.[22] Matthew the evangelist shows Jesus as the redeemer and Son of God in a unique sense,[23] but he betrays no further interest in calling the Christian believers "sons of God."[24] The SM is at this point different from Matthew's theology.

(4) Heinz Schürmann has interpreted the second petition of the Lord's Prayer, "Your kingdom come," and indeed all petitions of Jesus' prayer as implying a christology.[25] Accordingly, Jesus proclaimed the eschatological kingdom of God as being at hand. This then is said to mean that as eschatological salvation it is paradoxically present in Jesus' own conduct and destiny ("Geschick").

"Jesus understood the proclaimed kingdom, upon which he looked forward, on the basis of his unique relationship with God manifest in his looking upward as 'theologized'; this relationship with God is also (if one may say so) 'eschatological' in the sense that he connected it with his own destiny in the kingdom."[26]

---

[18]The difference is not to be minimized; see Luz, *Matthäus*, 1.341; Barr, "Abba," passim.
[19]See Matt 5:16, 45, 48; 6:1, 8, 14, 15, 26, 32; 7:11.
[20]Cf. "your (singular) Father" 6:4, 6, 18.
[21]See 5:9, 45; cf. 7:9.
[22]See Gal 3:7, 26-28; 4:4-6; etc. See Betz, *Galatians, ad loc.*
[23]See Matt 3:17; 4:3, 6; 8:29; 11:27; etc.
[24]Cf. 28:19: Christians are to be baptized "in the name of the Father and of the Son and of the Holy Spirit," but they are called "disciples," not "sons."
[25]Heinz Schürmann, *Das Gebet des Herrn als Schlüssel zum Verstehen Jesu* (Freiburg, Basel, Wien: Herder, [4]1981), 135-55: "Eine theologische Meditation über das 'eigentümlich Jesuanische' im Gebet Jesu."
[26]Schürmann, *Gebet*, 152: "Jesus verstand das verkündete Reich, auf das er ausblickte, von dem einzigartigen Gottesverhältnis seines Aufblicks her 'theologisiert' und dieses sein Gottesverhältnis (wenn man so sagen darf) 'eschatologisch' von seinem 'Basileia-Geschick' her."

Whatever the christological perspective thus described may be, one will have to say that it is formulated retrospectively. The mere expectation of the kingdom of God—even one's own involvement in it—does not as such imply a christology.

(5) Finally the title "Lord" (κύριος) is used in addressing Jesus in the episode of the last judgment (7:21-23).[27] While the use of the title certainly presupposes a christology, it is a christology which the Jesus of the SM rejects. He ridicules the devotion of gentile Christians who approach him by calling him "Lord, Lord!" (κύριε, κύριε) and who boast of spiritual achievements as benefits of their salvation. The fact is, however, that these Christians are refused by Jesus[28] because deluded by their christology they have neglected to "do the will of my Father who is in the heavens" and thus have become "workers of lawlessness" (7:23). They have been misled by false teachers (cf. 5:19; 7:15-20) to believe that a *kyrios*-christology can be a valid substitute for the teaching of Jesus concerning the Torah (cf. 5:19-20; 7:15-20, 24-27).

In conclusion, the SM not only lacks any christological affirmations, but even rejects those Christians who profess to have a *kyrios*-christology. In fact, there is no room for a christology in the SM. All that is needed for salvation and approval in the last judgment is hearing and doing the sayings of Jesus as contained in the SM because these sayings sum up his authentic interpretation of the Torah.[29]

---

[27]See my *Essays*, 125-57.

[28]In my *Essays*, esp. 151-54, I have attempted to show with considerable evidence that in the passage Matt 7:21-23 Jesus does not figure as judge but as advocate of his disciples. In their rebuttals, both Stanton ("The Origin," 188) and Carlston ("Betz," 54-55) rather quickly pass over this evidence. Admitting that there may be a difference here between the SM and Matthew's christology (cf. Matt 25:31-46) would of course jeopardize their theory of Matthean authorship of the SM. Their treatment is typical of those redaction-critics who interpret the theology of the evangelist into his sources and call this harmonisation sound method. Careful distinction between the theology of the sources and of the final redactor should, however, be one of the ground-rules of redaction-criticism.

[29]Part of this interpretation of the Torah is the doctrine of the forgiveness of sins (5:24; 6:12, 14-15). A petition to God is sufficient, and no sacrificial act on the part of Jesus is referred to. Again, this points to a difference between the SM and Matthew's soteriology (cf. Matt 20:28). Differently, Carlston, "Betz," 54 who uses 20:28 to contradict my interpretation of 5:17.

- II -

Adolf Schlatter's popular book *Der Einzige und wir anderen*, published in 1929, includes a chapter entitled "Das Bild Jesu nach der Bergpredigt" ("The Image of Jesus according to the SM").[30] Unassuming as this chapter is, it does present a highly important concept which could explain the absence of christology in the SM. Schlatter's keen eyes have of course detected this lack of christology. Taking it as a fact he simply sets out to explain it.[31]

Schlatter proceeds from a notion that has been around in New Testament scholarship for some time, the notion of the "image of Jesus."[32] As Schlatter puts it: As readers of the New Testament we carry within us the image of Jesus. In order that this image be protected against perturbation and confusion, the evangelists have done us the great service of preserving literarily that image which Jesus

---

[30] Adolf Schlatter, *Der Einzige und wir anderen* (Velbert: Freizeiten-Verlag, 1929), 149-62.

[31] When Schlatter first presented these ideas in his article "Die Christologie der Bergpredigt," *Der Kirchenfreund* (Basel) 13 (1879) 321-28, he regarded a christology as indispensable for the understanding of the SM (321, 327-28). In his later popular commentary, *Die Gabe des Christus, Eine Auslegung der Bergpredigt* (Velbert: Freizeiten-Verlag, 1928), he had changed his mind. According to this commentary, Jesus did not reveal a christology in the SM. Rather, Jesus glorified his Father through the gift he gave to the disciples (p. 5): "He made his disciples into people who hope." ("Er machte seine Jünger zu Hoffenden.") Different again is Schlatter's position in his *Der Evangelist Matthäus. Seine Sprache, sein Ziel, seine Selbständigkeit* (Stuttgart: Calwer Verlag, [6]1963 [[1]1929]), esp. 125-28, 130-31, 142, 198. In this last work Schlatter remains vague as to whether the SM is a work of Matthew (125, 130) or a pre-Matthean source (128, 142, 198). Does the SM have a christology (146) or not (143: the phrase 5:11 "for my sake" means "for God's sake")? He suggests that the universalism of 5:13 implies messianism and hence christology, but this he calls the "paradox" of "Jesus' self-consciousness" (146). On Schlatter's theology see Gottfried Egg, *Adolf Schlatters kritische Position, gezeigt an seiner Matthäusinterpretation*, Arbeiten zur Theologie 2:14 (Stuttgart: Calwer Verlag, 1968).

[32] It should be noted that even before Wilhelm Herrmann, *Der Verkehr des Christen mit Gott, im Anschluss an Luther dargestellt* (Stuttgart: Cotta, [5.6]1908), esp. 67-96, and Martin Kähler, *Der sogenannte historische Jesus und der geschichtliche biblische Christus* (Leipzig: Deichert, [3]1928), esp. 57-71, 99-114, the concept of the image of Jesus *(Bild Jesu)* played an important role in 18th and 19th century scholarship. Actually, as Eric Osborn has pointed out to me (*Ethical Patterns in Early Christian Thought*: [Cambridge: Cambridge University Press, 1976], 198), the concept of the image of Jesus goes back at least as far as Erasmus.

himself implanted in his disciples through his words which he entrusted to them. The benefit and purpose of reading the gospels is that as readers we can compare our image of Jesus with the one preserved in the gospels to make sure that ours remains "sober and true."[33]

This notion of the "image of Jesus" has played an important role in New Testament scholarship, but Schlatter does not indicate whether he is aware of it and which sources he has used to inform himself about it. Schlatter's reticence is unfortunate given the notion's wider applications.[34] It is well known from literary criticism generally that texts are capable of creating literary portraits of persons in readers.[35] One of the ways of creating such portraits is indirect, by speaking about someone else or even about the reader himself. The portrait intended then appears as a mirror-image of the one described. This concept is the one employed by Schlatter. "Which image of himself did Jesus give to his own at that time?" Schlatter asks.[36] The answer is that Jesus did not portray himself directly. Instead:

"Every word he spoke to his own at that time contributes to our question, even though he spoke about his work with his disciples only in such a way that he showed them what he made of them. He spoke with them of their calling, of what he enabled them to be. He gave them his commandments."[37]

His commandment, in turn, reveals his will and intent. "What he laid upon us as duties is alive in him as will and truth. By drawing for us the image of the disciple, as Jesus wants him to be, his own

---

[33]Schlatter, *Der Einzige*, 149: ". . .dass wir dasselbe mit dem zusammenhalten, was Jesus auf Erden gewesen ist, damit es nüchtern und wahr bleibe." For the importance of vision (*"Schakt"*) in Schlatter's theology see Egg, *Adolf Schlatters kritische Position*, 21-36, 115-21, also 88-89, 111.

[34]See Gustav Bebermeyer, "Literarische und bildende Kunst," *Reallexikon der deutschen Literaturgeschichte* 2 (1965), 82-103, esp. 102-03; Johannes Kollwitz, "Christusbild," *RAC* 3 (1957), 1-24; Hermann Funke, "Götterbild," *RAC* 11 (1981), 659-828, esp. 778-79 on "Götterbild und Christusbild."

[35]See the imaginative work by Bernard Frischer, *The Sculpted Word. Epicureanism and Philosophical Recruitment in Ancient Greece* (Berkeley & Los Angeles: University of California Press, 1982).

[36]Schlatter, *Der Einzige*, 149: "Welches Bild gab Jesus den Seinigen damals von sich selbst?"

[37]Ibid.: "Jedes Wort, das er damals zu den Seinigen sprach, gibt auch für unsere Frage einen Beitrag, obwohl er über sein eigenes Werk nur so mit den Jüngern sprach, dass er ihnen zeigte, was er aus ihnen macht. Er sprach mit ihnen von ihrem Beruf, von dem, wozu er sie tüchtig macht. Er gab ihnen sein Gebot."

way is communicated to us."[38] In other words, in the SM Jesus draws a character portrait of the true disciple, as he wants him to be. Schlatter is no doubt right that the SM intends to create such a character type in the minds of the readers. Thus the entire SM is engaged in character or ethos formation as it was understood in hellenistic education. If readers identify with this character type, the goal of the SM is achieved. In the text, the character type is represented positively by the "prudent man" as over against the "foolish man" (7:24-27), and the ethos by the Two Ways pattern (7:13-14). These types and patterns are presupposed throughout the SM. This image of the true and faithful disciple then is the mirror image of the master himself who presumably embodies the same virtues and character qualities. This mirror image reflects not only Jesus' own beliefs but also his way of life. This, Schlatter goes on to say, could be demonstrated from many other synoptic texts outside the SM.

What kind of picture does the SM draw? In Schlatter's view, it is a profoundly paradoxical picture: "It is an overwhelming power which is made visible here. Its measure is the total renunciation of every external means of power."[39] Contrary to the world which needs money for its activities of war, propaganda, briberies, and so forth, the Jesus who spoke with his disciples about the issues of money renounced it.[40] He also renounced all external means of publicity, name, fame, glory and splendor. Whereas in the world the greater one's gifts the higher one's rights and privileges are, Jesus, who has the rights of a king, lord and son, renounces such rights and privileges. He preaches abandonment of retaliation (5:38-42), violence (5:43-48), judgment (7:1-5) and other acts of power. The way of discipleship is the yielding of power, "inexhaustible and abundant" patience.[41] The cause and origin of such a demand is that Jesus himself possessed these qualities: "He himself was willing to endure tirelessly and without limit."[42] As a leader of his disciples Jesus acted contrary to worldly standards. "He did not present himself to them as the mighty shep-

---

[38]Ibid., 149-50: "Was er als Sollen uns auferlegt, ist in ihm als Wille und Wahrheit lebendig. Indem Jesus das Bild des Jüngers zeichnet, wie er ihn haben will, wird uns sein eigener Weg wahrnehmbar."

[39]Ibid., 150: "Es ist eine überwältigende Macht, die uns hier sichtbar wird. Ihr Mass ist der völlige Verzicht auf alle äusseren Mittel der Macht."

[40]Ibid., 150-52.

[41]Ibid., 152: "jene unerschöpfliche und überschüssige Geduld."

[42]Ibid.: ". . .weil er selbst zum unbegrenzten Dulden mit unermüdlicher Tatkraft willig war."

herd and protector who safeguards his flock against every form of danger and who surrounds them with peace and security."[43] Instead he renounced life for himself.

"In all firmness he denied life for himself and demanded the same from his disciples."[44] "'Blessed are you, if they persecute you.' When the disciples are being harrassed and chased away and if their way runs along the rim of death, then where is he? When the disciples are persecuted, he had become the first victim of death. On earth Jesus saw no room for himself and therefore prepared himself from the beginning for death."[45]

This picture is surely different from the popular ones showing Jesus "with a sunny disposition, full of high-flying ideals and moved by the most splendid of hopes, until then in the struggle with brutal reality the shadow of the cross fell on him."[46] Such a Jesus picture, Schlatter warns us, is a false one, "child's play, even if dressed up with a scholarly costume."[47] Those who knew Jesus have spoken differently. "They have told us that he prepared himself and his disciples for suffering and death from the beginning."[48]

Jesus' greatest sacrifice was that he who had the greatest calling possible gave up success and achievement in carrying out what he was called to do. "While they (sc. the disciples) looked up to him with the faithful expectation that glory would come forth from him which would lighten up the world, and power which would renew the earth," he gave it all up and left it to them: "It is you; I cannot be

---

[43] Ibid.: "Er hat sich ihnen nicht als der mächtige Hirte und Schirmherr dargestellt, der seine Herde vor jeder Gefahr beschützt und mit Frieden und Sicherheit umringt."

[44] Ibid.: "Er hat vielmehr mit aller Bestimmtheit auch auf das Leben Verzicht geleistet und dieses auch von seinen Jüngern verlangt."

[45] Ibid.: "'Selig seid ihr, wenn sie euch verfolgen.' Wenn die Jünger gehetzt und verjagt sind und ihr Weg sie am Rand des Todes vorbeiführt, wo ist er dann? Werden die Jünger verfolgt, so ist er zuerst des Todes Raub geworden. Jesus sah auf Erden keinen Raum für sich und hat sich von Anfang an zum Sterben willig gemacht."

[46] Ibid., 152-53: "In unserer Literatur ist ein Christusbild verbreitet worden, das ihn in seinen Anfängen als ein sonniges Gemüt beschreibt, von hohen Idealen erfüllt und von den herrlichsten Hoffnungen bewegt, bis dann im Streit mit der rauhen Wirklichkeit der Schatten des Kreuzes auf ihn fiel."

[47] Ibid., 153: "Das sind Kindereien, auch wenn sie sich mit einem wissenschaftlichen Kleide schmücken."

[48] Ibid.: "Sie haben uns gesagt, dass er sich und seine Jünger von Anfang an zum Leiden und Sterben bereitgemacht hat."

the one, I can be it only through you."⁴⁹ But they are only a small group: "He declared to his disciples that they must be able to be lonely."⁵⁰ Jesus also gave up his success in regard to the church.

"We would expect that he comforted himself that by having brought together only a small circle of disciples, he created something perfect, so that the intensity of his impact could compensate for what was missing in terms of expansion and magnitude. If he was able only to assemble a small community, it was at least a pure community!"⁵¹

Such an idea would however simply be an accommodation to worldly standards. Therefore: "The illusion of a pure community, however, did not enter into Jesus' mind."⁵² Instead he predicted false prophets and teachers (7:15-20, 21-23; cf. 5:19). "Thus, even in regard to his own circle of disciples Jesus gave up the idea to lead and rule them alone, so that they would only be filled with and shaped by his own endowment. Even among his own his work is being defiled and disturbed."⁵³

This leads to the deeper reason why there is no christology in the SM: Jesus had deliberately and in principle renounced it. As any good teacher he simply practiced what he taught. Making no claims about himself corresponds to the demand of self-denial and renunciation of money, name, power, rights and privileges, security and success. Yet, paradoxically, what appeared to be the absence of christology in the SM, *is* its christology. This is Schlatter's startling conclusion. In order to make it more plausible, he refers to the *kenosis* concept in Paul's doctrine about Christ: "He emptied himself" (Phil 2:7), and "He became poor" (2 Cor 8:9). Thus: "He presented himself to his

---

⁴⁹Ibid.: "Ihr seid es; ich kann es nicht sein, ich bin es nicht anders als durch euch."

⁵⁰Ibid., 154: "Er hat seinen Jüngern erklärt, sie müssten imstande sein, einsam zu sein."

⁵¹Ibid.: "Wir könnten erwarten, dass er sich über die engen Grenzen seines Erfolges damit tröste, dass er doch in seinem eigenen kleinen Kreis etwas Vollkommenes schaffe, so dass die Intensität seiner Wirkung einen gewissen Ersatz böte für das, was ihr an Weite und Grösse fehlt. Kann er auch nur eine kleine Gemeinde bilden, so wird sie doch eine reine Gemeinde sein!"

⁵²Ibid.: "Aber die Illusion einer reinen Gemeinde kam nicht in Jesu Sinn."

⁵³Ibid., 154-55: "So hat Jesus auch im Blick auf seinen eigenen Jüngerkreis darauf verzichtet, ihn allein führen und regieren zu können, so dass er nur mit dem erfüllt und durch das gestaltet wäre, was Jesu Gabe ist. Sein Werk wird auch unter den Seinigen durch fremde Hände befleckt und gestört."

disciples in his Sermon on the Mount as the one who divested himself,"[54] that is to say: he divested himself of a christology.

At this point Schlatter turns things around. "This is the revelation of his power."[55] Renunciation and self-denial are not the marks of weakness, but the signs of power. "Indeed, next to every No stands a Yes, next to every denial an attainment, next to the depth of lowliness the ascension to majesty."[56]

Jesus' real power is shown by facts. He who is without means lacks nothing: "Everything that he and his disciples need will be given to them."[57] According to Schlatter, 6:25-34 means that "He does not feel an alien, misplaced within nature, but he is at home in it as in his Father's property."[58] The man who can speak about the birds and the lilies as Jesus does is a rich man: "There he stands, the man of wealth, who has everything he needs for his work because he has the Almighty as his Father, and for this reason he is also entitled to offer the promise to his disciples: 'Everyone who asks receives.'"[59] (7:8). Schlatter then goes on to interpret the SM by way of Paul's so-called "antitheses" or paradoxes (cf. 1 Cor 4:11-13; 2 Cor 6:4-10; 11:7-10, 23-27; 12:10). Accordingly, renunciation of rights complies with God's rights; it is the rule of love because love means giving.[60] As a result, Schlatter can declare that Jesus' self-denial of a christology in the SM is in fact the revelation of his perfect love. It is through his love that he pronounces the beatitudes. As clear and uncompromising as these promises are, their giver remains in the background.

"The giver disappears, but the gift is there. He steps back into hiddenness, like the root burying itself in the ground but producing as the fruitbearing plant the community which he can address with the words: 'You are the light of the world' and 'You are the salt of the

---

[54]Ibid., 155: "Als der, der sich selbst entäusserte, trat er mit der Bergpredigt vor seine Jünger hin."

[55]Ibid.: "Das ist die Offenbarung seiner Macht."

[56]Ibid.: "Aber hier steht neben jedem Nein ein Ja, neben jedem Verzicht ein Erwerb, neben der Tiefe der Beugung die Auffahrt zur Erhabenheit."

[57]Ibid., 155-56: "Es fehlt ihm nichts; alles, was er und die Seinigen bedürfen, wird ihnen gegeben: 'Es wird euch hinzugetan werden'" (Matt 6:33).

[58]Ibid., 156: "Er fühlt sich in der Natur nicht fremd, sondern heimisch, weil dies alles seines Vaters Eigentum ist."

[59]Ibid.: "So steht er da als der reiche Mann, der alles hat, was er zu seinem Werk bedarf, weil er den Allmächtigen zum Vater hat, und darum ist er auch für seine Jünger zu der Verheissung ermächtigt: 'Jeder, der bittet, der empfängt.'"

[60]Ibid., 156-58.

earth.' Through them his illuminating and renewing power penetrates the world. He merely withdraws, in order to lift up his disciples as equipped to be bearers of grace for the world."[61]

Therefore, Jesus' obscurity in the SM is intimately tied up with his communion with his disciples. The passage 7:21-23 is a testimony to the eternal communion of Jesus and his faithful who do the will of his heavenly Father. "Wherein then lies the ground of Jesus' power, the basis of his ability to practice renunciation?"[62] The answer is again gained by a mirror reflection. The continuous references in the SM to God culminate in the commendation to serve God (6:24), and, therefore: "It is Jesus who serves God exclusively and completely."[63]

"In his Sermon on the Mount Jesus has told his disciples that it is God who forms and guides him. From God he attains everything, will and aim, power and success. Thus Jesus presents himself to his disciples as the one who receives his identity from God, is formed by God, and made complete by God."[64]

This is Jesus' power and authority which makes possible his renunciation of the world, including even the renunciation of christology. "Because Jesus' place is in God, it cannot, for that reason, be in the world; because he has his power from above, he cannot, for consistency's sake, seek it from below."[65] As Schlatter's meditation draws to its close, it more and more resorts to Paul's christology. He must admit that the doctrine of reconciliation through the blood of Christ is "not yet stated"[66] in the SM. But at least the question has been raised to which the cross will be the answer. In the SM, accord-

---

[61]Ibid., 158-59: "Der Geber verschwindet, aber die Gabe ist da. Er tritt in die Verborgenheit wie die Wurzel, die sich in den Boden senkt, aber sie erzeugt als ihr fruchtbringendes Gewächs die Gemeinde, der Jesus sagen darf: Ihr seid das Licht der Welt, ihr seid das Salz der Erde. Durch sie hindurch dringt seine erleuchtende und erneuernde Kraft in die Welt hinein. Er tritt nur so zurück, dass er seinen Jünger emporhebt als ausgerüstet zum Träger der Gnade für die Welt."

[62]Ibid., 159: "Was gibt uns die Bergpredigt für eine Antwort, wenn wir nach dem Grunde seiner Macht fragen, und nach dem Grunde, weshalb sie Jesus durch die Entsagung hindurch gewinnt und übt?"

[63]Ibid., 160: "Jesus dient ausschliesslich Gott."

[64]Ibid.: "Jesus hat mit seiner Bergpredigt seinen Jüngern gesagt, dass Gott es sei, der ihn gestalte und führe, aus dem er alles schöpfe und empfange, Willen und Ziel, Kraft und Erfolg. Als der durch Gott Bestimmte, von Gott Gebildete, durch Gott Erfüllte stellte er sich seinen Jüngern dar."

[65]Ibid., 161: "Weil Jesus seinen Standort in Gott hat, hat er ihn eben deswegen nicht in der Welt; weil er seine Macht von oben hat, kann er sie folgerichtig nicht unten suchen."

[66]Ibid.: ". . .in der Bergpredigt noch nicht ausgesprochen. . ."

ing to Schlatter, Jesus "represents God's law and God's grace simultaneously." "And even in the Sermon on the Mount Jesus speaks as the reconciler, just as later on the cross he acted as the reconciler."[67]

- III -

Despite its brevity and popular character, Schlatter's essay contains a number of brilliant ideas in need of further elaboration. This cannot be done at this point, but we will confine ourselves to a few considerations.

The idea that a text is designed in such a way that it indirectly creates a portrait of its author in the minds of the readers is in fact a literary device of enormous potential and importance for the gospel traditions. The portraits of Jesus generated by the gospel texts in the minds of the readers are indeed expressions of christologies: the christologies of the texts themselves, and the christologies of the readers. In the case of Schlatter, the image of Jesus he sees in the mirror of the SM is a mixture of what the text intends to communicate and of what Schlatter's own christology contributes. This phenomenon can also be amply documented from book art, where portraits of Jesus always conform to what was thought about Jesus at the time when the picture was drawn, despite the artist's familiarity with texts.

Schlatter's essay also contains a hypothesis concerning the origin of christology. Accordingly, Jesus refrained from making christological statements about himself by choice, not out of ignorance. As all good teachers do, he impressed his image into the minds and the memories of his disciples by letting the subject matter to be taught have the center stage. Only the poor teacher gets excited about himself; only the false teacher teaches himself. Jesus left it to his followers to conclude that he himself was what he taught. Jesus let the church work out these ideas and formulate christologies. This was a much more appropriate and effective method of revelation than engaging in what no doubt would have been taken as self-aggrandizement.

When we apply this idea to the SM, we must do so in terms different from Schlatter. We cannot, as he did, regard the SM as more or

---

[67]Ibid., 162: "Er vertritt Gottes Recht und Gottes Gnade zugleich. . .Er redet schon in der Bergpredigt als der Versöhnende, wie er nachher am Kreuz als der Versöhnende gehandelt hat."

less coming straight from the historical Jesus. The SM is a creation of the early Jewish-Christian church. Nevertheless, Schlatter was right in assuming that the SM intends to create a portrait of the teacher Jesus in the minds of the disciples, and that it accomplishes this goal indirectly by describing the faithful disciple, with whom the readers are to identify.

The portrait thus created, however, does not require explanation in terms of Paul's christology. At this point Schlatter even contradicts himself. If Jesus is the mirror picture of the faithful disciple, the relationship would follow the rule "As the master, so the pupil" (cf. Matt 10:24-25). Consequently, the portrait of Jesus would be that of the righteous teacher and prudent man (cf. 5:17-20; 7:24-26). Such a teacher can be expected with reason to serve as the advocate of his faithful followers in the last judgment (7:21-23). None of these propositions requires a Pauline christology, nor any other sort of christology; all of them are consistent with Jewish theological presuppositions. The portrait of Jesus in the SM, therefore, is non-christological, if christology presupposes the faith in Christ's crucifixion and resurrection as a saving event.

This non-christological portrait of Jesus is all the more remarkable, if the author of the SM is not Jesus himself but the early Jewish-Christian church. This church, as represented by the author(s) of the SM, intended a non-christological portrait of the master no doubt because they themselves held it in their minds. Confronted with existing gentile-Christian christology (cf. 7:21-23), the SM even insists on this non-christological portrait. This insistence must have special reasons. If we date the composition of the SM in the years around 50 A.D., the absence of a christology in the SM cannot be the result of not knowing a christology.[68] Other texts from the same period show

---

[68]In his perceptive review of my *Essays*, JR 67 (1987), 87-89, Ed P. Sanders raised two questions of importance for our problem. The first is, whether, given the literary genre of the SM, there is "reason to think that it therefore contains every idea important to its community." (89) In other words, there may be christological ideas, such as Jesus' death as atonement, held by the community but not stated in the SM. However, if the SM contains what is regarded as essential for the disciples to know, then a christology, if it were considered as such, would certainly be included. Also, there is no hint whatsoever in the text that a christology is presupposed or necessary. Jewish theology with its soteriology is fully sufficient. By contrast, it is Matthew, outside of the SM, who is explicit about christology and soteriology in a Christian sense of the terms. Sanders' second question has to do with the cause for the separation of Christianity and Judaism. If the SM has no christology, then why was there the split between Christianity

that christologies had developed by this time.[69] Therefore, the author(s) of the SM must have refused to develop a higher christology, rather than being simply ignorant of its possibility. If we ask about the reasons for such a refusal we are of course operating in the realm of speculation. Yet, some clues are worth considering. One of the reasons certainly was that the author(s) did not remember a Jesus other than the non-christological teacher of the Torah. This was the way he was, and this is the way he should be presented to the disciples learning the precepts of his teaching.

Another reason why christology was avoided may have had to do with the genre and function of the SM. When the group of Christian believers approach Jesus in the eschatological episode described in 7:21-23 they do so because they rely on their kyrios-christology and what they take to be soteriological benefits (prophecy, exorcisms, miracles). Trusting in this christology, however, was only the other side of their failure to do the will of the Father, as the SM understands it. Christological confidence, therefore, was the cause of their self-deception. That is to say, it is the nature of believing that

---

and Judaism? The answer is that according to the SM there is indeed no reason for a split. The persecution of the disciples (Matt 5:11-12) is caused by a false interpretation of Jesus' Torah interpretation (5:17-20). The SM tries to correct these misconceptions and refers as precedents to the persecution of the prophets of old (5:12). The eschatological scene (7:21-23) shows that the split is thought to come not between Christianity and Judaism but between Jesus' faithful disciples (i.e., faithful Jews) and gentile Christianity. Unfaithful Jews will be condemned, of course, as references to the tradition indicate (see 5:20, 26, 29, 30; 6:14-15; 7:1-2, 19, 21-23).

[69]The question of the christology of the SM is made more complicated by the Sermon on the Plain (Luke 6:20b-49). This passage (Luke 6:22) refers to the Son of Man: "for the sake of the Son of Man" (cf. Matt 5:11: "for my sake"), but does not identify Jesus with this eschatological figure (cf. Luke 7:34; 9:58). The question of this text is related to whether or not it was part of Q, sharing its christological views. The problem of the christology of Q, however, is equally vexed, so that no decision can be made. As far as I am concerned, the Sermon on the Plain existed first apart from Q and its reference to the Son of Man must be seen on its own terms first. This does not exclude secondary incorporation of the Sermon on the Plain into Q Luke, just as the SM was included into Q Matt. See also Athanasius Polag, *Die Christologie der Logienquelle*, WMANT 45 (Neukirchen-Vluyn: Neukirchener Verlag, 1977); Eduard Schweizer, "Jesus Christus I. Neues Testament," *TRE* 16 (1987), 671-726, esp. 697-98; John S. Kloppenborg, "Symbolic Eschatology and the Apocalypticism of Q," *HTR* 80 (1987), 287-306; Adela Yarbro Collins, "The Origin of the Designation of Jesus as 'Son of Man,'" *HTR* 80 (1987), 391-407; Migaku Sato, *Q und Prophetie, Studien zur Gattungs- und Traditionsgeschichte der Quelle Q*, WUNT 2:29 (Tübingen: J.C.B. Mohr [Paul Siebeck], 1988), esp. 301-02, 373-75.

one neglects the doing. This is a classic problem elsewhere in the New Testament as well, in particular in Paul's letters. Paul is under considerable pressure to have to emphasize both belief in Jesus Christ and ethical action. Perhaps, this is also the reason why the Epistle of James, highly critical of Paul precisely at this point, has almost no interest in christology.

If this consideration is true of the SM, the absence of christology would be a matter of intent, not ignorance. The total concentration of the SM on "hearing and doing" the sayings of Jesus as teacher of the Torah would only be diluted by a second focus of christology. Bad teachers, as 5:19 criticizes, would not only set aside Jesus' teaching but also replace it with their own teaching, presumably christologically motivated, and this would by necessity lead to the self-delusion 7:21-23 warns against. Christological faith would equal building one's house on the sand instead of on the rock (7:24-27).

It was the achievement of the evangelist Matthew to overcome the alternatives as envisioned by the SM. By inserting the SM into the account of Jesus' life, death, and resurrection, Matthew showed that Jesus lived out what he taught. Ironically, while the non-christological SM preserves the portrait of Jesus the teacher of the Torah, Matthew makes this portrait a part of a larger picture. Matthew changed the fixed portrait generated by the SM to the moving portrait of Jesus as this develops before the eyes of the reader following the sequences of events of Jesus' biography. But the biography of the Gospel keeps the focus on events and actions, into which are inserted speeches, debates, and other matters of doctrine. While in and through it all Matthew can present a fully developed christology, he can at the same time maintain the priority of "doing": In the final commission to the church, the risen Christ maintains what also the teacher of the SM had demanded: "Make disciples and teach them to keep all that I have commanded you." (28:18-20).

"BUT I SAY TO YOU . . ." CONCERNING THE FOUNDATIONS OF JESUS' INTERPRETATION OF THE LAW IN THE "SERMON ON THE MOUNT."

Hans Weder, *University of Zürich*

The interpreter who makes the Sermon on the Mount the theme of an interpretation of Jesus' understanding of the Law could be tempted to execute the task by historical description. That would be like an archaeologist who analyzes materials before sending them off to a museum. But the Sermon on the Mount — and the preaching of Jesus in general — is not a museum piece. The Sermon on the Mount is invested with a remarkable power, the power to engage the life of each successive generation. Numerous have been, and continue to be, the attempts to isolate this text from real life, either by relegating it to the garage, where remnants belong, or depositing it in a museum, where precious objects are preserved, but many a time the Sermon on the Mount has returned to life. Its remarkable power to shed light on life has led other generations to refer to it as the Word of God. Whoever respects this understanding will not be able to remain satisfied with historical description, but will move on to a theology of the New Testament.

Thus, a piece of New Testament theology will be the concern of what follows. However, New Testament theology can be taken as a "history of primitive Christian religion,"[1] that is, as description of the

---

[1] As in W. Wrede's famous thesis: "The name which suits the subject matter (i.e., of New Testament theology) is primitive Christian history of religion, or history of primitive Christian religion and theology." William Wrede, *Über Aufgabe und Methode der sogenannten neutestamentlichen Theologie*, Göttingen: Vandenhoeck & Ruprecht, 1897. Repr. in Strecker, *Das Problem der Theologie des neuen Testaments*, Darmstadt: Wissenschaftliche Buchgesellschaft, 1975, 153-54. Eng. tr., "The Task and Methods of New Testament Theology," in Robert Morgan, *The Nature of New Testament Theology*, London: SCM Press/Naper-ville, Ill: Alec R. Richardson, 1973, ??.

ideas and perceptions of some heterodox Jews of the first century after Christ. The Sermon on the Mount can indeed serve as a source that can inform us concerning the religion of Jesus and his disciples. But whoever engages more closely with this text encounters a completely different claim. The Sermon on the Mount provides more than information concerning the religion of Jesus; its claim goes far beyond that: Use of the word "God" in it calls the reader to engage in theology. Unexpectedly, the theme is no longer how one thought about God two thousand years ago; the theme is rather the understanding of God here and now: the problems and the truth of such an understanding. Past conceptions of God can then no longer merely be described religious historically: they have to be confronted by what the word "God" means among us today.

In particular, we cannot come to a halt at a theology, discourse concerning God, in a technical sense. Because, whoever reflects on God is drawn into elementary questions concerning human being. It is an old insight that knowledge about God always includes self-knowledge. Thus, whoever reflects on God in the framework of the New Testament is released into the universal realm of anthropological and philosophical thought. For with "God" the New Testament means a truth that is universal, addressing every human being. One is led by the texts into that practice of theology which Hendrik Boers calls "theology outside the ghetto." It is to Boers and his conception of such a theology that the following considerations are dedicated.

Engagement with New Testament texts always begins with historical description; it then moves through religious historical considerations to theology and from there to the elementary philosophical and anthropological questions. This movement will be carried out in what follows by means of an example. My theme is — seen descriptively — the basis of Jesus' ethical claim in the Sermon of the Mount, more precisely, this basis as it appears in the antithetical controversy with the Jewish Law.[2] Theologically it concerns the phenomenon of the will of God. The antitheses show that evidently a distinction should be made between the Law and the will of God. Evidently the will of God expects to be discovered in the Law. This process of discovery takes place before our eyes in Mt. 5:21-48. The further question has to be what phenomenon of life is represented by the Law and the

---

[2]We will consider this problem in connection with the "antitheses" in Mt. 5:21-48. For the historical and exegetical problems, see Luz, *Matthäus* 244-250, and Weder, *Rede* 99-102.

claim of Jesus. What demand is made by the claims of the antitheses? What is the nature of the authority presented here? Fundamentally, thus, it concerns the anthropological question to what degree the process of life as such is dependent on something like the will of God. Does the context of life itself entail speaking of the will of God?

1. The point of departure: "But I say to you . . ."

The point of departure for the following considerations is the remarkable formula "But I say to you." It is characteristic of the interpretation of the Law in the Sermon on the Mount. This formula is noteworthy first because it appears with beautiful regularity where Jesus' claim is set against the written Law.[3] The antithetical structuring goes back to Jesus in only two cases; in the other four cases it comes from the pre-Matthean tradition or from Matthew himself.[4] The structure of these antitheses reveals a strong formal consistency: (1) It begins with "You have heard it said (of old)." (2) A commandment of prohibition from the Torah. (3) To which Jesus answers with, "But I say to you," which (4) introduces one or more sayings of Jesus which interpret the Law critically. The consistency of this structure makes it clear that the formula "But I say to you" stands as a hinge between the Law and Jesus' newly discovered will of God.

The formula is also remarkable for the absence of any real parallels in the Palestinian and Hellenistic Jewish cultural environment.[5] *Materially* it can be compared with the introduction to the message of an emissary as it occurs in Old Testament prophecy. In its basic form it reads, "Thus says the Lord." (In some case additional designations of God follow.) The formula introduces the word which the prophet pronounces in the name of God. Characteristic of this introductory formula is that it is in the third person. The "I" of the prophet charac-

---

[3]It is not appropriate to speak here of an opposition, because the antitheses constitute in part an effective dismissal of the Law (for example, in Mt. 5:33-37, prohibition of purjury - swearing), in part also a positive interpretation which moves beyond the limits of the Law (for example, in Mt. 5:21-22: extending the command not to kill to a harmless swearing).

[4]The question of the exact tradition-historical development can be left aside here since the antithetical structure goes back to Jesus in at least two cases (see Luz, *Matthäus* 249).

[5]Käsemann, *Problem* 206, counts this formula "the most remarkable of all in the gospels" and correctly maintains: "There is no parallel for it on Jewish soil, and there can be none." For an historical evaluation of the formula, see also Schweizer, *Matthäus* 71.

teristically does not appear in it, and especially not with the emphasis with which the ἐγω is highlighted in ἐγὼ δὲ λεγο ὑμῖν. The formula makes clear that in the case of the prophet it concerns God's word rather than the prophet's. Formally the introductory formula is comparable with those that sometimes occur in rabbinic discussions concerning the Law. However, because of the formal similarity, the differences are all the more recognizable. With the formula, "But I say," a rabbi can distinguish himself from another interpreter,[6] but not from the Law itself, as Jesus does here. In addition, the rabbi in conformity with all the rules, justifies with quotations from Scripture why he distances himself from the rejected interpretation. Such a reasoning based on quotations from Scripture is absent from all six antitheses; a matter of great importance. Finally, for the rabbi it concerns an interpretation of the Law, its application to the world of experience, not a critical or even disavowing interpretation.[7] The rabbis interpret the Law *as* the will of God: Jesus discovers the will of God *within* the Law.

The Gospels themselves already take note of the peculiarity of Jesus' introductory formulas. Matthew, the final redactor of the Sermon on the Mount, presents the teaching of Jesus within the framework of the ἐξουσία. "The crowds were ecstatic concerning his teaching. Because he taught them like someone who had authority, and not like their scribes" (Mt 7:28b-29). In all probability the way in which Jesus opposed his discovery of the will of God to the Torah was decisively co-responsible for the supreme authority which was recognized in his teaching. The conclusion of the Sermon on the Mount is formulated in Matthew with a statement which he took over from Mark, where the authority of Jesus' teaching is recognized in an exorcism (Mk 1:27), expanded to his teaching in a synagogue and set in opposition to the teaching of the scribes (Mk 1.22). With the conception of authority Matthew thus addresses less the origin or foundation of the teaching of Jesus, than its effect. According to Matthew, the teaching of Jesus resulted in incomprehensibility and shock, which normally belonged to the well-attested effects of exorcisms and miracles. What about this teaching called forth such incredibility. Was it its violence? Was it because it broke all those containers in which the world and God were confined?

---

[6]See Luz, Matthäus 247, also note 13, with a few examples.

[7]"Jewish interpreters of the Law do not stand over against the Mosaic Law, but pose differing interpretations against each other" (Strecker, *Bergpredigt* 65).

Matthew himself gives an important hint at the religious historical orientation of the teaching of Jesus, namely, that in the "But I say to you" an authority comes to expression which distinguishes Jesus from the rabbis. As much as he was similar on many points — precisely with regard to teaching — he was different from them with regard to his *exousia*. What was this difference? Not infrequently inquiries have been made into the psycho-dynamic effects of this speaker: his fiery temperament overran the detached soberness of the Pharisaic scholars. It has also been suggested that the difference was one of degree: Jesus did have the same authority as the Pharisees, but he had more of it. The wording of the texts contradict at least the second of these theses. Jesus did not have more authority: it was a simple fact that he had authority in contrast with the Pharisees whose teaching was without it. Decisive for the teaching of Jesus is in any case the ἐξουσία. It reveals the dimension in which the "But I say to you" has to be understood.

2 Authority and Law

We receive the suggestion from the Matthean Sermon on the Mount that authority is an issue whenever the will of God is taught by human beings. Whoever pronounces the will of God — also whoever remains silent about it — confronts others with an incontestable command — or conceals it. Through this connection with the will of God what is commanded receives a certain dignity and authority. Who would risk to act against the will of God? It is for that reason that the question of authority arises of itself from the human interpretation of the will of God. Who gives a human being the right to designate certain prescriptions as the will of God? This question of authority is identical with the question of the substantiation which someone gives for her or his pronouncement of the will of God. In what follows we will thus inquire concerning the ἐξουσία which is exercised when the divine will is pronounced. We will concentrate on the relationship which exists between authority and the process of substantiation. Three more or less contemporary models from the same cultural environment will be contrasted against each other: the Pharisaic-rabbinic, the apocalyptic and that of Jesus.

2.1 The Pharisaic-rabbinic Model

The great passion of Pharisaic thinking and teaching is to let the will of God penetrate daily life in every detail.[8] It concerns the practical, concrete agreement of daily life with the will of God. Rabbinic work achieved admirable results in this regard.[9] The rabbis — by concentrating on the interpretation of Scripture — unmistakably distanced themselves from every fundamentalist attempt to insist on the letter and in that way violate life through the Law. Instead of a fundamentalist repetition of the commandments, rabbinic interpretation made their task the individual application of the commandments.[10] With that we have already reached the central point from where we can observe the authority which was practiced in this case.

In the Pharisaic-rabbinic area the will of God came to expression in a style which was *essentially* exegetical in the best sense of the term. The authority of the rabbi shows itself in no other way than through the given interpretation. The authority in this case is thus also of an exegetical nature. It depends entirely on the authority which it attributed to the Law itself. The aim of the interpretation is precisely to exclude any personal tone from that which comes to expression. In that sense one can say that the person of the interpreter plays no role in exegetical authority. We can recognize this in an obvious literal peculiarity: In Pharisaic-rabbinic interpretations of the Law the pronoun "it" (mostly concealed in a divine or some other passive) occurs far more frequently than "I." "It is prohibited," "it is permitted," "it is written." The rabbi has a derived authority. It extends precisely as far as the ἐξουσία of the Law. Therefore the rabbi presents the Will of God by grounding it in the Law.

This somewhat generally formulated thesis concerning the authority of the rabbis will be explicated further in what now follows. In this connection it is necessary to remind ourselves of certain characteristics of Pharisaic-rabbinic thinking. In the first place it is not an

---

[8]Thoma, *Christliche Theologie des Judentums* 97, points out that the Pharisees tried to live "in accordance with revelation and timeliness." "This was to be practiced by intensive attempts to relate God's revelation to every situation in life." Important for this is that God's revelation was in principle normative.

[9]Basically it was something like scientific interpretation (Schürer, *History II* 314-380 correctly refers to "Torah Scholarship") of the Law, an activity which gained for the rabbis a high esteem (so Schürer, 327).

[10]The rabbi is primarily obliged to interpret the Torah. As such it is a "necessity" for the Pharisaic way of life (so Meyer, *Tradition* 42).

accident that it was in the bosom of Pharisaism that *formal rules of interpretation* were first developed. They are attributed to Hillel, who was to become the model of an interpreter of the Torah in may other respects as well.[11] The phenomenon of the interpretation of the Law undoubtedly had already been important for centuries in early Judaism. But that *rules* of interpretation were developed meant taking a step beyond mere interpretation, because this meant the concern to free interpretation from the arbitrary whims of the interpreter. Rules of interpretation were developed because the power of the Law had to be protected against the counter power of the interpreter.

That the fundamental approach of Pharisaic-rabbinic authority was exegetical is also revealed by the reason that the same Hillel became renowned as a true interpreter of the Law. He succeeded in solving a difficult case by means of the interpretation of Scripture even though his solution was not foreseen by Scripture.[12] That the ἐξουσία belonged only to Scripture is also shown by the fact that in rabbinic education an unequivocal ruling was given for cases where two scriptural passages contradicted each other. In such a case a third passage of Scripture provided the solution. This same formal priority of Scripture is also shown in the pervasive misgivings about the written recording of oral interpretations of the Law. It is no accident that the Mishna was recorded only towards the end of the second century, and even then not without protest. For a long time there was resistance against the undermining of scriptural authority with the authority of scriptural interpretation. Finally this is in agreement with the understanding of the Law as an eternal reality. It was present from the beginning of creation, and it would survive the end of the world.[13] Pharisaic-rabbinic thinking shared this conception with almost all of ancient Judaism. It did of course not merely concern the temporal extent of the reach of Scripture, but far more its authority, on which even the end of the world could have no effect.[14]

---

[11]For the rules attributed to Hillel, see Bousset, *Religion des Judentums* 160; Schürer, *History II* 344, also note 21 (literature list). For the fame of the pair, Hillel and Shammai, see Schürer, 363-367.

[12]It concerns the question whether it is permitted to celebrate the Passover sacrifice even on the sabbath if the day of preparation fell on a sabbath. See Pesahim 6a and Bousset, *Religion des Judentums* 154-55.

[13]See Schürer, *History* II 314-21; Billerbeck I 244-47.

[14]Paul can be considered as an indirect witness for this dimension in his concern to limit the Law temporally in Galatians (cf. Gal 3:17-18). Paul observed ac-

It is evident that personal authority is neither called for nor desirable where it concerns in principle an exegetical understanding of the will of God. Consistent with this, the legend developed in rabbinic tradition which attributed the oral tradition (of the interpretation of the Law) to Moses, the Law-giver.[15] This fiction had the formal sense of maintaining in principle the superiority of the Law in relationship to its interpretation. Notwithstanding this formal sense the fiction had the effect that rabbinic interpretation began to dominate the Law of Sinai. Finally, we may now ask which place *experience* had in the total process of interpretation. Contrary to a fundamentalist procedure where the world of experience is devalued by a dogmatism of the biblical word, experience is taken seriously throughout in Pharisaic-rabbinic thought. This is shown by the program of interpretation to which the rabbinic tradition was indebted: the concern was that the commandments were interpreted for every possible situation. (This program has typically been designated with the not very fortunate concept of casuistry.) However, the importance which was attached to experience concentrated it on a single dimension: the world of experience became the fundamental area for the application of the Torah. Precisely by taking experience exegetically seriously, it lost its independence and became a field in which the interpreted Law was applied. Only the Law had a revelatory quality,[16] the world of experience had none. The world of experience was the place where what the Law commanded was realized. It was at best the place where revelation was illustrated, as is shown by the rabbinic parables: they are in principle exegetical[17] in the sense that they illustrate a saying

---

curately that the eternalization of the Law had no other purpose than to establish its universal validity.

[15]So in m Abot 1:1; an extended discussion in Billerbeck IV 446-449; also Bousset *Religion des Judentums* 157. For the discrepancy between the formal subordination of interpretation to the Torah and the factual dominance of interpretation, see Schürer, *History II* 341-42.

[16]This is not exclusively true for the Pharisaic-rabbinic form of interpretation, since it applied to the Jewish in general, probably since the days when Ezra read the Law to the people, and obliged them to do so (Neh 8-10). "The whole piety of the Israelite was primarily directed towards obeying in all its details, and with zeal and love, the God-given Torah" (Schürer, *History II* 314). Revelatory character was attributed only to the Torah in so far as it came completely from heaven and was handed over to Moses, or was at least dictated by God and was confirmed by the divine spirit (so Schürer, 325-16).

[17]See Lauer/Thomas, *Gliechnisse* 22-26. "Secular narratives and revelation texts together contribute to make one consciousness of what is meant by revelation in

from the Torah with a story that could be taken from the world of experience.

2.2 The apocalyptic model

The apocalyptic writings distinguish themselves with an understanding of revelation that can be described with the motto "heavenly journey." In the Greek apocalypse of Baruch, for example, the visionary is exalted to the fifth heaven. The higher he went, the deeper were his insights into the secrets of the truth (Gr Bar 2, 3, 4, 10, 11). This revelation from the various heavens are communicated by the visionary to his "brothers" upon his return.[18] In Ethiopic Enoch a similar idea is encountered of the visionary experiencing a heavenly vision (Eth En 1:2; 37:1).[19] His spirit ascended into heaven where all the divine secrets were revealed to him (71:1, 4). The same applies to the revelation source of the so-called Fourth Ezra. Here it is the angel Uriel who gives the divinely authorized revelation to the visionary. Ezra's task is to ask questions and to raise objections to which Uriel gives the correct answers. Ezra is the advocate of a disappointing and oppressing experience of the world: Uriel the representative of a divine revelation which clarifies everything.

Here in Fourth Ezra it becomes clear what is characteristic of the apocalyptic model: the human being as such is not capable of recognizing the divine truth. "You who are perishable cannot recognize the way of what is imperishable" (4 Ezra 4:11). The receiving of revelation through a heavenly journey coordinates with the lack of revelation in life on earth. The human experience of life on earth reveals nothing of the divine truth.[20] The role of the experience of life is rather that of objection which accuses the divine. Who cannot understand — with Ezra — that the experience of the world protests

---

its most profound sense" (26). Evidently the illustrations' *real* point of reference was not the Torah, but that which "was meant by revelation."

[18]Gr Bar 17. The visionary praises God for the honor which God bestowed upon him, and says, "And for that reason you too, my brothers, who have participated in such a revelation, should praise God . . ." Thoma, *Christliche Theologie des Judentums* 79-80, calls this the *esoteric* nature of apocalypticism.

[19]For the preponderance of visions in the apocalypses, see Vielhauer, *Einleitung* 408-409.

[20]This is also shown by the fact that the coming age is placed in sharp opposition to the present to the degree that every relationship it has to the latter is to put it to an end (see Vielhauer, *Einleitung* 412-14).

against God? But who still — with Uriel — wants to merely assert the divine against the facts?

Revelation always concerns the will of God. According to Fourth Ezra, God's will is laid down in the Law. Since being in the world does not have the quality of revelation it has relevance only as an argument against the Law, against the sense of God's will in the Law. Whoever listens to Ezra the visionary senses something of the weight of worldly experience. Nevertheless the Law is vindicated sharply against worldly experience by the angel of revelation, Uriel. For example, when Ezra objects that the Law is not functional because it did not lead Israel to life Uriel replies, *"Pereant enim multi praesentes, quam neglegatur quae anteposita est Dei lex."*[21] Ezra wants the Law to be tested by whether it leads to life. Against this the rule of revelation argues that for the sake of the unimpeachability of the Law one should accept that many will perish. Revelation does not allow itself to be disturbed at all by the downfall of humanity.

But since time immemorial it is true for the Law that it enhanced life, not that it destroyed it. This understanding of the Law is also not challenged in Fourth Ezra. The Law does bring life, but not in this age; only in the next.[22] The present, by contrast, is the time in which the human being fights with itself the battle to fulfill the Law. Doing the Law is in the mode of *waiting* on the life that comes only in the future eon.[23] In this way one could say that doing the Law was no longer the way of living but the way of waiting on life, because in this world real life does not take place; approaches (to life) and the ways of this world had become narrow. They require a view of the wideness of the coming world.[24]

There was a profound coordination between the nature of revelation and the way in which the relationship between life and the Law was determined. The source of revelation was moved to heaven: the receiver of revelation was a human being from a distant past. Thus we can say, revelation of the divine takes place, in the first instance, in the past and, secondly, through a heavenly emissary; in other

---

[21]"Rather let many of those living today perish than that the Law of God that had been laid down be disregarded" (4 Ezra 7: [7-8], 20).

[22]See Harnisch, *Verhängnis* 146-65.

[23]Thoma, *Christliche Theologie des Judentums* 76-77, considers it among the characteristics of the apocalyptic world view that it is to "strengthen the few who are trustworthy in their trustworthiness and motivate them to further endurance."

[24]4 Ezra 7:21-22.

apocalypses even through a heavenly journey of the visionary. The present is excluded in a double way as the source of revelation. That agrees completely with the understanding that the human being cannot direct its view to the present when it concerns the meaning of the Law, because that meaning — to lead to life — becomes revealed only in the future. "*Et quare non accepisti in corde tuo quod futurum, sed quod in praesenti.*"[25] Here the apocalypticist's conception of time is expressed succinctly. The authority of the visionary is grounded in the heavenly source of his knowledge.

2.3 Revelation of the will of God in the antitheses

From here we take a look at the grounding of the will of God in the antitheses of the Sermon on the Mount. Here too we maintain the leading question: what is the nature of the authority exercised here? The point of departure is the understanding that the antitheses are characteristic of the way in which Jesus brought the will of God to expression.

Jesus grounded his new discovery of the will of God in the Law with the plain "But I say to you." One might be tempted to subordinate this grounding to the model of authority as well. In that case one would have to consider the "I" of Jesus as an even higher authority than the two discussed above: higher than the authority of the Law; higher than that of a heavenly emissary.[26] At the level of the Gospel of Matthew such an understanding may be correct, because one could say that here the Son of God himself is the bringer of heavenly secrets. His interpretation is correct because he does it with the authority of the Son of God. But one should consider that the formula "But I say to you" already characterized the interpretation of Jesus of Nazareth, the human being. And what presupposed authority could

---

[25] "And why have you not taken the future to heart, but the present?" (4 Ezra 7:16).

[26] As far as I can see this is the common opinion of the interpreters. As representative the following two voices can be quoted: "Over against that (that is, against the rabbinic interpretation of the Law) Jesus stands remote from the Torah of Moses; his authority makes it possible for him to criticize the Law to the point of dissolving individual commandments and of establishing new precepts" (Strecker, *Bergpredigt* 65). Here the authority of the Lord is placed above the Law. In a similar way argues Käsemann, *Problem*, who reduces everything to the conception of the "claim;" the "only category" which can do justice to [Jesus'] claim is "that of Messiah." In both cases authority is immediately attached to the person of Jesus. As Kyrios or Messiah it is placed on a higher level that that of the traditional Jewish authorities.

this "I" have had which elevated him above the Law and heavenly knowledge?

In the present case one should, to my mind, abandon the attempt to understand the announcement of the will of God on the basis of the model of authority. By the model of authority I understand the Pharisaic-rabbinic and apocalyptic interpretations of the Law discussed above. Its characteristic is that it attributes a weight which lies outside itself to what is said. What is said carries weight in the one case because it agrees with the authority of the Law, in the other because it is of heavenly origin. In contrast Jesus does not revert to an external authority. He reverts solely to himself. That means that no external weight is attached to what is said, but that there is only the weight of what is said. That agrees well with the fact that in none of the antitheses does Jesus argue with the Hebrew Bible. His discovery of the will of God in the Law is to be found in the form of the pronouncement itself. For that reason he refrains from referring to supports in the recognized treasure of revelation. Jesus does not introduce external authorities, neither passages from the Holy Scriptures, nor renowned theological teachers, nor the heavenly origin of his knowledge. From this, to my mind, the conclusion follows that there is no longer any external authority that can or should support these pronouncements. Their truth exists solely in what they say. For that reason there is nothing which can add weight to these pronouncements except for the weight which the pronouncement themselves carry. And for that reason there is nothing which can move the hearers to do the will of God except the approval which these pronouncements seek from them.

It has always been maintained that Jesus represents an eschatological ethics here: the authority for his teaching is the kingdom of God which has come near in his person.[27] It is true that no direct relationship to the kingdom of God can be established in the antitheses of the Sermon on the Mount. In no instance does Jesus argue on the basis of the coming Kingdom of God, although it is of course correct that Jesus should be understood decisively within the framework of the Kingdom of God. And yet it is inaccurate to say that the coming

---

[27]So, for example, Strecker, *Bergpredigt* 74 (concerning the second antithesis): "Here Jesus brings to expression his authority which stands over against the Torah of Moses. His address grounds itself in the coming reign of God which has come near in his person. The eschatological justice which Jesus announces is therefore not oriented to this world but expresses the coming reign of God."

Kingdom of God provides the basis for the authority of his teaching. The actual point of Jesus' proclamation of the Kingdom of God is rather the extension of the coming Kingdom into the human present. For that reason his interpretation of the Law is an act of making the Kingdom present. Thus the Kingdom of God is not the answer to the question concerning the authority of Jesus' interpretation of the Law, but the Kingdom is the answer to the question about which time is realized in the teaching of Jesus. The Kingdom of God is not an external authority *behind* what Jesus teaches; rather it appears *in* his interpretation of the will of God. And the power which the Kingdom of God exerts in the present is nothing other than the power of what is said.

With his teaching Jesus claims a space of freedom in which only what is said counts. Matthew correctly calls this space ἐξουσία, the space in which one can find the freedom to depend on the evidence of what is said, and so on the approval of the one who is addressed. Now the question becomes how Jesus came to claim for himself such a space of freedom. The space of freedom is in constant danger of deteriorating to an area of arbitrariness. Thus such a space of freedom can be claimed only by someone who does not speak arbitrarily. That Jesus' discovery of the will of God is not arbitrary can be seen where it is most incisive, in the command to love one's enemy (Mt 5:43-48).

Here the commandment of Scripture to love the neighbor is contrasted with love of one's enemies by means of the simple "But I say to you." Here too the weight of this commandment rests on the evidence that love — when it is thought through to the end — should extend to enemies. The evidence of the claim rests upon itself. But in verse 45 it is founded in another way as well: love of one's enemies — at least for those who can read the book of nature[28] — is, as can be seen from rain and sunshine, what makes God be available for the bad and the good, the righteous and the unrighteous. One can call this argument creation-theological. It would be more accurate to speak of the foundation of the love of one's enemies in the daily *experience* of creation, in the experience of daily life.[29] Evidently skepti-

---

[28]For the problem of the ambiguity of the book of nature, see Weder, *Rede der Reden* 147-49.

[29]Betz, *Kosmogonie* 108 attaches particular weight to this. He observes correctly that the appeal is not made to the history of creation in Genesis, but to "what is there for every eye to see and to evaluate critically." "What is good about the order of creation can thus be confirmed by the experience of daily life: . . . This is given by the experience of the goodness of nature, and everyone who lives in

cism about the traditional theology of creation no longer allows reliance on it. It is most interesting that neither the absolute authority of heavenly knowledge (apocalypticism) nor the authority of the Law (Pharisaism) are used against this skepticism. Instead what is used here is life experience itself. With that Jesus focuses on exactly that domain in which speaking about God is ready to hand and where his evidence can be found.

This reverting to the experience of creation in daily life recurs in the Sermon on the Mount like a *cantus firmus*, making clear what is involved at the deepest level in the discovery of the will of God.[30] The demand to love one's enemies emerges from the love which appears in the image of the sun and rain which comes to the good and the evil (Mt. 5:43-48). The demand to speak the truth and nothing but the truth every time (and not only under oath) emerges from the fact that people are endowed with language (Mt 5:33-37). The demand to practice good will emerges from the fact that there is still time before the end when all that will remain is the δίκη, the final judgment.[31] From the living relationship between man and woman emerges the demand to consider it as indissoluble and unique.[32] Important about this appeal to the given is that it is not a theology of creation, but makes everyday life experience the source of ethically correct behavior; the everyday experience of life as sun and rain, as gift and speech, as having time.

These natural factors are nevertheless certainly not unequivocal. They can never represent an authority which compels everyone to obey — as if they were a natural law. Even when the book of nature is opened the word still carries no other weight than what it says, because from the book of nature many different things could also be

---

awareness of it can attest to it." Concerning the interchange between the order of creation and the daily experience of creation Betz expresses the interesting supposition that there is a strong skepticism about the order of creation. (Such skepticism, according to Betz, is also shown by apocalypticism and Jewish apologetics.)

[30]For this perspective on the Law, see Weder, *Hermeneutik* 295-304.

[31]In Mt 5:25-26 what was originally a terminology of judgment has become a metaphor for the human way of life (so Strecker, *Bergpredigt* 71), and so for the bestowal of time to live which claims good will from those who are so bestowed. (It is not appropriate to speak of a "spiritualizing," *contra* Strecker, 71).

[32]In this regard it is worth referring to Mk 10:2-9 as well, another Jesus tradition. This text is particularly remarkable since Jesus does not appeal to Scripture, but to the "beginning," to the reality of creation itself which can be experienced by everyone.

read. Jesus' words gain their own weight by uncovering the experience of God's creativity in the midst of the diffusion of life experiences which contradict each other. The word, which seeks to elicit evidence for what is demanded, must first perform an act of disentanglement. The creativity which is the source of doing good is not obvious. It first has to be discovered, because it is the secret of everyday life.

3. Conclusions

In conclusion the attempt must be made to draw a few results from these deliberations.

3.1 At the outset the question was asked what the life-phenomenon of the will of God is. It can now be answered: the will of God is a (theological) concept for the demand inherent in what is given in life. To meet this demand is to accept what is given. One can presume that the life that is given is forfeited when its claim is not heeded.

3.2 The authority of the claim is the same as the authority of the given. That means, on the one hand, that there is no compelling power because what is given has no compelling authority over the recipient. Since what is given is not present in the figure of a claim or of something apodictic, but of a given, no power in the world can prevent the given (and so also its claim) from being rejected. The claim of the given is as a result a "weak" claim. When what is offered is present in the figure of the given which I need in order to live, it means, on the other hand, that every attempt to distance oneself from the given, once it has been recognized, is meaningless. The question concerning a space where the claim of the given cannot reach me is senseless since the entire area of my life is within what is given. Thus the question, what is still allowed in view of the will of God, is no longer meaningful; this question does not ask about the ethical but the limits of the ethical;it asks not for the space of love but for the limit where love can readily end. Now this question is replaced by the question about what the experience of life claims.

3.3 On the basis of the notion of what is commanded or the will of God, the alternative of heteronomy or autonomy has presented itself in recent times. Our deliberations should show that this is a false alternative. Does Jesus' interpretation of the Law by way of uncovering the claim of the given bind me to a heteronomy or does it address me concerning an autonomous behavior? What else can an autonomous ethical decision want other then coordination with the ἕτερος νόμος of the given? And by what could a heteronomous ethical decision be substantiated if not by the νόμος which is impressed on every human being itself (αὐτός) by the work of Jesus?

3.4 Finally I would like to ask the question — in parentheses — concerning the epistemological relevance of the reflection on the "But I say to you" of the Sermon on the Mount. The "life phenomenon" of God's will as it was uncovered by Jesus as the claim of the given shows unmistakenly that all that is given also wants to be perceived in terms of its demand (its ἐντολή). To what degree does this take place in our everyday life (practically) and theoretical concepts? Or to what degree is perception in the contemporary period confined to the one question, what can *I* do with the given? Which of *my* demands can it fulfill? To discuss such epistemological considerations extensively would contradict the claim that time is limited; for that reason they will be broken off here.

Männedorf, August 30, 1988
Hans Weder

LITERATURE

Hans Dieter Betz, "Kosmogonie und Ethik in der Bergpredigt," in *Studien zur Bergpredigt*, Tübingen: J.C.B. Mohr (Paul Siebeck), 1985.

Wilhelm Bousset, *Die Religion des Judentums im späthellenistischen Zeitalter*. Handbuch zum Neuen Testament 21. 3rd ed. (by Hugo Gressmann) Tübingen: J.C.B. Mohr (Paul Siebeck), 1926.

Wolfgang Harnisch, *Verhängnis und Verheissung der Geschichte. Untersuchungen zum Zeit- und Geschichtsverständnis im 4. Buch Esra und in der syr. Baruchapokalypse*. Forschungen zur Religion und Literatur des Alten und Neuen Testaments. Göttingen: Vandenhoeck & Ruprecht, 1969.

Ernst Käsemann, "Das Problem des historischen Jesus," ZThK 15 (1954), pp. 125-153. Repr. in Ernst Käsemann, *Exegetische Versuche und Besinnungen*, Göttingen: Vandenhoeck & Ruprecht, 1960, Vol. 1, pp. 187-213.

Ulrich Luz, *Das Evangelium nach Matthäus*. Evangelisch-Katholischer Kommentar zum Neuen Testament. Zürich: Benziger, Vol I, 1985.

Emil Meyer, *Tradition und Neuschöpfung im antiken Judentum*. Dargestellt an der Geschichte des Pharisäismus. Berlin: 1965.

Emil Schürer, Geza Vermes, and Fergus Millar, *A History of the Jewish People in the Age of Jesus Christ (175 B.C.-A.D. 135)*. Edinburgh: T. & T. Clark, Vol II, 1979.

Eduard Schweizer, *Das Evangelium nach Matthäus*. Das Neue Testament Deutsch, Göttingen: Vandenhoeck & Ruprecht, 13th ed, 1973.

Clemens Thoma, *Christliche Theologie des Judentums*. Aschaffenburg: P. Pattloch Verlag, 1978.

Clemens Thoma and Simon Lauer, *Die Gleichnisse der Rabbinen. Erster Teil: Pesiqta deRav Kahan (PesK). Einleitung, Uebersetzung,*

Parallelen, Kommentar. Judaica et Christiana Bd. 10. Bern and New York: P. Lang, 1986.

Philipp Vielhauer, "Apokalypsen und Verwandtes," in Edgar Hennecke/Wilhelm Schneemelcher, *Neutestamentliche Apokryphen*. Tübingen: J.C.B. Mohr (Paul Siebeck), Vol II, 4th ed. 1971, pp. 405-27.

Hans Weder, *Die "Rede der Reden". Eine Auslegung der Bergpredigt heute*. Zürich: 2nd ed. 1987.

Hans Weder, *Neutestamentliche Hermeneutik*. Zürcher Grundrisse zur Bibel. Zürich: Theologischer Verlag, 1986.

William Wrede, *Über Aufgabe und Methode der sogenannten neutestamentlichen Theologie*, Göttingen: Vandenhoeck & Ruprecht, 1897. Repr. in Strecker, *Das Problem der Theologie des neuen Testaments*, pp. 81-154.

THE MARTYRDOM OF THE SON OF MAN
Theodore W. Jennings Jr., *Independent Scholar*

The question of the origin (background), referent (single or generic) and content (meaning) of the son of man sayings in the Gospel of Mark is a much vexed one. I will not attempt here to review the vast literature on this subject.[1] I will however attempt to show that those son of man sayings which are often taken to be predictions of Jesus' passion actually function in the Gospel of Mark to propose a program of action which has already been actualized in a preliminary way by John the Baptist and which it is hoped the readers of the gospel (successors of the disciples) will understand and actualize in their own continuation of the mission of Jesus (and John).

The action proper of the Gospel of Mark begins with Jesus' announcement of the arrival of the reign of God. The announcement and enactment of that reign is represented as the mission of Jesus, a mission shared from the beginning and at virtually every point with the disciples. Through the narrative we learn that the arrival of God's kingdom entails the liberation of the sick from disease, of the blind from darkness, of the paralyzed from immobility, of the despised and outcast from their friendless isolation. Within the narration of this messianic program we hear for the first time of the son of man who ignores the religious distinctions and institutions which have become obstacles to the humanism of the divine reign. These passages do not suggest the special identity of Jesus (that remains "hidden") but do point toward the emergence of a new humanity associated with Jesus which acts as if the barriers between God and humanity were already overcome; thus as capable of forgiving sin (2:10), and as "lord of the sabbath" (2:27-8).

---

[1] Boers has surveyed much of this material in *The Diversity of New Testament Christological Concepts and the Confession of Faith* (Bonn, 1962) pp68-85, and in "Where Christology is Real." *Interpretation* 26 (1972) pp 300-327.

It has been long recognized that a decisive turn occurs in the narrative in the early part of chapter eight which ushers in a section characterized by what are often called the passion predictions, themselves framed as sayings concerning the son of man. Although it is often supposed that the earlier son of man sayings do not have exclusive reference to Jesus, the sayings of this section (roughly chapter eight through ten) are generally regarded as referring exclusively to him and his destiny. The sayings most often noted here are 8:31; 9:31; and 10:33-4.

Taken together these sayings produce both a general and a detailed picture of the fate of the son of man which serves as a pattern for the narration of the fate of Jesus from 14:43 to 16:8. In general the picture is of suffering, death and resurrection. However we may also indicate the subfeatures of this description. The specific features are:

1) Betrayal. The same word may be (and often is) translated as "delivered up" and "arrested". (9:31; 10:33)

2) Rejection by religious authorities (specified as elders, chief priests and scribes in 8:31; and as merely chief priests and scribes in 10:33.)

3) Condemnation. (mentioned only 10:33)

4) Suffering many things (8:31) specified as "they will mock him and spit upon him and scourge him" in 10:33 where it is also specified that it is the gentiles (nations) who do this, i.e., the secular as opposed to specifically religious authority

5) Execution. (in 8:31; 9:31; 10:34)

6) Resurrection "after three days."(8:31; 9:31; 10:34, see also 9:9)

Keeping these six features in mind as well as the fact that they constitute not a rigid formula but a set of elements which may enter into different combinations we turn to an examination of the way in which the destiny of the son of man is represented in the narrative by characters other than Jesus. There is no question that the story of Jesus' fate in Mark 14:43- 16:8 corresponds tolerably well to the description, though by no means in a mechanical way. But is Jesus the only one who meets this fate? Is the suffering son of man only to be identified with Jesus?

1. The Martyrdom of John

The exact nature of the relation between the mission of Jesus and that of John is nearly as vexed a question as that of the proper interpretation of the son of man sayings. Boers has in any case suggested that the NT texts which have a Christological interest in maintaining the uniqueness of Jesus and his mission nevertheless also betray through the traditions they transmit a very different picture in which the mission of Jesus is a continuation of that of John.[2] I believe that this picture of continuity is in fact reinforced by a consideration of the way in which Mark portrays the martyrdom of the baptizer as in conformity with the destiny of the son of man.

The relation between the fate of John and that of the son of man is made the subject of explicit comment in Mark 9:11-3

> And they asked him, "Why do the scribes say that first Elijah must come?" And he said to them, "Indeed, Elijah, coming first, will restore all things; and how has it been written of the son of man, that he should suffer many things and be treated with contempt? But I tell you that indeed Elijah has come, and they did to him as they pleased, as it has been written about him."

This passage follows from the account of Jesus' metamorphosis in which he was seen in the company of Elijah and Moses and in which the disciples were instructed by a voice from the skies to pay attention to Jesus as "my beloved son." This passage is notoriously difficult. It does not say, although it strongly implies, that John the baptizer is to be understood here as the returned Elijah. This impression is strengthened when we recall that the description of John in 1:6 corresponds to that of Elijah in 2 Kings 1:8. It then appears that the coming of Elijah in the person of John, together with his suffering already belongs to the past. But that is not all that is maintained here.

For the saying links the fate of Elijah/John to that of the son of man. Jesus claims that "it has been written that the son of man [will] suffer many things and be set at naught." And of Elijah/John he says "they did to him as they pleased, as it has been written about him." That is, Elijah/John has already fulfilled the destiny of the son of man. The suffering of John, to be considered in a moment, is the suf-

---

[2] *Who was Jesus? An Interpretation of the Christological Passages in the Synoptic Gospels.* (San Francisco: Harper & Row, 1989) especially chapter 2.

fering of the son of man. Put simply, John the Baptist is the son of man.

The references to the written here are also puzzling. We know of no written traditions which speak of the suffering either of Elijah or of the eschatological son of man. So far as we know the only place where it was written that the son of man must suffer was in the preceding chapter of this gospel! It is often supposed that the reference to the written must be a reference to the suffering servant oracles of Isaiah (i.e., 42:1-4; 45:1-6; 50:4-11; and especially, 52:13-53:12). These of course do not refer to the son of man nor to Elijah but to the servant of Yahweh whose humiliation and suffering heals those who regard that suffering. Certainly there are other texts of the New Testament which apply these passages to Jesus and regard them as an anticipation of his redemptive suffering (e.g., Matt. 8:17; Acts 8:32-33; 1 Peter 2:21-25). If that is what Mark has in mind here then we have a radical re-interpretation of the son of man and Elijah expectations by way of these being connected to the suffering servant poems. But we must notice that if the reference to the written does intend to make us think of the suffering servant poems then the significance of this is that the suffering servant is John! It is his death then which marks him as bruised for our transgressions, it is by his stripes we are healed!

Finally we notice that the mission of the returned Elijah is to "restore all things". Thus John, if he was the returned Elijah, had as his mission the restoration of the earth. It is this John who has been set at naught, just as Jesus who has the same mission (dramatically enacted in the cleansing of lepers, the restoration of sight etc.) will also, in the same way be, or seem to be, set at naught.

We are faced with three possibilities. Either Mark has carelessly and inadvertently been led to suggest that John is the messiah, the son of man and so on,(the whole thing is a mistake) or Mark is saying that John rather than Jesus is the son of man, or Mark is saying that somehow both are.

The possibility of a mistake may be readily eliminated by a consideration of the detailed way in which, according to Mark, John's fate corresponds to that which is fitting for the son of man. We noted earlier six features of the fate of the son of man. How do these square with what Mark otherwise tells us of John?

1.) Betrayal. Jesus' mission begins with the betrayal of John (1:14). This correspondence is usually covered over in the translations which obscure the fact that the same word is used of John here as is otherwise used of the son of man (9:31; 10;33; 14:21; 14:41) and of Jesus (14:18; 14:42).

2.) Rejection by religious authorities. Jesus has said of the son of man that he will be rejected by the elders, chief priests and scribes. When Jesus enters Jerusalem following his attack upon the temple he is accosted by "the chief priests and the scribes and the elders" (11:27) who demand to know what authorization he has for his outrageous actions. In the course of Jesus' reply we are informed that these religious authorities did not accept the message and mission of John (11:31). The connection between the fate of Jesus and that of John is further reinforced by the way in which Jesus links his authority with that of John (11:29-30)

3) Condemnation. This is only a separate item in 10:33 and is included in the account of John's death.

4) Suffering many things. This is claimed with respect to John in the passage already discussed from 9:11-3.

5) Execution (by political authority.) This is the subject of the long narrative in Mark 6:17-29.

6) Resurrection (after three days). There is no narration of an actual resurrection appearance of John. But this is also true for Jesus. Jesus' resurrection is reported in 16:6. But we are also informed three times of the report that John has returned from the dead (6:14, 6:16, 8:28.) It is true that in the case of the account of the metamorphosis of Jesus on the mountain we are presented with what appears to be a kind of resurrection appearance (9:3). But if we regard it in this way then we must also recall that one of the other figures who appears there is Elijah (9:4) who, we are subsequently led to believe, has returned as John. That is, if we have a disguised resurrection appearance for Jesus then we also seem to have one for John.

The fate of John corresponds not only in general, but in detail to that which is specified as appropriate for the son of man. The distribution of these characteristics makes clear that Mark has not made a mistake in suggesting that John is the son of man in 9:11-13. Mark has carefully suggested that the vocation of the son of man is actualized not only by Jesus but also by John. The new humanity of the son of man is a class with at least two members. Are there any more?

2. The Martyrdom of the follower

We have noted that the mission of Jesus began with the notice of the fate of John which we now recognize as the beginning of his martyrdom or passion. Similarly the account of the launching of the independent mission of the twelve in chapter six is connected with the conclusion of John's martyrdom. This linkage is reinforced by the way in which Mark employs the narrative technique of "sandwiching" the account of John's death between the beginning (6:7-13) and the conclusion (6:30) of that mission. Thus already at that early point in the narrative the similarity in their fate is signalled.

This similarity is further emphasized in the paralleling of the statements concerning the fate of the son of man with statements concerning the "cost of discipleship"[3] Thus the initial statement concerning the fate of the son of man (8:31) is followed by the clarification of the vocation of the disciple

> If anyone would come after me, let him deny himself and take up his cross and follow me. For whoever would save his life will lose it; and whoever loses his life for my sake and that of the gospel's will lose it. (8:34-5)

Similarly the second statement concerning the fate of the son of man (9:31) is followed by the assertion:

> If anyone would be first, he must be last of all and servant of all. (9:35).

The final passion "prediction" (10:33-4) is followed by a discourse on the theme of greatness which expands on the saying of 9:35:

> Whoever would be great among you must be your servant, and whoever would be first among you must be slave of all. For the son of man came not to be served but to serve and to give his life a ransom for many.(10:43-5).

In this last saying the comportment of the follower is directly modeled upon that of the son of man. The son of man serves as paradigm for the disciple with respect to a life of service. In the case of the son

---

[3] cf Robert C Tannehill "Reading it Whole: The Function of Mark 8:34-35 in Mark's Story" *Quarterly Review* 2 (Summer, 1982) 67-78; and "The Disciples in Mark" *Journal of Religion* 57 (1977) 386-405.

of man this service takes the ultimate form of giving one's life as a ransom for many. This appears to apply to the disciple as well. This is so first because of the way this saying concerning service carries forward the earlier assertion concerning the disciples' surrendering of life in order to gain it and by the suggestion in that earlier passage that the disciple is to take up the cross. We may note that the emphasis upon self-denial and service is immediately intelligible as practice and discipline for prospective martyrs. One cannot undertake this role of witness unless one is trained in the concrete, regular and rigorous practice of turning against one's own self interest, self preservation or self assertion.

The juxtaposition of the sayings concerning the son of man and those concerning the followers of Jesus already indicates the parallel between their fate and that of the son of man. But this parallel is brought out in other ways as well. This can be seen if we return to the characteristics noted earlier of the fate of the son of man and ask how this corresponds with what is said of the disciple.

1) Betrayal. In the case of Jesus this betrayal is portrayed as coming from within the ranks of his adopted family (3:35) of disciples (3:19). But concerning the disciples themselves the "apocalyptic discourse" warns: "And brother will betray brother to death, and the father his child, and children will rise up against parents and have them put to death; and you will be hated by all for my name's sake." (13:12-13) If anything the theme of betrayal is even more strongly emphasized in the case of the disciple that in that of the son of man.

2). Rejection by religious authorities. In the case of Jesus this is the theme of the narrative of his trial. The disciple is warned: "But take heed to yourselves; for they will deliver you up to councils and you will be beaten in synagogues" (13:9.)

3) Condemnation. We noted that this is not usually a separate item. Here it is implied in the notion of trial: "and when they bring you up to trial and deliver you up..." (13:11). It is noteworthy that this being tried and handed over is not presented as a possibility (if) but as a certainty (when).

4) Suffering. The theme of suffering is represented both by the statement that "...you will be hated by all for my name's sake ..." (13:13) as well as by various sayings concerning persecution (4:17; 10:30)

5) Execution. The execution of the disciple is foreshadowed in the saying concerning the cross in 8:31. It is also the theme of the inter-

change between Jesus and the sons of Zebedee which precedes the saying concerning true greatness in 10:43-45. In that interchange Jesus assures the brothers that "The cup that I drink, you will drink; and with the baptism with which I am baptized you will be baptized." (10:39). The cup which Jesus drinks is the cup of woe as is clearly indicated in his Gethsemane prayer (14:36). His baptism is a baptism in blood. Thus the follower is summoned to share the fate of the son of man.

6) Resurrection. The resurrection of the follower is only mentioned in connection with the return of the son of man who "will send out the messengers [angels] and gather his elect from the four winds, from the ends of the earth to the ends of heavens." (13:27). However we should also recall the saying that those who lose their lives for the sake of the gospel will save their lives (8:35) and the assertion that in the midst of sufferings those who endure to the end "will be saved". (13:13)

The fate of the disciple corresponds both in general and in detail to that of the son of man.

This parallel is developed in other ways as well. In the sayings which first indicate this parallel in suffering Jesus points to the connection between himself and the son of man in the following way:

> "For whoever is ashamed of me and of my words will the son of man also be ashamed when he comes in the glory of his Father with the holy angels [messengers]." (8:38)

This is as close as Jesus comes in this central section to an explicit identification of himself with the son of man. But this identification remains indirect. Those who are repelled by his words will find themselves repelled by the son of man. Is any thing like this said of the disciple? In the teaching occasioned by the appearance of an exorcist not connected with the disciples Jesus maintains:

> For truly I say to you, whoever gives you a cup of water to drink because you bear the name of Christ, will by no means lose their reward." (9:41)

This saying is not isolated since the reception of the disciple is also emphasized as determinative in 6:11.

Just as a repudiation of Jesus and his words leads to a being repudiated by the son of man, so also the welcoming of the disciple, even in the most simple terms, leads to weal. In neither case, it should be noted, is what at stake something like what we normally associate with faith. It has more to do with the question of hospitality (cup of water) or repugnance.

This review has shown that there is a detailed paralleling of the disciple with the son of man. The son of man serves as a paradigm for the disciple. Of course this was already indicated by the way in which it was the freedom of the disciple with respect to the sabbath which led to Jesus' saying that the son of man is lord of the sabbath (2:28). Thus the disciples have already acted the role of the son of man with respect to this freedom just as they are called to take on this role with respect to service and suffering, being repudiated by religious and secular authority, dying and rising.

3. The New Humanity

We have seen that the statements concerning the fate of the son of man serve as a paradigm which has already been actualized by John, is being actualized by Jesus and is to be actualized by the disciple. It thus cannot be maintained that these sayings apply exclusively to Jesus, that they serve simply as predictions of his passion. They rather serve to indicate the appropriate or fitting destiny of those who are involved in the messianic mission indicated at the beginning, that of announcing and enacting the inbreaking of the divine reign. I wish now to show how these results illuminate features of these sayings and of the Gospel of Mark in general before turning to a final consideration of the way in which Mark's view of the son of man may serve to clarify aspects of human life "outside the ghetto" of specifically Christian belief and identity.

In the first place it is already quite clear that "son of man" does not designate a single subject but includes a certain plurality. This plurality does not seem to be "all humanity" but neither is it connected exclusively to Jesus. It begins at least with John and it includes the disciples as well. This corresponds to the initial depiction of the son of man in Daniel 7:13 as the designation of a new human-like empire which will replace the totemic or beastly empires (7:3-8). The son of man appears to designate those who play a part in the messianic mission of announcing and enacting the reign of God beginning at least with John (although earlier with the prophets according to 12:1-5) and continuing through all those who follow in this mission toward martyrdom.

It is now clear that the sayings concerning the son of man are not to be understood as predictions at all. They are prescriptive rather than predictive. These sayings describe not a miraculous foreknowledge of a contingent future but the specification of what is fitting or appropriate for a class of subjects which are included in the son of man. This means that these sayings appear to indicate a program or strategy which applies to "whoever would come after" Jesus.

This may be clarified if we focus our attention on what *appears* to be the difference between Jesus and his predecessors (possibly including John). In his temple discourse Jesus repeats, in allegorical form, the tradition of the fate of the prophets at the hand of religious and political authority (12:1-5). This fate could have been regarded as an anomaly (people should respond to God's messengers, God should protect his messengers). However the tradition cited by Jesus has at least gone beyond the notion of the suffering of God's messengers as an anomaly to the view that it is predictable. That is, those who rebuke the powerful can expect that they will meet with virulent opposition. (It is possible that John had recognized this and so expected to be rejected and possibly killed).

What appears to be distinctive in Jesus' view is a threefold advance. In his view (as represented by Mark) the dismal fate of the messenger of God is represented as not simply an anomaly nor a regrettable if predictable pattern but as in some sense fitting or necessary. That is, it corresponds to the divine will; it is somehow essential to the divine strategy of accomplishing the divine reign. This is actually thematized in Jesus' agony in the garden in which the fate of martyrdom is directly linked with the divine will (14:36) but is already implicit in the sayings concerning the fitting or appropriate end of the son of man. What it means for this to be an essential part of the coming of God's reign we will discuss below.

On the basis of such a recognition of the necessity of martyrdom the action of Jesus appears in Mark's narrative to be deliberately calculated to bring this fate upon himself. Jesus' trial and execution is by no means represented as a consequence of a miscarriage of justice but the result of provocative tactics on the part of Jesus. Thus the determination to go to Jerusalem (10:32ff), the provocation of Jesus' kingly ride to the gates of the city (11:1-10) the blockade of the temple (11:15-6) with its allusion to Jeremiah's characterization of the temple as a refuge for bandits (Jer. 7:11)— a characterization which led to Jeremiah's imprisonment and the demand for his execution (cf. Jer.

26:7ff)— all seem calculated to provoke the alarm of the centers of power in Jerusalem.

This strategy is further exhibited in Jesus' confrontational tactics in "dialogue" with the various representatives of the Jerusalem power structure. In these dialogues he manages to systematically alienate the scribes, priests and elders (11:27ff), the Herodians and Pharisees (12:13ff) and the Sadducees (12:18ff). His behavior at the trials continues this pattern in that Jesus does not seek to rebut the charges against him (14:61; 15:5), and, when the evidence of the witnesses against him is unconvincing, speaks in such a way as to convict himself (14:62; 15:2). In all of these ways the behavior of Jesus is that of one who is pursuing a deliberate strategy of provoking martyrdom. The fate of Jesus then appears to be the result of his own provocation. This serves to contrast with the apparently arbitrary features of John's death (which has been portrayed as the result of palace intrigue in Herod's court.)

But Jesus does more than turn the recognition of the fittingness of the fate of the son of man into a deliberate strategy. He also trains disciples or "understudies" to continue this strategy. That is the significance of the insistence on the parallel between his fate and that of the disciple. From the very beginning Jesus has called some persons to share with him in his mission. This participation initially takes the form of accompanying him but quickly assumes the form of proclamation, healing and exorcism; that is, assumption of the characteristic features of his Galilean mission. But from 8:31 on Jesus is also explicitly preparing his followers not only for his own martyrdom but for theirs as well. This means that in the aftermath of his own execution they are to carry on the messianic mission which includes the strategy of martyrdom.

The notion that the suffering of the son of man is a strategy being recommended to (the followers of) the disciples casts light on the much debated "messianic secret of Mark's Gospel. Of course Jesus' identity has never been a secret for the reader of the narrative. It is announced at the very beginning (1:1). But there is a prohibition directed against the proclamation of the messianic identity of Jesus. This prohibition does more than prevent the proclamation of a messiah without the cross. It prevents a Christian confession of Jesus as Christ which does not recognize what it means to follow this Jesus, to live and die in solidarity with him. What is at stake for Mark is the way in which a Christian confession of Jesus may actually serve to circumvent or evade the strategy of martyrdom. Mark's concern here is by no means without foundation. For it is clear that the tendency to focus upon the suffering and death of Jesus as if it were the dying of a mystery cult figure was a possibility not only in the first century but continues to be a basic characteristic of Christianity through the ages.[4] By identifying Jesus as the Christ or as son of God it is quite easy to slip into supposing that his suffering was exceptional in the sense that it serves to exempt the follower from suffering, from persecution, from provocation of the principalities and powers, from the condemnation of the respectable and the suppression of the powerful. Then Christianity can become the pillar of the status quo rather than the witness to the transformation of all things, the coming of the divine reign of justice, generosity and joy. It is this sort of confession which must at all costs be interdicted for it is satanic (8:33).

This does not absolutely preclude the confession of Jesus as the messiah or his acclamation as the son of God. These titles themselves are not contested but rather are "deconstructed" by way of being tied to the son of man strategy. Precisely in so far as Jesus is the one who recognizes and discloses the necessity of this fate, precisely as the one who transforms it from fate to strategy, precisely as one who makes this strategy not a singular event but a continuing, indeed permanent vocation for those who are called to participate in this messianic mission, to that extent the titles son of God and messiah are justified. That is, they are justified precisely in so far as they do not serve to open a gulf between Jesus and the follower but serve to express an absolute and unwavering loyalty to this one and his mission and his strategy of martyrdom.

In this way it can also be said that Jesus *is* the son of man. That is, he is the one who makes this suffering into the strategy of martyrdom and propagates this strategy through his disciples. He is in this sense the "first born of many brethren" as Paul suggests in another connection (Rom. 8:29).[5]

---

[4]It will be evident that I disagree with Boers' view ,in "The Unity of the Gospel of Mark" [*Scriptura* 1981], which views Mark as a cultic myth. Boers modifies this view (in "Reflections on the Gospel of Mark: A Structural Investigation" *SBL 1987 Seminar Papers* pp. 255-67) to agree that the disciples are to imitate Jesus in suffering service to humanity but does not realize that this renders the notion of a cultic myth superfluous in accounting for the structure of the Gospel.

[5]The relation between this reading of the son of man in Mark and the Pauline notion of Jesus as the second Adam is one both of a certain continuity and of tension. Also interesting in this regard is the view which Paul takes of his own

We may also note that this reading of Mark places it in the context of persecution and so emphasizes its rhetorical purpose of persuading the Christians to accept martyrdom not only as a necessary evil but as a deliberate strategy of imitating Christ.

Now this loyalty can finally only be justified if it is clear in what sense the coming of the divine reign of justice, generosity and joy actually requires this strategy rather than another. What is the connection between the son of man strategy and the messianic mission?

The enactment of the coming of God's reign leads at every point to confrontation with the guardians of the status quo. This is true whether one thinks of solidarity with despised groups, of disregard for religious customs and distinctions, or of putting human welfare above even the most sacred religious institutions. Thus provocation is inherent in the enactment of the reign of God from the very beginning.

This provocation is an extension of the way in which the enactment of the reign of God entails the healing of disease and the exorcism of demons. The coming of God's reign means the overcoming of all that disfigures or distorts creation and especially the one created to be the divine image and likeness. Thus the far more pervasive, if less visible, forces of religious, social and political injustice, arrogance and violence must also be overthrown. This overthrow is not simply the setting up of a new power structure but the abolition of power structure as such (9:42-4). Thus it cannot be accomplished through the imitation of the tactics of domination, but only by the inversion of these tactics, i.e., by martyrdom.

The strategy of martyrdom is explicitly aimed at the very foundation of society, that is, at the pretension on the part of these structures to themselves represent the divine will and authority. The strategy of martyrdom serves to strip these authorities of their pretended divine legitimation and expose them as the torturers, the murderers of God.

The son of man then designates the new humanity which corresponds to the new creation, the reign of God. But this new humanity is not produced by divine fiat. Rather it is produced by the suffering of those who are called to participate in this mission of liberating the earth. By taking on this mission, the gospel is proclaimed to all the earth. The witness of those who accept the paradigm of the son of

---

sufferings as an image of those of Jesus. The formal similarity of these Pauline notions to the role of the son of man in Mark suggests that the views I have ascribed to Mark are not wholly without parallel in the other writings of the NT.

man serves to spread the good news of God's coming (and the way of God's coming) to all nations (13:10).

4. A Ransom for Many

In the Gospel of Mark it is Jesus who recognizes that the coming of God's reign means that those who bear witness to that coming must take on the role of the son of man, the new humanity which suffers and dies on the road to this reign. As the one who both discloses, enacts and promotes this strategy Jesus is the messiah, the son of God. But this does not by any means legitimate Christian claims to an ex officio connection to this messianic mission, still less to an exclusive relation with it. The Christian acknowledgement of Jesus as the messiah may very well conceal an attempt to escape this mission as in the case of Peter's confession. What is of utmost importance is not the paying of metaphysical or eschatological or soteriological compliments to Jesus, but the following of him on this mission, the participation with him in the vocation of the son of man, the participation in the witness of martyrdom. It is this which bears a relation to the coming of that reign which he announced and enacted.

But this means that the following of Jesus is not found even primarily within the precincts of the church. It is found wherever there are those who place their own lives in jeopardy in order to actualize a more human future, a future worthy of the image and likeness of God. In our own time the son of man strategy has undergone a new birth. As the cycle of violence and arrogance has become increasingly transparent some have chosen the path of a militant martyrdom, of a refusal of violence which entails a refusal of the structures of violence, a confrontation with them and a provocation of them. This son of man strategy was reborn in the life of Gandhi, first in South Africa and then later in his ancestral India. It has continued in South Africa with the work of such figures as Chief Albert Lutuli and Steve Biko. It has been associated in the U.S. with the name of Martin Luther King, Jr. The spirit is seen today in the work of human rights activists in Poland and Chile. Wherever people dream of a new era in which the structures of domination and division, the powers of avarice and arrogance and violence, are overcome, there they also take up, consciously or unconsciously, the son of man strategy.

And when they do so men and women begin to be delivered from resignation to the way things are, begin to hope for a future of justice and joy, they begin to see the demonic forces of our world for what they are and to turn their back upon them. The evidence of early Christianity as well as the evidence of committed movements of our own day demonstrate that wherever the son of man appears, wherever this surrender of life for the sake of a new humanity occurs, there many are ransomed from bondage. The saving work of the son of man is to be found not within the ghetto of confessional or religious Christianity but in the world of this witness to the coming of a future worthy of human hope.

Theodore W. Jennings, Jr.

V
Translation and Transformation

PAUL OUTSIDE THE CHRISTIAN GHETTO
Stories of Intercultural Conflict and Cooperation in Acts
Robert C. Tannehill, *Methodist Theological School in Ohio*

In *Theology out of the Ghetto* Hendrikus Boers prompted New Testament exegetes to consider the dangers of religious exclusiveness and to search for resources within the New Testament that can lead us beyond this exclusiveness. "In religious exclusiveness," he reminded us, "a captive God functions to isolate the believer" from nonbelievers.[1] There is a prophetic quality to Boers' book. He saw ahead of time that a dormant issue was in fact a key issue. The role of religion in the present political scene underscores the correctness of his insight, for we can now see clearly that exclusive religion, religion that encourages imperial attitudes by believers and consigns nonbelievers to the hostile darkness, makes peaceful settlement of political disputes almost impossible. To survive, the world needs a large infusion of tolerance.

Concern over religious exclusiveness has been one motivating factor in my study of Luke-Acts. I am convinced that Luke-Acts has a vision of God's saving purpose that can help Christians to embrace the world, for, guided by Second Isaiah, it understands God's saving purpose as potentially universal, encompassing "all flesh." This saving purpose underlies the whole narrative and is emphasized for the reader at the beginning through Simeon's oracle (Luke 2:30-32) and the banner quotation from Isa 40:3-5 in Luke 3:4-6. God's salvation is for both Jews and Gentiles, that is, for all. But it is being brought to the world through the mission of Jesus and his witnesses. Here problems arise, problems that Luke-Acts does not hide. The mission produced conflict and rejection, both among Jews and Gentiles. The Christian mission moved out of its ghetto into the larger world, but

---

[1] See *Theology out of the Ghetto*: A New Testament Exegetical Study Concerning Religious Exclusiveness (Leiden: E. J. Brill, 1971), 105.

partially for this reason, it became separated from its Jewish parent. Christianity became a threat to Judiasm, and strong barriers were the result. Far from being a simple success story, Acts highlights the tragedy of Jewish rejection.[2] Instead of uniting Jews and Gentiles, Christianity became a religion in competition with Judaism, and the protective barriers on both sides became strong.

The culture and government of the Greco-Roman world, guided by values quite different than the Christian movement, were also potential sources of conflict. This essay concerns the ways in which Paul interacts with Greco-Roman culture and government according to Acts. I hasten to add that I cannot discuss this subject fully here. Full discussion would obviously require treatment of Paul's response to the religion of Lystra (Acts 14:11-18) and the idols and philosophers of Athens (17:16-34), and consideration of Paul's relation to Roman officials after he is seized in Jerusalem (21:27–26:32).[3] Instead I wish to focus on some other passages, which I will approach in a different way than commentaries usually do in order to highlight their importance for our subject. I am referring to 1) four passages in Acts 16-19 in which Paul and other Christians are publicly accused and 2) the sea voyage to Rome in Acts 27. The first four passages are scenes of conflict. The last passage is a suggestive example of cooperation across religious lines. In both cases attention to certain aspects of narrative composition will help us to understand the importance of the material.

I. The Public Accusation Type-Scene

In four sites of Paul's later missionary work — Philippi (16:19-24), Thessalonica (17:5-9), Corinth (18:12-17), and Ephesus (19:23-40) — we find scenes that present a similar sequence of events. The sequence contains three basic elements: 1) Christians are forcefully brought before officials or a public assembly. 2) An accusation is made, and this accusation is highlighted by direct quotation. 3) The result of this attempt to curb the Christian mission is narrated. Thus in Philippi the owners of the girl with the oracular spirit drag Paul and Silas to the magistrates (16:19) and state their accusation (16:20-

---

[2] See Robert C. Tannehill, "Israel in Luke-Acts: A Tragic Story," *Journal of Biblical Literature* 104 (1985), 69-85.

[3] For comment on these passages, see Robert C. Tannehill, *The Narrative Unity of Luke-Acts: A Literary Interpretation*, vol. 2 (Philadelphia: Fortress Press, forthcoming).

21). As a result, Paul and Silas are beaten and imprisoned (16:22-24). In Thessalonica Jews raise a mob and come looking for Paul and Silas (17:5). Not finding them, they drag "Jason and some brothers" to the magistrates (17:6) and make their accusation (17:6-7). The officials are disturbed and require Jason and the others to post a bond (17:6-7). In Corinth the Jews bring Paul before the tribunal of Gallio, the proconsul (18:12), and accuse Paul (18:13), but Gallio refuses to accept the case (18:14-16). The scene in Ephesus is the most independent in construction. Here the narrator presents a longer and more dramatic scene, and the first two elements of the type-scene are rearranged. The accusation is stated first, in a speech by Demetrius to other members of his trade (19:25-27). In this case the accusation motivates action against Christians, which follows. People rush together into the theater, seizing Gaius and Aristarchus, companions of Paul, along the way (19:29), and forming an impromptu public assembly (ἐκκλεσία, 19:32). After much confusion and uproar, the secretary (γραμματεὺς) of Ephesian government succeeds in calming the people and dissolving the assembly.

The similarities among these scenes justify speaking of a public accusation type-scene. We may speak of a type-scene when a basic situation, with similar characters and plot-elements, recurs several times in a narrative. The analysis of type-scenes is similar to the analysis of genres in form criticism, but my interest, like that of Robert Alter, who introduced the term,[4] is not in the preliterary history of traditional genres but in a narrator's employment of type-scenes to suggest similarity, with variation, in a narrative. Type-scenes can be used as an important literary technique. The recurrent type-scene suggests that the situation is common or characteristic, while the variations in the type-scene both fight monotony and teach us to look for similar situations in varying costume. The public accusation type-scene in Acts, with its four examples in four consecutive chapters, shows the narrator's strong concern with the way that the Christian mission appears to the outside world and the effect those perceptions may have on Christians.[5]

---

[4]See *The Art of Biblical Narrative* (New York: Basic Books, 1981), 47-62. On type-scenes in Luke, see R. Tannehill, *Narrative Unity*, 1:18, 105, 170-171.

[5]In her dissertation Marie-Eloise Rosenblatt discusses "the public confrontation type-scene" in Acts. Her category overlaps with mine, although it is defined somewhat differently and includes a somewhat different list of passages. See "Under Interrogation: Paul as Witness in Juridical Contexts in Acts and the

The accusation is a central element in the scene. It is highlighted through direct discourse and expresses what Paul and his supporters represent to opponents, both Gentiles and Jews. These opponents see the Christian mission as a threat to established society. In most cases they express their accusation in a way likely to arouse their audience and move them to action against the Christians. This public accusation may not completely coincide with their private motives, as indicated by the narrator. Thus in Philippi the narrator first indicates that Paul's opponents, when they seize Paul and Silas, are reacting to their financial loss through the exorcism of the slave girl. But in their statement to the magistrates they present Paul and Silas as a threat to society. They say, "These men, who are Jews, are unsettling our city, and they are proclaiming customs which it is not lawful for us, who are Romans, to accept or practice" (16:20-21). The customs that made Rome great are being threatened by some troublesome Jews, who, it is well known, follow a very distinct set of customs. Paul and Silas, the accusers claim, are openly advocating Jewish customs in a Roman colony. Note that Paul and Silas are attacked as missionaries of Judiasm. By Jews Paul is attacked for failing to uphold the Mosaic customs (21:20-21,28). Thus he is caught between two suspicious communities, each regarding him as an advocate of the opponent's position. In Philippi the charges are accepted by the local magistrates. Paul and Silas are beaten and imprisoned.

While Paul has frequent disputes in synagogues, in the four cases we are examining the dispute either does not begin or does not remain in the synagogue community. It spills over into the public sphere and is brought to city officials, the provincial governor, or the public assembly. Jews may or may not be involved as accusers. Of the four scenes under consideration, Jews are accusers in the second and third (Thessalonica and Corinth), while Gentiles are accusers in the first and fourth (Philippi and Ephesus). This provides a neat balance that may be deliberate. Jews are not the sole source of trouble for Paul's mission. Gentiles also feel threatened by his mission and take action aginst him. To both Jews and Gentiles Paul is a troublesome outsider who advocates teachings and behavior that threaten their way of life.

From Philippi Paul travels to Thessalonica. Here the public accusation scene grows out of his preaching in the synagogue. Paul has

---

Implied Spirituality for Luke's Community" (Ph.D. dissertation, Graduate Theological Union, 1987), 193-205.

some success there, but jealous Jews form a mob, set the city in an uproar, and appear at Jason's house in hopes of capturing Paul. When they can't find Paul, they drag Jason and some others to the magistrates. Just as the validity of the accusation in Philippi was undermined when the narrator indicated that the accusers were acting out of selfish economic motives, so the accusation of these Jews is undermined by indications that they are acting out of jealousy (17:5). Furthermore, they form a mob from "some evil men" hanging around the market place and set the city in an uproar. When they then accuse Christians of "upsetting the world," the lack of evidence of deliberate disturbances by Christians contrasts starkly with the accusers' own behavior. The Jews have their private reasons for opposing Paul and his supporters, while the public accusation is designed to move Gentile magistrates to action. It portrays Christians as a threat to Roman society. It goes a step further than the accusation in Philippi. Christians are not only a threat to social stability because they are "upsetting the world"; they are also a direct threat to Caesar's rule, for "all these persons are acting against the decrees of Caesar, saying that there is another king, Jesus" (17:7). This charge and the preceding one in Philippi would be plausible to outsiders with little acquaintance with Christianity. Clearly the narrator intends this extreme charge to be an expression of either ignorance or malice. However, Acts also shows awareness of realistic reasons for tension between the Christian way and its Roman environment, including government officials.[6] In the scenes we are examining, the accusations are not followed by defense speeches. We are left to speculate about the grains of truth that may lie behind the charges that arise from ignorance and malice.

In Thessalonica the magistrates are disturbed by the charges and require Jason and the others to post a security bond. While the charges have some effect, the result is not nearly as severe as in Philippi. The four public accusations in Acts 16-19 have varied results, and they illustrate various attitudes among officials. The Philippian magistrates are fully taken in by the charges, with serious results for Paul and Silas. The Thessalonian magistrates are more cautious. In Corinth the proconsul Gallio will dismiss the charges out of

---

[6]Richard J. Cassidy provides a helpful discussion of Paul and Roman authorities in Acts, showing that the picture does not fit the theory of political apologetic. See *Society and Politics in the Acts of the Apostles* (Maryknoll, NY: Orbis Books, 1987), 83-157.

hand, probably with contempt for the accusers. In Ephesus the charges lead to a large public protest but no legal action or bodily harm, due in part to the intervention of a city official. There is no attempt in Acts to stereotype officials. They may or may not protect Christians against attacks. The variety of the local scene is retained in this aspect of the narrative. A sense of the varied local situation is further encouraged by the use of titles appropriate to the particular locations (στρατηγοὶ for Philippi [16:20],[7] πολιτάρχαι in Thessalonica [17:6]), naming a particular proconsul in Corinth, and referring to the temple of Artemis and the theater in Ephesus. The accusations, the attitudes of the officials that respond to them, and the results vary from place to place.

The officials of Roman society do not form a monolithic front of opposition to the Christian way, but those who protect it may have their own reasons for doing so. The scene before Gallio in Corinth may well be intended to illustrate the Lord's protection of Paul, promised in the vision in 18:9-10. At the same time, it is probable that Gallio's own motives in this scene are less than admirable. The Jews bring Paul to Gallio and make their charge: "This fellow is inciting people to worship God contrary to the law" (18:13). There is some uncertainty here whether Roman law or Jewish law is meant, and Hans Conzelmann believes that Luke pictures the Jews as deliberately ambiguous in an attempt to deceive Gallio.[8] This strains credulity, however, The Jews speak of worshiping God (using the singular). It is unlikely that any official would forget that Jews have their own way of worship according to their own law. It seems, then, that the Jews are straightforwardly appealing to Gallio for protection of their religious community against a disturbing intruder. The Jewish concern may have a basis in the earlier narrative. Paul left the Corinthian synagogue for the house of Titius Justus, a "worshiper of God (σεβομένους τὸν θεόν)" (18:7). This devout Gentile would not be bound to observe the Jewish law as a Christian, while the local Jews may have hoped that he and others would accept the life of Judaism. The complaint in 18:13 could be a direct result. Paul is telling such

---

[7]See Walter Bauer, *A Greek-English Lexicon of the New Testament*, translated and adapted by W. F. Arndt and F. W. Gingrich, 2nd edition revised and augmented by F. W. Gingrich and F. W. Danker (Chicago: University of Chicago Press, 1979), 770: "This title was not quite officially correct" for the officials of the Roman colony of Philippi "but it occurs several times in inscr[iptions] as a popular designation for them."

[8]See *Acts of the Apostles* (Hermeneia; Philadelphia: Fortress Press, 1987), 153.

people that it is possible "to worship God (σέβεσθαι τὸν θεόν)" apart form the law, robbing the Jewish community of present supporters and potential converts.

Gallio's refusal to intervene may have been the correct decision, but the final verse of the scene suggests that he is acting less from legal wisdom than from contempt for Jews. He not only refuses to intervene in Jewish disputes but also refuses to rescue a Jew being attacked in his presence. While the attackers are not clearly specified, the Jews as a group are driven away from Gallio's tribunal in 18:16. Therefore, when Sosthenes is attacked before the tribunal in 18:17, it would seem to be the work of Gentile onlookers who share Gallio's attitude toward Jews, not the work of Jews taking out their frustrations on their leader. Paul benefits from Gallio's refusal of the Jews' appeal, but not because Gallio is a virtuous governor. A sense of the complexities of good and evil in human affairs appears in this scene.[9]

The effect of Christianity on Greco-Roman religion is a thematic issue in the last of the public accusation scenes. The episode begins with the speech of Demetrius and ends with the speech of the secretary. In both cases we must understand the speech in light of the person who is speaking. Demetrius the silversmith, speaking to the people of his trade, brings the accusation against Paul, and his speech is carefully crafted to move his audience to action. He cites the threat to their trade from Paul's influence and adds that reverence for the temple of Artemis and for Artemis herself are threatened (19:25-27). Here, as in the Philippi scene, the commercial motive of the accuser undermines his moral stance. However, the concern about Artemis and her temple is picked up by his hearers and the larger population of Ephesus. Inspired by a mixture of local pride and devotion to Artemis, the crowd in the theater spends hours shouting "Great is Artemis of the Ephesians." Then the government secretary intervenes. He rejects the position of Demetrius and denies that the Christians apprehended by the crowd have committed sacrilege against Artemis' temple or blasphemed her (19:37). Although he defends Christians, he does not speak from a Christian point of view but as a city official who shares its dominant culture. He points out the danger to the city of being accused of riot or revolt, a concern that would

---

[9]It is wrong to interpret Luke-Acts itself as anti-Jewish. See R. Tannehill, "Israel in Luke-Acts," 69-85, and idem, "Rejection by Jews and Turning to Gentiles: The Pattern of Paul's Mission in Acts," in *Luke-Acts and the Jewish People*, ed. Joseph B. Tyson (Minneapolis: Augsburg Books, forthcoming).

weigh heavily on a city official. His remarks about Ephesus and Artemis also reflect his place in the local establishment. He refuses to take the concern of Demetrius and the crowd seriously. He is sure that no one fails to recognize Ephesus' claim to fame as "temple keeper of the great Artemis." These things are "undeniable," he says (19:35-36).

These opening words of the official's speech can be interpreted either as strategic flattery to quiet the crowd or as the smug assurance of an establishment figure who thinks that Paul's mission cannot possibly affect the dominant culture. In the latter case, he is naive, from the perspective of Acts as a whole. Demetrius pointed to Paul's strong influence in Ephesus and the province of Asia and reported that Paul has been saying, "Gods created by hands are not gods" (19:26). Here Demetrius' report fits what we find elsewhere in Acts. In 19:10 we were told that Paul worked in Ephesus for two years, "so that all those inhabiting Asia heard the word of the Lord, both Jews and Greeks." In an earlier example of his preaching, Paul stated that human attempts to represent the divine by images of gold, silver, or stone are signs of pagan ignorance of God (17:29-30). Thus the larger narrative indicates that Demetrius has good reason to be worried about Paul's effect on his trade and Ephesian religion, while the city official is either blind to the problem or chooses to ignore it in order to soothe the crowd. The worried reaction of Demetrius and the crowd hints at the potentially shattering effect of the Christian mission on the religious culture of a place like Ephesus. The episode is remarkable in that Christians have a very small role in it. We are asked to view the effect of the mission through the eyes of Demetrius, the crowd, and the city secretary, an approach that requires subtle sifting of characters' points of view in order to discern the implied author's.[10]

These four examples of the public accusation type-scene in Acts provide narrative images of conflict between the Christian mission and both Jewish and Gentile society, conflict important enough to demand the attention of government officials. While the accusations may reveal ignorance and malice, and arise from self-interested mo-

---

[10]The implied author is a mental construct, based on a reading of the work, of the kind of person who would write this work, which affirms certain values, beliefs, and norms. The implied author may closely resemble the real author, but there may also be differences, for authors may write in order to purify themselves, becoming more consistent, noble, radical, etc., than they are in real life.

II. The Storm at Sea

tives, there is a core of hard reality behind the conflict. In some ways the Christian movement does threaten both Jewish and Gentile society, raising the question whether peaceful coexistence is possible.

It is remarkable that the implied author chooses to tell in such vivid detail the story of storm and shipwreck in Acts 27. It is doubly remarkable when we note that Paul is only intermittently in the focus of attention. It will be helpful to begin with the hypothesis that Acts 27 is a unified narrative in which the parts contribute fittingly to the whole, for we will discover good evidence to support this view. Furthermore, this approach will help us to recognize that this story of a storm at sea is more conducive to theological reflection than commonly assumed.

In the early part of the chapter there are numerous signs of a difficult and dangerous voyage.[11] These include Paul's explicit warning of loss of the ship and loss of life (27:10). This warning is not heeded, and the ship is caught by the great storm. As the storm continues, the "we" narrator indicates that "all hope of our being saved" was dissolving (v. 20). At this low point in the narrative, Paul intervenes a second time.[12] Although he reminds his audience of their failure to listen to his previous advice, his main purpose is to revive the hope and courage of a company that has lost hope.[13] He urges them "to cheer up" or "take heart" (εὐθυμεῖν, v. 22; cf. v. 25). Paul can encourage others because he himself has been encouraged by an angel, who said, "Do not fear" (v. 24), and assured him that it is still God's plan for him to reach Rome and stand before Caesar. Furthermore, the angel said, "God has granted you all those sailing with you." The whole ship's company will be rescued, a major modification of what Paul

---

[11]The following discussion parallels much of my treatment of Acts 27 in *Narrative Unity*, vol. 2.

[12]Reinhard Kratz notes that Acts 27 shifts between scenes that heighten the danger and scenes in which Paul responds to this danger. See *Rettungswunder: Motiv-, traditions- und formkritische Aufarbeitung einer biblischen Gattung* (Europaeische Hochschulschriften 123; Frankfurt a. M.: Peter Lang, 1979), 323.

[13]A speech in the midst of the storm is a convention of storm scenes, as Susan Marie Praeder indicates. She says, "The usual place for such speeches is at a high point in the storm and a low point in the fortunes of the sea travelers." Paul's speech is unusual in conveying a message of hope. See "Acts 27:1–28:16: Sea Voyages in Ancient Literature and the Theology of Luke-Acts," *Catholic Biblical Quarterly* 46 (1984), 696.

expected according to his earlier warning in v. 10. If the author were simply interested in bringing Paul to Rome under divine protection, it would be an unnecessary complication to refer to the rescue of all, especially since this requires correction of Paul's previous warning. This announcement is a key to understanding the rest of the episode, for it determines what must happen, and the acts of sailors, soldiers, and Paul are to be judged in light of it. From this point on, no method of escape is acceptable that doesn't include all. Opportunities arise for the sailors to escape, abandoning the rest (v. 30), and for the soldiers to escape after killing their prisoners (v. 42). These plans are thwarted, in spite of the risk involved in trying to get the large ship close to shore and allowing prisoners to swim for their lives when they might escape. These plans are wrong not only because they endanger Paul but also because they offend against the divine plan of saving all.

Paul identifies the angel as "an angel of the God whose I am, whom I also serve" (or "worship," v. 23). He refers in this way to his own God because the majority of his audience has other gods. Thus the "all" who are promised rescue consist primarily of pagans who do not worship the one God. Nevertheless, God has decided to rescue them.

There is no indication that Paul's encouraging message has an immediate effect on his audience. The narrative continues with the approach of the island, which, although it fits Paul's prediction in v. 26, produces fear (v. 29), not encouragement. The sailors are afraid that the ship will run aground against sharp rocks. Paul's efforts to revive hope are successful only after a further intervention, when the ship's company finally does take heart (εὔθυμοι...γενόμενοι, v. 36), as Paul had earlier urged (vv. 22, 25). With the approach of land, the technical skills of the sailors, also noted previously in the narrative, come into play. They sense the approach of land. They confirm that shallows are approaching by taking soundings. Then they throw out four anchors from the stern to keep the ship from drifting onto rocks in the middle of the night. In all of this they are acting for the benefit of the whole ship's company. Then, however, they do something that both demonstrates disloyalty to the rest of the seafarers and failure to trust Paul's promise that God would provide a way for all to be saved. They try to "flee" from the ship in a small boat, on "pretext" of stretching out further anchors from the bow. Paul recognizes their plan in time, tells the centurion and soldiers, and the soldiers cut the ropes, letting the boat drift ashore. This is a drastic move, since the boat might have been useful the next day. If nothing is done, however, the boat will only help the fleeing sailors, who are abandoning the others in a ship they cannot handle. The ship can carry all, and the divine plan is that all should be saved. The sailors are needed to sail the ship. Without them there is no hope of bringing it safely to shore. The boat must be sacrificed so that all will have a chance. Paul's alertness and the soldiers' swift action make it possible for all to reach safety.

Already in v. 21 we were told that the ship's company was not eating. Seasickness in the storm could have been the cause, but there may also be a link between the loss of hope in v. 20 and the failure to eat in v. 21. The latter view is strengthened by the scene in vv. 33-38, for which v. 21 is preparation. Paul urges all to eat and begins to eat himself. The decision of the others to eat is accompanied by a change of mood; all were "taking heart" (v. 36). It is Paul who causes this change. So we find Paul, shortly before the final effort to reach shore safely, urging all to take nourishment and break their long fast. He supports his exhortation with a reason, which includes a renewed promise that all will be saved. They must eat, for it will contribute to their "salvation, for a hair from the head of none of you will perish" (v. 34). It is finally this promise plus Paul's own action that overcomes the hopelessness indicated in v. 20, replacing it with new hope and courage.

Paul takes the lead and begins to eat. The description of this is remarkable, for it echoes accounts of other significant meals in Luke-Acts: "Taking bread, he gave thanks (εὐχαρίστησεν) to God before all, and breaking it, he began to eat" (v. 35). The sequence of taking bread, giving thanks or blessing, and breaking the bread is also found in Luke 9:16 (Jesus feeding the multitude), 22:19 (the last supper), and 24:30 (the meal at Emmaus). Furthermore, the church's meal celebration in Acts is called the breaking of bread (Acts 2:42, 46; 20:7, 11). The reference to giving thanks makes Acts 27:35 particularly close to Jesus' last supper, while the reference to the number of participants and the indication that they were filled in vv. 37-38 are reminiscent of the feeding of the multitude (Luke 9:14, 17). The details of Paul's actions in Acts 27:35 are not necessary parts of the narrative. They could easily have been omitted if they did not have special significance. The narrative invites us to picture Paul doing what Jesus did and what the church does: give thanks to God by breaking bread and eating.

Paul's meal, then, is as sacramental as any other meal in Luke-Acts. However, the fact that Paul is eating with pagans has proved troublesome for this interpretation. Bo Reicke, who argued for the sacramental associations of this scene in 1948, nevertheless added that it could not be a real Lord's Supper, since Paul is eating with pagans. Rather, Paul is allowing the people in the ship to participate in a prefiguration of the Christian Lord's Supper as preparation for later discipleship.[14] The absence of an indication that Paul distributed the bread over which he had given thanks is probably significant, Gerhard Schneider, who recognizes the eucharistic associations of this scene, is technically correct in saying that it does not depict a common meal, for Paul eats his food and the rest of the company other food.[15] To that extent the privacy of the church's celebration is maintained. The remarkable thing, however, is the effect that Paul's eucharist has on his non-Christian companions. By eating before them, Paul finally achieves his goal of encouraging them. They take nourishment and strengthen themselves for the final effort to reach shore safely.

The promise of rescue for all in v. 24 is echoed by repeated references to all in vv. 33-37. Paul urges all to take nourishment (v. 33). He promises that a hair of none of them will perish (v. 34). He gives thanks before all (v. 35). Then all take heart (v. 36). Finally, v. 37 indicates, "All the lives in the ship, we were two hundred seventy six." The "we" in the voyage to Rome generally refers to a small group of Christians. Here, however, the entire ship's company becomes a single "we" as the narrator numbers the company so that readers will know what "all" means. Even though the boundary of the church is not completely eliminated, the meal on the ship is an act that benefits all, Christian and non-Christian, and an act in which community is created across religious lines.

The meal can do this because of its association with God's promise for all. In v. 34 Paul repeats the angel's promise of v. 24 in other language. Then Paul takes bread and gives thanks to God. In the present context Paul's thanksgiving has particular significance. It is thanksgiving especially for God's promise of the rescue of all. Therefore, it is also an act of trust in this promise in spite of the im-

---

[14]See "Die Mahlzeit mit Paulus auf den Wellen des Mittelmeers Act. 27, 33-38," *Theologische Zeitschrift* 4 (1948), 408-9.

[15]See *Die Apostelgeschichte*, 2 vols. (Herders theologischer Kommentar zum Neuen Testament 5; Freiburg: Herder, 1980, 1982), 2: 396.

mediate danger. There may even be a play on words to support a connection with the promise. The angel announced that God "has graciously granted (κεχάρισται)" all to Paul. In response Paul "gave thanks (εὐχαρίστησεν)."[16] Paul's gratitude and trust are infectious. The others take heart and eat, showing the first signs that they, too, believe in the promise.

Even though the others do not share Paul's food, celebrating eucharist "before all" so that all will eat shows a remarkable concern to benefit non-Christians through a central Christian practice. The use of the hyperbole of the hair of the head in v. 34 is also remarkable. It parallels a promise of Jesus in Luke 21:18, but there the promise applied to persecuted disciples. Here the promise is stretched to include all, in accordance with the repeated references to the salvation of all in the voyage narrative.

Paul told the centurion and soldiers, "Unless these [sailors] remain in the ship, you cannot be saved" (v. 31). Paul also urged the others to eat because this would contribute to their "salvation" (v. 34). He is referring, of course, to being saved or rescued from the sea. These verses are part of an emphasized theme, for there are seven references to being saved from the sea in this section of Acts, using the verbs σῴζω (27:20, 31) and διασῴζω (27:43, 44; 28:1, 4), and the noun σωτερία (27:34). The rapid repetition of the same word in 27:43, 44; 28:1 is a particular sign of emphasis. These words are found in other accounts of sea voyages in ancient literature.[17] Therefore, ancient readers would not find them to be unnatural in their context. But Susan Praeder rightly discerns a double sense in these words. She emphasizes that narratives are both created from and read in light of a real world context of "experience and imagination" that enters literary expression. Two such contexts have taken literary shape and are particularly relevant to reading Acts 27:1–28:15: the imaginative experience of ancient sea voyages expressed in sea voyage literature and the imaginative experience of first century Christianity as expressed in Luke-Acts.[18] These two contexts suggest a double reading of the thematic emphasis on salvation or rescue. In the former context the hope for rescue from the sea is a natural part of the experience of

---

[16]See S. Praeder, "Sea Voyages," 698.

[17]See Susan Marie Praeder, "The Narrative Voyage: An Analysis and Interpretation of Acts 27-28" (Ph.D. dissertation, Graduate Theological Union, 1980), 245-56.

[18]See "Narrative Voyage," 95-99, 183-312.

a sea voyage, when danger arises. The salvation or rescue may come from various human and divine sources. In the latter context salvation takes on a special significance. It is not only the hope of those in a storm at sea but the purpose of God for all humanity, as announced at the beginning of Luke (2:30-32, 3:6). The emphasis on salvation in Luke-Acts gives to the emphasis on salvation in this sea voyage a second, symbolic sense.[19]

The narrative hints at a second sense by emphasis within the story of the voyage and by the theological importance of the terms "save, salvation" in Luke-Acts as a whole. However, the narrative does not determine for us how far we should take its suggestion. Even if we wish to remain close to the Lukan world of thought, there are two interesting possibilities to consider. First, not only does the emphasis on salvation in the voyage echo the emphasis on salvation in Luke-Acts as a whole but the insistence that all the ship's company must be saved echoes the promise that "all flesh will see the salvation of God" in Luke 3:6.[20] Thus the fulfillment of God's promise to Paul that all those in the ship will survive the storm becomes a sign in miniature of God's promise of salvation for all flesh, which has not yet been fulfilled. Paul is conscious that he is speaking mainly to pagans when he shares God's promise with those on board the ship.[21] This unconverted audience is promised salvation from the sea. Paul makes no reference to faith in Jesus Christ as a precondition. God graciously grants salvation to all on the ship, not because of their works or their faith, but simply because it fits God's purpose. In fact, the whole narrative of the voyage to Rome is remarkable for the absence of any indication that Paul proclaimed Jesus either to his companions on the ship or to the people of Malta. The benefits that God brings through Paul do not depend on acceptance of this message. In

---

[19]G. Schneider, *Apostelgeschichte*, 2:396, n. 107, recognizes that the use of the term elsewhere in Acts suggests that σωτερία in v. 34 is "transparent" to a meaning larger than rescue from the sea. On the use of the word group "save, salvation" in Luke-Acts, see Augustin Goerge, *Études sur l'oeuvre de Luc* (Sources bibliques; Paris: Gagalda, 1978), 307-20. George, however, regards the occurrences in the voyage to Rome as simply profane uses.

[20]On Luke 3:6 see R. Tannehill, *Narrative Unity*, 1:40-42, where I argue that seeing God's salvation means recognizing it and responding to it, which shades over into personal participation in it. In the Lukan context Luke 3:6 (= Isa 40:5) refers to participation in salvation by both Jews (including Jewish outcasts) and Gentiles.

[21]As noted above, Paul in v. 23 must distinguish the God he is talking about from other deities.

Rome Paul will continue his work as a missionary. He has not changed his mind on the importance of this work. But the voyage narrative presents a more comprehensive vision of God's saving work, which is not limited to those who hear and accept the gospel. The mission continues within the context of this vision.

To be sure, there is little evidence outside Acts 27 that Luke-Acts anticipates the salvation of every individual. One could argue that in the context of Luke-Acts the promise to "all flesh" is a promise to large numbers of people of all kinds, but not necessarily to every individual. Indeed, the reference to "as many as were ordained to eternal life" in Acts 13:48 suggests that there are some who are not ordained to eternal life. However, if salvation in Paul's voyage to Rome does have a second level of meaning, this section of Acts represents a new boldness of hope that anticipates salvation (in some sense) for every individual of a pluralistic community and views persons such as Paul as mediators of this promise. We cannot assume that the implied author reached theological clarity on this issue and held one view consistently. Furthermore, the nature of this salvation is not clarified. The larger Lukan context suggests that it has a second level of meaning that exceeds rescue from a storm, and the voyage narrative indicates that this salvation reaches even unconverted pagans. These observations still leave various options of interpretation, stretching from the view that Christianity is an occasional benefactor of society at large to a universalism that includes every creature in God's ultimate salvation.

Reflection on this story of the salvation of all may also move in a second direction. In the voyage narrative a remarkable amount of attention is given to the cooperative relationship between Paul and Julius the centurion and to the contributions that various parties – the sailors, Julius, and Paul – make to finally reaching safety. God's role in events is explicit only at one place: Paul receives a message from God through an angel (vv. 23-24). This message is important because it conveys a promise that enables humans to take heart and because it points to the goal toward which humans must work. Human decision and action are crucial in reaching this goal. As Paul said to the centurion, "Unless these [sailors] remain in the ship, you cannot be saved" (v. 31). Therefore, the soldiers must act. Human actions that work toward the rescue of all are acceptable contributions to the realization of God's purpose, while actions that seek the safety of one's own group while abandoning others will block this purpose until corrected. When the parties in the ship work together cooperatively for the good of all, dangers are avoided and the ship's company is finally saved. In the ship Paul and his Christian companions are a small minority within a largely pagan company, but survival depends on each party acting for the good of all. Paul does this when he warns Julius that the sailors are abandoning the ship and when he eats before all. Julius does this when he stops the soldiers from killing the prisoners, who might escape (vv. 42-43). The sailors do this when they stick to their tasks in the ship. Working together and for each other, they reach the safety that God had promised.

The implied author's interest in such a narrative could arise from concern about the role of a Christian minority in Roman society. The Christian movement is very important in the eyes of the implied author, but it will remain a minority for the foreseeable future. The possibility of salvation in the social and political sphere depends on Christians and non-Christians being willing to follow the lead of Paul, Julius, and the sailors, when they are acting for the good of all. Perhaps the Christian prophet, like Paul, will have a special role in conveying an understanding of what is possible and promised by God, but non-Christians also have important roles.

Following the meal the rejuvenated company moves into action. Remaining cargo is cast overboard so that the ship will have the best chance of passing over shoals. The efforts of the sailors (mentioned simply as "they" in vv. 39-41) are described in detail. In spite of their previous attempt to abandon the ship, they now do their duty for the good of all and steer the ship toward a beach. But this is not a familiar harbor. The ship runs aground, and the stern begins to break up. Paul has helped by prophetic encouragement, enabling the company to respond to their situation in light of the divine promise. The sailors have done their part by protecting the ship in the storm and taking it as far as possible toward the beach. But still there is danger. Not only is the ship breaking up, but the soldiers decide to kill the prisoners, lest they escape. The soldiers, like the sailors, forget in the crisis that God's promise is for all, and they plan to save themselves by eliminating others. The community of all with mutual responsibilities is about to be violated a second time. At this point Julius the centurion makes an important contribution to the rescue. "Wishing to save Paul," he stops the soldiers and organizes the escape from ship to shore, making it possible for all to reach safety. Julius' friendship with Paul makes a crucial difference at this point, saving not only

Paul but the other prisoners. His friendly attitude was demonstrated at the very beginning of the voyage (v. 3), and the relationship was probably strengthened when Paul helped the soldiers and then the whole ship's company in vv. 31 and 33-36. Paul is a benefactor of the others on this voyage,[22] but he is also benefited. His benefits return to him as the centurion intervenes to save his life. Of course, this is part of God's care for Paul, who must stand before Caesar (v. 24), but the narrative gives careful attention to the ways that other persons contribute to and are benefited by this aspect of God's purpose. The storm narrative ends with a significant summary: "And thus it happened that all were saved (διασωθῆναι) upon the land"(v. 44). "Thus," i.e., through these human actions, God's promise was fulfilled.

In the narrative of Paul's mission in Acts, we find stories of intercultural conflict and also a remarkable story of cooperation. The stories of conflict are, of course, narrated from a Christian point of view and tend to present Paul's opponents in a negative way. The opponents act from commercial motives (16:19, 19:25-27) or cause civil unrest while accusing Christians of upsetting the world (17:5-6). Nevertheless, it would be naive to assume that a religion can be vital without causing conflict. If avoidance of conflict is the primary value, the status quo is ratified and the prophetic function of religion is nullified. The stories of conflict we have examined (and other parts of Acts) provide images of a bold messenger who is willing to challenge religious cultures that have become tired or corrupt, while accepting the negative reaction that will follow. These narrative images have continuing usefulness. But one of the results of such a missionary challenge may be the revival of the other religion in reaction, and religious conflict easily gets out of hand. Therefore, it is important that there is also a model of interreligious cooperation in Acts which encourages us to find a way to bring all to safety from the dangers that threaten our world. This narrative also reminds us that the divine promise ultimately is for all; it therefore transcends all of the religious perspectives that inspire and divide us.

---

[22]Emphasized by Gerhard Krodel, *Acts* (Augsburg Commentary on the New Testament; Minneapolis: Augsburg Publishing House, 1986), 470.

THE PASTORAL EPISTLES — PAUL AND WE
J. Christiaan Beker, *Princeton Theological Seminary*

I.   The importance of the Pastoral Epistles should not primarily be attributed to their theological depth or creative thought. Rather their importance may be phrased as follows: the Pastoral Epistles illustrate the problem of the relation of the *"original"* to its *"translation"*, i.e., the problem of the transmission of tradition, and its hermeneutical consequences. This problem arises whenever a tradition is considered not simply as an archeological deposit — buried in the historical past — but as an *authoritative* tradition, transmitted to subsequent generations as a *viva vox* — as hermeneutically relevant and as such to be appropriated.

The problem thus focuses on the *transmission of tradition*, whether defined in terms of the relation of the "original" and its "translation", or in terms of the relation of "authenticity" and "relevance."

Now, ever since the Reformation and subsequent historical scholarship (beginning with J. S. Semler and F. C. Baur in the 18th and 19th century), the focus of attention has been directed — on the basis of the "reforming" principle of the Reformation and on the basis of the search for historical veracity and integrity — to only one aspect of the problem of the transmission of tradition, i.e. the *recovery of the original*, so as to be able to undo the anachronisms which the history of tradition had created. In this way Luther fought for the *"claritas Scripturae"* and the *simplicity* of God's Word in Scripture overagainst the layers which scholastic tradition had imposed on the text of the Scripture. In like manner historical scholarship endeavored to elucidate the true historical framework and content of the text overagainst the dogmatic impositions of ecclesial interpretations.

However invaluable and necessary the *recovery of the original* is for the hermeneutical task of permitting the original its critical and innovative function, i.e., for the sake of a truthful appropriation, allowing the original to exercise its rightful claim on subsequent readers, a second aspect of the matter, i.e., a different perspective on it, is equally important. From this perspective concentration does not focus on the recovery of the authentic tradition, but rather on the process of tradition itself, i.e., on the question of *what happens to the original in the course of its transmission* [i.e., the *traditio* of the original *traditum*]. It is the problem of the appropriation of tradition, once this tradition is considered to be authoritative and relevant for times and situations which differ from those of the original authors and their text.

In other words, the problem addresses the question of what actually occurs in the transmission of tradition and its appropriation and raises questions like the following: (1) how *much* of the tradition *can* in fact be *appropriated* for new generations and situations?; (2) how much *accommodation* must *necessarily* take place?; (3) to what extent does accommodation transgress into *distortion* and essential loss of meaning?; and finally (4) — related to the first question — how selective is the appropriation of tradition and is this selectivity not just an oversight, but simply a *necessity* in the process of the transmission of tradition?

II.   The importance of the Pastoral Epistles is directly related to this issue. We have here before us a collection of three letters — written at the same time [they never circulated separately] at the end of the 1st century A.D., ostensibly for churches in Ephesus and Crete in order to assist church leaders in their task of preaching, guidance and organizational planning. We should be aware that the letters have a twofold pseudonymous character: they are written supposedly by Paul to supposedly two of his most intimate co-workers, Timothy and Titus, who are located respectively in Ephesus and on Crete. Moreover the authority of the letters is based on Paul and his teaching — and what is more — on Paul's authority alone. In other words, orthodox Christianity and what constitutes the authoritative gospel are exclusively identified with the gospel of Paul. There is no appeal to other apostolic leaders or to the Jerusalem authorities [but cf. *Lk-Acts*]. In other words, the author intends to convey to his churches *the unique authority of Pauline tradition* in order to establish the *true continuity* of Paul's gospel for subsequent generations, i.e., for the time after Paul's departure and death, when the *viva vox* of the apostle and his letters — for Paul always the substitute for his personal presence — could no longer be heard.

The Pastoral Epistles therefore illustrate what I above delineated as the second aspect of the problem of tradition. In other words, I will not focus on the usual procedure of critical scholarship, i.e., a comparison of the Pastoral Epistles with Paul's authentic letters so as to establish a theory of "the fall from the true Paul." My primary interest is not to demonstrate to what extent the Pastoral Epistles miss the mark, compared to the imaginative and creative thought of Paul.

Rather I will focus my attention on the transmission of tradition and its appropriation in new situations. This issue is all the more interesting, with respect to the Pastoral Epistles, since we can trace its problems not simply within church history in general, i.e. between the canonical Scriptures and later extra-canonical interpretations, but rather within the canon of the New Testament itself. Moreover, the issue is quite relevant for us — 20th century interpreters of Paul — as well, when we reflect on how we in fact handle the issue of the transmission of Pauline tradition. Thus it may well turn out that our generally low estimate of the Pastoral Epistles may in fact teach us a very valuable lesson. For we — in our own appropriation of Paul's gospel — may be much closer to the Pastoral Epistles than we think. Thus the Pastoral Epistles compel us to reflect on the relation of the original and its translation, i.e., on how we handle the issue of the transmission of authoritative tradition.

III.   A. The Pastoral Epistles — like we — face the problem of how to convey the *viva vox* and authority of Paul to new problems and new times, i.e., they face the problem of the transmission of tradition. Succinctly, how is it possible to establish *continuity* of tradition within the inevitable *discontinuity* of historical existence.

Moreover, the Pastoral Epistles — like we — are aware of the hermeneutical problem of *coherence* and *contingency*: they do not simply recreate the various oppositions which Paul faced in his churches, but rather attempt to apply Paul's theological convictions to the new contingent problems they face in their churches.

In this context we must pay particular attention to important factors which are constitutive for the transmission of tradition — as they are exemplified by the Pastoral Epistles, especially, their description of Paul.

B. First of all, the figure of Paul is inextricably bound up with the *reputation* of the apostle in the area of Asia Minor, where the Pastoral Epistles were produced, i.e., in the area where Paul had worked extensively. Therefore, the picture of Paul is heavily influenced by the historical *impact* of Paul on the awareness of the Pastoral Epistles. In other words, we deal with the authority of Paul, as this had been established not only by his letters but primarily by his missionary work. Thus it comes as no surprise that when we trace the picture of Paul in the Pastoral Epistles that picture is *a composite* of allusions/references to the Pauline letters and of Pauline legend, of stories and anecdotes about Paul. It is interesting to observe here the similarity and dissimilarity of the Pastoral Epistles with the Book of Acts. The picture of Paul in Acts is also composed of various legends and narratives about Paul — as these circulated in the various regions of Asia Minor and Greece. However, whereas the Pastoral Epistles clearly know the Pauline letters and probably know them in their collected form, Acts is totally silent about the letters of Paul.

The manner in which history impacts on the transmission of tradition surfaces here. Paul is an established-authoritative apostle for the author of the Pastoral Epistles: his credentials are beyond dispute. History has confirmed his importance and the appeal to his authority does not need to be argued within the churches of the Pastoral Epistles. And so we notice that the picture of Paul which the Pauline corpus manifests, undergoes a fundamental *change* in the Pastoral Epistles. Whereas the Paul of the authentic letters argues for his apostolic authority, which is challenged and even denied by many of his contemporaries, the Paul of the Pastoral Epistles argues from his already self-evident authority.

(ii) This change affects as well *both* the *substance* of Paul's thought, *and* the manner of his *argumentation*. The method of argument and the content of Pauline thought in the Pastoral Epistles manifests the curious phenomenon, that although the author *intends* to be faithful to the authority of Paul — his final product deviates so sharply from Paul's *thought* and from his *argumentation* that it can hardly be called "Pauline thought." In other words, the Pauline intent of the author turns out to be only *formally* Pauline, whereas *materially* it is basically non-Pauline.

(iii) In terms of the *method of interpretation*, we notice that the intricate manner in which the historical Paul integrates the coherence of his gospel with the various contingent situations of his missionary churches undergoes a profound change. Paul's hermeneutic continuously attempts to conjoin the coherent aspects of his gospel to the relevant contingent situations of his churches, so that the coherence of his gospel cannot be abstracted from its encounter with contingency. Thus the relation of coherence and contingency never becomes a matter of a simple casuistic application of a fixed authoritative body of teaching to contingent situations. In other words, the coherent flexibility of Paul's gospel is inseparable from the demands of the contingent situations which he faces, so that the coherent base of Paul's gospel cannot be ascertained apart from its relation to contingent situations. It is, therefore, the intricate confluence of coherence and contingency, which constitutes the *dialogical character* of Paul's hermeneutic.

However, in the Pastoral Epistles this confluence is broken apart. Dialogue is displaced by monologue and vilification: the Pauline gospel has now become a "deposit of truth" (*paratheke* I 6:20) and "sound doctrine" (*hygiainousa didaskalia* I 1:10; II 4:3) and the opponents of the author are not addressed in terms of their theological claims, but are instead vilified and stereotyped, e.g., "men, depraved in mind and bereft of the truth" (I 6:5); "evil men and impostors" (II 3:13); "empty talkers and deceivers" (Titus 1:10).

Therefore, the coherence-contingency *interaction* of Paul is here broken apart by the *bifurcation* of a fixed "timeless" coherence and a spurious contingency, which the author does not consider worthy of serious consideration.

(iv) When we turn from the hermeneutic of the Pastoral Epistles to their presentation of *Paul's thought*, an interesting phenomenon draws our attention. The intent of the author is to be faithful to Paul and to Paul alone as the paradigm and prototype of Christian truth (I 1:16; I 2:7; II 1:11-12). There are not only direct allusions to the Pauline letters, but also an abundant use of Pauline terminology and conceptuality (e.g., *pistis; dikaios; dikaiosune; dikaioo; agape; elpis; sozo; soter; parakalo; paraklesis; charis; eirene*).

However, an important feature of the transmission of tradition is evident here, i.e., changes occur in the meaning of specific words and concepts. They are due to the inevitable historicity of language, i.e., to the fact that inherited words and concepts must now function within a different context. In other words, the new religious worldview of the Pastoral Epistles requires an adaptation of Pauline language and thought for an entirely new context.

The author of the Pastoral Epistles is not interested in an archaeological expedition to search for the original-historical Paul. Rather he desires the Pauline gospel to be a relevant "word on target" for the new situations which his churches face. Its relevance must be asserted in the face of two dangers: inner-ecclesial dissent ("the danger from within") and the pressures of Roman society ("the danger from without").

The author intends to save the church for orthodoxy and therefore appeals to the unique authority of Paul who is for him not only the source of the gospel of Christ, but also the source of authentic tradition [cf. Paul as *protos* (I 1:16)]. However, his appeal to this unique Pauline tradition is deflected by a worldview which is entirely different from its original Pauline context. The worldview of the author is shaped by an Hellenistic-Christian conceptuality and piety. It centers on the conceptuality of an *epiphaneia*-Christology (cf. also, both God and Christ as *soter*) and on a piety, characterized by (non-Pauline) terms such as *eusebeia, semnotes*, "a quiet and peaceable life" (I 2:2); *agathe syneidesis* (I 1:19); "*epignosis aletheias*" (I 2:4); "*hygianouse didaskalia*"; *paratheke*, etc.

IV. What then is the positive function of the Pauline tradition and its transmission in the Pastoral Epistles? In order to understand this positive function, we must attend to the contingent factors which shape the author's argument.

The post-apostolic situation of the church of the Pastoral Epistles is characterized by several theological, sociological and political factors, which makes its appeal to Paul intelligible.

The Church is no longer able to maintain its sectarian character, i.e., to be a contra-society in the Pauline sense. It needs to secure a stable position within the structures of Roman society and an ongoing world, and struggles to adapt itself to its new status, i.e., of how to be "*in mundo, sed non mundi.*" And in the midst of this struggle, it must face not only the mode of its relation to Roman society at large, but also the dissolution of its cohesion by internal theological dissent. This latter issue is so prominent in the Pastoral Epistles that we may properly call them polemical letters directed against Christian heretics.

The basic intent of the author is to meet the threat of dissolution with the demand for stability, i.e. to destroy the threat of a Jewish-gnosticizing heresy with an unswerving commitment to the inherited truth of the Pauline tradition. Moreover, "the danger from within" is to the author's mind closely related to "the danger from without." Although it is difficult for us to gain a precise picture of the opposition — due to its imprecise description by the author of the Pastoral Epistles — it seems likely that if the opposition wins the upper-hand with its emancipatory convictions and deviant behavior, the danger from Roman officials and society at large will threaten the very existence of the church. The author's appeal to Paul and his gospel must be understood in this context. Pseudepigraphy serves here to *contemporize* Paul and his authority, so as to demonstrate the vacuity of the opponents' position and to undermine their propaganda within the church (especially successful — it seems — with women). Moreover, the introduction of Paul as a *viva vox*, who entrusts his gospel to his intimate co-workers, also strengthens the hand of the author in establishing his own position as the truly Pauline position, i.e., as incontestable orthodoxy. This is all the more significant because the churches, which he addresses, were originally Pauline foundations and are aware of their indebtedness to Paul. Thus the appeal to Paul is all the more impressive, because "Paul" not only hands down mandates for future generations and thus insures the continuity of tradition, but also is represented as the one who predicted long ago the heresies which have now become reality. Moreover, II Timothy is cast as the last will and testament of Paul, who from his death-cell instructs his successors to conserve the *paratheke* (II 1:14) and to suffer for the truth of the gospel (II 4:5.17).

V. We may call the theology of the Pastoral Epistles *"Epigonen"*-theology, a theology which without creativity of its own appeals to theological figures of the past. What are we to think of a theology which, fearful in the face of opposition, withdraws into its own inherited-established setting, in order to find there its security? Moreover, what has become here of the transmission of tradition, even while we fully recognize the historicity of tradition and the necessary changes it entails? Has the author of the Pastoral Epistles succumbed to a form of traditionalism, which posits authoritative claims without critically evaluating them and "translating" them for his own time with its new situations and demands?

In whatever manner we answer these questions, the Pastoral Epistles raise an important question for us: how do we handle the transmission of tradition? Shall we dismiss the burden of tradition altogether and opt for radically new models which promise relevance for our time? Or shall we embrace "traditionalism" as the only way to be faithful to tradition? The Pastoral Epistles give us notice that a critical evaluation of the tradition is our never-ending task. For it is only in our risky translation of the original that the original can come to speech again, albeit in a new language. And one of the greatest contributions to Biblical scholarship of the person we honor in these pages is his untiring devotion to this task.

TEXT AND CONTEXT
"THE GOSPEL" ACCORDING TO MARK I: 14-18*
Jean Delorme, *Université de Lyon*

Sacred texts such as the gospels are inseparable from a tradition of reading. It is for this reason that, perhaps more than any other texts, they run the risk of becoming imprisoned in a system of interpretation that the sociological requirements of reading groups tend to make rigid over time.

Classical biblical criticism emerged and developed in large part as a reaction against inveterate habits of reading, or rather, of not reading, because received interpretation preceded and prevented attention to the text. Criticism's goal was to liberate the text and restore it to its original milieu, to its first context (historical, literary, sociological, cultural). We sought to make today's readers contemporaries of the first readers or hearers of Jesus. Or as Hendrick Boers says,[1] we wanted to translate ourselves into the language and the world of people from a vanished past, believing that this alone could give us the key to the texts.

One could wonder whether all the work in this direction resulted in anything more than an enclosure of the Gospels behind a wall that prevents understanding—prevents archeological understanding, I should say—by all but an aristocracy of experts. In order to fill in the moat separating the citadel from ordinary mortals, hermeneutics was given the task of making the message "current," the message being the interpretations accepted in the circle of specialists. These interpretations became the required link between the reader and the text; they tended to take the place of the text, as if they were not themselves the

---

*Translated by James Creech

[1] Cf. Boers, Hendrick, "Traduction semantique/transculturelle de la parabole du bon Samaritain," in *Parole-Figure- Parabole: Recherches autour du discours parabolique*, ed. Jean Delorme, (Lyon, France: Presses Universitaires de Lyon, 1987), 87-102.

product of a certain hermeneutic elaboration. As for making the message "current," that effort was often based on analogies in historical or existential situation linking the first receivers of the message with those of today, or on philosophies or theologies erected as "canonical" re-writings of the Scriptures. In any case, the letter of the text was subsumed into another discourse considered more "current."

Interest in the historical reception of texts could allow us to avoid this back-and-forth between interpretations which invoke the original cultural context and those which are concerned with the world of today. The text has outlived its contemporaries. It has been read by other people, in other places and in other epochs. Before concluding from this that we have drifted onto another course, often judged to be unfortunate in the name of the "literal historical meaning" which is posited as the rule for truth, it behooves us to reflect on the links connecting text and cultural context. The question concerns just as much the "primitive" context, as we can reconstruct it, as it does the subsequent contexts in which the text went on to show itself, and can yet show itself, to be a text still speaking and acting.

The gospels have traversed and are still traversing different cultures. This fact should be sufficient to indicate that they have a consistency all their own and that, in a manner of speaking, they stand up well under wear and tear. The text is not an empty receptacle which merely fills up with the liquid into which it is immersed (with the vase already imposing its form on the liquid). It cannot be adapted to just any context and it does not lend itself to just any interpretation. It can be *interpreted* on the basis of a context (original or acquired), but it also can become the *interpreter* of its context, able to modify the way we understand and appreciate that context.

I take as an example Jesus's word which is found in Mark 1:15: *"The time has been fulfilled, and the reign of God has drawn near. Repent and believe in the gospel."* God knows (and the computer now is able to know, too) how many times each word of this text has been studied in the literary and cultural context in which Jesus and/or the disciples lived! And yet, its signifying force does not come first to this text from its context. We must take into account the structuring that it imposes upon the cultural elements that it borrows. On the other hand this micro-text is closely linked to an introductory note which places it in the time and space of Jesus (verse 14). These two constitute a small semantic cell which in turn forms mutually interpretative links with the context given by the book of Mark.

That is where I propose to look in order to specify the kind of action and reaction which can occur between a text and a cultural context. That could shed light on the problem of transcultural translations of "the gospel."

1. The Formulary of "the Gospel" According to Mark 1:15.

"The time has been fulfilled, and the reign of God has drawn near." The two verbs are in the perfect in Greek: a double transformation has been realized in the past and its result remains. Then two imperatives specify for potential hearers what must be done: "Repent and believe in the gospel."

It is not necessary to know in advance how all these words were used in the discourses from the time of Jesus or the gospels to notice the straight-forward construction of this sentence: there is what is done and here is what is to be done. Moreover, it is an utterance addressed to "you," which supposes a speaking "I" and a "here" and a "now" of the utterance. What is done and declared to be objectively accomplished outside of "you" affects the "here and now" of this "you" who is being invited to realize a subjective transformation.

This structuring gives the text its cohesion. It is determinative for the particular meaning assumed here by words that it causes to signify in relation to each other.

1.1. "The time has been fulfilled, and the reign of God has drawn near."

We have good reason to point out that the linguistic and cultural context knows temporal representation as a measure to be fulfilled. The measure of time can be a matter of nature, as the time to give birth (Luke 1:57, 2:6), or a matter of God's design (Galatians 4:4, or Ephesians 1:10), as is here the case since "the reign of God" is approaching. A divine will was inscribed within time: it is realized, there is no more delay. And the "fulfilled" or accomplished time is not *chronos*, the time which passes and whose good or bad quality depends on that of events. Rather it is *kairos*, the opportune or favorable time, the "right time," here marked by a fortunate event, bearer of a beneficent intention. The word "evangel" (εὐ - αγγέλιον) suggests the same thing, since here it manifestly designates the "good news" of this event.

The figure of the "reign of God" and its arrival is also well documented. It is easy to cite Biblical and Jewish texts that speak of it in various guises and in diverse senses. We also know that βασιλεία can also be translated as "reign," "kingdom," or "royalty," according to whether the text privileges the quality and sphere of "king" ("royalty"), its exercise ("rule"), or the territory in which it is exercised ("kingdom"). Because Mark 1:15 does not explain the expression ἡ βασιλεία τοῦ θεοῦ, we could conclude that the text supposes that readers are familiar with it. But do we have to begin by situating it within the culture of the time? Because of the variety of its uses in the texts that were then known, we run the risk of transporting into Mark a definition imported from somewhere else. And we are only deferring the problem, since when speaking of God the figures of king, rule and kingdom are in any case metaphors. These approximations are trying to represent a relation between God and the human world which can be full of hidden surprises. The story of Mark, precisely, has several in store for us. It is fortunate therefore that it says less about them than the Biblical or Jewish texts preceding or contemporary. Rather than approaching the text with a previously established notion of the "reign of God," it is better to be attentive to the place and the function that the text gives it: it is a figure that the text declines to explain and interpret.[2]

If we limit ourselves to what is said, we notice that it proposes to "you" a new space-time. The two propositions, "The time has been fulfilled, and the reign of God has drawn near," must be read together, in mutual relationship to each other. The first privileges time and gives it the spatial figure of a full measure. The second speaks of an approach which can be inscribed just as well in space as in time, although it privileges space (that is why we could translate it as: "the kingdom of God has drawn near," as in the case of clearly spatial expressions such as "to enter in the kingdom of God," "not to be far from the kingdom of God," but the dynamism of the approach pleads in favor of "reign.")

There is a remarkable difference between the two propositions . The measure of time is filled; there is no more time for a delay. But

---

[2]I use the word "figure" to designate a linguistic expression, not one that takes on a *figural* or metaphorical meaning, but one that offers a *figurative* representation of the world of "reality" outside of language. In a text, figures are ordinarily organized in *figurative trajectories* [*parcours figuratifs*], (for example, the approach of the reign of God, or the arrival of Jesus in Galilee to proclaim the gospel...).

although "the reign has drawn near," it is not stated that it has arrived "here and now."³ However great the proximity, it is not coincidence. (If one translated "the reign of God is there," it would be necessary to maintain the difference between "here" and "there.") The scene at Gethsemane offers a parallel case (14:41-43). The figures of time ("The hour has come") and of space ("he who will betray me has drawn near," ἤγγικεν) are linked there as well . Distance has become so minimal and so close to being nil that Jesus can speak in the present of the Son of man betrayed, and of the one who betrays him. In the same way, the actualized proximity of the "reign of God" is such that the time for delays is past. But in the case of Judas, distance is cancelled as Jesus is speaking ("And while he was yet speaking, Judas Iscariot, one of the Twelve, came"), while "the reign of God" does not manifest itself when its proximity is affirmed. The realization of its approach is a verbal, not a visual object.

This utterance positions its audience in the present of a completed time, gone full term, and in a "here" that is minimally distant from the "reign of God." There is no more delay, but what is so close is not shown and does not coincide with the "here-and-now" of sense experience. This non-coincidence reserves an interval for repentance and for receiving the utterance, without allowing the urgency of the call to be diminished.

1.2. "Repent and believe in the gospel"

These two imperatives constitute a single directive with two connected aspects. For potential hearers they specify the reaction that is expected of them in the new space-time that is being announced to them. Here again, we could recall the cultural rootedness of "repentance," "faith," and "the gospel." It is more important to grasp a rootedness, deeper than cultural rootedness, in the structures of language and utterance.

"The gospel," the good news that was just announced, is given to be "believed." That underscores its quality as an utterance addressed

---

³This complex figure of a completed time and of an approach that the utterance proclaims without a visible spatial manifestation, vastly exceeds the sempiternal debate about the imminence or the presence of the Kingdom according to verse 15 (cf. the commentaries on this point). Instead of using these terms to posit a choice that in any case is premature, it is better to look to the narration for clarification of this figure through the representation that it will give of Jesus' activity. That will be its way of interpreting it.

to someone. It offers no evidence for what it affirms. It claims truth for what it says, but its truth is awaiting to be "believed," which is to say, taken on as true by hearers. This truth has all the fragility of the utterance, but also the force of a summons addressed to listening subjects, challenging them to take charge of themselves and to commit themselves in relation to this truth by making it their own, and by bringing them the sanction of the true.

"Repentance" in Greek implies knowledge (*noein*) after the fact (*meta-noein*) and change in relation to the past recognized as regrettable. This figure is close to that of "conversion," which evokes a turning around (in LXX and in the *NT apo-strephein*, "to turn away from," or *epi-strephein*, "to turn towards," which correspond to the Hebrew *shub*). They are frequently parallel and can appear synonymous. (Compare to Jeremiah 8:6, and 31:18-19 in Hebrew and Greek; Isaiah 46:8 in Greek; Acts 3:19; 26:20.) However "conversion," in a spatial image, indicates more spontaneously the new orientation of a behavior, while "repentance" is inscribed in time where it marks a rupture.

The call to repentance precedes the call to faith. As with faith, repentence is determined by the content of the "good news." It underscores the change that has intervened in time. It is no longer a matter of preparing oneself for the future according to the message of John the Baptist (1:4-8), but of adapting to the present. To the degree that "the gospel" brings us to recognize the negative and superseded aspect of the past, it becomes urgent for us to tear ourselves away from it.

1.3. The Structure of "the gospel"

It is hard to imagine an evangelizing discourse reduced to two affirmations followed by two imperatives. The conciseness of the statement in Mark 1:15 has the advantage of highlighting a fundamental structure that no rhetoric should obscure.

a. Utterance addressed to a hearer

"The Gospel" is not formulated in impersonal terms, in factual or descriptive tones, nor is it a general affirmation to which everybody assents without doubting its truth (like, "the earth is round"), nor even is it a narration in the third person that could stand by itself, independently of the narrator and of its reception by a hearer. "The gospel" is utterance by an "I" to a "you." It is not reserved for an individual addressee: the "you" here is in the plural. But the repentence and faith that is required of this "you" calls for a personal step to be taken. It is up to each hearer to constitute him or herself as addressee, without monopolizing it at the expense of others. When one takes this step, one speaks not of oneself but of "the gospel." One does not say: "believe me," but "believe in the gospel." One does not seek to pass for the origin or the guarantor of what one says, nor as the agent of the transformation that one is announcing. The event that has fulfilled time, and the approach of "the reign of God," are the affair of an Other and depend upon "God." And is up to this "you" to orient him or herself to the new situation.

b. Happy utterance

The call "to repent" might seem paradoxical in the context of a "happy announcement." "Good news" by definition presumes to offer something "good" to the hearer, to respond to expectations, to bring something satisfying. Here, however, as hearers we are first invited to change, which supposes that we are not immediately apt to receive the news and to recognize it as good news. "The gospel" situates us in a new space-time. The "good" that is proposed does not correspond to the natural inclinations of a prior way of living. Although the "good" anticipates desire, that desire may be one which is awakened without receiving immediate satisfaction, since "the reign of God" is a verbal promise whose object the hearer does not possess. If so, "repentence" is not a simple condition to be fulfilled before receiving the good news; it is called upon to last as long as "the reign of God" continues to be governed by an utterance to be proclaimed and to be believed (the two verbs are in the present imperative).

c. Utterance to be believed

This quality of "the gospel" is emphasized by the brevity of its enunciation. The absence of any appeal to reasoning, of any attempt to persuade makes it seem abrupt. It pushes the risk of utterance to the limit. Whoever speaks it thereby undertakes a commitment, and this speaker cannot dispense the listener from personally having to reckon with what is thus heard. An accord is required between them, an accord that enables agreement as to the truth of the utterance that is offered and received.

This accord does not consist in the hearer's being willing to defer to the bearer of the message. The bearer says nothing about him or her self, but only proposes an utterance that is other. It is this utterance which becomes the *locus of* believing: "believe in the gospel."[4] It is inside this utterance that the believing subject enters into the space-time which is revealed to that subject, and here that one situates oneself in relation to the Other of whom it is said that He preceded one in the here-and-now of one's existence. If the hearer welcomes the utterance of the speaker announcing the "gospel," their mutual accord is established in their common relation to this Other.

2. "The Gospel" and Jesus

Thus we see that "the gospel" according to Mark 1:15 has a certain semantic autonomy. It can be read in itself. It resists readings which one might want to impose on it from the outside. One could, perhaps even one should, turn to the cultural context of the period to clarify words and figures that are used. But Mark 1:15 hinges these figures together in a manner that gives them a new consistency, a new orientation. Based on its structures, it requires redefinition of "the reign of God," the repentence and the faith of which it speaks and about which the texts of the period may also speak, only differently.

But in Mark this "gospel" does not stand alone. It is reported in a context and it needs that context. Since it is an utterance addressed to others, it requires at least an introduction that presents the speaker. For the moment we will restrict ourselves to the immediate context formed by verse 14 and will will try to specify what happens between this verse and "the gospel" cited in verse 15. Here it is possible to observe how text and context react upon each other.

Of course, the case of relations between text and cultural context is very different. Here it would be better to speak of *co-text* rather than context, since verse 14 belongs to the same textual ensemble as verse 15. Even so, semantic exchanges occur between them in the

---

[4]We know that the construction *pisteuein en* is found neither in classical Greek, nor in the papyri, but that it is found in the Septuagint, and that it may go back to a semitic construction (cf. J. C. Doudna, *The Greek of the Gospel of Mark*, SBL Monographs 12, Philadelphia 1961, pp. 23, 79). "The gospel" is an object of "believing" insofar as it announces an invisible transformation about which we can only speak. It is in this sense, and not because of purely linguistic considerations, that we say that it becomes the site of "believing."

form of a reciprocal interpretation which in turn might suggest ways of understanding the exchanges occurring on a larger scale within the same cultural ensemble.

The introduction of verse 14 can be reduced to this: "And after John had been delivered up, Jesus came into Galilee, preaching the gospel of the reign of God, and saying. . . ." It is not much, but it is enough to allow this introduction and "the gospel" quoted next to clarify each other mutually.

2.1. Jesus the "evangelist" and his addressees

a. It may seem superfluous to point out that the introduction identifies Jesus as the "I" implied in the utterance addressed to "you." But in this utterance nothing requires that it be pronounced by Jesus. In a narration, it is not inconsequential for an utterance to pronounced by one character or by another. Jesus, in verse 14, has already been on the scene since verse 9, and he will remain there throughout the whole book. We will have to link what is recounted about him and what is quoted from his words.

By attributing to him the role of proclaimer of "the gospel of the reign of God," verse 14 makes Jesus "God's" messenger and confers upon him the authority to speak about "God."[5] This specification is pertinent for the reader and affects the reading of "the gospel" cited. But that "gospel," on the other hand, shows how Jesus understands his role. He speaks of "God" and his "reign" while claiming no authority of his own, no title which could make us believe him. He says nothing of his own experience, of his history. He effaces himself so that only what he is announcing remains. His silence on this score should be noted for the proper interpretation of his role as "God's evangelist." The direct quotation and the introduction interpret each other mutually.

b. On the other hand, the introduction furnishes no information on the subject of the "you" to whom the utterance is addressed. Since the proclamation of "the gospel" includes a temporal duration (the verb is a present participle), the hearers do not have to be indicated. It is nonetheless the case that the effacement of the historical addressees

---

[5]The genitive τοῦ θεοῦ can be subjective and refer to the origin of "the gospel," or it can be objective and designate "God" as the one about whom "the gospel" is speaking. This ambivalence must be respected since verse 14 favors the first interpretation and verse 15 the second.

fits perfectly with what we noticed concerning this "you": the hearer is charged with the responsibility of constituting him or herself as the addressee of the message by taking it personally. It is therefore unnecessary to give the hearer a specific identity.

Just as it is important to link "the gospel" to the word of Jesus, it is equally important not to bind it to a determinate image of an audience. The role proposed to "you" is available for whoever will want to take it on and the text remains open beyond any particular audience. On this point, the utterance we have quoted and the introduction support each other and comment upon each other mutually. "The gospel" is not a circumstantial utterance limited to some specific situation, and the activity which Jesus is undertaking must be extended in time and space.

2.2. The Space-Time of "God's gospel"

The relationship of reciprocal interpretation is even more distinct in the matter of the space-time of "the gospel." The new situation that it announces presupposes that a transformation has intervened before one speaks of it. But "the gospel" says nothing of the moment or the place of this change. This silence makes all the more remarkable the relationship between the givens of space and those of time in verses 14 and 15:

(Time)	(Space)
"After John had been delivered up	Jesus came into Galilee
The time has been fulfilled	the reign of God has drawn near."

Nothing allows us to identify the "historical" event narrated in verse 14, and the invisible, "transhistorical" event presupposed in verse 15. It is not Jesus's arrival in Galilee after John had been delivered up, which fulfills time and sets in motion the approach of "the reign of God." But because of the difference between the two events, each makes the other signify.

The historical event does not merely assign a date and a geographical situation to the proclamation of a message. It has something to do with what this message affirms. It inserts into history the event which it is not possible to show, and about which it is possible only to speak. It gives it a concrete value within the world of humanity, without which "the gospel" would be "an empty word."

Conversely, the invisible event illuminates the other. It wrests the introduction of verse 14 from the banality of a simple, chronological and topographical notation. It changes the quality of the space and the time in which Jesus's intervention is inscribed. It gives that intervention the value of a sign. At this point in Mark's text, "the gospel's" message offers the audience no other guideline than Jesus' activity, among them, at that moment. That confers a new signification upon the turning point marked by Jesus' sermon after John is delivered up, and by the change in space of the utterance which, from the Judean desert, passes into the cities and villages of Galilee.

3.3. A Signifying Cell

In Mark 1:14-15, then, we are faced with a signifying unit which places in relation to each other two micro-texts that are different enough for signification to circulate from one to the other. The one does not absorb the other, nor is it reduced to the other. We can speak of a hermeneutic circuit between the two. This complex signifying unit makes "the gospel" attributed to Jesus appear to be inseparable from the action which is begun at the time of its proclamation.

The relationship between the two is dynamic in the sense that each is waiting to be reinterpreted in the light of the other. This internal dynamism is comparable to that of a living cell. It grounds the possibility of a reinterpretation of "the gospel" through adaptation to variable contexts. One can become aware of this within the book of Mark.

3. The Interpreting and Interpreted "Gospel" in Mark

The hermeneutic operativity of "the gospel" according to verses 14-15 in Mark works in comparison both to what precedes and to what follows in the rest of the book.

a. Jesus' proclamation follows John's, but his "gospel" marks a certain rupture between the two proclamations. Thus we must reread in its light what we are told about the Baptist. This narrative was at first presented in light of what "is written in Isaiah the prophet" (verses 2-3). John is preparing the way and announces the coming of the one who is to follow. But if the narration establishes that he will be Jesus, neither John nor Jesus say as much. The narration establishes a continuity between them that is for the reader's use. But there are so many things that are unforeseen, so many differences in this continuity, that it requires, in order to be recognized, that John's activity be reevaluated on the basis of what happens to Jesus and what Jesus says that is not announced or anticipated by the precursor. "Repentence," for example, comes to signify in verse 15 something other than the meaning given it by John. In order for John's ministry to dispose the reader for proper understanding of Jesus' ministry, John himself must be understood in the light of Jesus' ministry.

The same must be said of the narration of the events which followed the baptism of Jesus by John. "The gospel" of verse 15 does not speak of them and they are unknown in Galilee. The reader alone knows of them and can thus link these secret events to what Jesus said of a transformation realized in time and space. The descent of the Spirit in Jesus and the commentary upon it by the heavenly voice thus offer a possible interpretation of "the gospel" proclaimed by Jesus.[6] But Jesus does not say that time has been fulfilled for him, nor that "the reign of God" has approached him. And if we must link what happened in the desert and what he says, the substitution of the figures is remarkable . Those of "fulfilled time" and of the "reign of God at hand" reinterpret those of the events on the desert. These events themselves are awaiting comprehension in the light of what begins with "the gospel" of Jesus in Galilee.

b. Henceforth, "the gospel" will never be taken up again in the way it is formulated in 1:15. And yet, because there is reciprocal interpretation between what it affirms and Jesus' activity which proclaims it (verse 14), its content sheds light in advance on the development of this activity . "The gospel" of the beginning invites us to recognize the sign of the approach of "the reign of God" in what happens to Jesus and through him . But in return, this approach will be reinterpreted by the narration of his life, of his death, of his resurrection. In "the gospel" this narration will tend to take the place of the annunciation of "the reign of God drawn near." "The gospel" is inseparable from Jesus ("for my sake and for the gospel's sake," 8:35;

---

[6]As constructed in Mark's narration, the events in the desert after Jesus' baptism represent functionally, and for the reader, his secret investiture and the establishment of his competence for the activity that he is starting in verse 14. Figuratively they represent an intervention of "God" (of the "Heavens") which the reader cannot avoid linking to the intervention that "the gospel" represents in verse 15; hence, in their differences, there exists the possibility of mutual illumination and semantic exchanges between these events.

10:29) and it is suggested that it will have to speak of him after his death (13:10; 14:9). It is predictable from the first words of the book onward: "the gospel" which begins in 1:1 is the gospel "of Jesus Christ" and it is the beginning of the narration that concerns him. But this narration will not erase Jesus' announcement in verse 15. It will allow it to be understood differently than is possible at the beginning. The rhetorical figures in which it is expressed and those of Jesus' activity and passivity are called upon to illuminate each other. The call for repentence and faith at the beginning contains something which, in the continuation of the narration, will return in other expressions that translate it and make its importance explicit.

The hermeneutic tension that we have seen in verses 14-15 thus works between these verses and the rest of the book. If in the course of the book "the gospel" adapts itself to context, it is not surprising that it should be able to adapt itself to still other contexts as well.

4. Text and Context

This inquiry could be pursued outside of Mark. By changing the formulation, "the gospel" conserves a certain structural form and a fundamental semantic investment:

—It remains tied to the "Jesus event," which itself is formulated and interpreted in various ways;

—it is an utterance that is addressed to someone, that is waiting to be taken up by a hearer and that, calling forth a profound desire, keeps the hearer open beyond immediate satisfactions;

—it invites the hearer to recognize in the spatio-temporal situation a qualitative change capable of reorienting personnel existence.

This structural definition of "the gospel" is more durable than its linguistic manifestation which necessarily passes through words, metaphors and the discursive procedures of a culture. It grounds the possibility of transcultural translations.

A text can be translated into a language other than the one in which it was written, but it can also be translated within its own language since any language offers several possibilities for manifesting a semantic organization. The problem of translation is never purely linguistic. Two different languages can belong to a homogeneous cultural area. But within a community speaking the same language, diverse cultures can coexist. Since no text is produced independently of a cultural context, to translate is to displace the text from one cultural context to another. In any case, another text is produced, a text which is no more separable from a culture than was the first. The text/cultural context relationship is not the privilege of the text to be translated. It also affects the new, "transculturated" text.

It seems to me that the case of "the gospel" according to Mark 1:14-15 can offer a useful model for studying this relationship. This text refers to a whole cultural context that is sufficiently known. It is easy to understand it and to comment upon it based on conceptions and expectations of its time. But this text exists by virtue of its own forms. These allow it to detach itself from the cultural milieu to which it belongs and to transform what it receives from that milieu by reinterpreting it.

This text is itself constructed as a cell within which elements interpret each other mutually. It becomes a principle of reinterpretation at the heart of the book to which it belongs: it receives meaning from it and furnishes meaning to it, it interprets its figures and its own figures are interpreted by others in the course of the book. Text and co-text cooperate and "the gospel" transforms itself without losing its structure and its hermeneutic dynamism.

"The gospel" is subject to receiving varied expressions according to the cultures into which it is itself received. It can be comprehended and discussed in the context of discourses from settings other than the one which produced it. If it is intended for "all the nations," then it calls for rewritings in other languages, in other figures. Today, the discourses of "liberation," of "development," of "peace," of "human rights" offer it new possibilities of expression.

If it is really a question of translations then these translations will favor semantic exchanges. These exchanges do not dilute a content which has become unrecognizable in the translator's discourse. They do not lead to a mixing in which the contributions of the text and the context are blended together. Rather an exchange takes the form of a reciprocal interpretation. If such an exchange favors a renewed understanding of "the gospel," then in the light of this gospel it must also permit us to understand differently the figures and themes that are received from our context.

I have taken the example of a particular text. Certainly not all texts offer the same resistance to being used and not all have the same type of relation with the cultural context. Some only reflect it and have only historical or sociological interest. But there also exist innovative texts which, without escaping ambiant culture, detach from it enough to contest it or to surpass it. The context allows historical commentary on such texts; it does not furnish the key to them. On the other hand, they can indeed provide a key for a different appreciation of the context. What happens when they pass from one culture into another? For the major texts of humanity, the question is worth the asking.

LOVING BACH IN THE WORLD OF TORTURE
Dorothee Sölle, *Union Theological Seminary/University of Kassel*

Several years ago I gave a lecture on "The Suffering Creature and the Suffering God as a Theme of Art and Theology" during the Nürmberg Organ week. For reasons evident in the text, it remained very fragmentary and I've now revised it in honor of Hendrikus W. Boers with the hope that all of us will develop an "aesthetic of resistance" and learn to listen to the voices of the scourged and tortured, yet not without also hearing, making and interpreting classical music.

When I began to work on this lecture and was looking about a little in the aesthetic music literature on the subject, I received a call from friends who worked with Chilean refugees. They asked me to fly to Santiago as part of a European delegation to become informed about the hunger strike of relatives of the disappeared; the disappeared have been estimated at around 2500. I was very uncertain what I should do: remain at my writing desk, meditate on suffering, art and theology, or fly to Santiago to stand by those who are being tortured or who wait until perhaps one of the tortured comes back? It turned out I couldn't say no to this request. Thus I now stand before you as someone who is possibly less prepared in an academic sense of the word but may be more prepared in an existential sense.

This may also have been true for you—I will not decide between religion and politics because I can't distinguish between religion and politics, between the suffering God and the tortured people. I can't withdraw from God to hide from suffering; I can't make God my protection and my mighty fortress over against those outside. I will not let myself be separated from the suffering. And when religion does this—separates us from the those who suffer, by giving us a different language or a higher certainty which the suffering cannot have—then it is time that we become free of this religion. I try to preserve my life in co-suffering (συμπαθεία). I will not adhere to this self-protection, this self-division, this moving in suitable connections, this accustoming oneself to injustice because it is so common and occurs everywhere. I will not choose. How can I ever love Bach and myself, even for only one day, by accustoming myself to the torture, even if only by forgetting it?

I am a child of facism that came to power in a culture which radically separates art, religion and morality from politics and business. The SS-leaders in Auschwitz listened to Beethoven when they came home from the gassing. There was no contradiction for them and no problem; these were simply separate planes. The example may be extreme. But isn't this separation, this "one after the other", this classification, one of the deepest characteristics of our culture? Both art and religion are becoming private, free time occupations. They are subjectivized and their privatization is their destruction. We separate, we select, we classify. Instead of sympathy we endure an advancing apathy which is based on the separation of spheres. I despair more and more in this culture of separation, disconnection and irreconcilability. It is a culture made by men and ruled by men. It is hostile to women, hostile to children and, in a profound sense for which the curriculum of our schools represents only a tiny example, hostile to art.

I will not classify; I will communicate. I will not give myself to the classification machinery because classifying and dividing always aims at ruling! "*Divide et impera*" is the most important principle of this culture in which we live. Selecting is one of its basic scientific ideas and whoever knows the context in which selection abundantly appeared for the first time in the German language, on the ramps of Auschwitz, where those still able to be used for work were selected from those to be gassed, will understand what horror can strike when one sees the mechanisms of selection which rule in our schools and universities. Separation and selection help us to screen ourselves from the suffering of the creature rather than to sense it. They help in the business of distancing the suffering from ourselves. If music is one of the self-expressions of suffering then these mechanisms make us "unmusical."

For the sake of the greater sympathy, for the sake of our capacity for compasssion, we must not accept the vigorously promoted separation of religion and art on the one hand from economy and politics on the other hand. The separatist division of the spheres of life makes us incapable of suffering and so impoverishes us.

I'd like to make that clear in a specific example, the separation of liturgy from aesthetics. There is no question that that this separation once represented a progressive element, the liberation of artists from the rule of the church, the freeing of art as an independent sphere of play, its emancipation from religious dependence. Suffering is then no longer understood and interpreted in this context as God's suffering but as a human experience shown or plotted in the medium of music. Music after the Enlightenment could not have the same metaphysical quality as before the Enlightenment in so far as it liberated itself from the institutional tie to the church in the framework of a rising middle-class culture. The question is whether or not we are standing at the end of this middle class epoch. From Franz Kafka we have the phrase that writing is a form of prayer; this phrase shakes the middle class thesis of a separation of liturgy from aesthetics, as does Penderecki's music. Why does Penderecki speak about Hiroshima and Auschwitz? One of the passages which struck me most as I recently heard his 'Lukan Passion' was the realization of the phrase "he helped others" for which Penderecki uses harmonious murmering and childish prattling. When people participate in the Crucified, they don't know exactly how to divide private from public.

If the separation of areas of life is a characteristic of middle class culture, then the new post-middle class interest might be a liberation of both art and religion from their subjectivist privatization, making them again media of communication and collective remembrance, media in which we can again speak together about the most important experiences of our life.

Is there a theological language that can overcome the separatism of culture? I understand my work as work in the medium of theology aimed at overcoming the separation of art and politics, liturgy and aesthetics. I don't try to aestheticize or to theologize the sufferings of people in the sense of justifying or minimizing this suffering. In my opinion the two most important languages of humanity, theology and music, have the task of communicating precisely where other forms of communication are no longer possible. The need for unity, for a language in which I don't have to separate the experiences I had in Chile from those about which I speak in Nürmberg, is a growing need. If separatism is the characteristic of a culture hostile to humanity in which we live, reunification is the characteristic of the new culture that we seek.

The autonomy of the arts was a legitimate theme as long as theology and religion provided norms of rule. But when this changed, when the private neuroticization of religion (to speak with Freud), shrivelled up to the "I'm o.k., you're o.k.", a new definition of the relationship of art and theology became necessary. They are now allies since they are exposed in different ways to the same strangulating grip of technicist separation. Both are irrelevant for the gross national product; both could be omitted without marked disturbance. Speaking in a marxist way, theology and art are the oldest refusals to produce exchangeable goods. They have "use-value" but not "exchange value". They produce durable works—something with which one can live, something which quenches need, not something one produces for continued sale as a mere exchangeable commodity. As theologians, philosophers and artists, we produce something which, from the point of view of the market is useless and superfluous. It doesn't let itself be marketed as an exchange good for this would be to abandon its nature. However in a culture in which all public relationships are ordered under the point of view of exchangeable goods and consequently only go so far as relations to purchasable and salable things go, religion and art have this reduced private character. What is new—in the crisis of middle class culture that we are now experiencing—is that they stand together and are threatened together.

Theology and art both labour in this profound attempt not to grow silent but to commune together over our most important concerns. Both theology and music take away from suffering its muteness, its being cut off and its bestial or petrified character. Both move us to tears. Let us put the question this simply: what makes us cry? The Roman liturgy knows the petition for the gift of tears. I don't mention this as an historical remembrance but to denounce a culture which only allows tears to women and children, just as it concedes religion to them. When will we all learn to cry again? And when will we be able to cry together?

ANNOTATED BIBLIOGRAPHY

Annotated Bibliography of Works by Hendrikus W. Boers

The following is an annotated bibliography which proceeds in chronological fashion. Brief biographical notes are included where relevant. Books and articles are usually summarized. Reviews are marked with (R).

1962

Boers completes the dissertation and goes to the Candler School of Theology at Emory University in Atlanta, Georgia as Assistant Professor of New Testament.

The Diversity of New Testament Christological Concepts and the Confession of Faith, Dissertation published privately in accordance with the requirements for promotion at the Friedrich-Wilhelm University of the Rhine, Bonn, 1962

An historical critical investigation of christological titles and formulations from the Synoptics, the speeches in Acts and the hellenistic hymns of Phil. 2:6-11 and Col. 1:15-20. The concepts available to the Palestinian community did not adequately convey what had been experienced in the ministry of Jesus thus their use materially contributes to the reworking of this memory. For Luke the focus of faith is not christology but the action of God in raising Jesus and bestowing the spirit. The categories of gnostic hymns were appropriated in the hellenistic context without being grounded in the traditions concerning Jesus. Thus there is no unbroken continuity in the christological confession but a series of adaptations of existing categories appropriate to each new cultural setting. These adapted categories materially contribute to christology at the same time that they are transformed by the process of adaptation.

1964
"Christians and the Civil Law" *Christian Advocate* 8/26, pp 11-12

The failure of Christians to actualize Christian justice meant that injustice had to be remedied through civil justice. But the latter still leaves room for the actualizing of Christian justice in the area of race relations.

1965

"Analysis and Reply on Luke 9:57-67," (with Arthur Wainwright), *Junction* 1/2 (December 1965) pp. 23-7

The three sayings of this text are analyzed to demonstrate the working of form- and redaction criticism. Boers shows that there is a shift from Jesus' call for commitment to the reign of God to the evangelist's call for commitment to Jesus.

1966

"The Meaning of the Resurrection" *Junction*, 1/4 (April, 1966) pp7-14

An historical-critical evaluation not only of the appearance and empty tomb traditions but of the meaning which was assigned to the resurrection of Jesus as the sign of God's impending victory. The scandal of the non-occurence of this victory cannot be mitigated (as in Luke, John or Hebrews) but must be held fast (as the protest of Jesus in Mark 15:34 or that of the saints in Rev. 6:9) if we are to retain the sense of Paul's "hope against hope."

1967

"Herbert Braun's Quest for what is Essentially Christian" *Journal for the American Academy of Religion (JAAR)* 35, pp350-61

Presents Braun's comparative method of studying the NT in its 1st century environment. Although regarding Braun's method as exemplary concludes that Braun's description of a constant NT anthropology actually seems to fit John best, still leaving open the question of a common denominator of NT texts.

"Apocalyptic Eschatology in I Corinthians 15. An Esssay in Contemporary Interpretation," *Interpretation* 21 (1967) pp 50-65

Enters the debate among Barth, Bultmann, Braun and Käsemann concerning the role of apocalyptic in the theology of Paul with reference to 1 Cor 15. Concludes (with Käsemann) that Paul's apocalyptic can not be reduced to an existential interpretation. Rather it locates salvation within the context of cosmic transformation from which it cannot be arbitrarily separated. But this leaves unresolved the question of how this can be understood today since apocalyptic categories are not transparent for us.

1968

"Commentary on Louie Dupré's 'Secular Man and his Religion,'" *Philosophy and the Future of Man. Proceedings of the American Catholic Philosophical Association* 42 (1968) pp. 93-96

> What is unclear for "secular man" is how "religious man" ascribes ultimate reality to that which appears to be derivative from appearances and events. [i.e., how the predicate "divine" becomes the substantive "god."]

(R) "H. R. Balz, *Methodishce Probleme der neutestamentliche Christologie*", *Journal of Biblical Literature* [*JBL*] 87 (1968) pp467f.

1969:

> Boers' first sabbatical at Univ. of Bonn, devoted to the study of Plato; becomes Associate Professor at Emory

"Psalm 16 and the Historical Origin of the Christian Faith" *Zeitschrift für die neutestamentliche Wissenschaft* 60 (1969) pp. 105-110

> The Psalm may have originally functioned to suggest that the messiah would not die but after the death of Jesus it suggests that the messiah is not abandoned to death but is with God. This makes the resurrection appearances psychologically possible. But these appearances then render the Psalm superfluous until it can be re-interpreted in terms of the appearances. It appears that the cross is the basis of a faith not reducible to a self-understanding but which entails an understanding of the whole of reality on the basis of the cross.

1970

"Jesus and the Christian Faith: New Testament Christology since Bousset's *Kyrios Christos*," *JBL* 89 (1970), pp 450-456

> The problem of a NT theology raised by Bousset still needs to be addressed. It cannot be avoided either by assuming the correctness of a christology (Cullmann) nor by concentrating on the synoptics in order to give the (false) impression of continuous development (Fuller.)

"Dialogue: Where is the Revolution?" (with Mack B. Stokes), *Junction* 5 (1970) pp. 20-30

> The revolution in modern consciouness means also a revolution in the way in which God is spoken of, and this entails a revolution in theological education.

(R) "Marshall D. Johnson, *The Purpose of the Biblical Genealogies with Special Reference to the Setting of the Genealogies of Jesus*," *Interpretation* 24 (1970) pp. 512f.

(R) "Jan Lambrecht, *Markus Interpretator: Stijl en Boodschap in Mc. 3,20-4,34*" *JBL* 89 (1970) p. 249

1971

Theology out of the Ghetto: A New Testament Exegetical Study Concerning Religious Exclusiveness, Leiden: E. J. Brill, 1971.

> Is a theology based upon the NT restricted in significance to those who accept the Christian confession? Can Christianity address the world as a partner in discussion or only as an audience? In answer Boers presents an exegetical study of NT texts which break out of the pattern of Christian exclusiveness. The parables of Jesus are not intended to disclose the identity or role of Jesus but to interpret or disclose the truth about the human situation in the world. The kingdom of God does not describe some future reality for Jesus (as for John) but is the determinative illumination of the present human situation. Matthew develops a critique of christology in emphasizing that it is not confession but works of mercy and justice which determines one's standing. In Romans 4 Paul temporarily escapes religious exclusiveness in order to argue that faith is a form of trust and hope open to the Christian and non-Christian alike. Boers concludes: "In religious exclusiveness a captive God functions to isolate the believer from his fellow man as fellow man. In all three of our examples [Jesus, Matthew, Paul] a freed God functioned to open the way to the recognition of the fellow man."

"Dimensions in Theological Education," (with Gene Tucker), *Junction* 6, pp. 6-20

> Reflections on theological education as a humanistic enterprize.

1972

"Where Christology is Real. A Survey of Recent Research on New Testament Christology," *Interpretation* 26, pp. 300-327

> Surveys the most important issues of NT Christology research, especially focused on the son of man and the Christological hymns (updating the discussion of the Dissertation.) Claims for the special dignity of Jesus cannot be anchored in the words of Jesus himself but must be assessed in their own terms, on the basis of the question, what comes to expression (about human existence) in them. Their validity is not historical but philosophical.

"Historical Criticism versus Prophetic Proclamation," *Harvard Theological Review* 65, 393-414

> Identifies the identity crisis of NT research as the dissolution through historical-critical inquiry of the relation between the Jesus of history and the self-understanding of faith. The crisis is clarified by means of a reflection on Plato's view of the relation between the logos of the poet and that of the philosopher.

"Sermon: What God Did not Do," *Junction* 8, pp. 24-28

> In his protest against abandonment (Matt. 27:46) Jesus becomes the voice of every human and provokes a hope which is beyond illusion.

1973

"Die Theologie des Paulus im Lichte der Philosophie Platons," in Hans Dieter Betz and Luise Schottroff (eds), *Neue Testament und christliche Existenz. Festschrift für Herbert Braun zum 70. Geburtstag am Mai 1973*, Tübingen: J.C.B. Mohr (Paul Siebeck), pp. 57-77.

> What happens to a religious system of thought like the Pauline when its foundation, belief in the intervention of God in history, has ceased to be meaningful? The framework of confidence in the return and reign of Christ has shown itself to be an illusion. Yet the illumination of human existence based on this illusion proves itself to have continuing value. Paul's apocalyptic Christology serves in much the same way as Plato's myth of the cave in that it provides Paul with a means of countering the escapist tendencies of the Corinthian opponents.

(R) "W.S. Duvekot, *Heeft Jesus zichzelf voor de Messias gehouden?*" JBL 92 pp. 130-32

(R) "Vincent Taylor, *The Passion Narrative of ST. Luke: A Critical and Historical Investigation*," Interpretation 27, pp. 112-114

(R) "Hans Dieter Betz, *Der Apostel Paulus und die sokratische Tradition: Eine exegetische Untersuchung zu seiner 'Apologie' 2 Korinther 10-13*," Interpretation 27 pp. 488-490

1974

(R) "Charles Davis, *Temptations of Religion*, and C. Leslie Mitton, *Jesus: The Fact Behind the Faith*," Religion and Life 43 pp. 508f.

(R) "Gordon D. Kaufman, *God the Problem*," *The Candler Review* 1, pp30f.

1975

Study of linguistics while serving as translations consultant for the United Bible Societies in Angola and Mozambique [74/75]

1976

"The Form Critical study of Paul's Letters. I Thessalonians as a Case Study," *New Testament Studies* 22 pp. 140-58.

Review of the scholarly discussion of the problem of the structure of the letter. The problem can be resolved if 2:13-16 is regarded as an interpolation in which case the letter is paranetic aimed at commending and exhorting the community.

(R) "The Realia of History and the Historical Task,. Review of S. Safrai and M. Stern, editors, *The Jewish People in the First Century: Historical Geography, Political History, Social, Cultural and Religious Life and Institutions* Vol. I", *Interpretation* 30 pp. 74-77

(R) "John B. Cobb, Jr., *Christ in a Pluralistic Age*", *The Candler Review* 3 pp. 26f.

1977

Promoted to Professor at Emory.

"The Contemporary Significance of the New Testament," *JAAR* 45 (Abstract: p. 69) *Supplement* pp. 1-33

An attempt to clarify what is at stake in the differing views of the law in Matthew and Paul and the differing views of the role of savior in Paul and John. Matthew emphasizes the fulfilling of the fundamental intention of the law as necessary to salvation. Paul agrees but finds that this can not be done without the intervention of a savior. But John's view of the role of a savior leads humanity away from itself to a participation in the divine while for Paul the savior abandons the sphere of divinity in order to orient our existence to true humanity. The views of Paul thus are a creative synthesis not only of Pharasaic and gnostic ideas, but also of apocalyptic, stoic and mystery religion concepts. Understanding NT texts by uncovering differences and convergences among themselves and with other hellenistic currents opens up their significance for our time as well, as responses to the most fundamental questions of human existence.

1978

"Sisyphus and his Rock. Concerning Gerd Theissen, *Urchristliche Wundergeschichten*," Semeia 11 pp. 1-48

Analysis of Theissen's argument with a detailed critique of the use of structural linguistics. Theissen is faulted for using a too restricted sample (not taking into account the miracle stories of hellenistic culture) and for not taking into account the way in which a narrative whole (eg the Gospel of Mark) determines the meaning of its parts.

1979

What is New Testament Theology? The Rise of Criticism and the Problem of a Theology of the New Testament Philadelphia: Fortress [Dutch translation: Kampen: J.H. Kok, 1980; Japanese translation: Tokyo: Kyo Bun Kwan, 1985]

If NT theology cannot be simply the collection of verses to illustrate a given dogmatic system but must actually allow the NT to stand over against such systems so as to challenge and correct them then some means of identifying the meaning of these texts prior to dogmatic appropriation is required. The discipline of NT theology was clarified by Gabler as the presentation of all the teachings of the NT ("true" NT theology) and the identification of those teachings with a permanent validity ("pure" NT theology). In this way NT theology mediates between the religion of the NT and the task of dogmatic theology. The task of a true NT theology was further developed by D.F. Strauss as a history of early Christian doctrine while the *religionsgeschichtliche schule* understood this as a study of primitive Christian religion within the context of hellenistic religion (Wrede, Bousset). Schlatter protests that NT documents cannot be understood merely historically since this violates their character as address. Thus historical and theological inquiry cannot be separated. The development of a "pure" NT theology is exemplified in Bultmann's development of a theology based upon Paul and the attempt of Braun to identify the basic anthropological problematic of the NT as a whole. The problem of a NT theology is that the texts do not present us with a set of clear and consistent ideas about God and the world. A NT theology cannot be found in the texts but must be constructed on the basis of the texts.

(R)"Henry R. Moeller, *The Legacy of Zion: Intertestamental Texts Related to the New Testament*," Interpretation 33 pp. 218f.

(R) "Peter Thomas O'Brien, *Introductory Thanksgivings in the Letters of Paul*," JBL 98 pp. 303f.

1980

"Interpreting Paul: Demythologizing in Reverse," in Peter J. Opitz and Gregor Sebba (ed.s) *The Philosophy of Order. Essays on History, Consciousness and Politics in Honor of Eric Voegelin*, Stuttgart: Klett-Cotta, pp. 153-172.

> Maintains that in Paul there is an attempt to hold together the principle of works (Matthew) and grace (John) thus making Paul in this respect the canon within the canon. Paul recognizes that either principle by itself is contradicted by reality and so risks contradictory formlations to hold them together. The interpretation of Paul should not proceed by an attempt to resolve this tension philosophically but by attention to the mythic polarities which govern the text. The structuralist analysis of myth by Levi-Strauss is decisive in this regard.

"Language Usage and the Production of Matthew 1:18-2:23," in Richard Spencer (ed.), *Orientation by Disorientation: Studies in Literary Criticism and Biblical Literary Criticism in Honor of William A Beardslee*, Pittsburgh: Pickwick Press, pp. 217-234

> Making use of the language theory of Saussure, Chomsky, Halliday and van Dijk which suggests that the meaning of a text unit depends upon the whole into which it is integrated and the way in which the integration is accomplished, Boers shows that the text may be viewed as a redaction of traditional material so as to produce a genuinely new narrative. Even in dependence on other traditions Matthew is more an author than an editor.

"Discourse Structure and Macro-Structure in the Interpretation of Texts: John 4:1-42 as an Example," in Paul J. Achtemeier (ed.), *Society of Biblical Literature [SBL] 1980 Seminar Papers* Chico California: Scholars Press, pp. 159-182.

> A preliminary study of this text (see 1989) that identifies the macro-structure (van Dijk) which serves as the global contraint determining the production of the text of John 4 accounting for what on the surface appear as breaks or discontinuities in the narrative. The resulting analysis of John's text and the view of existence it presupposes is contrasted with the perspectives of Luke and Matthew.

(R) "Herbert Braun, *Jesus of Nazareth: The Man and His Time*," *Interpretation* 34 pp. 208-212

(R) "Thaddee Matura, *La Radicalisme évangéligue: Aux sources de la vie chrétienne*," *JBL* 99 pp. 456f.

1981

81/82 work on semantic analysis of texts at the Centre pour l'Analyse du Discourse Religieux in Lyon, France

"The Unity of the Gospel of Mark," *Scriptura* 4 pp. 1-7

Beginning with the observation that NT scholarship is too often concerned with scholarship instead of understanding, Boers focuses on the question of Jesus' identity in Mark 8:27-33 in order to argue that the narrative is a progressive disclosure of the mystery of Jesus' identity as crucified and risen lord of the community. The narrative is thus construed as a cultic myth which leads to the manifestation of this mystery in the worship of the community. The resurrection of Jesus is not narrated since it is to be experienced in the cultus of the community.

1982

"The Problem of the Jews and the Gentiles in the Macro-Structure of Romans," *Neotestamentica* 15, pp. 1-11 [Also in *Svensk Exegetisk Ærsbok* 47 (1982) pp. 184-196

If Romans is viewed as an exposition of the doctrine of justification by faith then the argument reaches its climax already in 3:24. It should rather be seen as presupposing this doctrine and dealing with the question of the salvation of Israel raised by the doctrine. This structure is highlighted by the rhetorical questions of chapter 3-11. Faith then is the basis for existence for both Jews and gentiles and 15:7-13 is the paranetic culmination of the argument.

(R) "James Barr, *The Scope and Authority of the Bible*," *Biblical Theology Bulletin* [BTB] 12 p. 61

1983

"The Meaning of Christ in the New Testament: A Structuralist-Semantic Study," Luise and Willi Schottroff (ed.s), *Die Auslegung Gottes durch Jesus. Festgabe für Herbert Braun zu seiner 80. Geburtstag am 4. Mai, 1983*, Mainz 1983, pp. 17-56. [see below, 1984]

(R) "James D.G. Dunn, *Christology in the Making*," *Journal of Religion* 63 pp. 79-82.

(R) "Edward Schillebeeckx, *Interim Report on the Books JESUS and CHRIST*," *Interpretation* 37, pp.100f.

1984

"The Meaning of Christ in Paul's Writings. A Structuralist-Semiotic Study" *BTB* 14 pp. 131-144.

(A slightly revised version of "The Meaning of Christ in in the New Testament, 1983) Beginning with a catalogue of "figures (the ways the text actually speaks of Christ) which present the relation to Christ, the act of Christ, the effect of Christ with the incidence of such sets of figures in Paul's writings. These figures are then translated into themes which in turn are organized into polarities. Ultimately the most basic polarities are those of individual (life and death) and community (good and evil). Paul refuses to abolish either of these. The seeking of the good is not a life or death matter but an "opportunity" based on the securing of life through Christ.

"Polarities at the Roots of New Testament Thought," *Perspectives in Religious Studies. Essays in Honor of Frank Stagg* 11/4 pp. 55-75.

The limitations of the existentialist interpretation can be overcome through an appropriation of the analysis of myth from Levi-Strauss and the generative trajectory of Greimas. This approach is illustrated in relation to Romans 4: 18-22 and the resulting clarification of Paul's view is contrasted with the way in which Matthew emphasizes the basic (horizontal) polarity of good and evil while John emphasizes the vertical polarity of life and death. Paul holds these in tension. The NT does not give us a doctrine but rather a (religious/mythic) framework for the Christian understanding of human existence.

1985

(R) "E.P. Sanders, *Paul, the Law, and the Jewish People*," *Interpretation* 39, pp. 322-324.

1987

(edited with Helen Sebba) *Creativity: Lectures by Gregor Sebba* Atlanta: Scholars Press

An edited transcript of four lectures (of six given and ten planned) on the theme of human creativity in art, literature, science and mathematics by Boer's long time friend.

"Traduction sémantique/transculturelle de la parabole du bon Samaritain," Jean Delorme (ed.), *Parole-figure-parabole*, Lyon: Presses Universitaires de Lyon, pp. 87-101. [Also in *Sémiotique et Bible* 40, pp 18-29.

Distinguishes the deep structure of the parable and shows that while this structure is translatable, the concrete meaning of settings (road from Jericho to Jerusalem) and figures (priest, levite and samaritan) are not. Either one must translate oneself into the original story by means of historical investigation and imagination or one must replace the concrete settings and figures with others drawn from a different culture or discourse. Then the general meaning may persist but the concrete meaning is quite different. Examples of the transcultural transformation of the deep structure of the parable are the Philippians hymn and the Gospel in Solentiname.

"Reflections on the Gospel of Mark: A Structural Investigation" *SBL 1987 Seminar Papers* ed Kent H. Richards Atlanta: Scholars Press pp. 255-267

From a consideration of the beginning, ending and center of Mark, Boers concludes that the narrative prepares for the recognition of the identity of the crucified Jesus in the proclamation and cult of the community. This is elaborated through a consideration of the roles played by figures in the narrative. The narrative also aims at persuading followers to immitate the role of suffering service to humanity.

(R) "Herbert Braun, *Jesus-der Mann aus Nazaret und seiner Zeit*, *JBL*, 106, pp. 129-131
(R) "John Dominic Crossan, *Sayings Parallels: A Workbook for the Jesus Tradition*", *Interpretation* 41 428-430.
(R) "J. Christiaan Beker, *Suffering and Hope: The Biblical Vision of the Human Predicament*," *Theology Today* 44 pp. 476f.

1988

"Neither on This Mountain nor in Jerusalem": A Study of John 4 Atlanta: Scholars Press, 1988

A study which aims at developing a "metaphysics" of the NT text in the sense of identifying the fundamental structures from which the text is generated and which give it its unity. To this end Boers proposes a semiotic analysis of the text, employing and adapting a "generative grammar" derived from Greimas. This grammar is employed here not deductively but inductively, in so far as it serves to illuminate John 4 and its apparent ruptures and fissures. Boers uses both a syntactic (narrative) and semantic analysis to arrive at a "deep structure" and the designation of a fundamental micro-universe in terms of which the text may be understood. The proceedure is then reversed to show how this structure governs the generation of the text as we have it. Through this double analysis Boers demonstrates the unity of the text which aims at exposing the superior value of an obedience that issues in human solidarity and universal integration thereby transcending concerns of self-preservation (sustenance) and overcoming divisions between groups.

"The Foundations of Paul's Thought: A Methodological Investigation—The Problem of a Coherent Center of Paul's Thought" *Studia Theologica* 42 (1988) pp. 55-68

> The recognition that Paul was not a systematic thinker leads to the question of whether there is nevertheless a coherent core or center to his thought which lends it a certain unity. Barth identified this core with the infinite qualitative distinction between time and eternity. But Bultmann showed that this left unexplained certain features of Paul's thought for which the distinction between meaning and the means of expression (and hence the programme of demythologizing) was necessary. Käsemann noted that Paul's thought could not be reduced to existential categories but must include the historical-social and that the justification of the sinner could be understood as a theme unifying these dimensions. Beker and Patte have carried forward this discussion by developing ways of distinguishing between the surface and the depth of Paul's thought. What must be proposed is that, for Paul, the center of his thought is a contradiction in the most fundamental grammar of his thought between the existential (faith) and social (works) micro-universes. Thus the "coherent center" of Paul's thought is this contradiction which Paul refuses to surrender.

1989

Who Was Jesus? An Interpretation of the Christological Passages in the Synoptic Gospels San Francisco: Harper & Row,

> An essay that guides the non-specialist in a reading of the texts which aims at making clear how the critical study of NT passages proceeds. Rather than entering into discussion with contemporary scholarship (as in 1962 and 1983/4), the book discusses the texts themselves so that the reader is led into an historical critical inquiry directly. The result of this inquiry is a picture of Jesus' mission which has its origin in that of John the Baptist, regarded by Jesus as the one who had inaugurated the reign of God. On this basis Jesus celebrates the presence of this reign through an abandonment of ascetic practices and through open friendship with the outcast and despised. This shocking behavior is regarded as a threat by religious and political authorities, leading to his execution. But his gruesome death makes him a symbol for what his befriending the outcast meant. In this way he becomes the symbol for and witness to the presence of this solidarity and celebration. It is this which then engenders the christological reflections of his followers, reflections which in turn engender the NT texts. In spite of the confessional orientation of these texts the essential humanism of Jesus' mission still comes to expression in and through them.